Dialogue on the Threshold

SUNY series in Contemporary Continental Philosophy
———————
Dennis J. Schmidt, editor

Dialogue on the Threshold
Heidegger and Trakl

IAN ALEXANDER MOORE

Front Cover. Trakl's sketch of himself as a monk, courtesy of the Forschungsinstitut Brenner-Archiv, Sammlung Trakliana, call number 243-001-004.

Published by State University of New York Press, Albany

© 2022 State University of New York

All rights reserved

Printed in the United States of America

No part of this book may be used or reproduced in any manner without written permission. No part of this book may be stored in a retrieval system or transmitted in any form or by any means, including electronic, electrostatic, magnetic tape, mechanical, photocopying, recording, or otherwise without the prior permission in writing of the publisher.

For information, contact State University of New York Press, Albany, NY
www.sunypress.edu

Library of Congress Cataloging-in-Publication Data

Name: Moore, Ian Alexander, author.
Title: Dialogue on the threshold : Heidegger and Trakl / Ian Alexander Moore.
Description: Albany : State University of New York Press, [2022] | Series: SUNY series in contemporary continental philosophy | Includes bibliographical references and index.
Identifiers: LCCN 2022009661 | ISBN 9781438490670 (hardcover : alk. paper) | ISBN 9781438490687 (ebook) | ISBN 9781438490663 (pbk. : alk. paper)
Subjects: LCSH: Heidegger, Martin, 1889–1976. | Trakl, Georg, 1887–1914.
Classification: LCC B3279.H49 M5858 2022 | DDC 193—dc23/eng/20220808
LC record available at https://lccn.loc.gov/2022009661

10 9 8 7 6 5 4 3 2 1

For Lisa

Contents

List of Images — xi

Acknowledgments — xiii

Abbreviations — xv

Note on Translations — xxi

Introduction — 1

Chapter 1
"The Poet of Our Generation": Heidegger Reads Trakl — 7
  1. Discovering the Poet (Thanks to a Journal for the
    Avant-Garde) — 9
  2. Lecturing at a Luxury Resort — 12
  3. Speaking of Language — 18
  4. Celebrating Trakl, Saving the West — 21
  5. *Post eventum* — 30
  6. Annotating the Trakl Bible — 32

Chapter 2
Language of Bread and Wine — 45
  1. Gesture, the Inexpressible, and the Speaking of the
    Unspoken — 47
  2. Language of Earth and Sky — 50
  3. Digression on Christianity — 63
  4. Language of Body and Blood — 72

Chapter 3
For the Love of Detachment 81
1. The Problem of Polysemy 82
2. Heidegger's Placement of Detachment 83
3. *Abgeschiedenheit* in (Our?) Middle High German 103
4. Heidegger's Early Acquaintance with Detachment 105
5. Deconstructing Detachment 106
6. *Pour l'amour de l'Abgeschiedenheit* 108

Chapter 4
Pain Is Being Itself 111
1. Heidegger's *On Pain* 112
2. Ernst Jünger: On or beyond Pain? 115
3. *Via doloris heideggeriana* 117
4. *Zum Schmerz selbst!* 119
5. The Gentle Gathering of Pain 123
6. *Algos*: An Etymological Excursus 130
7. In the Name of *Schmerz* 132
8. "ein gewaltiger Schmerz": Trakl's "Grodek" 134

Chapter 5
Poetic Colors of the Holy: Trakl with Pindar 143
1. Chrusology, Ontology, Hierology 146
2. Sacré bleu 152
3. A Heideggerian *Farbenlehre?* 162
4. (Un)holy Madness: Trakl with Hölderlin and Celan 163

Chapter 6
Geschlecht 171
1. "A Grand Discourse on Sexual Difference" 176
2. The Wild Blue Game 189
3. Humanimality 194

Chapter 7
Spirit in Tatters 201
1. The Promise 202
2. The Promise, Painfully Broken 202
3. "Grodek" Redux 208

Postscript 211

Appendix 1
Heidegger's Trakl Marginalia   215
  1. Background   215
  2. Marginalia in the Zurich Edition   218
  3. Marginalia to "Into an Old Family Album"   232

Appendix 2
Heidegger's Occasional References to Trakl   239

Appendix 3
References to Trakl's Works in "Language in the Poem"   271

Appendix 4
Selected Poems by Trakl   277
  Abendländisches Lied / Song of the Occident   278/279
  An den Knaben Elis / To the Boy Elis   278/279
  An Novalis / To Novalis   280/281
  Das Herz / The Heart   280/281
  De profundis / Out of the Depths   282/283
  Der Tau des Frühlings / The Dew of Spring   284/285
  Frühling der Seele / Springtime of the Soul   284/285
  Geistliche Dämmerung / Spiritual Twilight   286/287
  Gesang des Abgeschiedenen / Song of the Departed One   288/289
  Grodek / Gródek   288/289
  Herbstseele / Autumn Soul   290/291
  Hölderlin / Hölderlin   292/293
  Im Winter (Ein Winterabend) / In Winter (A Winter
    Evening)   292/293
  In ein altes Stammbuch / Into an Old Family Album   294/295
  Karl Kraus / Karl Kraus   294/295
  Klage / Lamentation   294/295
  Passion / The Passion   296/297
  Nachtergebung / Surrender to the Night   298/299

Notes   301

Works Cited   353

Index   381

Images

1. Cover of the journal in which Heidegger's "Language in the Poem" first appeared. Courtesy of *Merkur: Deutsche Zeitschrift für europäisches Denken*.   16

2. Invitation to the Kommerell celebration at Bühlerhöhe. Courtesy of the Deutsches Literaturarchiv Marbach, call number HS.1989.0010.07111.   19

3–4. Invitation to the Trakl celebration at Bühlerhöhe. Courtesy of the Forschungsinstitut Brenner-Archiv, Nachlass Ludwig von Ficker, call number 48-25-5.   24–25

5. Heidegger's marginal note following Trakl's "Grodek," in his personal copy of *Die Dichtungen*, ed. Horwitz, located in the Martin-Heidegger-Archiv der Stadt Meßkirch. Photograph by I. A. Moore, permission granted by Alfred Denker.   97

6. Manuscript of Trakl's "Grodek." Courtesy of the Forschungsinstitut Brenner-Archiv, Nachlass Ludwig von Ficker, call number 99/46-1.   142

7. Trakl's ex libris and manuscript of the poem "Hölderlin," in his personal copy of Hölderlin's *Dramen und Übersetzungen*. Courtesy of Hans Weichselbaum and the Trakl Gedenkstätte.   168

8. Trakl's self-portrait. Courtesy of Hans Weichselbaum and the Trakl Gedenkstätte.   188

9. Heidegger's marginalia to Trakl's "Into an Old Family Album," in his personal copy of *Die Dichtungen*, ed. Schneditz. Courtesy of Arnulf Heidegger and the Deutsches Literaturarchiv Marbach. 233

Acknowledgments

In 2016, while conducing archival research in the Meßkirch castle, I noticed, inconspicuously placed on the bottom shelf of one of the library's bookcases, a faded blue volume with a barely legible sticker on the spine. It read: *Georg Trakl, Die Dichtungen*. Opening this old copy of Trakl's poems, I was surprised to see numerous annotations in Heidegger's hand. One was particularly striking. Next to Trakl's harrowing poem about the battle of Gródek, Heidegger had drawn a diagram suggesting that the "flame of spirit" had the potential to lead not only to searing insurrection but also to gentle *Gelassenheit* ("releasement," "letting be")—perhaps *the* term of art of Heidegger's later thought. The late-medieval philosopher and mystic Meister Eckhart, on whom I was working at the time, had coined the term as a synonym for the word *Abgeschiedenheit* ("detachment," "departedness"), a word that, on Heidegger's interpretation, had served as the center point of Trakl's entire body of poetic work. Curiously, despite his deep acquaintance with the medieval thinker, Heidegger never mentions Eckhart or releasement in his two main essays on Trakl. I knew that I had discovered something important here, something that, as far as I was aware, no one had ever mentioned in the secondary literature. But I had to finish my dissertation. I was not yet ready to delve into the strange world of Trakl's poetry, let alone the even stranger world of Heidegger's commentary on it.

Fortunately, two years later, Katie Chenoweth and Rodrigo Therezo invited me to give a lecture at Princeton University for a conference they were organizing on Jacques Derrida's recently discovered seminar sessions on Heidegger's reading of Trakl. Drawing on Derrida's work, I began to develop an interpretation of Heidegger's remarkable, enigmatic relation to the poet, which I expanded on a few months later for a conference on Heidegger and national humanism, held at Texas A&M University under the direction of Adam Rosenthal. It was from these two conferences that the present book was born.

I am grateful, first and foremost, to the conference organizers. For their comments and critiques, I thank the participants at these conferences, as well as those at the Southwest Seminar in Continental Philosophy, the Society for Phenomenology and Existential Philosophy, and the Heidegger Circle, where I presented earlier versions of selections from this book.

David Krell has provided encouragement and inspiration throughout this project. My thanks to him, as well as to Charles Bambach, Peg Birmingham, Richard Capobianco, Alfred Denker, Chris Eagle, Ilit Ferber, Francesco Guercio, Werner Hamacher (†), Arnulf Heidegger, Heinrich Heidegger, Tobias Keiling, Elissa Marder, Rainer Marten, Josh McBee, Will McNeill, Mary Moore, Michael Portal, Jim Roi, Denny Schmidt, Chris Turner, Peter Trawny, Alan Udoff, Karl von der Luft (who also prepared the index), Friedrich-Wilhelm von Herrmann, and two anonymous reviewers. Thanks also to the archivists at the Deutsches Literaturarchiv in Marbach, Germany, and at the Forschungsinstitut Brenner-Archiv in Innsbruck, Austria, especially Ulrich von Bülow and Markus Ender. Although, due to the COVID-19 pandemic, I was unable to accept the research fellowship that the German Literary Archive had awarded me, I am grateful for the institution's support of my project, as well as for making unpublished documents available to me remotely.

Portions of this book appeared previously in "For the Love of Detachment: Trakl, Heidegger, and Derrida's *Geschlecht III*," *International Yearbook for Hermeneutics* 18 (2019): 233–256; "The Promise of Pain: (Di)spiriting the *Geist* of Heidegger's Trakl," *Política común* 14 (2020), https://doi.org/10.3998/pc.12322227.0014.002; "Georg Trakl's Poem 'Hölderlin,'" *Journal of Continental Philosophy* 1, no. 2 (2021): 304–317; "Heidegger's Trakl-Marginalia," *Research in Phenomenology* 51, no. 1 (2021): 99–122; "Poetic Colors of the Holy: Heidegger on Pindar and Trakl," in *Heidegger and the Holy*, ed. Richard Capobianco (Lanham, MD: Roman & Littlefield, 2022), 63–83; and "Pain Is Beyng Itself: Heidegger's Algontology," *Gatherings: The Heidegger Circle Annual* 12 (2022): 1–39.

Abbreviations

DD	Trakl, Georg. Die Dichtungen: Gesamtausgabe, mit einem Anhang Zeugnisse und Erinnerungen. Edited by Kurt Horwitz. Zurich: Die Arche, 1946.
GA	Heidegger, Martin. Gesamtausgabe. Frankfurt: Klostermann, 1975–.
GA 1	Frühe Schriften. Edited by Friedrich-Wilhelm von Herrmann. 1978.
GA 3	Kant und das Problem der Metaphysik. Edited by Friedrich-Wilhelm von Herrmann. 1991.
GA 4	Erläuterungen zu Hölderlins Dichtung. Edited by Friedrich-Wilhelm von Herrmann. 1981.
GA 5	Holzwege. Edited by Friedrich-Wilhelm von Herrmann. 1977.
GA 7	Vorträge und Aufsätze. Edited by Friedrich-Wilhelm von Herrmann. 2000.
GA 8	Was heißt Denken? Edited by Paola-Ludovika Coriando. 2002.
GA 9	Wegmarken. Edited by Friedrich-Wilhelm von Herrmann. 1976.
GA 10	Der Satz vom Grund. Edited by Petra Jaeger. 1997.
GA 11	Identität und Differenz. Edited by Friedrich-Wilhelm von Herrmann. 2006.

GA 12	Unterwegs zur Sprache. Edited by Friedrich-Wilhelm von Herrmann. 1985.
GA 13	Aus der Erfahrung des Denkens. Edited by Hermann Heidegger. 1983.
GA 14	Zur Sache des Denkens. Edited by Friedrich-Wilhelm von Herrmann. 2007.
GA 15	Seminare. Edited by Curd Ochwadt. 1986.
GA 16	Reden und andere Zeugnisse eines Lebensweges. Edited by Hermann Heidegger. 2000.
GA 18	Grundbegriffe der aristotelischen Philosophie. Edited by Mark Michalski. 2002.
GA 19	Platon: Sophistes. Edited by Ingeborg Schüßler. 1992.
GA 24	Die Grundprobleme der Phänomenologie. Edited by Friedrich-Wilhelm von Herrmann. 2nd ed. 1989.
GA 26	Metaphysische Anfangsgründe der Logik im Ausgang von Leibniz. Edited by Klaus Held. 1978.
GA 27	Einleitung in die Philosophie. Edited by Otto Saame and Ina Saame-Speidel. 1996.
GA 29/30	Die Grundbegriffe der Metaphysik: Welt–Endlichkeit–Einsamkeit. Edited by Friedrich-Wilhelm von Herrmann. 2nd ed. 1992.
GA 31	Vom Wesen der menschlichen Freiheit: Einleitung in die Philosophie. Edited by Hartmut Tietjen. 1982.
GA 34	Vom Wesen der Wahrheit: Zu Platons Höhlengleichnis und Theätet. Edited by Hermann Mörchen. 2nd ed. 1997.
GA 39	Hölderlins Hymnen "Germanien" und "Der Rhein." Edited by Susanne Ziegler. 3rd ed. 1999.
GA 40	Einführung in die Metaphysik. Edited by Petra Jaeger. 1983.
GA 41	Die Frage nach dem Ding: Zu Kants Lehre von den transzendentalen Grundsätzen. Edited by Petra Jaeger. 1984.
GA 42	Schelling: Vom Wesen der menschlichen Freiheit (1809). Edited by Ingrid Schüßler. 1988.

| GA 45 | Grundfragen der Philosophie: Ausgewählte "Probleme" der "Logik." Edited by Friedrich-Wilhelm von Herrmann. 1984. |

| GA 49 | Die Metaphysik der deutschen Idealismus: Zur erneuten Auslegung von Schelling: Philosophische Untersuchungen über das Wesen der menschlichen Freiheit und die damit zusammenhängenden Gegenstände (1809). Edited by Günter Seubold. 2nd ed. 2006. |

| GA 52 | Hölderlins Hymne "Andenken." Edited by Curd Ochwadt. 2nd ed. 1992. |

| GA 53 | Hölderlins Hymne "Der Ister." Edited by Walter Biemel. 2nd ed. 1993. |

| GA 54 | Parmenides. Edited by Manfred Frings. 2nd ed. 1992. |

| GA 55 | Heraklit. I. Der Anfang des abendländischen Denkens. II. Logik: Heraklits Lehre des Logos. Edited by Manfred S. Frings. 3rd ed. Frankfurt: Klostermann, 1994. |

| GA 58 | Grundprobleme der Phänomenologie (1919/20). Edited by Hans-Helmuth Gander. 1993. |

| GA 60 | Phänomenologie des religiösen Lebens. 1. Einleitung in die Phänomenologie der Religion. 2. Augustinus und der Neuplatonismus. 3. Die philosophischen Grundlagen der mittelalterlichen Mystik. Edited by Matthias Jung, Thomas Regehly, and Claudius Strube. 1995. |

| GA 65 | Beiträge zur Philosophie. Edited by Friedrich-Wilhelm von Herrmann. 1989. |

| GA 66 | Besinnung. Edited by Friedrich-Wilhelm von Herrmann. 1997. |

| GA 68 | Hegel. 1. Die Negativität: Eine Auseinandersetzung mit Hegel aus dem Ansatz in der Negativität (1938/39, 1941). 2. Erläuterung der "Einleitung" zu Hegels "Phänomenologie des Geistes" (1942). Edited by Ingrid Schüßler. 1993. |

| GA 70 | Über den Anfang. Edited by Paola-Ludovika Coriando. 2005. |

| GA 71 | Das Ereignis. Edited by Friedrich-Wilhelm von Herrmann. 2009. |

GA 72	Die Stege des Anfangs. Edited by Günther Neumann. Forthcoming.
GA 73	Zum Ereignis-Denken. Edited by Peter Trawny. 2013.
GA 74	Zum Wesen der Sprache und zur Frage nach der Kunst. Edited by Thomas Regehly. 2010.
GA 75	Zu Hölderlin—Griechenlandreisen. Edited by Curd Ochwadt. 2000.
GA 76	Leitgedanken zur Entstehung der Metaphysik, der neuzeitlichen Wissenschaft und der modernen Technik. Edited by Claudius Strube. 2009.
GA 77	Feldweg Gespräche (1944/45). Edited by Ingrid Schüßler. 1995.
GA 78	Der Spruch des Anaximander. Edited by Ingrid Schüßler. 2010.
GA 79	Bremer und Freiburger Vorträge. Edited by Petra Jaeger. 1994.
GA 80	Vorträge. Edited by Günther Neumann. 2016, 2020.
GA 81	Gedachtes. Edited by Paola-Ludovika Coriando. 2007.
GA 83	Seminare: Platon–Aristoteles–Augustinus. Edited by Mark Michalski. 2012.
GA 84.1	Seminare: Kant–Leibniz–Schiller. Part 1. Edited by Günther Neumann. 2013.
GA 85	Vom Wesen der Sprache: Die Metaphysik der Sprache und die Wesung des Wortes: Zu Herders Abhandlung "Über den Ursprung der Sprache." Edited by Ingrid Schüßler. 1999.
GA 86	Seminare: Hegel–Schelling. Edited by Peter Trawny. 2011.
GA 87	Nietzsche: Seminare 1937 und 1944. 1. Nietzsches metaphysische Grundstellung (Sein und Schein). 2. Skizzen zu Grundbegriffe des Denkens. Edited by Peter von Ruckteschell. 2004.
GA 90	Zu Ernst Jünger. Edited by Peter Trawny. 2004.

GA 94	Überlegungen II–VI (Schwarze Hefte 1931–1938). Edited by Peter Trawny. 2014.
GA 95	Überlegungen, VII–XI (Schwarze Hefte 1938/39). Edited by Peter Trawny. 2014.
GA 97	Anmerkungen I–V (Schwarze Hefte 1942–1948). Edited by Peter Trawny. 2015.
GA 98	Anmerkungen VI–IX (Schwarze Hefte 1948/49–1951). Edited by Peter Trawny. 2018.
GA 99	Vier Hefte I und II (Schwarze Hefte 1947–1950). Edited by Peter Trawny. 2019.
GA 100	Vigiliae und Notturno (Schwarze Hefte 1952/53 bis 1957). Edited by Peter Trawny. 2020.
GA 102	Vorläufiges I–IV (Schwarze Hefte 1963–1970). Edited by Peter Trawny. 2022.
GIII	Derrida, Jacques. Geschlecht III: Sexe, race, nation, humanité. Edited by Geoffrey Bennington, Katie Chenoweth, and Rodrigo Therezo. Paris: Seuil, 2018.
GS/LF	Stroomann, Gerhard, and Ludwig von Ficker. Unpublished correspondence available in the Forschungsinstitut Brenner-Archiv, Nachlass Ludwig von Ficker, call numbers 041-048-023–027, and Sammlung Forschungsinstitut Brenner-Archiv alt., call numbers 47/4.34.2–29.
HKA 1, 2	Trakl, Georg. Dichtungen und Briefe: Historisch-kritische Ausgabe. Edited by Walther Killy and Hans Szklenar. Vol. 1. 3rd ed. Salzburg: Otto Müller, 1974. Vol. 2. Salzburg: Otto Müller, 1969.
MH/LF	Heidegger, Martin, and Ludwig von Ficker. Briefwechsel 1952–1967. Edited by Matthias Flatscher. Stuttgart: Klett-Cotta, 2004.
SZ	Heidegger, Martin. Sein und Zeit. 19th ed. Tübingen: Niemeyer, 1993.
ÜdS	Heidegger, Martin. Über den Schmerz. Jahresgabe der Martin-Heidegger-Gesellschaft, 2017–2018.

Note on Translations

All translations of Heidegger, Trakl, and Derrida's *Geschlecht III* are my own, as are translations of works for which I do not specify an English edition in the abbreviations or in the list of works cited. When quoting unpublished material, I provide the original either in the body of the text or in the notes. Unless otherwise indicated, for Bible passages, I cite from the *Novum Testamentum Graece*, the 1545 Lutherbibel, and the 1769 King James Version.

Introduction

With the discovery and recent publication of Jacques Derrida's seminar sessions on Martin Heidegger's lecture "Language in the Poem," the Austrian poet Georg Trakl (1887–1914) has been receiving more attention in continental philosophy than ever before.[1] Previously, many scholars in this tradition, to say nothing of philosophy more broadly, shied away from Heidegger's bizarre reading of the melancholic, incest-ridden expressionist, who died at twenty-seven of a cocaine overdose in a psychiatric ward in the early days of World War I. In the words of David Krell, who, like no other, has been facing the abyss of this reading for over four decades,

> Heidegger's own discussion of Trakl's poetry remains startling, bewildering, so that it is no exaggeration to say that the extended essay on Trakl ["Language in the Poem"] is of an order of difficulty that is unmatched by any of Heidegger's other essays. Compared to it, "Time and Being" (1962) and the *Beiträge* (1936–38) are child's play.[2]

There are numerous reasons for this difficulty, not least of which is Trakl's own poetry, with its disconnected, dream-like images of rot and sexual perversion, female monks and shit-stained angels. Through decontextualization and selective etymology, Heidegger radically reinterprets the sense of Trakl's words. For example, *fremd* does not mean "strange," but Old High German *fram*, "on the way." *Geist* does not mean "spirit," but Indo-Germanic *gheis*, "to be outside oneself." Even the ordinary sense of "sense" changes. *Sinn*, in Heidegger's reading, fundamentally means "direction," not "meaning." Heidegger situates the entire body of Trakl's poetic work under the banner of such sense. Trakl's poetry, he claims, is in the process of cutting itself off from the corrupt and degenerate cast of contemporary humanity and moving toward a new homeland, or rather to the homeland that has always been held in store for it but has long been forgotten. Heidegger has, in short, turned Trakl into a sort of Hölderlin for the twentieth century, without, however, mentioning Hölderlin even once in his two lectures on Trakl.

And yet, for all its idiosyncrasies, Heidegger's work on Trakl has led to a sort of "canonization of the lyric poet": hardly anyone writing on Trakl after 1952 has been able to escape Heidegger's influence, for good or ill.[3] What is more, Trakl's fraught poems compelled Heidegger to take up underrepresented themes in his philosophical oeuvre, such as sexual difference, pain, and madness, and even to blur the boundaries between the animal and the human.

But what compelled Heidegger to think about Trakl? Why, after never mentioning the poet in any of his writings, does Heidegger come to deliver two lectures on Trakl in the early 1950s? Why, only at that point in time, does the philosopher discover that this Austrian *enfant terrible* not only ranks among the few great poets, but is "the poet of our generation" and "the poet of the still-hidden land of evening"—the poet, in other words, who keeps the story of the secret Germany alive?[4] And what bearing does this discovery have on the interpretation of Trakl and on Heidegger's own trajectory?

Drawing on little-known sources such as Heidegger's marginalia in his personal copies of Trakl's poems, the present study endeavors to answer these questions by reconstructing and continuing Heidegger's dialogue with Trakl. I argue that Heidegger was at once attracted to Trakl and apprehensive about immersing himself in Trakl's world. For Trakl was not just a philosopher's poet. He was also a poet of pain and putrefaction, a poet of incest and sexual difference, a Christian poet, a poet of love in death and death in love. In his reading of Trakl, Heidegger laid hold of things he could not quite mold into his matrix. Rather than letting them be, he repurposed them or simply let them go. Yet, at times—and even despite himself—he let Trakl's poetry affect his lifework. Even if Heidegger manipulates Trakl to serve his own ends, there are moments when the poetry gains the upper hand. Impressions to the contrary, their dialogue is not, therefore, unanimous.[5]

Following an initial historical-philological chapter, this book explores six sites in which poetry, not philosophy, prevails. I use these sites as opportunities to reflect not just on the productive and problematic tensions that pervade Heidegger's reading of Trakl, but more broadly on the thresholds that separate philosophy from poetry, gathering from dispersion, the same from the other, and the native from the foreigner. To take Trakl's work seriously is to accept his invitation to cross these thresholds. This volume, the first of its kind in English, French, or German, accordingly aims to contribute not just to the study of Heidegger and Trakl but also, more modestly, to the "old quarrel [*diaphora*] between philosophy and poetry."[6]

Chapter 1 provides an overview of Heidegger's engagement with Trakl and situates this engagement within the broader context of Heidegger's corpus and sociopolitical milieu. I explain why Heidegger started to write about Trakl in the early 1950s and why he came to see him as a poet who was pivotal, not only for his own thought and for that of his generation, but for the West as such. The chapter offers the first substantial reconstruction of the setting and background for Heidegger's Trakl lectures, namely, the Black Forest spa Bühlerhöhe and its charismatic head Gerhard Stroomann, the influential postwar periodical *Merkur* (*Mercury*), and the circle of authors connected to the avant-garde journal *Der Brenner* (*The Burner*), in which many of Trakl's poems first appeared. Heidegger reacts strongly against these authors' interpretations of Trakl's work, as can be seen in his marginalia to their tributes to the poet. In the final section of the chapter, I show how these marginalia help to reveal the distinctiveness of Heidegger's reading of Trakl, especially as regards the topics of Christianity, sexual difference, and the interplay of biography, autobiography, and hagiography, all of which receive further treatment in later chapters.

Chapter 2 offers a close reading of Trakl's poem "A Winter Evening" and Heidegger's interpretation of it in the three versions of his lecture "Language" (1950, 1951, 1959). I argue that, although Trakl marks a point of departure for a second distinct turn in Heidegger's thinking—this time toward the self-speaking of language, where Heidegger also develops a unique theory of difference—Heidegger effaces or questionably repurposes crucial elements in Trakl's song, such as its search for a uniquely Christian redemption. For Trakl, poetic language is mainly a matter of expiation, which has important implications, ignored by Heidegger, for how to understand the meaning of things like bread and wine, and hence the meaning of being.

Chapter 3 turns to Heidegger's second text on Trakl, "Language in the Poem," from 1952. Heidegger claims that all of Trakl's poetry is gathered around the concept of *Abgeschiedenheit*, "detachment" or "departedness," which Heidegger interprets both as a departure from the degraded present of the Occident (*Abendland*) and as a departure toward a proper dwelling place, toward the land of evening (*Abend-Land*). This is a promised land, but the promise is made, not to all those who would believe, but to the few who have ears to hear the elemental power of the German language. Heidegger harnesses the etymologies of nearly every key German word for his earth-bound interpretation; however, he does not explore the history of the very word that supposedly centers Trakl's entire corpus. Taking inspiration from Derrida's way of reading other important terms in "Language in the Poem," I show how the ancestry of *Abgeschiedenheit* both undermines Heidegger's appeal to an exclusive land and language and opens up the possibility of an inclusive, anarchic love that is more in accord with the spirit of Trakl's poetry. This chapter also includes a close reading of the entirety of Trakl's "Springtime of the Soul," from which Heidegger takes the famous line, "The soul is something strange on earth," although he questionably passes over the poem's staging of incest and the pain it causes the narrator.

Chapter 4 examines what Heidegger does have to say about pain in his two texts on Trakl and in a selection of notes recently published in a limited German edition under the title *On Pain*. While it is remarkable that Heidegger places pain on the same level as other key terms in his effort to understand being, he shrinks back from its most radical, rending implications, as articulated in Trakl's late poem "Grodek."

Chapter 5 brings Trakl into dialogue with the ancient Greek lyricist Pindar, the only poet, besides Trakl, whom Heidegger names in his two lectures on his Austrian contemporary. I show how, for Heidegger, both the gold of Pindar's victory odes and the blue (together with gold) of Trakl's expressionist poems articulate essential aspects of the holiness of being: gleaming presence in the case of gold, and sheltering concealment in the case of blue. I raise some questions as to whether Heidegger's work on poetic color could accommodate poetic accounts of sacrilege, which leads to a discussion of the extent to which madness can be considered holy in Trakl's work. I ultimately argue that the word "madness," which Trakl seems purposefully to misspell in a recently discovered poem titled "Hölderlin," resists the sense of gentle gathering that Heidegger locates in Trakl's poetry and in Hölderlin and his madness. Trakl is, rather, a precursor to Paul Celan.

Chapter 6 explores the polysemous word *Geschlecht* ("gender," "tribe," "generation," "species") in Heidegger's reading of Trakl. Heidegger is interested initially in how Trakl appears to distinguish between a corrupt humanity, in which difference entails dissension, and a unified humanity to come, in which difference would resolve its dissonance, without thereby dissolving *as* difference. However, Trakl's poetry prompts Heidegger to address other differences, including those of sex, of species, and, less directly, of race. In this chapter, I explore several possibilities that Heidegger opens but either leaves undeveloped or soon forecloses: that ontological difference is bound up with sexual difference, that Heidegger is not necessarily committed to the male/female binary, and that he loosens the barriers between the human and the animal that he had erected earlier in his career.

Chapter 7 considers the larger arc of "Language in the Poem." Juxtaposing Heidegger with Friedrich Schelling, I show how Heidegger's analyses of spirit and evil militate against the sort of salvation he proposes. Trakl, too, is in search of spiritual redemption, but his is a redemption inextricably mediated by atonement and the necessity of enduring the decay and deprivation of existence, the trauma of being in the world. As Trakl's friend and patron Ludwig von Ficker once wrote, "Trakl looked straight through the hell of his life (never beyond it!) into the actuality of the distant heaven."[7] Or, to apply Celan's language: Trakl's poetic work "does, certainly, make a claim to infinity, it attempts to reach through time—through it, and not out beyond it."[8]

The volume concludes with four appendixes. The first reproduces some of Heidegger's marginalia in two of his personal copies of Trakl's poetry. The second provides chronologically organized evidence for Heidegger's engagement with Trakl, beyond the two texts he wrote on the poet. The third documents which poems Heidegger references in "Language in the Poem." In the fourth appendix, I offer new translations of eighteen poems by Trakl that have been important for my interpretation of his work.

Chapter 1

"The Poet of Our Generation"
Heidegger Reads Trakl

Das Traklsche Gedicht ist für mich ein Gegenstand von sublimer Existenz. Nun erschütterts mich erst recht, wie die von Anfang an flüchtende, in ihrer Beschreibung leise ausgesparte Gestalt imstande war, das Gewicht ihres fortwährenden Untergangs in so genauen Bildungen zu beweisen. Es fällt mir ein, dass dieses ganze Werk sein Gleichnis hätte in dem Sterben des Li-Tai-Pe: hier wie dort ist das Fallen Vorwand für die unaufhaltsamste Himmelfahrt. [. . .] Eine neue Dimension des geistigen Raums scheint [. . .] ausgemessen und das gefühls-stoffliche Vorurteil widerlegt, als ob in der Richtung der Klage nur Klage sei—: auch dort ist wieder Welt.[1]

—Rainer Maria Rilke

Ficker sandte mir heute Gedichte des armen Trakl, die ich für genial halte ohne sie zu verstehen. Sie taten mir wohl. Gott mit mir![2]

—Ludwig Wittgenstein

Philosophers and literary critics have long been fascinated, perplexed, and even appalled by Heidegger's reading of Trakl in his two lectures on the poet: "Die Sprache" ("Language"), from 1950, and "Die Sprache im Gedicht: Eine Erörterung von Georg Trakls Gedicht" ("Language in the Poem: A Discussion of Georg Trakl's Poem"), from 1952. Derrida considered the second lecture to be "one of Heidegger's richest texts:

subtle, overdetermined, more untranslatable than ever," but also "one of his most problematic." Alain Badiou has spoken of the "heavy-handed and fallacious recourse to the sacred in the most questionable of [Heidegger's] poetic analyses, especially those of Trakl"—analyses that led Walter Muschg to call Heidegger "a language-criminal." Yet, there is little doubt that, as one scholar put it in 1977, "the impact that Heidegger's capricious formulations had on the image of Trakl in the community of readers was so strong, so absolute, that he recast the image of the expressionist poet almost overnight."[3] Heidegger's lectures also inaugurated what might be called a second distinct turn in his own trajectory, this time toward the self-speaking of language, which would exercise profound influence on no less a poet than Paul Celan, whose own work we will have occasion to encounter in the pages that follow.[4] (English readers often do not realize that the Trakl lectures comprise the first two chapters of the opus magnum of this turn, *Unterwegs zur Sprache*, since the English translation, *On the Way to Language*, omits the lecture "Language" and inexplicably relegates "Language in the Poem" to the final chapter. Such decisions, together with the lax and often misleading translation of the latter text, no doubt contributed to the broad failure to appreciate Trakl's importance for Heidegger in Anglophone scholarship, at least until recently.)[5]

Heidegger's later work on language, however influential on people outside academia, nevertheless marked a crossroads in professional philosophy: if there was a time when philosophy professors in Germany were readily able to draw on Heidegger and poets such as Hölderlin in their lecture courses, Heidegger's two talks on Trakl "tore," in Otto Pöggeler's words, "the thread connecting contemporary philosophical endeavors with Heidegger." The violence of this image parallels the perceived violence of Heidegger's own hermeneutics. Pöggeler himself claimed that it was quite difficult to discern whether Heidegger's first Trakl lecture had anything to do with the poet, whereas Hannah Arendt saw the second lecture as marking a shift in Heidegger's interpretative practice: if the putative violence of his earlier interpretations of poets and philosophers was actually, she wrote, "no different from the so-called 'distortions' of Picasso"—that is, "Heidegger does not say what was unsaid by the author (as he sometimes seems to mean), but rather catches sight of the space of the unsayable"—his reading of Trakl, despite "very significant things" happening in it, ultimately "blew up" the poet's work, "rather than bringing it to life." But Trakl's friend and patron Ludwig von Ficker, the editor of the journal for avant-garde literature and cultural critique *Der Brenner*, found Heidegger's engagement with Trakl to be one of the greatest gifts and recompenses in Ficker's life. It even put one addict on the path to recovery.[6]

How to explain these paradoxes? How, moreover, could Heidegger go so far as to call Trakl "the poet of our generation" and "the poet of the still-hidden land of evening,"[7] that is to say, *the* poet of Heidegger's present and *the* poet of his and of every Westerner's possible future—a future that is supposed to bring us back to a primal past that lies deeper than any chronological reckoning—how could Heidegger make these claims and at the same time abandon his quest to grasp and develop what he deemed was "only a groping" in his lectures (MH/LF: 91)?[8]

Answers to these questions will emerge throughout the course of the book. What I would like to do in this chapter is to prepare for them by reconstructing Heidegger's broader engagement with the poet, not just in his two lectures but in texts that were unavailable or unknown to the above-mentioned commentators, such as Heidegger's marginalia in his personal copy of the Zurich edition of Trakl's poems. Until (or unless) Heidegger's complete *Nachlass* becomes available to researchers,[9] it will be impossible to provide a complete picture of this engagement. There is, nevertheless, enough material to trace more than its outlines.

§1. Discovering the Poet
(Thanks to a Journal for the Avant-Garde)

Several times in his corpus, Heidegger recalls his first encounter with Trakl's poetry. It occurred in Summer 1912, as he was paging through the influential journal *Der Brenner* in the academic reading room of the Freiburg University library. As Heidegger writes in a letter to Arendt from December 1952, a couple months after the delivery of his second Trakl lecture: "I was taken back to the year 1912, when as a student I [. . .] came across Trakl's poems for the first time. They haven't let go of me ever since."[10] He provides a similar account in another recollection from the same year, which he read aloud before presenting the lecture; only, this time, he adds that he purchased "the first Trakl poems" in 1913, by which he must mean Trakl's first volume, titled *Gedichte*.[11]

Now, although Trakl's poems may well have "accompanied [Heidegger] constantly" in the intervening years,[12] Heidegger, as far as I know, does not actually mention Trakl in his writings until 1950. Nor is there any evidence that he subscribed to *Der Brenner* between 1911 and 1954, as scholars sometimes claim.[13] Although Heidegger does not devote much attention to other German poets, with the exception of Hölderlin, until rather late in his career, in his early texts he at least mentions Novalis (in 1915–1916; GA 1: 399), Stefan George (in 1919–1920; GA 58: 69), Rainer Maria Rilke (in 1927; GA 24: 244–246), and Eduard Mörike (in 1913; GA 16: 31). The only other German poet who plays a major role for Heidegger, but to whom he does not refer until 1946–1947 (GA 97: 215), is Johann Peter Hebel; however, Heidegger never, to my knowledge, claims he had been under Hebel's influence since his school days, nor does he name Hebel "the poet of the still-hidden land of evening."[14] Perhaps the following question will be irrelevant when more of Heidegger's writings, and especially his correspondence, become available, but at present we ought therefore to ask: why, if Heidegger found Trakl so important as to mention him alongside the paragon poet Friedrich Hölderlin (GA 12: 87–88; see also GA 1: 56 and GA 100: 33–34), did he wait until he was a sexagenarian to put Trakl's name to paper?

I do not wish to deny possible allusions to Trakl in Heidegger's early work. I believe I can, for instance, hear Trakl's melancholy tone in some of Heidegger's juvenilia, such as his 1916 "Abendgang auf der Reichenau" ("Evening Stroll on Reichenau Island"):

> Seewärts fließt ein silbern Leuchten
> zu fernen dunkeln Ufern fort,
> und in die sommermüden, abendfeuchten
> Gärten sinkt wie ein verhalten Liebeswort
> die Nacht.
> Und zwischen mondenweißen Giebeln
> verfängt sich noch ein letzter Vogelruf
> vom alten Turmdach her—
> und was der lichte Sommertag mir schuf,
> ruht früchteschwer—
> aus Ewigkeiten
> eine sinnjenseitige Fracht—
> mir in der grauen Wüste
> einer großen Einfalt.[15]

*

> Seawards flows a silver gleam
> on to distant, darksome shores,
> and into the summer-weary, evening-damp
> gardens sinks, like a word of love held back,
> the night.
> And one last bird call
> from the old tower roof
> is caught between the moon-white gables—
> and what the luminous summer day brought me
> rests, fruit-heavy—
> from eternities
> a freight beyond sense—
> for me in the gray desert
> of a great simplicity.

But it is hard to know, since I believe I can also discern the voices of Novalis and Meister Eckhart, both of whom influenced Trakl and the early Heidegger.[16] Thus, the question remains: if Trakl had been crucial for Heidegger, would not Heidegger have seen fit to record Trakl's name *at least once* before 1950? In other words, how seriously should we take Heidegger's recollections? Was Trakl's poetry more vivid in Heidegger's memory than it had been in his life? Might this have something to do with Heidegger's attempt to reinvent himself after the catastrophe of the Third Reich? Trakl, the drug-addicted Austrian expressionist, was, after all, less politically compromised in the early German republic than Hölderlin—"the most German poet," in Norbert von Hellingrath's words.[17] And yet, even though Heidegger interprets Trakl in the wake of Hölderlin, without, incidentally, ever mentioning Hölderlin himself in the Trakl lectures, it is not as though Heidegger had completely stopped speaking in public about his favorite poet after the war. For example, he delivered a lecture on Hölderlin (". . . dichterisch wohnet der Mensch . . ." [". . . poetically the human dwells . . ."]) around the same time (1951) and at the very same place he first delivered his two lectures on Trakl (1950, 1952).

Perhaps, then, Heidegger felt so close to Trakl that he preferred to keep it a secret? A more likely explanation is that Heidegger recognized

Trakl's importance as "the poet of our generation" only in the 1950s, and this discovery brought his earlier acquaintance with Trakl's poetic work into greater relief.[18] (Now that I am writing a book on Heidegger and Trakl, I can look back at certain moments as having more significance than I accorded them at the time: my discovery of Trakl and of Heidegger's second lecture on the poet in the summer of 2012, when I saw the biopic *Tabu: Es ist die Seele ein Fremdes auf Erden* in a small Freiburg cinema; or finding Heidegger's personal copy of Trakl's poems in 2016.) In any case, even if I cannot close the gap between Heidegger's biographical claims and the absence of textual evidence to support them, it is possible to explain why Heidegger started to write about Trakl in the early 1950s and why he came to see him as vital for the destiny of the West. The story begins with a spa in the Black Forest.

§2. Lecturing at a Luxury Resort

In 1949, Gerhard Stroomann (1887–1957), the physician and charismatic head of the posh resort and sanitarium Bühlerhöhe, located in the vicinity of Baden-Baden in the northwestern Black Forest, began a sensational lecture series there that would go on to feature some of the most prominent German-speaking intellectuals and artists of the day, including Heidegger. Like the Bayerische Akademie der Schönen Künste and the Club zu Bremen, the invitations to Bühlerhöhe gave Heidegger a venue to present his ideas publicly at a time when he was prohibited from doing so at the university. (Technically, the ban was lifted in 1949, but he had not yet been granted emeritus status; thus, he could not teach until obtaining this status in the winter semester of 1951–1952.) Heidegger found his affluent and powerful audience members, however, to be quite different from the ivory tower of academia—although some of them no doubt literally traded in tusks. In the words of Georg Britting, who gave a reading of Trakl's poems after Heidegger's second lecture on the poet in 1952: "It was *very* highbrow, tempered by Black Forest trout and fried chicken. [. . .] I]t was swarming with counts and princesses, a bit snobbish."[19]

Despite his irritation with the crowd, Heidegger nevertheless participated frequently in the events, both as a speaker and auditor, and he was even somewhat of a patient: "We spent eight days," he once wrote, "recovering well at Bühlerhöhe." Judging from recollections by Stroomann and others, Heidegger's lectures were a great success: "each time there was the utterly exceptional excitement with which people inundated his lecture, his appearance at the lectern, as with no other contemporary figure."[20]

One might wonder why Heidegger's presence was in such high demand after the war, or why Heidegger would be sought out at the very venue where Konrad Adenauer, the first chancellor of the Federal Republic of Germany, liked to vacation. Heidegger's philosophy hadn't been particularly important in the latter days of the Third Reich, and the denazification proceedings during the Allied Occupation had deemed him unfit to teach, which, among other things, led to his mental breakdown in 1946. Many West Germans were nevertheless seeking to come to terms with their complicity in the Shoah and to find a way forward after power had been returned to them in 1949. To this end, they believed it necessary to make space for a variety of voices, including—and, in some cases, especially—conservative philosophical ones. Stroomann's invitations to Bühlerhöhe met this need, and in particular his first invitation, where Heidegger repeated a four-part lecture that he had previously delivered to a similarly prosperous and conservative crowd in Bremen. In this long lecture, titled "Einblick in das was ist" ("Insight into That Which Is") but better known as the "Bremen Lectures," Heidegger borders on blaming technology for the Holocaust, even as he gives his bureau- and technocratic audiences a peculiar means to salvation: they must not flee the "danger" of technology, but instead find a "saving power" (Hölderlin) in its very essence (GA 79: 72).[21]

These ideas would have resonated with Stroomann, who resisted the increasing technologization of medicine and sought to heal the whole person and even the whole society through culture and the arts. Indeed, he saw it as his (secular) spiritual mission to keep the artistic fire alive. One year after the Nazi collapse, he wrote: "How much of the holy flame remains depends on the luminosity and heat of this flame—on the priestly-pure—on the greatness of talent, of 'genius,' and on much else besides."[22] The invitation letter to Bühlerhöhe for Heidegger's lecture "'. . . poetically the human dwells . . .'" provides an explanation for how Stroomann's series at the sanitarium serves this spiritual-intellectual end:

Our *efforts* are not lectures and events. / On "*Wednesday Evenings*" [as Stroomann titled the series, even though many of the monthly "efforts" took place on weekends] we attempt to serve the *spirit* [Geist] in a chaotic, deeply imperiled time; to make, in the words of Richard Benz, a "*cosmos*" palpable, "in which the sensitive human being" is capable of "living."[23]

Stroomann promoted culture and the arts, especially German-language expressionist poetry, not only through his lecture series at Bühlerhöhe but also through his affiliation with the registered association of the "Kreis der Freunde europäischen Denkens" ("Circle of Friends of European Thinking"), of which he served as co-chairman, together with the German lawyer and politician Karl Geiler.[24] Its advisory board included José Ortega y Gasset and T. S. Eliot. A brochure that Stroomann sent to Ficker in August 1954 describes the aim of the organization as follows: "to support the creation of valuable representatives of the European life of the mind [Geistesleben], in particular those who stand for the freedom of the individual human being against all collective slogans, and to promote their publishing activity."[25] The brochure goes on to explain the organization's connection to the highly influential monthly periodical *Merkur: Deutsche Zeitschrift für europäisches Denken* (*Mercury: German Journal for European Thinking*), which it describes as a sort of middle ground between a rightwing return to the old and a leftwing insistence on the new:

> More than ever, we must confront the split into a thoughtless restoration, on the one hand, and a questionable activism, on the other, with a medium for publication that preserves substance and at the same time holds itself open to the new. For genuine continuity emerges only where old and new, tradition and project of the hour, continually prove themselves before one another.
>
> European thinking means seeing and preserving the connection in space and time: the connection with our history and that between the peoples. In this sense, European thinking is fatally threatened today by utopias that are alien to history and by the split between East and West. Associations

and organizations for European unity on the political level cannot banish the threat without individuals who exemplify with binding force the stance of the "good European" of yesterday and tomorrow.[26]

Heidegger, for his part, was never much of a European, let alone a "good one" (Nietzsche's phrase). Yet Heidegger did benefit from *Merkur*, which dedicated itself to rehabilitating politically tainted figures such as Gottfried Benn, Ernst Jünger, and Carl Schmitt, even while it provided a forum for radically opposed figures such as Theodor Adorno, Jürgen Habermas, Paul Celan, and Martin Buber. As one of the co-editors of the journal wrote in July 1948, just as Romance-language-scholar Hugo Friedrich was working on making "French editions of new texts by Heidegger" available: "Why not work on the German ones for *Merkur*?" "*Merkur*," he continues, "*must* get Heidegger going again. Getting people going again in this way [will be] a primary theme in the future."[27] The journal got Heidegger going again by publishing the philosopher Max Bense's positive review of Heidegger's "Brief über den Humanismus" ("Letter on Humanism") in 1949, and by publishing two of Heidegger's own texts in the ensuing years: "Was heisst Denken?" ("What Is Called Thinking?") in 1952, and his second Trakl lecture, under the title "Georg Trakl: Eine Erörterung seines Gedichtes" ("Georg Trakl: A Discussion of His Poem") in 1953.[28] The editors of "the leading journal for intellectuals"[29] did not, for all that, silence Heidegger's dissenters, although on one occasion they did try, unsuccessfully, to get an author to mitigate his critique. I am referring to Buber's "Religion und modernes Denken" ("Religion and Modern Thinking"), which appeared in February 1952. After reading the article, Heidegger censured Buber as unphilosophical, although he enthusiastically praised a different text Buber published in the journal six months later, "Hoffnung für diese Stunde" ("Hope for This Hour"), which even compelled Heidegger to comment on the essence of atonement (*Sühne*) as the bringing about of stillness (*Stille*).[30] Heidegger's remarks on Buber suggest that he kept up with the journal. He thus would have followed its advocacy on behalf of Trakl, which, alongside Heidegger's own lecture on the poet, included the printing of previously unpublished poems, articles on Trakl and on his literary remains, and an account of the last issue of *Der Brenner* and the latter's support of Trakl.[31]

MERKUR

DEUTSCHE ZEITSCHRIFT FÜR EUROPÄISCHES DENKEN

Julius Ebbinghaus	*Verfassungsgeschichte oder politische Entscheidung?*	201
Felix Somary	*Deutschland zwischen den zwei Weltmächten* . . .	210
Edgar Salin	*Der Gestaltwandel des europäischen Unternehmers* . .	214
Martin Heidegger	*Georg Trakl. Eine Erörterung seines Gedichtes* . .	226
Marguerite Yourcenar . . .	*Hadrian an Marc Aurel*	259

*

CHRONIK: Winfried Merlin, Gelebtes Utopia. Brief aus dem Kibuz 276

*

KRITIK: *Jean Wahl*, Karl Jaspers zum 70. Geburtstag 291
Eduard Rosenbaum, Verfassungen als Derivat der Kohle? 292
Otto v. Taube, Carl J. Burckhardt. Reden, Aufzeichnungen, Erzählungen 295
Karl August Horst, Autobiographie einer Bibliothek 298

DEUTSCHE VERLAGS-ANSTALT
STUTTGART

VII. Jahrgang 1953   **61**   *Drittes Heft*

Image 1. Cover of the journal in which Heidegger's "Language in the Poem" first appeared.

To return to Bühlerhöhe, Heidegger sojourned or lectured at the sanitarium numerous times in the 1950s. Here is what I have been able to determine about his activity there:[32]

March 25–26, 1950, during an eight day stay: delivery of "Insight into That Which Is"

October 7, 1950: delivery of the first Trakl lecture "Language," at a celebration in honor of Max Kommerell

February 24, 1951: delivery of an introduction to a poetry reading

May 2, 1951: participates in the discussion of a lecture by Kurt Bauch titled "Der Weg Picassos" ("Picasso's Path")

July 7–8, 1951: participates in a conference on psychosomatic medicine, with lectures by Gustav Richard Heyer, Medard Boss, and Immo von Hattingberg

October 6–7, 1951: delivery of "'. . . poetically the human dwells . . .'" and participation in the discussion the following day; public exchange with José Ortega y Gasset

October 4–5, 1952: delivery of "Georg Trakl: A Discussion of His Poem" and participation in the discussion the following day

January 24, 1953: participates in a discussion of a lecture by Emil Preetorius titled "Vom Künstlerischen in der Kunst und seine Wandlung mit Bildern aus jetzt und früher, aus West und Ost" ("On the Artistic in Art and Its Transformation, with Images from Today and Earlier Times, from West and East")

March 13, 1954: letter from Heidegger, Clemens von Podewils, and Stroomann to the poet Gottfried Benn, sent from Bühlerhöhe;[33] presumably attends the lecture by Preetorius titled "Das Beispiel Japans, mit westlichen und östlichen Bildern" ("The Example of Japan, with Western and Eastern Images")

> March 14, 1954: attends—and walks out on—a causerie by the actors Gustaf Gründgens, Elisabeth Flickenschildt, and Antje Weisgerber, titled "Das Theater und die moderne Kunst" ("Theater and Modern Art")
>
> May 11, 1955: participation in a celebration of expressionist poet Ernst Stadler, during which, at Heidegger's recommendation, Beda Allemann gave a lecture titled "Über das Dichterische" ("On the Poetic")[34]
>
> July 30–31, 1955: conversation with Podewils, Preetorius, and Walter Friedrich Otto about plans for Heidegger's future lectures on language

Note that nearly all of Heidegger's activities at Bühlerhöhe involved the promotion of poetry and art, and that it was there that he delivered his two lectures on Trakl. Thus, one must take the name "Bühlerhöhe" and everything it stands for into consideration when one is trying to understand Heidegger's relation to the Austrian poet. In the next two sections, I will summarize Heidegger's Trakl lectures and provide further information about their context.

§3. Speaking of Language

Heidegger delivered the first version of "Language" for a celebration at Bühlerhöhe in memory of literary scholar Max Kommerell, who had himself been a frequent patient at the resort and had died six year earlier. On the invitation to the celebration, Stroomann wrote:

> We are honored to commemorate and to bring to living effect a mind who was closely connected to us through his many sojourns at Bühlerhöhe up to his early death. With the wealth of his ideas and the force of his being, *Max Kommerell* (February 25, 1902–July 25, 1944) would have lent his support to our intentions. His quite special, intellectually, infinitely attractive appearance lives on among his many friends. Most recently, as a literary historian in Marburg, he enchanted scholarship and the youth with his astoundingly rich work. His poetic mission reached the broader public for the first

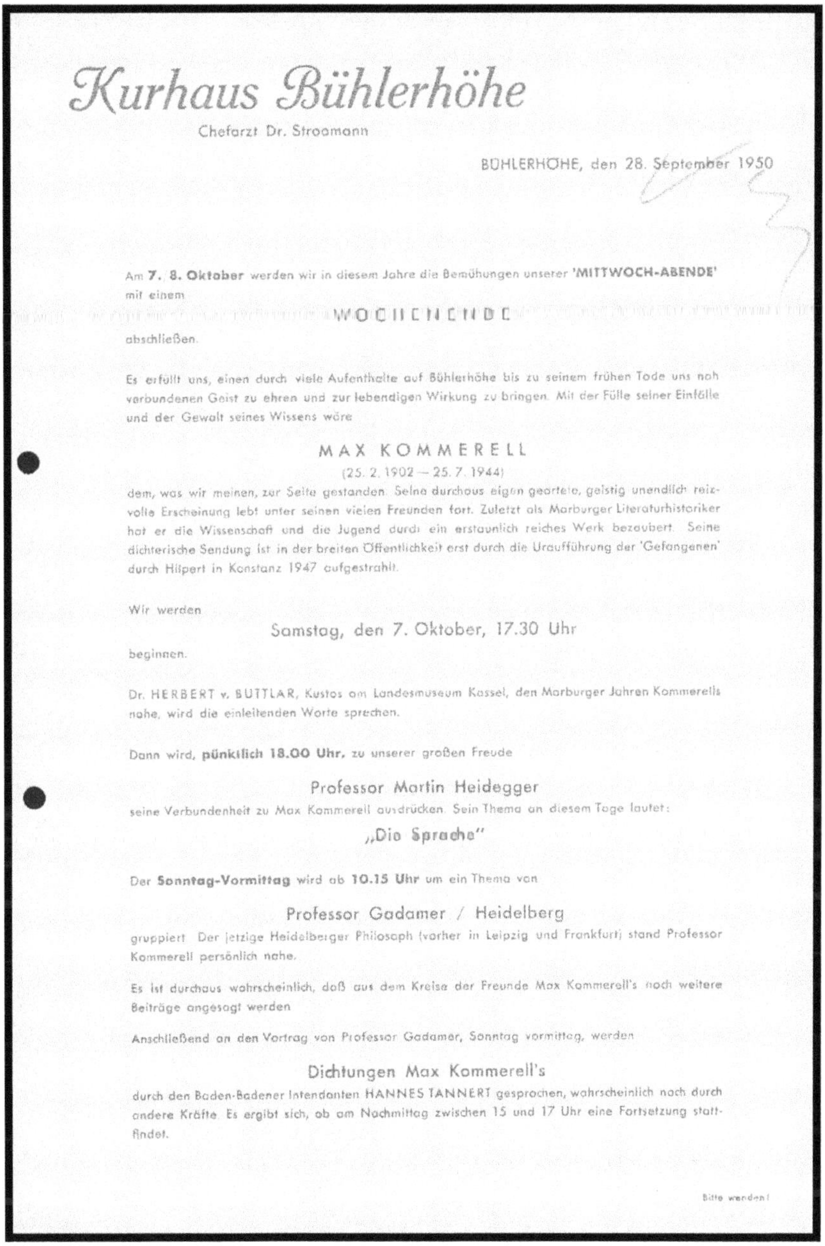

Kurhaus Bühlerhöhe

Chefarzt Dr. Stroomann

BÜHLERHÖHE, den 28. September 1950

Am **7. 8. Oktober** werden wir in diesem Jahre die Bemühungen unserer **'MITTWOCH-ABENDE'** mit einem

WOCHENENDE

abschließen.

Es erfüllt uns, einen durch viele Aufenthalte auf Bühlerhöhe bis zu seinem frühen Tode uns nah verbundenen Geist zu ehren und zur lebendigen Wirkung zu bringen. Mit der Fülle seiner Einfälle und der Gewalt seines Wissens wäre

MAX KOMMERELL
(25. 2. 1902 — 25. 7. 1944)

dem, was wir meinen, zur Seite gestanden. Seine durchaus eigen geartete, geistig unendlich reizvolle Erscheinung lebt unter seinen vielen Freunden fort. Zuletzt als Marburger Literaturhistoriker hat er die Wissenschaft und die Jugend durch ein erstaunlich reiches Werk bezaubert. Seine dichterische Sendung ist in der breiten Öffentlichkeit erst durch die Uraufführung der 'Gefangenen' durch Hilpert in Konstanz 1947 aufgestrahlt.

Wir werden

Samstag, den 7. Oktober, 17.30 Uhr

beginnen.

Dr. HERBERT v. BUTTLAR, Kustos am Landesmuseum Kassel, den Marburger Jahren Kommerells nahe, wird die einleitenden Worte sprechen.

Dann wird, **pünktlich 18.00 Uhr,** zu unserer großen Freude

Professor Martin Heidegger

seine Verbundenheit zu Max Kommerell ausdrücken. Sein Thema an diesem Tage lautet:

„Die Sprache"

Der **Sonntag-Vormittag** wird ab **10.15 Uhr** um ein Thema von

Professor Gadamer / Heidelberg

gruppiert. Der jetzige Heidelberger Philosoph (vorher in Leipzig und Frankfurt) stand Professor Kommerell persönlich nahe.

Es ist durchaus wahrscheinlich, daß aus dem Kreise der Freunde Max Kommerell's noch weitere Beiträge angesagt werden.

Anschließend an den Vortrag von Professor Gadamer, Sonntag vormittag, werden

Dichtungen Max Kommerell's

durch den Baden-Badener Intendanten HANNES TANNERT gesprochen, wahrscheinlich noch durch andere Kräfte. Es ergibt sich, ob am Nachmittag zwischen 15 und 17 Uhr eine Fortsetzung stattfindet.

Bitte wenden!

Image 2. Invitation to the Kommerell celebration at Bühlerhöhe.

time when [Heinz] Hilpert premiered [Kommerell's play] *The Prisoners* in Konstanz in 1947.

The main attraction at the celebration was Heidegger's lecture, which took its point of departure from Trakl's "Ein Winterabend" ("A Winter Evening") and from Kommerell's seminal essay on Heinrich von Kleist, "Die Sprache und das Unaussprechliche" ("Language and the Inexpressible"). I will briefly discuss the latter, along with a couple other works by Kommerell, in the next chapter. Although Heidegger does not mention Kommerell in the published version of his lecture, there is a fascinating, albeit brief, reference to the literary historian's essay in the original version of "Language" delivered at Bühlerhöhe (GA 80: 1000). There, Heidegger contrasts his own understanding of language as the speaking of the unspoken with Kommerell's emphasis on the inexpressibility and ineffability that lie at the heart of poetic utterance.

Kommerell was more explicitly at the center of the other presentations. The classical archeologist Herbert von Buttlar said some introductory words about Kommerell's connection and eventual break with the hermetic circle that formed around the poet Stefan George. The philosopher Hans-Georg Gadamer discussed Kommerell and the latter's then-unpublished work on the novelist Karl Immermann. And the director and actor Hannes Tannert gave a reading of some of Kommerell's poetry and prose.[35]

Heidegger's lecture "Language," for its part, does not aim to interpret Trakl in himself but rather uses Trakl to develop Heidegger's own distinct approach to language. In an unpublished letter to his brother from September 28, 1950, Heidegger relates that he had been working on the topic for his talk ever since summer 1939, when his Japanese student Kuwaki Tsutomu was still taking classes with him (and, I might add, when Heidegger held a seminar on Johann Gottfried Herder's theory of language, GA 85).[36] Heidegger expresses his frustrations with having to condense at least four lectures' worth of material into a one-hour presentation. Rather than remain at the superficial, programmatic level, he says that he decided to focus on a single poem by Trakl, of which the audience would have copies.[37]

In this lecture, Heidegger endeavors, not to speak *about* language, but to let language *itself* speak. For Heidegger, "A Winter Evening" is not about earthly pilgrimage and religious salvation, as one might expect. Rather, it articulates the fundamental relation between things and the world, or what Heidegger elsewhere calls "the fourfold" of earth, sky, divinities, and mortals. This articulation allows for a difference that does abolish intimacy. Language speaks such difference in the poem. Only in hearing this can we learn to dwell properly.

In the coming years, Heidegger will become even more emphatic about the need to listen to language. He will also claim that it is necessary for us to listen to Trakl specifically.

§4. Celebrating Trakl, Saving the West

Heidegger's second and final lecture on Trakl, "Language in the Poem," took place just under two years after "Language." He delivered it at the express request of Stroomann, who had organized a two-day commemorative event in honor of Trakl. Stroomann began planning the event as late as April 1951. On multiple occasions he described it as his "favorite idea." He wanted to use his influential venue to bring renown to Trakl, as he had been doing for Heidegger. In a letter to Ficker from January 5, 1952, Stroomann writes: "For me, [Trakl] is the great Austrian talent since Hofmannsthal and the last truly original force in lyric poetry. [. . .] I am sure that *Martin Heidegger*, whose great time has come and who signifies another philosophical epoch after Hegel and (differently) Nietzsche, will speak [at the event]."[38] Indeed, Trakl (along with Heidegger) was so important to Stroomann that he had initially planned to have the Trakl celebration take place in July on his (Stroomann's) sixty-fifth birthday, although he ended up postponing until October because both he and Heidegger fell ill.

In the same letter, Stroomann again pleads with Ficker to speak at the event—Ficker had previously turned him down due to reasons of health—and asks the old patron of Trakl for advice as to who should contribute to the celebration. Ficker eventually agreed to attend, but only as an auditor, and recommended both the poet Emil Barth, who had previously written on Trakl in *Merkur*, and the actor and theater director Kurt Horwitz, who had edited the Zurich edition of Trakl's poems, which I will discuss in detail below.[39] Stroomann communicated with Heidegger about Ficker's recommendations, and, by June, Stroomann was able to provide Ficker with concrete details about the forthcoming event: "[Heidegger] will call his lecture 'Das Gedicht Georg Trakls' ['The Poem of Georg Trakl'] and bring his insights [to bear on the relation] between thinking and poetizing [*Dichten*]. Emil Barth will give the introduction. Kurt Horwitz will read the verses: all invited according to your suggestions."[40]

By early September, however, both Barth and Horwitz had backed out. To replace Barth, Ficker suggested Eduard Lachmann, the novelist and, later, professor of German literature who would, in 1954, publish the controversial *locus classicus* for the Christian interpretation of Trakl, *Kreuz und Abend* (*Cross and Evening*).[41] It took Stroomann a while to agree. He insisted that Lachmann provide no more than a biographical introduction to Trakl so as to prepare the audience for Heidegger's "tremendous statement in honor of the poet." It seems, in other words, that he did not want Lachmann to offer his own interpretation of Trakl, which would stand in tension with Heidegger's reading and thereby turn the event from a celebration into a debate. Heidegger, who had been keeping Stroomann apprised of his own developing interpretation, was also involved in the assessment. While Heidegger valued Lachmann's editorial efforts on behalf of Hölderlin, Stroomann relates that "we [Heidegger and Stroomann] do not love his essay [on Trakl and Hölderlin] in the Salzburg Trakl edition."[42] To preempt conflict, Stroomann and Heidegger demanded that Lachmann write his introduction under the close eye of Ficker.

Horwitz, for his part, was replaced by the poets Friedrich Georg Jünger (the brother of author Ernst Jünger) and Georg Britting (a member of the Bayerische Akademie der Schönen Künste). Clemens von Podewils, general secretary of the Bayerische Akademie, was present at the event, although it appears he did not join Jünger and Britting in reading Trakl's poems aloud, as had been planned. I do not know whether it materialized, but Stroomann's idea was to have them read the poems that Trakl had himself selected for the one reading Trakl gave during his lifetime: "Die junge Magd" ("The Young Maid"), "Sebastian im Traum" ("Sebastian in Dream"), "Abendmuse" ("Evening Muse"), "Elis," "Sonja," "Afra," "Kaspar Hauser Lied" ("Kaspar Hauser Song"), and "Helian."[43] Here, in any case, are the details that Stroomann sent out in the official program on September 22, 1952 (which, because of Heidegger's close involvement in the planning of the event, I will quote at length):

> Within the framework of the "Wednesday-Evenings," the tribute to the poet Georg Trakl, which we had to postpone at the beginning of July, will take place on the weekend of October 4–5, 1952 at the health resort Bühlerhöhe.
>
> Georg Trakl is one of those individuals in German literature who accomplished his work early on in life. He died in World War I in 1914 at the age of twenty-seven. His brief years coincide with the life and work of Stefan George, Hugo v. Hofmannsthal, and Rainer Maria Rilke. This last great poetic movement was passionately accompanied by literary circles

and circles resembling religious orders, by much publicity, and by interest on the part of publishers and private individuals.

Georg Trakl's difficult life and poetic activity were carried out in solitude with the support and under the protection of Ludwig v. Ficker in Mühlau near Innsbruck. There the poet's soul found a home. Ludwig v. Ficker is the editor of the intermittently appearing journal *Der Brenner*, in which almost all of Trakl's poems first appeared; the first editions of his books [appeared with the publishing house run by] Kurt Wolff. The "Brenner Circle" is one of the most productive cultural convergences, with minds such as Theodor Haecker and Karl Kraus, and the poets Theodor Däubler, Josef Leitgeb, and Paula Schlier, among others. A veritable paragon for all similar efforts.

Georg Trakl's poetry, its vast lyrical substance and form, expresses much decay and melancholy: "In the age of the world night, the abyss of the world must be experienced and endured. But for this it is necessary that there are those who reach into the abyss" (Martin Heidegger) [quotation from "Wozu Dichter?" ("Wherefore Poets?")].

Professor Martin Heidegger will speak in honor of Georg Trakl on Saturday, October 4, 1952 at exactly 6 p.m. "Georg Trakl: A Discussion of His Poem" / Beforehand, at 4:15 p.m., the *Privatdozent* [unsalaried lecturer] Dr. Lachmann from the University of Innsbruck will provide an introduction: "Biographical Outlines for a Picture of Trakl" / To our great joy, Ludwig v. Ficker will take part in the tribute to Trakl. / There will be a pause after the lecture by Dr. Lachmann, before Martin Heidegger speaks. / In the late evening, around 9 p.m., poets who are present will honor Georg Trakl by reading some of his poems. / Likewise, on Sunday morning, October 5, 1952, at 10:15. / Afterwards, we are planning on having time for a discussion, in which Ludwig v. Ficker and Professor Heidegger will be present. / We need precise acceptances as space is an issue and we have to strive to limit the number of participants so as to have a productive gathering.

The event, reported on by numerous journals and newspapers, turned out to be a veritable *cause célèbre*. Among the numerous attendees (which, alongside Britting, Ficker, Heidegger, F. G. Jünger, Lachmann, and Podewils, included the editors of *Merkur* Hans Paeschke and Joachim

Images 3 and 4. Invitation to the Trakl celebration at Bühlerhöhe.

LUDWIG v. FICKER wird zu unserer tiefen Freude an der Ehrung Trakl's teilnehmen.

Nach dem Vortrag von Dr. Ladimann ist eine Pause vorgesehen, ehe Martin Heidegger spricht.

Am *** *** *** *** *** *** Dichter zu Ehren Georg Trakl's aus seinen Gedichten.

Ebenso Sonntag vormittag, am 6. Oktober 1952, 10.15 Uhr.

Dornach ist an eine Aussprache gedacht, bei der Ludwig v. Ficker und Professor Heidegger zugegen sind.

Wir benötigen genaue Zusagen, da die Platzfrage überspannt ist und wir im Sinne produktiver Zusammenseins eine Beschränkung der Teilnehmerzahl anstreben müssen.

                                                                                Prof. Dr. Straomann

Zu diesem Abend fährt ein SONDER-OMNIBUS: ab Bühl, Reithausplatz 14.30 Uhr, ab Baden-Baden Ludwig-Wilhelm-Platz 15 Uhr. Rückfahrt etwa gegen 23 Uhr über Baden-Baden nach Bühl.
Rückfragen bitten wir an Fräulein Radtke zu richten (Telefon Baden-Baden 60919, Bühl 1375).
Um Antwort auf anliegender Karte wird gebeten.

Moras), several were outraged at Heidegger's idiosyncratic, even violent interpretation of Trakl, in which, in the words of one commentator, Heidegger "expressed only his own thought."[44] Although, in the 1930s, certain Marxists, most prominently György Lukács, had seen expressionism as a precursor to fascism, Kurt Horwitz's daughter Ruth Horwitz couldn't reconcile Heidegger's commitment to National Socialism in 1933 with his declaration of an early admiration for Trakl and for the expressionism of *Der Brenner*, which the Nazis had banned.[45] She was also irritated by the format and Heidegger's manner of proceeding. In a letter to Ficker, she relates that, after Heidegger's lecture on Saturday evening, there was no opportunity for a public exchange; then, in the discussion period the following morning, Heidegger expressed his amazement that no one had noticed his omission of an important stanza in Trakl's poem "Herbstseele" ("Autumn Soul") about God. Horwitz continues:

> When the theme of Trakl's relation to Christ, to God, was at least shyly hinted at by the helpless priest from Vienna [Alfred Focke], Heidegger mopped under the table all the questions that could have subsequently arisen with the lapidary sentence: "God is there!" (In Trakl's poem.) [. . .] I feel this sort of intellectual exchange [*geistigen Auseinandersetzung*] to be dishonest [*unlauter*]: it dazzles; still more, it bluffs. Heidegger secured himself in all directions by announcing the evening before that the theme of religion, Christ, God, was very difficult to grasp in Trakl, and that a direct pronouncement on these things ran the danger of simplification and banalization. The aforementioned stanza of the poem "Autumn Soul" was precisely not spoken about—(it is very simple and very great!). Then on the next day it is suddenly and solemnly explained: "*God is there.*" No, here my heart can't take it![46]

On the other hand, many in the audience were enraptured, not least Ficker himself. In a letter to one of the *Merkur* editors, Ficker describes Heidegger's lecture as one of those "irruptions of light that matter today." Elsewhere he treats the celebration at Bühlerhöhe as an act of providence, as one of the most important events of his life. For it not only planted the seed for an abiding friendship with Heidegger but also provided the occasion for Ficker to give the first improvised speech of his life, a speech so moving it brought Heidegger to tears.[47] As Heinrich Wiegand Petzet describes it:

The audience in the hall had sensed that here someone was speaking who had sympathetically experienced the sorrow and solitude of a poet. [. . .] [I]t was actually not a lecture, but an address, a human consolation, from which Trakl poignantly came forward. [. . .] It was a confession—of truth. Who could ever forget how, in simple sentences, the last years, days, and hours of the poet were unveiled, how the friend told of the sad departure [Abschied], and then—with almost trembling voice, as though everything were happening at that moment for the first time—read aloud the testimony of [. . .] Trakl's loyal military servant [Matthias Roth]: the irrevocable, laden though it was with the burden of a world that had been perverted into something inhuman? What Ludwig von Ficker presented, quivering in the recollection of what he had once lived through, and at the end summarizing it with a reading of Trakl's "Grodek," because his own words threatened to fail him: here an experience of things that withdraw from rational touch was spoken.[48]

However one interprets the content and context of the Trakl celebration, the event at Bühlerhöhe had, by 1977, elevated Trakl to canonical status.[49] I will discuss this reception in more detail in later chapters, but for now let us turn to Heidegger's "Language in the Poem" to see why it has been so provocative.

What is initially striking about this lecture, in contrast to "Language" from 1950, is that Heidegger is forced to think specifically about a single poet, rather than just using a poem to work out a larger point, as was the case with his earlier talk. The name of the poet cannot vanish. Nonetheless, Heidegger contends that the person still can. He admits from the outset that his reading will seem one-sided to historians, biographers, psychoanalysts, and sociologists. Biography, apparently, is irrelevant to the dialogue between thinker and poet, although, as we will see, this will not stop Heidegger from seeking out information about Trakl's life and chronology, nor from using what he learns to suit his own ends.

In Heidegger's lecture, nearly every key term takes on a new and unfamiliar sense, or rather, the putatively proper sense of nearly every key term is resurrected from the ancient tombs of language—the German language above all. The word *Erörterung* from the subtitle does not mean "discussion," but "emplacement" or "situating." But we must be careful, for *Ort* does not merely signify one spatial coordinate among others, or even one locale; it marks the site at which all of Trakl's poems are gathered together, like the tip, or in Old High German the *ort*, of a spear. We are thus dealing, ultimately, not with poetic creations but with what Trakl has gathered together of being and condensed (*ge-dichtet*) into song, into a single *Gedicht*. The title of Heidegger's lecture accordingly takes on a new sense: not "Language in the Poem," but "Language in the Poetic Work," or even more loosely: "Language in the Condensed Word of Being: An Emplacing of Georg Trakl's Poetic Work." The place of this *Gedicht*, according to Heidegger, is *Abgeschiedenheit*.

Oddly, unlike so many other words throughout his lecture, Heidegger does not trace the origins of *Abgeschiedenheit*, which dates back to the late thirteenth century, when the mystical philosopher Meister Eckhart used it to exhort the soul to own up to its essential detachment from time, space, goals, and language. This is not to say that Heidegger subscribes to its more common sense, however, which refers to the state of having departed from this life, whether literally, as in death, or metaphorically, as in joining a cloister. We can hear something of these senses in the final stanzas of Trakl's "Autumn Soul":

> Bald entgleitet Fisch und Wild.
> Blaue Seele, dunkles Wandern
> Schied uns bald von Lieben, Andern.
> Abend wechselt Sinn und Bild.
>
> Rechten Lebens Brot und Wein,
> Gott in deine milden Hände
> Legt der Mensch das dunkle Ende,
> Alle Schuld und rote Pein. (HKA 1: 60)

*

> Fish and game soon slip away.
> Blue soul, darksome wand'ring, soon did
> Sever us from loved ones, others.
> Evening changes sense and image.
>
> Bread and wine of proper living,
> God, into your mild hands
> Layeth man the darksome ending,
> All the guilt and scarlet torment.

Heidegger, in contrast, reads the soul's departure not as a departure *from* the earth but as a point of departure for properly moving *toward* the earth. As for the last, unmistakably Christian stanza, he does not try to secularize (or paganize) it, as he did with bread and wine in the lecture "Language"; he ignores it altogether and cites only from the previous stanza in his second lecture on Trakl. And even when he brought up the end of the poem in the discussion period the day after his lecture, he claimed it pertained to the "others" from the third stanza, not to the earthbound soul. "Transcendence," he is reported to have said, "would no longer be necessary here, since 'God is indeed present,'" "'God is there!'"⁵⁰ Recall that it was this claim that especially irked Ruth Horwitz.

We can get a sense for the radicality of Heidegger's interpretation by examining how he avails himself of etymology to interpret a line from Trakl's "Frühling der Seele" ("Springtime of the Soul"). There, Trakl sings of the soul as *ein Fremdes auf Erden*, "something foreign or strange on earth." Heidegger, however, would have us hear *fremd auf* as Old High German *fram ūf*: the soul is "*on the way to* the earth." Thus, according to Heidegger's etymological rereading, Trakl is not concerned with the soul's salvation in heaven, with the soul alone trembling before God alone, hungering for the bread of life and thirsting for the wine of the blood shed for it. The soul is, admittedly, subordinate to *Geist* (Trakl's line continues with the syntagm *Geistlich dämmert . . .*), yet *Geist* does not mean *pneuma* or *spiritus*, let alone the Holy Ghost, but rather the archaic *gheis*, that which, as such, stands ambiguously outside of itself: on the brink of insurrection, but also on the brink of gentleness and peaceful gathering. We, however, currently live in the throes of *Geist*, or better, in the throes of *Geist* qua *spirit*, having forgotten its original twofold essence in favor of the abstracted and absolutized Good of Plato and the abstracted and absolutized God of Christianity, as well as their techno-scientific counterparts.

Our Western *Geschlecht* has grown decadent and corrupt. But a new dawn looms on the horizon. The time beckons when the sexes, tribes, generations, and species—*Geschlecht* means all of these things and more—will no longer strike out into violence and warfare but will be folded back into the gentle and harmonious doubleness of times past, or rather of the primeval time before time that marks the time to come, provided we heed its summons.

If there is a single sense to all these old and new senses, it is sense in the spatial sense of direction. The soul, Heidegger contends, is on the way to a promised land with very specific features. It is a land cut off from the degenerate race of Occidental metaphysics and its progeny. But it is not therefore Oriental or otherworldly. It is rather an *Abendland* held in store for us, or more accurately, for some of us. This *Abendland* is the place for those with ears to hear the proper sense and heed the proper direction of this word—not "Occident," but "land of evening"—and of all the German words Heidegger has been discussing, or rather situating. It is the place of the authentic, secret Germany (GA 16: 290, GA 94: 155).

§5. *Post eventum*

Heidegger continues to mention Trakl in the final decades of his career, although most of his later references to the poet are fleeting or undeveloped. While Heidegger's correspondence with Ludwig von Ficker, which began after both men spoke at the Trakl celebration in 1952 and ended with Ficker's death in 1967, centers primarily on the poet, the letters are not especially substantive. Heidegger and Ficker would send each other gifts, such as photos of Trakl as a child and of his bust and grave (which Heidegger put on his desk, possibly alongside a picture of Trakl's sister Grete[51]), or copies of their recent publications and texts by others on Trakl.[52] Ficker even sent Heidegger the autographed manuscript of Trakl's poem "Afra." Given Heidegger's apparent lack of interest in biography, the most puzzling thing about the correspondence is how eager Heidegger is to learn from Ficker about "our poet" Trakl; on two separate occasions, they even visited Trakl's gravesite together, which was profoundly moving for Heidegger (MH/LF: 49, 53–55, 146–147). This tells us, at the least, that Trakl was frequently on Heidegger's mind after the events at Bühlerhöhe, even if he did not find the space or time to develop his thoughts into another major lecture on the poet. Indeed, when, in June 1964, Ficker sent a personal invitation to Heidegger to hold the memorial lecture at a ceremony in November for the fiftieth anniversary of Trakl's death, Heidegger regretfully declined, saying it would take too much work to do justice to the poet in view of Heidegger's trajectory and the contemporaneous state of the world:

> In order to be able to say something even remotely worthy, it would require an entirely new reflection [*Besinnung*], which, with my work process, would have demanded at least a year. For what was attempted and ventured earlier at Bühlerhöhe

was only a groping. Today I see the uniqueness of Trakl's poetry much more clearly, but also recognize the conceptual and linguistic perplexity and lack of means when it comes to speaking in correspondence with it [*ihr zu entsprechen*]. I thus would not want to repeat what I had said earlier or say something that is entirely insufficient. But I must also, at the same time, remain on my path, which, with age, is becoming easier, but precisely thereby all the more difficult in view of the uncanny change in the world to which the human is exposed. And, at my age, there is not much time remaining for alert and acute thinking. Thus, it is the necessity [*die Not*] of the task that compels [*nötigt*] me to decline. (MH/LF: 91–92)[53]

Nevertheless, there are a few noteworthy topics to which Heidegger connects Trakl's poetic work in other writings. During the summer semester of 1952, as Heidegger was getting ready for his trip to Bühlerhöhe to present his second Trakl lecture, he cites from Trakl's "Das Gewitter" ("The Thunderstorm") to support the idea that the German word *Seele* signifies not just "the principle of life" but also "the essential sway of spirit [*das Wesende des Geistes*], the spirit of spirit, the little spark of the soul in Meister Eckhart" (GA 8: 153). Around this time, he also connects Trakl's repeated use of the phrase *Es ist* ("It is" or, less literally, "There is") in the poem "Psalm" with the soundless and extra-logical speaking of what lies before us (GA 8: 209). While doing so, as though in passing, Heidegger thwarts convention and uses the word *schweigen* transitively, in the sense of holding something in silence or even silently bringing it into being. Typically, it just means "to be silent." Heidegger seems to have taken the transitive usage from Trakl, for, in several other texts, Heidegger discusses precisely this peculiar usage in the Austrian's work, citing the poems "Im Dunkel" ("In the Dark") and "Abendlied" ("Evening Song").[54] A decade later, Heidegger returns to the *Es ist* of Trakl's "Psalm" and "De Profundis," comparing it with the French *Il y a* in Arthur Rimbaud and with the German idiom *Es gibt* (GA 14: 47–49; MH/LF: 81).

Other topics for which Heidegger draws on Trakl include the idea of language as essentially a saying qua showing (GA 12: 242), the *Lichtung* or "clearing" of being (GA 14: 80 and 80n12), and Nietzsche's idea of the Dionysian, which, Heidegger claims, Trakl was able to "twist free from [*Verwindung*]" (MH/LF: 53). There is also, finally, an important letter from 1972 that Heidegger wrote to the young French scholar

Jean-Michel Palmier, who had sent him a copy of his massive—and massively inaccurate—study entitled *Situation de Georg Trakl*, which Heidegger had encouraged Palmier to undertake as a doctoral thesis several years prior.⁵⁵ In this letter, Heidegger says that, aside from the preface to the second volume of the 1969 historical-critical edition of Trakl's work, Palmier is the only one who understood "the sense of my exposition."⁵⁶ Indeed, Palmier seems to have understood it so well that his critical remarks on Heidegger's interpretation could find an amenable audience in the philosopher himself. This is due, in no small part, to the fact that Palmier's overall analysis is chiefly indebted to Heidegger, even if it is not up to the philosopher's level.⁵⁷ Heidegger says Palmier's remarks are "quite justified, above all with respect to the figure of the 'Stranger' [*l' 'Étranger'*] and other figures." Palmier criticizes Heidegger for three main reasons: for being too quick to conflate the stranger with the soul and with Traklian figures such as Elis and the unborn; for seeing a division of the species (stranger vs. corrupt *Geschlecht*) in "Autumn Soul," rather than the opposition between innocence and evil; and (3) for Heidegger's astounding disregard for Trakl's distress over his fallen comrades at Gródek, which, Palmier stresses, we must turn to history (or in Heidegger's language, to historiography) in order to appreciate.⁵⁸ Yet, one should question whether Heidegger's concession pertains to this last point. Heidegger praises Palmier for his ontological, as opposed to existenti*ell* or anthropological, reading of the concept of *Verfallen* ("falling prey") in *Being and Time*, which Heidegger links to Trakl's poem "Verfall" ("Collapse"); however, Heidegger retains his general skepticism about biography. He asks Palmier about the extent to which he (Palmier) is oriented to the biographical (which Palmier says we cannot ignore, at least when it comes to certain works by Trakl),⁵⁹ instead of, like Heidegger, being oriented to something that lies deeper and makes possible any appreciation of the biographical, namely, the work. This contrast between biography and work is a major issue in Heidegger's marginalia to the appendix of the Zurich edition of Trakl's poems.

§6. Annotating the Trakl Bible

Heidegger's marginalia are significant because they shed light on how Heidegger's reading is situated in, or rather against, the general reception of Trakl's work at the time, especially by those who had some connection with *Der Brenner*.⁶⁰ If Trakl-biographer Otto Basil was right to identity these individuals as a "sort of religious community"—"a Trakl-church" that, "with its hierarchy of interpreters and commentators, claimed not only primacy in Trakl-scholarship, but also infallibility of judgment and the halo of orthodoxy"[61]—then it would not be altogether inappropriate to call the Zurich edition, with its hagiographic tributes and arrangement of Trakl's poems according to the last testament of the poet-saint, a sort of Trakl Bible. On this interpretation, which I present with only partial irony, Heidegger would be its apostate scholiast.

Before I examine Heidegger's marginalia, it might prove helpful to say a few words on why I believe it is legitimate to draw on such a source, especially since I will be doing so not just here but throughout this book. I have four reasons. First, Heidegger considered his annotations to many of his own books, as well as to those of Ernst Jünger (GA 90), to be worthy of inclusion in his *Gesamtausgabe* (*Collected Works*). Heidegger was therefore not, as such, opposed to the philosophical import of the medium. Second, in his lecture course on Hölderlin's "Andenken" ("Remembrance"), Heidegger draws on what one might call Hölderlin's self-marginalia in order to determine the very essence of poetry. In Heidegger's reading, the poet's variants on the word *undichtrisch* ("unpoetic") in the manuscript of the fragment "Das Nächste Beste" were not mere alternatives, but rather something of a gloss, an attempt "to clarify" what the word and, accordingly, its unnegated counterpart actually meant (GA 52: 163).[62] Third, Heidegger wrote far less on Trakl than he did on Hölderlin. Marginalia may not be the next best source for elaborating prose, but they do provide hints when the latter is lacking, and, in this case, we lack evidence of Heidegger's serious engagement with the Brenner Circle elsewhere. Fourth, is it not possible that the intimacy and directness of marginal notes could be more revealing, more honest, than countless pages of commentary?[63]

It is unclear whether Heidegger wrote all of his marginalia to the appendix of the Zurich edition before or after he composed his two lectures on Trakl. Even if he did so afterward, this does not mean he was unacquainted with some of its contents before then. Most simply, this acquaintance could have come from reading the Zurich edition earlier on, which he refers to in both of his lectures on Trakl, even singling out the appendix in "Language in the Poem" (GA 12: 15, 36n1). Another possibility is that Heidegger had read some of this material elsewhere. Eight of the texts of the appendix are taken, as a whole or in part, from the first edition of Ficker's pious memorial to the poet, the edited collection *Erinnerung an Georg Trakl*, from 1926:

1. Ludwig von Ficker, "Lebensdaten" ("Biographical Dates")
2. Karl Kraus, "Zum Dank für den 'Psalm'" ("With Thanks for the 'Psalm'")
3. Rainer Maria Rilke, "Aus den Briefen, die er im Februar 1915 an den Herausgeber des 'Brenner' richtete" ("From the Letters That He Sent to the Editor of *Der Brenner* in February 1915")
4. Erwin Mahrholdt, "Aus einer Studie über Georg Trakl" ("From a Study on Georg Trakl")
5. Karl Borromäus Heinrich, "Die Erscheinung Georg Trakls" ("The Phenomenon of Georg Trakl")
6. Hans Limbach, "Begegnung mit Georg Trakl" ("Encounter with Georg Trakl")
7. "Brief des Bergarbeiters Matthias Roth aus Hallstatt zum Tode seines Herrn" ("Letter from the Miner Matthias Roth from Hallstatt on the Death of His Master")
8. Josef Leitgeb: "Am Grabe Georg Trakls: Ein Gedicht, gesprochen anlässlich der Beisetzung der Gebeine des Dichters auf dem Friedhof von Mühlau am 7. Oktober 1925" ("At the Grave of Georg Trakl: A Poem, Spoken on the Occasion of the Burial of the Bones of the Poet at the Mühlau Cemetery on October 7, 1925").

The Zurich edition also contains:

1. Ludwig von Ficker, "Die letzte Begegnung mit Georg Trakl" ("The Last Encounter with Georg Trakl")
2. Emil Barth: "Zu Trakls letztem Gedicht: 'Grodek': Schlusswort einer Schrift zum Gedächtnis von Trakls 50. Geburtstag am 3. Februar 1937" ("On Trakl's Last Poem: 'Gródek': Concluding Words of a Text in Memory of Trakl's Fiftieth Birthday on February 3, 1937")
3. Ludwig von Ficker, "Aus einem Brief vom 12. Juni 1945 an den Herausgeber" ("From a Letter to the Editor from June 12, 1945")
4. Kurt Horwitz, "Nachwort" ("Afterword").

At any rate, whether the marginalia date from before or after his lectures, they provide precious evidence of the uniqueness of Heidegger's reading, especially when it comes to the themes of Christianity, *Geschlecht*, and the interrelation of biography, autobiography, and hagiography.

Let us begin at the end of the volume, with editor Kurt Horwitz's afterword. Horwitz explains that his goal in compiling the texts that comprise the appendix was twofold: he wanted "to let the image of a poet more clearly come to the fore," and he wanted "to point to the existentially Christian dimension in Georg Trakl's essence, a dimension that distinguishes him essentially from the highly celebrated poets of his epoch—Rilke, Hofmannsthal, and George" (DD: 229).[64] It is significant that these two objectives are precisely what Heidegger resists in his reading of Trakl. Heidegger actively opposes the value of biographical depiction (GA 12: 15, 33), and at nearly every turn he tries to undermine or, at best, underpin the Christian(-Platonic) reading by recourse to an ontological one (GA 12: 25, 35–36, 41, 54–55, 72–73). It should therefore come as little surprise that Heidegger drew a large question mark next to Horwitz's interpretive justification for his editorial focus:

> [Trakl] has answered the decisive question of the Gospel clearly and distinctly: "What do you all hold about Christ? Whose son is He?" [Matthew 22:42] In his poems, bread and wine and the angels do not merely show up as sweet and beautiful images. His melancholy, his solitude, and his despair are absolutely <u>conditioned</u> [*bedingt*] by Christianity. (DD: 229)

Heidegger underlined the word *bedingt* ("conditioned") here, apparently because, on his reading, Christianity is not the condition for the possibility of understanding the place of the poetic work; rather, if there is a Christian element in Trakl's oeuvre, it is intelligible only on the basis of a prior, and therefore pre-Christian, determination of the place of the poetry. "Trakl's melancholy, his solitude, homelessness, and despair," are not, as Horwitz claims, "that of an essentially Christian poet in an un-Christian age" (DD: 230); Christianity or, at best, Christendom, for Heidegger, is rather of a piece with the machinations and mendacity of the metaphysical age.

We can interpret another marginalium in the appendix in a similar fashion. The fourth text in the appendix is an excerpt from what one scholar has called the "most striking" representation of the image of Trakl projected by the Brenner Circle, namely, Erwin Mahrholdt's substantial study "Der Mensch und Dichter Georg Trakl" ("The Man and Poet Georg

Trakl") (1925).[65] In contrast to Heidegger's anti-Platonic interpretation, Mahrholdt contends that Trakl's profound Christian suffering led him to espouse a dualistic metaphysics of good versus evil, heaven versus earth. Experiencing these oppositions within his own person,

> [Trakl's] watchword was to purify oneself and bear oneself up to God [. . .]. To tell people what they no longer knew: that their soul is something foreign on earth [*ein Fremdes auf Erden*], is something divine, worthy of the highest care, and to sing to them of its golden stillness. (DD: 202–203)

Heidegger drew a line in the margin next to Mahrholdt's interpretation of the soul as something strange or foreign on earth, no doubt because of its diametrical opposition to Heidegger's own interpretation of Trakl's verse ("Es ist die Seele ein Fremdes auf Erden") in his second lecture on the poet. Recall that Heidegger reads *fremd* not as "foreign to," but as *fram*, "on the way to," the earth (GA 12: 37). Heidegger's articulation of the standard approach to this verse reads like an ironic gloss on Mahrholdt's account. Heidegger writes:

> Suddenly, with this sentence, we find ourselves in the midst of a commonplace notion. This notion presents us with the earth as the terrestrial, in the sense of the transitory. The soul, in contrast, is considered to be what is intransitory, supra-terrestrial. Ever since Plato's doctrine, the soul has belonged to the super-sensuous. If, however, it appears within the sensuous, then it is only as something that has been cast out [*verschlagen*] into it. Here, "on earth," it does not have the right cast [*Schlag*—a word related to *Geschlecht*]. It does not belong on the earth. Here, the soul is "something foreign." The body is a prisoner of the soul, if not something worse. Thus, there apparently remains no other prospect for the soul than to leave behind the realm of the sensuous as soon as possible, a realm that, seen from a Platonic perspective, is not truly existent and is only decay. (GA 12: 35–36)

In the next paragraph of Mahrholdt's study alone are five additional moments that sharply contrast with Heidegger's hermeneutics. Mahrholdt writes:

Looming alongside this Christian submission and cloistral, inner detachment [*Abgeschiedenheit*] is the most terrible fear that [Trakl's] beloved human race [*Menschengeschlecht*] could at some point completely perish [*untergehen*]. Just as the boy hated the relentlessly forward-rushing and all-devouring times and threw himself in the path of furiously hurrying people and animals, so, in the midst of the absurdity [*Wahnwitz*] of the war and of the greedy destruction, the poet plaintively exclaims: the icy wave of eternity would devour the golden image of man. (DD: 203)

First, Mahrholdt reads *Abgeschiedenheit* in its religious sense, as involving both disconnectedness from earthly decay and departure toward heavenly restoration, not in the sense of setting out in the direction of a new German homeland. Second, Mahrholdt emphasizes Trakl's concomitant compassion for the world he wishes to flee (see the poem "Grodek"), whereas Heidegger claims that Trakl would have jubilated over the deaths that checked the propagation of the degenerate race (GA 12: 61–62). Third, Mahrholdt uses the word *untergehen* in the catastrophic sense of extinction, not, as Heidegger does, in the sense of "going (back) down" into a realm that precedes the putrescent *Geschlecht* and awaits the unborn (GA 12: 38, 50–51, 70). Fourth, Mahrholdt reads Trakl's late poem "Klage" ("Lamentation"), from which he takes the words "the icy wave of eternity would devour the golden image of man," as though spoken from the mouth of a prophet; it is a jeremiad quite compatible with Christianity, or at least its older testament. Heidegger, however, asserts that the "icy wave of eternity" is not only *non*-Christian, "it is not even Christian despair" (GA 12: 72). Finally, here, as well as in the very title of his study, "The Man and Poet Georg Trakl," Mahrholdt follows the maxim, *like person, like poetry*, while Heidegger gives primacy and pride of place to the poem itself.

Mahrholdt's biographical approach is exemplified in another passage annotated by Heidegger:

Trakl bore within himself both of the dangers of genius that Weininger speaks of, those of crime and madness:[66] he subdued the criminal element early on, even if it often reared up in his severe and, as it were, petrified face and scared people off; to the death, however, he feared falling entirely into madness, which had already at times grabbed hold of the infinitely melancholic one. Blooming behind this slag was a truly benevolent and faithful human being, recognizable in his mildness and purity only through the <u>untarnished reflection of his essence</u>, the poetry [*das ungetrübte Abbild seines Wesens, die Dichtung*]. (DD: 200–201)

Heidegger underlined the phrase *ungetrübte Abbild seines Wesens* ("untarnished reflection of his essence"), and drew a question mark next to it in the margin. Again, what Heidegger is opposing is the idea that poetry reflects the person, whether purified or not.

Despite this, Heidegger shows particular interest in the person of Trakl. He drew lines in the margins next to Mahrholdt's comments that Trakl's "head was somewhat bent by the torture of his blinding consciousness," and that "[t]he senseless spirit of power and commerce that wrecked Germany was foreign to him, together with the West's idealism about sports and its craving for happiness" (DD: 200–201). Heidegger did the same for a passage from a 1926 text by Trakl's friend Karl Borromäus Heinrich, the dedicatee of the poems "Gesang des Abgeschiedenen" ("Song of the Departed One") and "Untergang" ("Downfall"). Heinrich relates "that gloom and madness [*Trüb- und Wahnsinn*] did not speak from [Trakl's] countenance, but rather love, compassion, unspeakable suffering, in addition the mighty stillness of the gazing human being" (DD: 207). And, in Hans Limbach's 1914 recollection of his encounter with Trakl, Heidegger took note of passages in which Limbach emphasizes Trakl's reticence:

> Trakl responded only briefly and seemingly unwillingly, and when one of the questions appeared to come too close, he shrank back in a timid and almost hostile way. [. . .] [B]y all appearances, it was embarrassing for him to have to justify himself. [. . .] Trakl's essence was characterized by the profoundest reticence. (DD: 210)

To be sure, Heidegger takes up many of these themes in his writings on Trakl, including the importance of silence and stillness (especially GA 12: 26–30, 75); *Wahnsinn*, not as madness, but as being without (*wana*) modern sensibility (*Sinn*) (GA 12: 49, 67, 76); and compassion, or rather, contra Heinrich, its inverse, a certain disdain (GA 12: 61–62).

But Heidegger is also interested in the way Trakl the man does or does not embody them.

There is perhaps something more at play here than biographical fascination. Derrida notes that Heidegger's reading of Trakl bears Heidegger's own signature or distinctive mark: as Trakl's *Fremder* ("foreigner," "stranger") has a determinate trajectory and destination, so too does Heidegger in his interpretation; indeed, it is one and the same destination, that of the *Abendland*, the "land of evening" that is more primordial and futural than all notions of the West or Occident (GIII: 87, 89, GA 12: 73–77). Derrida hesitates to call Heidegger's reading autobiographical in any conventional sense of the term, but I wonder whether Heidegger did not see aspects of himself—or aspects of how he would have liked to have seen himself—in the poet: reticence; reluctance to justify himself; aversion to mass culture and its pursuit of happiness; having, as Hölderlin said of Oedipus and Heidegger said of Hölderlin, "one eye too many, perhaps" (GA 4: 47).

Moreover, we might wonder about Heidegger's stance on the hagiographic tendencies—and tendentiousness—of the Brenner Circle when it came to Trakl.[67] Heidegger would presumably balk at the biographical justification for sainthood, its attractiveness notwithstanding. But Heidegger does not hesitate to include Trakl in his own heterodox canon of the blessed. Trakl is a "great poet," and great poets poetize *only* from out of one *single* unspoken poem (GA 12: 33). This poem, like the parables of Jesus or Fichte's appeal to the German nation, is audible only to one "that hath ears to hear" (Matthew 11:15, et passim).[68]

Earlier I suggested that, at best, Heidegger might be critiquing Christendom and not Christianity as such. This reading would require a large helping of hermeneutic charity, but it would not be baseless. Heidegger does appear to be open to the possibility of an emplacement of the Christian dimension; it is just that such an emplacement would be derivative of Heidegger's prior ontological emplacement, and—if this is even possible—it would not be able to use "the concepts of metaphysical theology or those of ecclesiastical theology" (GA 12: 72). As Heidegger said around the time when he was preparing his second lecture on Trakl: "If I were to write another theology, as I am sometimes tempted to do, the word 'being' would not be allowed to appear in it" (GA 15: 437). Another prohibited word would, presumably, be "transcendence," which, as I mentioned earlier, Heidegger is reported to have addressed during a discussion the day after the delivery of his second Trakl lecture at Bühlerhöhe. In any case, Limbach's report, which Heidegger marked up extensively, is an important source for any effort to think seriously about Trakl's Christianity.

In a diary entry reproduced in part in the appendix of the Zurich edition, Limbach relates that, on January 13, 1914, he had gone with the author Carl Dallago, for whose writing *Der Brenner* was actually founded in 1910, to Ficker's home, on which occasion Limbach first met Trakl.[69] That evening, before turning to the subject of religion, the outspoken Dallago had been grilling Trakl with a host of disparate questions, completely insensitive to Trakl's reserved, even detached nature. In Limbach's words, which Heidegger drew an arrow next to, "D. had no sense for [Trakl's] way of being and laid into him more and more" (DD: 210).

Noting similarities in their poetry, Dallago asked Trakl about Walt Whitman, whom Trakl said he found to be pernicious. This surprised Dallago and led to another barrage of questions. Ficker intervened, noting a major opposition between the two poets: whereas Whitman affirms life in all its complexity, "Trakl is a pessimist through and through" (DD: 210). Yet Dallago would not relent. He asked whether Trakl did not, after all, have any "joy in life," whether his creative work did not bring him any "satisfaction." "'Certainly,'" Trakl responded, "'it's just that one must be mistrustful of such satisfaction'" (DD: 210–211). We now arrive at the turning point in the conversation, in which Trakl's faith comes to the fore. In his marginalia, Heidegger drew an arrow to mark off what comes next:

> Extremely astonished, D. leaned back in his chair.
> "Why don't you simply enter a cloister, then?," he asked finally, after a short silence.
> "I'm a Protestant," Trakl answered in a muffled tone.[70]
> "Pro-te-stant?," asked D. slowly—"I certainly wouldn't have thought that!—You should at least not live in the city, then, but in the country, where you would be farther removed farther from the hustle and bustle of people and closer to nature!"
> "I have no right to escape from Hell," Trakl retorted.
> "But Christ also escaped from it."
> "Christ is God's Son!," answered the former.
> D. hardly knew how to contain himself.

"So then you also believe that all salvation comes from him? You understand 'God's Son' in the proper sense of the word?"

"I'm a Christian"—answered Trakl.

"Okay,"—continued the former—"then how do you explain such non-Christian phenomena as the Buddha or the Chinese sages?"

"They, too, received their light from Christ." (DD: 211)

The spirit in which Heidegger took note of this report is difficult to ascertain, although Trakl's replies do bear a noble simplicity and immanent orientation. In any event, Trakl's God is hardly the transcendent *causa sui* of the theologians (cf. GA 11: 77).

Trakl grew even more weary and withdrawn as the conversation went on. Dallago asked about the decline of humanity since the age of the ancient Greeks, suggesting thereby that that age had marked the pinnacle of human achievement. Trakl replied by resetting the parameters: humanity had never, and could never have, sunk so low as since the appearance of Christ. Limbach relates that, at this point in the exchange, Dallago, refusing to consider Trakl's mood, "brought up Nietzsche as a final trump" (DD: 211). Heidegger drew two lines in the margin next to this. Limbach does not report what exactly Dallago said, but it was such as to elicit a brusque response from Trakl: "'Nietzsche was mad [*wahnsinnig*]!'" (DD: 211). When Dallago asked for clarification, all Trakl could bring himself to do was to chalk it up to the same sickness from which Maupassant suffered, namely, syphilis. Trakl said this even though, according to Limbach, "the demon of falsehood seemed to glisten in [Trakl's] eyes" (DD: 211).[71] Outraged, Dallago rejected Trakl's contention outright, exclaiming that Trakl had to know there was more to Nietzsche's madness than the mere pathophysiology of a sexually transmitted infection. Trakl fell silent. A while later, he turned back to Christ, touching on the relation of the sexes and the possibility not of the "*One Geschlecht*" of the lovers in Trakl's poem "Abendländisches Lied" ("Song of the Occident"), but of the "one flesh" from Genesis (2:24) and from Jesus's gloss on it (Matthew 19:4–6; Mark 10:5–9):

"It is unheard of"—[Trakl] began—"how Christ solves the deepest questions of humanity with every simple word! Can

> the questions regarding the community between man and woman [*Mann und Weib*] be solved more completely than through the command: *They shall be One Flesh?*" (DD: 212)

Later in the evening, Trakl spoke with Limbach about Dostoevsky and about Russia, where Limbach had been living for the past couple of years. Trakl must have still been thinking about the relation between man and woman, since, with respect to the character Sonja from *Crime and Punishment*,

> [Trakl] uttered the beautiful words—again with wildly glistening eyes—"The hounds who assert that woman only seeks sensual pleasure should be struck dead! Woman seeks *her justice* [or *righteousness*, Gerechtigkeit] as well as each of us do!" (DD: 212)

There are, to conclude, two things worth noting about this passage, which Heidegger marked with two lines in the margin and a ">"-shaped figure, perhaps thereby signaling its special significance for him. First, this passage, together with the one from Genesis above, displays Trakl's opposition to the hugely influential book by Otto Weininger from 1903, *Geschlecht und Charakter* (*Sex and Character*)—so influential, in fact, that no intellectual in the Austro-Hungarian empire writing in the years before the onset of World War I could theorize *Geschlecht* without having been affected, however indirectly, by this work. In contrast to Trakl, Weininger deprecated women's inherent lack of justice—they were, for him, a symbol of totipotent nothingness—and advocated celibacy as a means to escape their corrupting influence on men's moral ascent.[72] However, even if there is discord between the sexes in the present age, the solution is not to dissolve difference altogether; rather, what is needed, according to Heidegger, is a thinking that would do justice to a gentler sexual difference (see chapter 6). Remarkably, Heidegger moves in this direction in his second lecture on Trakl (GA 12: 41, 46, 63, 74). But, and this is the second point I would like to make, to do justice to this topic requires a consideration of justice, *Gerechtigkeit*, itself. Or, if we are to take the Christian dimension seriously, it requires a consideration of *righteousness* (another possible rendering of *Gerechtigkeit*; compare the Greek *dikaiosunē*). Despite a possible moment of recognition in his marginal note here, Heidegger effectively ignores this theme in his reading of Trakl, as he does the theme of love. These themes are nevertheless crucial for Trakl, as we can read in the following words from one of his letters to Ficker:

> Too little love, too little *Gerechtigkeit* and mercy, and always too little love; all too much hardness, haughtiness, and all sorts of criminality—that is what I am. I am certain that I refrain from evil only out of weakness and cowardice and thereby further defile my malice. I yearn for the day when the soul will no longer want and be able to dwell in this unholy, soulless body that is tainted with melancholy; when the soul will leave behind this figure of derision that is made of excrement and putrefaction and is but an all-too-faithful reflection of a godless, accursed century.
>
> God, only a small spark of pure joy—and one would be saved; love—and one would be redeemed. (HKA 1: 301)

Love, justice, God, salvation—these topics, and many others, will occupy us in the following chapters on Heidegger's engagement with Trakl's poetic language. Trakl was clearly of great importance to Heidegger. Whether and to what extent Heidegger allowed his own thinking to be transformed by this relationship remains to be seen.

Chapter 2

Language of Bread and Wine

Und so, wie man in der eigenen Wahrheit lebt, in der Wahrheit eines fremden Wesens zu leben ist Liebe. Von dieser Wahrheit abzuweichen ist die Gefahr aller Sprache.[1]

—Max Kommerell

si on veut accéder au Lieu des textes, d'où procèdent les textes dits métaphysiques ou chrétiens, il faut cesser de croire à une certaine univocité et les lire comme on lit Trakl, en leur faisant le même crédit.[2]

—Jacques Derrida

To a Western ear, perhaps no two words carry more symbolic weight than "bread" and "wine." Together, these words appear frequently in Trakl's poetry, often in conjunction with God or the Eucharist:

Und es leuchtet ein Lämpchen, das Gute, in seinem Herzen
Und der Frieden des Mahls; denn geheiligt ist Brot und Wein
Von Gottes Händen. (HKA 1: 79)

*

And a little lamp, the good, shines in his heart
And the peace of the meal; for hallowed are bread and wine
By the hands of God.

> Hier Evas Schatten, Jagd und rotes Geld.
> Gewölk, das Licht durchbricht, das Abendmahl.
> Es wohnt in Brot und Wein ein sanftes Schweigen
> Und jene sind versammelt zwölf an Zahl. (HKA 1: 24)

> *

> Eve's shadow here, the hunt and crimson coin.
> Clouds, broken by the light, the Evening Meal.
> A gentle silence dwells in bread and wine,
> And they are gathered, twelve in number.

But there are also pagan and sinister connotations to the syntagm:

> In reinen Händen trägt der Landmann Brot und Wein
> Und friedlich reifen die Früchte in sonniger Kammer. (HKA 1: 40)

> *

> In pure hands the peasant carries bread and wine
> And the fruits ripen peacefully in the sunny chamber.

> Schweigende versammelten sich jene am Tisch; Sterbende brachen sie mit wächsernen Händen das Brot, das blutende. Weh der steinernen Augen der Schwester, da beim Mahle ihr Wahnsinn auf die nächtige Stirne des Bruders trat, der Mutter unter leidenden Händen das Brot zu Stein ward. (HKA 1: 83)

> *

> Silent ones, they gathered to eat; dying ones, with waxen hands they broke the bread, the bleeding bread. Woe, the stony eyes of the sister, when at table her madness trod the nocturnal brow of the brother, under the mother's suffering hands the bread became stone.

In this chapter, I will orient my interpretation of Heidegger's first lecture on Trakl, which bears the deceptively simple title "Language," by the following questions: if, as Heidegger argues, it is not Trakl but language itself that speaks in the poem "Ein Winterabend" ("A Winter Evening"), what, precisely, does it say, and particularly what does it say about bread and wine? Does it say or want to say just one thing (monophony)? If there are multiple voices, how do we discern the dominant one (homophony)? Or might language speak two or more truths simultaneously, without regard of rank (polyphony)? Are bread and wine "things" in Heidegger's sense of the term—that is to say, sites where earth, sky, mortals, and divinities come together? Or are they rather, or perhaps additionally, symbols (or substances) of Christ's body and blood? Should we not listen for both possibilities in the poem?

Before turning to Heidegger's lecture, it will be helpful to begin with a consideration of the work of Max Kommerell (1902–1944), in whose honor Heidegger composed and delivered "Language" for the first time in October 1950.

§1. Gesture, the Inexpressible, and the Speaking of the Unspoken

Judging solely from *Unterwegs zur Sprache* (*On the Way to Language*), one would be justified in thinking that Kommerell's work played little to no role in the composition of Heidegger's lecture "Language." The only reference to the literary scholar appears at the end of the volume, where Heidegger specifies that his lecture "was delivered in a first version at Bühlerhöhe in memory of Max Kommerell" (GA 12: 259). However, given Heidegger's utmost respect for Kommerell—the "most significant literary historian and poet," "the only one in his field with whom I could have fruitful dialogues at times about the historical destiny [*Bestimmung*] of thinking and poetizing"[3]—one would be justified in expecting more research to be available on their relationship. While several scholars have examined their fascinating exchange on Hölderlin, no one in the secondary literature, to my knowledge, has brought them together on the theme of language specifically.[4] It is important to do so here, albeit briefly, because the recent publication of the first draft of "Language" proves that Heidegger was in critical dialogue with Kommerell—"certainly," in the words of Giorgio Agamben, "the greatest German critic of the twentieth century after Benjamin, and perhaps the last great personality between the wars who still remains to be discovered."[5]

To start, I would like note a few things about Kommerell's theory of gesture, which Heidegger will allude to and attempt to deepen in his first lecture on Trakl. I should also note, in passing, that Heidegger did not turn to Trakl because of Kommerell's work on the Austrian poet. In fact, Kommerell hardly wrote anything about his contemporaries. At issue, rather, is the ultimate status and agent of language. In his book on the Romantic writer Jean Paul, Kommerell describes three levels of linguistic gesture. The first is the gesture of the soul, where one "says oneself" without reference to the body. The second is the gesture of nature, which emerges as a response to the insufficiency of the first. At this second level, one imaginatively imposes meaning on the jumble of exteriority and thereby finds a way to express one's interiority. The third, highest, gesture Kommerell calls "pure." It is the condition for the possibility of the other two. Pure gesture is completely self-referential, unencumbered by external ends, "the pure possibility of speaking itself."[6] It therefore cannot be expressed by means of that which it makes possible. In the opening of his 1937 essay "Die Sprache und das Unaussprechliche: Eine Betrachtung über Heinrich von Kleist" ("Language and the Inexpressible: A Consideration of Heinrich von Kleist"), Kommerell expands on this last idea, casting it in terms of the unsayable (*Unsagbare*) that lies at the heart of all speech:

> Just as, among animals, the human is the one who speaks [*der Sprechende*], so, among humans, is the poet the one who speaks. The measure of expression [*Aussprechens*] seems to be limited for humans, infinite for poets. And yet the unsayable grows with the ability to say things; the most beautiful poets win us over through what wants to remain mute in them and yet is there between the words.[7]

Kommerell provides further clarification in a later text devoted to the essence of the lyric poem:

> it should not be denied that, in the utterance [*Aussage*] of the lyric poem, which, making us blissfully happy, discloses the scope of possible speaking, only the unsaid and unsayable are present in the middle of what is said, a silence in the speaking. It must be this way; for, if the poem is a first speaking, it indeed rips the words out of what has not yet been uttered, and it necessarily lives in the midst of silence. The words have something startled about them, so freshly have they been

broken from the quarry of stillness. They are rare, valuable, and numbered; because the scope of the unsaid is so much greater than the sayable, the poem is short. For its words are not a selection from the wide compass of the spoken and of what has become language, but rather the rare exception, won from the silence of the soul that has been moved.[8]

For Kommerell, then, the gestural core of language is not expressed in spoken and written words, even though it is mutely present in the spaces between those words, especially the words of poetry. Poets do not simply select from the stone heap of language and rearrange it for their own ends. Their souls are moved to form the building blocks of speech in the first place. "Language," Emerson once said, "is fossil poetry."[9]

The problem with modernity is that we no longer have a sense for gesture. Kommerell writes that Jean Paul, for example,

wanted to stir the laughter of the gods over the fair of life and instead stirred a shudder over the rift in his spirit, which is a rift in the modern human being: the human being who has lost the path of spirit into life, who has lost his gestures.[10]

Kommerell's work is, among other things, an attempt to reawaken his readers to the significance of gesture and to salvage it for the future.

As I will show in the next section and in chapters to come, Heidegger's interpretation of Trakl implicitly draws on many of Kommerell's ideas and terms—stillness, silence, gesture, rift—in order to recall the deeper, gestural dimensions of language. But Heidegger also explicitly distances himself from his deceased friend in the first draft of "Language," no doubt partly because of Kommerell's basic orientation to the human being, rather than to being itself. But there is a finer point of contention in the lecture's only direct reference to Kommerell, which disappears by the second version.[11] Heidegger writes:

so long as we represent language solely in view of the expressed, we always find language's limit only at the unexpressed. Those who think more deeply next recognize the enigma of language in the inexpressible [*Unaussprechlichen*]. But language speaks as the speaking of the unspoken. The latter is the abyss on which all that is inexpressible already rests, on which everything ineffable [*Unsägliche*] sustains itself.

> Nevertheless, Max Kommerell said his most beautiful thing where he thought on his path into the farthest. This is, in my judgement, the treatise whose title reads: "Language and the Inexpressible." May what has been said in his memory remain the echo of the last conversation that moved us on a common path over a Black Forest summit. (GA 80: 999–1000)[12]

Kommerell, in other words, did not go far enough. Although he saw the inexpressible and its presence in the poetic work as foundational for any genuine consideration of language, he did not pay sufficient attention to a still more profound paradox: the fact that language does not just shelter but *speaks* the unspoken. Later, in "Language in the Poem," Heidegger explains this by comparing the relation between Trakl's individual poems (*Dichtungen*) and his single unspoken Gedicht to the undulations of a wellspring: just as the source is not the wave but nevertheless manifests itself in, and is indicated by, each wave, so the Gedicht is not the poem but nevertheless speaks itself in and is said by each poem (GA 12: 33–34).[13] In the context of the earlier lecture "Language," however, which I would like to examine now, Heidegger uses a different phrase for the speaking of the unspoken, one he will return to again and again throughout his corpus, including in a 1960 speech for Ludwig von Ficker (GA 16: 563–564). The speaking of the unspoken, he writes, is the *Geläut der Stille*, the "peal of stillness." As Hans-Georg Gadamer recalls:

> It was at Bühler Höhe [sic] when Heidegger, in memory of my deceased friend Max Kommerell, used a beautiful and gripping metaphor for language as the pealing of stillness [*Läuten der Stille*]. Then a clever audience member said: "That was a new theory of reason." Indeed, reason is already being thought of as the secret pre-structuring of thoughts from the perspective of verbalization [*Verwortung*] in language.[14]

§2. Language of Earth and Sky

The lecture "Language" sets itself a bold task. It aims not merely to point out a few aspects of language. It aims not merely to form a concept of what language in general or what the essence of language is, where what we say about it would, by definition, and impossibly, have to differ from that about which we speak. "Language"—simply titled—will not talk *about* language (the German *erörtern* in its everyday sense). It will not so much put *language* in its proper place (*erörtern* in the idiosyncratic sense that Heidegger will ascribe to the verb in "Language in the Poem," GA 12: 33–34) as it will endeavor to move *us*, to bring (*er-*) us to the place (*Ort*) where language is itself always already speaking (itself),[15] even if we mostly fail to hear it over the white noise of progress and pings of information transfer (GA 12: 10, 17; cf. 139). Before we speak—let alone write code—*die Sprache spricht*.

But how to hear such speech? The question is not, *what* is language? The question is, rather, *how* language is, how it resonates before—or better, under—the giving of reasons and the tracing of causes.[16] If we are to begin to answer this question, we must learn to listen differently. Heidegger exhorts us to train our ear on tautology ("language itself is language") and on poetry above all else (GA 12: 10). My remarks in this section, like Heidegger's in "Language," will focus on poetry.[17]

We can, according to Heidegger, listen for the speaking of language in what has been spoken. But this must not be something said and done. It must still speak to us. In Heidegger's idiomatic German, *das Gesprochene* must be more than what the nominalized past participle would suggest to the average ear, more than "the spoken." It must be heard as a gathering and sheltering (*Ge-*) of a still-present speaking (*Sprechen*):

> In the spoken [*Im Gesprochenen*], the speaking does not cease. In the spoken, the speaking remains sheltered. In the spoken, speaking gathers the mode [*Weise*] in which it endures and that which endures on the basis of it—its enduring [*Währen*], its essencing [*Wesen*]. But, for the most part and too often, we encounter the spoken only as a past instance of an act of speaking. (GA 12: 13–14; cf. 24)

Incidentally, this very explanation already serves as an example of learning to hear differently. The rhetorical anaphora creates expectation, and "the spoken," by its fourth iteration, no longer speaks to us in the same way as it did in the beginning. Heidegger also anticipates his later play on *Weise* as way and tune (GA 12: 28–29; compare the English "mode" as manner and as musical scale), and, for those with ears to hear, he exploits—or lets be sounded—the etymological connection between

Währen and *Wesen* (cf. GA 7: 31–32). Heidegger's own language, in short, bears some of the traits of poetry that he will soon develop.

The advantage of a poem, Heidegger asserts, or at least of a poem deserving of the name *Gedicht*—not something that has been created by a *poiētēs*, but a gathering (*Ge-*) of what has been said (*dictum*) and made dense (*dicht*)—is that it contains "the purely spoken" or, in other words, "that wherein the consummation of speaking, which is proper to the spoken, is for its part something inceptive [*anfangende*]" (GA 12: 14). Heidegger leaves this as a bald assertion, but it relates to what we heard earlier. In poetry especially, the speaking is not over and done with. A proper poem, like language itself, is not simply a vehicle for conveying a message. Language continues to speak (itself) in the poem. Still more, it inaugurates (*anfängt*). Indeed, it captures (*fängt*) us and sets us on the path to (*an-*) our proper abode. "To follow language out in thought [*nachdenken*]," writes Heidegger, "means to arrive at the speaking of language in such a way that this speaking properly comes to pass [*sich . . . ereignet*] as what grants sojourn to mortals" (GA 12: 11).

Of all possible poems, which one will guide us? Which will help us to *nachdenken*, to "think after," "according to," and "in the direction of" the speaking of language? Is not any decision going to seem arbitrary at the outset? Heidegger responds circularly:

> Here there remains only one choice that is nevertheless protected against sheer arbitrariness. Whereby? By means of what has already been thoughtfully intended [*zugedacht*] for us as what essentially holds sway [*das Wesende*] in language, provided we thoughtfully follow out the speaking *of language*. In accordance with this bond, we choose, as something purely spoken, a poem that, more readily than others, can help us in our first steps to experience what is binding in that bond. (GA 12: 14)

Our choice of the poem is to lead us to what is essential about language. But this can succeed only if what is essential about language is already addressing us, only if we already have and hear it—a circle, to be sure, but not necessarily a vicious one, or at any rate not one to be avoided. We must use language in order to speak about it. We therefore presuppose the very thing we are trying to explain. Rather than shrinking back from this circle, or simply letting our legs hang over the edge, we must, as Heidegger puts it in *Being and Time*, "leap originally and wholly" into it (SZ: 315).[18]

To elucidate this, Heidegger chooses the poem "A Winter Evening," citing it in both main versions before finally naming its author. He waits to do so because, on his view, Trakl is less the creator of the poem than a conduit for the self-speaking of language. If anything, the poem belongs to being, not to the man. As Heidegger writes: "Georg Trakl composed the poem [*Gedicht . . . gedichtet*]. That he is the poet remains unimportant, this is the case here, as with every other greatly successful poem. In part, the great success even consists in its being able to disown the person and name of the poet" (GA 12: 15; cf. 33). Heidegger performs this repudiation by never mentioning Trakl's name again in the lecture. The final version of the poem reads:

EIN WINTERABEND

Wenn der Schnee ans Fenster fällt,
Lang die Abendglocke läutet,
Vielen ist der Tisch bereitet
Und das Haus ist wohlbestellt.

Mancher auf der Wanderschaft
Kommt ans Tor auf dunklen Pfaden.
Golden blüht der Baum der Gnaden
Aus der Erde kühlem Saft.

Wanderer tritt still herein;
Schmerz versteinerte die Schwelle.
Da erglänzt in reiner Helle
Auf dem Tische Brot und Wein. (HKA 1: 57)

A WINTER EVENING

When the snow falls on the window,
And the evening bell tolls long,
There's a table prepped for many
And the house arranged just so.

Several in their pilgrimage
Come on dark paths to the gate.

Golden blooms the tree of grace
Rising from the earth's cool sap.

Wanderer steps in, so still;
Pain has petrified the threshold.
There in purest brightness gleam
On the table bread and wine.

It is curious, however, that, before proceeding to cite an earlier version of the poem, Heidegger writes that it derives from a letter to the famous satirist and cultural critic Karl Kraus, whose name therefore appears even before that of Trakl. What, from Heidegger's philosophical perspective, would Kraus have to do with the poem's great success, especially when Trakl the man does not matter? Further, why does Heidegger even cite this more overtly religious earlier version when he will never mention it again in his commentary, let alone its connection to Kraus? Is it, too, greatly successful? If not, why does it appear in "Language"? If so—or if it is really all just one poem, as one might expect from Heidegger's use of the singular after his citations ("Das *Gedicht* hat Georg Trakl gedichtet," GA 12: 15; emphasis added)—then shouldn't the Kraus version factor into the interpretation?

I will return to these questions later in the chapter. For now, I will simply follow Heidegger in citing the variant verses in the earlier version, which Trakl eventually titled "Im Winter" ("In Winter"). These variants will also play an important role later on in my interpretation. In lieu of verses 3–4 of the second stanza and the entirety of the third stanza, the earlier version of Trakl's poem has:

Seine Wunde voller Gnaden
Pflegt der Liebe sanfte Kraft.

O! des Menschen bloße Pein.
Der mit Engeln stumm gerungen,
Langt von heiligem Schmerz bezwungen
Still nach Gottes Brot und Wein. (HKA 1: 211)

*

His wound so full of grace is
Tended by love's gentle might.

Oh! sheer agony of man.
He who strove with angels mutely,
Reaches, vanquished by holy pain,
So still, for God's bread and wine.

Heidegger begins by presenting—and promptly dismissing—a superficial reading of "A Winter Evening," which highlights the poem's prosody and rhyme scheme, its aesthetic beauty and descriptive power (GA 12: 15–17). According to this reading, the poet is using the tools of his trade to express his emotions (despair, hope) and depict the worldview (Christianity) that informs them. "The third stanza," for example, "invites the wanderer to leave the dark outside and to enter the brightness within. The houses of the many and the tables of their quotidian meals have become a house of God and an altar table" (GA 12: 16). All of this, in Heidegger's view, relies on the traditional conception of language as expression, and it will not allow us to hear how language speaks itself in the poem.

One might wonder whether Heidegger does not move too quickly here. Does the form of a poem have no bearing on its content? Is sound unrelated to sense? Even beyond these commonplace categories, is the language of Christianity necessarily superficial? Does not language speak here, too? Might not language even speak here above all?

Heidegger does not entertain such questions. He instead moves on to an analysis of the first stanza of "A Winter Evening," which, on his reading, gives us a new sense for time and space. The punctual and punctilinear tolling of the bell is stretched, and time slows down—or better, it is not so much time that changes as our attention. The poem calls us to experience time, not as a series of points, but, to draw on Augustine and the earlier Heidegger, as distention and contraction, as what is primordially, albeit for the most part inconspicuously, outside of itself (*ek-statikon*). The poem also calls things forth into presence. But this is not the presence of objects perceived at objectively measurable distances from one another. It is rather an active "presenc*ing* [*Anwesen*]" that is at the same time "held out toward" and "sheltered in the direction of absenc*ing* [*Abwesen*]" (GA 12: 19). The call, accordingly, does not tear nearness out of farness, but preserves remoteness and absence even as things come close, similarly to how, as Heidegger phrases it elsewhere, *lēthe*, "concealment," still prevails in any event of disclosure, *a-lētheia*. In bringing things to presence, the poem allows things to do their thing; or, in Heidegger's language, it allows things *to thing*. Genuine things gather together what, earlier that year at Bühlerhöhe, Heidegger had referred to as the "fourfold" of earth and sky, divinities and mortals—or more simply, as "the world" (GA 79: 12).[19] Here is how Heidegger brings these ideas together in his reading of the first stanza (note the polytheistic shift from the singular neuter "divine" to the plural "divinities"):

> The snowfall brings humans under the sky that is dusking into night. The tolling of the evening bell brings them, as mortals, before the divine [*das Göttliche*]. House and table bind mortals to the earth. Thus summoned, the things that have been named gather, in their midst [*bei sich*, "at their home"], sky and earth, mortals and divinities [*die Göttlichen*]. The four are an originary-unified to-getherness. [. . .] Things, by thinging, bear forth world [*tragen . . . Welt aus*]. (GA 12: 19)

In tacit reference to Kommerell, Heidegger proceeds to tie the word *austragen*, "to deliver" (a letter, a child), to the more explicit language of bearing in German, which he then, questionably, links to gesture: "Our old language names *Austragen*: *bern*, *bären*, whence the words '*gebären*' ['to bear'] and '*Gebärde*' ['gesture']. Thinging, things are things. Thinging, they gesticulate [*gebärden*] world" (GA 12: 19; see also GA 12: 51).[20] In chapter 6, we will return to Heidegger's maternal language here and elsewhere in his reading of Trakl. At present, I will just note that Heidegger has shifted Kommerell's idea of pure gesture to an ontological, epiphanic register, on which Heidegger's lecture will continue to move.

Regarding the second stanza of "A Winter Evening," Heidegger contends that the wanderers who open it are not the morally wayward. They are not seeking the solace of religious redemption. They are rather the few, called to be capable of death—not individual demise, but "the most extreme concealment of being" (GA 12: 20). They do this, not primarily for themselves, but for the complacent many, so that the latter may break from their presumption and learn properly to dwell. The tree of grace, for its part, has nothing to do with the Edenic Tree of Life, let alone the tree that is the Cross of Christ. It is instead a *thing*, emerging from the solid earth thanks to the gifts of celestial rain and sunlight, and in turn bearing "the fruit that falls unearned: the salvific holiness that is propitious to mortals" (GA 12: 21). The golden blooming of the tree might recall various images from the Bible: the Tabernacle, Solomon's Temple, the New Jerusalem of Revelation. It might remind one of the

Evangelische Christuskirche in Salzburg, where Trakl was baptized; where, rising up from the altar, there is a white cross from 1867 with leaf-like top and sides ("trefoil"), on which a golden figure of Jesus hangs; and where, today, one can find a plaque near the entrance on the north side of the church commemorating Trakl with a reproduction of "A Winter Evening." Heidegger, however, will hear none of this. To explain the gold of the poem, he turns, of all places and poets, to Ancient Greece and the pagan Pindar—incidentally, the only poet he mentions in the lecture besides Trakl, and one of the few authors he mentions at all[21]—as if Trakl had had Hölderlin's Greek. At the beginning of the 5th Isthmian, which I will discuss in greater detail in chapter 5, Pindar invokes Theia, the Titan goddess and mother of Sun, Moon, and Dawn:

> Μᾶτερ Ἀελίου πολυώνυμε Θεία,
> σέο ἕκατι καὶ μεγασθενῆ νόμισαν
> χρυσὸν ἄνθρωποι περιώσιον ἄλλων.[22]
>
> *
>
> Mother of Sun, many-named Theia,
> on your account humans judge gold
> mighty far beyond other things.

Heidegger provides a powerful, if idiosyncratic, gloss on the last phrase of the invocation:

> At the beginning of this ode, the poet names gold *periōsion pantōn*, that which, like a ring around everything that is present, gleams above all through all, *panta*. The gleam of the gold shelters everything present, bringing it into the unconcealment of its appearing. (GA 12: 21)

If the first stanza of "A Winter Evening" beckons things to bear forth world—understood thoughtfully as the fourfold, not metaphysically as created *mundus*, secularized *universum*, or the cosmic totality of everything present (GA 12: 21)—the second stanza proceeds from the opposite direction: it beckons world to grant things their essential sway and shine.

In the third stanza, we hear how these modes of beckoning relate. Things and world do not stand opposed to one another. There is, to be sure, a difference, but it is not such that they would lack intrinsic connection. Heidegger says they are *geschieden* but not *getrennt*; there is, we could say, a scission without a sundering. In 1952, Heidegger will hearken back to the language of cutting when he uses the term *Abgeschiedenheit* ("detachment," "departedness," or, more literally, "the state of having cut oneself off") to characterize the site around which all of Trakl's poetry is gathered. Here, in the first Trakl lecture, he uses this language to develop a distinctive theory of difference. He says that things and world are intimately connected by means of a unique middle, which he clarifies with the use of the Latin preposition *inter* and what he admits is the corresponding German *unter*. This is already striking, given his typical deployment of pejorative Latinate terms in contrast to positive Germanic ones, especially in his later thought. Just a few paragraphs later, for example, he will contrast this theory of intimate difference with mental *Distinktionen* and external *Relationen* (GA 12: 22). Such intimate inter-mediacy is not inter-dissolution or inter-flation, but is only possible as inter-section or inter-scission; it is only possible as a literal *Unterschied*, the most common word for difference in German. As Heidegger puts it, using Germanic words that are hardly translatable without recourse to Latin:

> The intimacy of world and thing is not a melting together. Intimacy prevails only where what is intimate, world and thing, purely sects/cises itself [*sich scheidet*] and remains sected/cised. In the middle of the two, in the between of world and thing, in their *inter*, in this *Unter-*, prevails the section/scission [*Schied*]. (GA 12: 22; cf. GA 80: 995)

Heidegger proceeds to expand on this notion of *Unter-Schied* by again turning to the terminology of bearing in Greek and German: *diaphora*, "difference" or, literally, "carrying through"; *Austrag*: "carrying out" or "carrying to full term." He then endeavors to read it in line with verse, "Schmerz versteinerte die Schwelle." Although in the simple past tense (or possibly the subjunctive), he says we should hear the verb *versteinerte* as still enduring in the present, like the still-present speaking of what has been poetically spoken (*das Ge-sprochene*). Pain has not just hardened the threshold, which is another word for the just-developed middle; pain is still present and active, harden*ing* the threshold, making it the reliable and enduring center of support for the differential inter-section of thing and world. Indeed, pain just *is* (transitively) this inter-section. To explicate this, Heidegger draws on yet another set of terms, which I will discuss in greater detail in chapter 4:

> Pain cleaves [*reißt*]. It is the cleaving. Only, it does not cleave asunder into splinters that drive apart. To be sure, pain does cleave apart, it cises, but it does so in such a way that it likewise draws everything to itself, gathers everything into itself. [. . .] Pain is the jointure of the cleaving. It is the threshold. It bears out the between, the middle of the two that have been cised into it [*in sie Geschiedenen*]. Pain joins the cleaving of the inter-scission. Pain is the inter-scission itself. (GA 12: 24)

What, finally, of the last lines of the stanza? Is Trakl referring to the barrier of sin and the need for a repentant faith to cross over and partake of the healing power of Holy Communion? By this point, Heidegger's answer should not come as a surprise: *No, Trakl is not talking about the body and blood of Christ, he is talking about things. He is talking with Hölderlin.*[23] "Bread and wine are the fruits of heaven and earth, bestowed on mortals by the divinities" (GA 12: 25).

Heidegger arrives at this conclusion by way of two subtle grammatical alterations. (1) He turns the object of the prepositional phrase "in purest brightness" into the subject of Trakl's final lines. It is not, in the first place, bread and wine that gleam on the table. It is, rather, brightness itself that gleams on the threshold: "The cleaving of the inter-scission lets the pure brightness gleam" (GA 12: 25). Heidegger is not simply saying that there must be a medium in which objects can appear. He is instead drawing attention to the inceptive brightness itself. World and things—bread and wine—shine only as a *result* of this pure epiphany: "Through the brightening up [*Auf-Heiterung*] of world in its golden gleam, bread and wine likewise come to gleam forth" (GA 12: 25). Heidegger has, in short, shifted the focus from *that* which shines to pure and simple *shining*, from the significance of beings to the sense of *being*. Although the language of being is largely implicit in the Trakl lecture,[24] the ontological register becomes evident when we consider Heidegger's contemporaneous commentary on the nineteenth-century poet Eduard Mörike's "Auf eine Lampe" ("On a Lamp"). Provoking what has been called "probably the most famous interpretative controversy in German studies, which has not ended to this day,"[25] Heidegger criticized literary critic Emil Staiger's interpretation of the meaning of the word *scheint* in the final verse of Mörike's poem:

> Was aber schön ist, selig scheint es in ihm selbst.

In Staiger's lecture "Die Kunst der Interpretation" ("The Art of Interpretation"), which Heidegger attended one month after delivering "Language" at Bühlerhöhe, Staiger proposes that we should hear *scheint* as "seems": "Yet what is beautiful seems to be blissful in itself." Heidegger, however, argues that *scheint* has the sense of "shines," which would make *selig* an adverb:

> The articulation and the "rhythm" of the final verse have their weight in the "is." "Yet what *is* beautiful" (*is* an artistic formation of the genuine sort), "*shines* blissfully in itself!" "Being-beautiful" ["*Schön-Sein*"] is pure "shining." [. . .] Here, the "is" does not have the worn-down meaning of the copula [. . .] Here, the "is" has the meaning of "essentially holds sway" ["*west*"].[26]

It would take me too far astray to analyze, let alone to try to adjudicate, Staiger's and Heidegger's arguments for their respective readings. What interests me here is how Heidegger brings the individual poem—not just Mörike's, but any poem deserving of the name—to the level of being, thus to his own, and not necessarily the individual poet's, lifelong preoccupation. We can see a similar maneuver in one of his interpretations of the aforementioned ode by Pindar:

> "Being" means nothing other than this shining [*Scheinen*], which provides, not mere "semblance" ["*Anschein*"], but that wherein gold, as gold, is merged and, as so merged, arrives and, arriving in the gleam, essentially presences [*an-west*] as itself. "Gold"—that is, in a certain way, this pure presencing itself, such that, in it, beings are "more in being" [*das Seiende "seiender" ist*]. (GA 78: 68)

Heidegger's ontological interpretation certainly sheds new light on the work of Trakl, Mörike, and Pindar. Whether this light does not overwhelm the work's own internal illumination is, as we will see, another matter.

(2) The other grammatical alteration I would like to address appears right after Heidegger cites verse 9 of "A Winter Evening." Depending on how you hear *tritt*—as indicative or, like Heidegger, as imperative[27]—the wanderer either "steps in, so still" or is called upon to do so ("Wanderer, step stilly in"). In any case, still*ness* becomes the destination for Heidegger. At first, he acknowledges that "[t]he verse does not say" wherein the wanderer enters. This might already seem suspect. Although it is literally true that that the *verse* does not say, the context is not opaque: the wanderer takes or is invited to take refuge in a hospitable home or church, perhaps during Christmastime. In keeping with his nominalizing tendencies, however, Heidegger immediately moves to the level of abstraction, thereby effacing the concrete means to its attainment. The verse, he claims, "calls the entering wanderer into stillness" (GA 12: 23). Stillness and, especially in the first version of the lecture, the unspoken become the focus of the final pages of "Language."

Let us begin with the unspoken. Recall that Heidegger had criticized Kommerell for his failure to look more deeply into "the enigma of language." With his discussion of the inexpressible in the writings of Kleist, Kommerell had gone further than most; however, he did not see how, in Heidegger's words, "language speaks as the speaking of the unspoken," which "is the abyss on which all that is inexpressible already rests, on which everything ineffable sustains itself" (GA 80: 999). We are now in a position to understand what Heidegger means. The third stanza of "A Winter Evening" invokes the difference or inter scission between thing and world without naming it as such. "Language," Heidegger explains in the first version of the lecture, "speaks by bringing the spoken under the protection of the unspoken [*ins Ungesprochene hütet*], so that the latter will remain the dimension as which the speaking of language spans the difference" (GA 80: 999; cf. GA 12: 25). What is said in the poem, in other words, is said not just on the basis of difference, which would be true for all language, however hackneyed; it is also said in direct, albeit tacit, reference to difference. Like the wave and the water, like the peal of an evening bell.

We can also understand difference in terms of stillness, which we should not confuse with soundless inactivity. *Die Stille*, Heidegger says, using one of his favorite tautological grammatical constructions—*die Stille stillt*, "stillness stills," "stillness satiates," or even, as I will revisit in chapter 6, "stillness suckles" (GA 12: 27). But it does not still or satiate something already present at hand. It exercises a unique sort of causality, something other than mechanism or teleology, so as to let things and world *be* in the first place. Difference, as stillness, "stills things *into* their thinging and stills world *into* its worlding" (GA 12: 26; emphases added). It calls them into intimacy. This call, Heidegger concludes, is the *Geläut*, the "peal" or, literally, the "gathered sounding," of stillness, as which language speaks.[28]

For Heidegger, Trakl's poem is concerned with the differential interscission of world and things. Through it, language speaks. Through it, we can learn to hear the self-speaking of language. Only in so hearing can we speak in accordance with language. Only then can we properly dwell. Only then, to speak once more with Pindar, can we become who we are.

∾

Heidegger's reading is, no doubt, one of a kind. He has found a poem that confirms his deepest convictions about language, or perhaps better put: that has allowed his relationship—the properly human relationship—with language to come to the fore in language. Like most Heidegger scholars, I might be willing to leave it at that, were it not for the following three difficulties.

First, a couple years after delivering "Language" for the first time, Heidegger turned more explicitly to Trakl himself, not just to another one of his poems. It was then a matter of interpreting the poetic work of "Georg Trakl," as "Language in the Poem" was initially titled. In 1959, Heidegger finally published "Language" as the first chapter of *On the Way to Language*. "Language in the Poem: A Discussion/Emplacement of Georg Trakl's Poem" was the second. We therefore ought not to treat the first as though it had no bearing on how Heidegger contends we should understand the second, and therefore on how we should understand the poet.

Second, Heidegger believes that Trakl is the poet of his generation—not Rilke, not Benn, not Hofmannsthal, not even, if we stretch the dates, George, to say nothing of poets of other languages. Trakl is "the poet of an Occident—of the land of evening—that is still concealed" to us (GA 12: 77). On Heidegger's own terms, the stakes could not be higher. The salvation of our very being depends on whether we discover this promised land and learn to indwell it. To this end, it is crucial that we hearken unto the words of the poet. But it is also crucial, I believe, that we try to discern whether Heidegger hears him rightly. By this I do not just mean measurable or calculative correctness: for instance, the word "stone" is important because it appears more than thirty times in Heidegger's main copy of Trakl's poems; "gold" has both positive and negative connotations for the poet; before a youthful literary circle, Trakl once read aloud from "Der hässlichste Mensch" ("The Most Contemptible Human") without mentioning the author; after they rejected it, he exclaimed it had been written by Nietzsche and walked away in contempt.[29] Heidegger is therefore correct to focus on stones and ambiguous colors, and it makes sense that he would refer to Nietzsche and the philosopher's poetic *Zarathustra* (GA 12. 41, 50, 59, 71). By "rightly," I also mean to consider whether Heidegger does justice to Trakl, whether his hermeneutics moves with the spirit of Trakl's poems, even if it often violates their letter. Trakl may well be the poet of the land of eventide, but we should not assume that he and Heidegger understand the same thing by these words. Perhaps Trakl is saying something that Heidegger does not have ears to hear.

Third, if there is a biblical echo in my language of the previous paragraph, it is because I cannot help but hear the Bible in Trakl's "A Winter Evening."[30] Before I turn to my own interpretation of this poem, it will be useful to examine how Heidegger handles Trakl's ostensible Christianity and how the philosopher understands Christian faith more broadly—a faith he once referred to as one of the "two thorns" in his flesh, the other being his failed Nazi rectorate.[31] Ultimately, I want to take the topic of Christianity as an opportunity to bring Trakl into critical dialogue with Heidegger, which will then open onto other sites of confrontation.

§3. Digression on Christianity

In chapter 1, I noted Heidegger's aversion to Christian interpretations of Trakl. Recall, to take one example among many, that, in his personal copy of the Zurich edition of Trakl's poems, Heidegger drew a large question mark next to editor Kurt Horwitz's claim that, "[i]n [Trakl's] poems, bread and wine and the angels do not merely show up as sweet and beautiful images. His melancholy, his solitude, and his despair [*Verzweiflung*] are absolutely conditioned by Christianity" (DD: 229). Heidegger's aversion is due, in no small part, to Christianity's complicity with what he calls the Platonic, and therefore metaphysical, separation of spirit and soul from body, heaven from earth, eternity from time, truth from appearance.

Heidegger tries to find a place in Trakl's poetry that precedes and exceeds these dichotomies. One of Trakl's terms for this place is the German *geistlich*, which, despite its Christian and ecclesiastical connotations ("spiriual" and "clerical"), retains a hypo- and hyper-metaphysical sense in Heidegger's reading. It is this sense that Heidegger believes he can make out in Trakl's poems (GA 12: 54–56).

In "Language in the Poem," Heidegger acknowledges that Trakl must draw on the vocabulary of Christianity. Trakl is a transitional figure. Even though the poet intimates a coming race, he, like Heidegger himself, has not entirely left behind the old, degenerate *Geschlecht* and its language. However, contra Horwitz, this does not mean that Christianity *conditions* Trakl's work.

When it comes to Trakl's Christianity, Heidegger at first cautions restraint. In his most extended discussion of the topic, he writes:

> Whether Trakl's poetry [*Dichtung*], to what extent and in what sense it speaks in a Christian manner, in what way the poet was a "Christian," what "Christian," "Christianness," "Christendom," "Christianity" mean here and in general—all this involves essential questions.

Yet Heidegger immediately explains what one would have to do before trying to answer such questions:

> The discussion/emplacement [*Erörterung*] of these questions remains suspended in the void, however, so long as the place of the poetic work [*Ort des Gedichtes*] is not thoughtfully made out. Furthermore, their discussion/emplacement requires a thoughtful reflection, for which neither the concepts of metaphysical nor those of ecclesiastical theology suffice.
>
> A judgement about the Christianity of Trakl's poetic work would, above all, have to consider thoughtfully his two last poems "Klage" ["Lamentation"] and "Grodek." It would have to ask: why, in the extreme distress of his last saying, does the poet not call on God and Christ here, if he is such a decided Christian? Why, instead, does he name the "swaying shadow of the sister" and her as the "greeting one"? Why does the song end, not with the confident prospect of Christian redemption, but with the naming of the "unborn

grandchildren"? Why does the sister also appear in the other last poem "Lamentation" [. . .]? Why is "eternity" called here "the icy wave"? Is that thought in a Christian manner? It is not even Christian despair [*Verzweiflung*—the same word Horwitz had used]. (GA 12: 72)[32]

In the tenth session of *Geschlecht III*, Derrida poses a number of questions in response to Heidegger's interpretation of Trakl's last two poems and to his peculiar denial of their Christian despair.[33] Are the concepts of Christianity unequivocal and unequivocally derivative, such that they could never stand at the source of true poetry? Heidegger is often happy to salvage words and schemas from the Christian tradition, just not the tradition itself. But what if they were inextricable? What, moreover, if Heidegger's own discourse, which mimics many of the characteristic gestures of Christianity, were itself inseparable from it? Does the absence of obvious Christian language entail the absence of Christian commitment? Is silence about the letter incompatible with a hearkening unto the spirit? Might Trakl's silence be a telling silence? Moving on to the figure of the sister, is it necessarily the case that, in calling on her, Trakl is not also calling on Christ? After all, in poems such as the first version of "Passion," the figure of the sister is not merely a symbol for Christ, but actually seems to merge with him, as Richard Detsch has shown in a chapter on the role of incest in Trakl's work.[34] If this is too much of a stretch, could she not at least be a cipher for Jesus's mother, whom Trakl, despite his Protestantism, often invokes in his poetry, and on whom many a Christian calls—and is called on to call—in times of distress? ("Only she," writes Thomas Aquinas, "lifted the curse and carried the blessing and opened the gate of Paradise; therefore, it is fitting that her name is *Maria*, interpreted as *stella maris*, for, just as sailors are directed to port by the star of the sea, so Christians are directed to glory by Mary.")[35] In any case, what does it mean to be a *decided* Christian? Might Christianity, as Kierkegaard said and as Heidegger well knew, instead always be a matter of *becoming* a Christian rather than having a fixed identity *as* one (GA 49: 73)? Would this act of perpetual becoming, would even the claim to identity, be free of doubt or despair? Even Jesus could be said to have despaired on the Cross. And what to make of the fact that the despair in the poem "Lamentation"—if despair it be—is presented in the subjunctive mood, which Heidegger passes over (as does Derrida)?

> Des Menschen goldnes Bildnis
> Verschlänge die eisige Woge
> Der Ewigkeit. (HKA 1: 94)
>
> *
>
> The golden image of man
> *Would* be devoured by the icy wave
> Of eternity.

Finally, and here I must quote Derrida directly:

> Christ, the son of God, is the brother of all men and all women, at the same time as he is the image or intercessor of the father. But a brother whose virility is never simply manifest or unilateral, a brother who presents himself in an aura of universal homosexuality, or in an appeased, pacified sexual difference [. . .], a brother, therefore, who is perhaps not other than a sister [. . .], perhaps without manifest desire in the space where desire makes war [. . .] but not without tender desire, a relation to the other as double homosexuality, a reflection without appropriation of the desire of the other [. . .]. And who can tranquilly affirm that this is not the essence of the relation to Christ, the essence or at least the destination, the destiny that is searched for, that to which every Christian experience of the holy family, even of the family simply, is on the way? (GIII: 114–115)

However one might end up answering these questions—some of which we will return to later in the chapter and in those to follow—here I just want to remark that, although Heidegger may seem hermeneutically cautious in the two passages from "Language in the Poem" cited above, and especially the first one, he has actually already decided on the status of Trakl's Christianity. I say this, because, on Heidegger's own terms, genuine Christianity, as opposed to institutionalized Christendom, is not a derivative matter. Shortly after delivering his two lectures on Trakl, Heidegger explained to a group of philosophers and theologians: "Within thinking, nothing can be accomplished that would prepare for or have a say in what occurs in faith and grace. If I were so addressed by faith, I would close up shop."³⁶ If, therefore, faith has nothing to do with the thinking of being, then faith and the thinking of being cannot legitimately be placed into an order of priority or implication. It is accordingly impossible to establish Trakl's faith on the basis of an antecedent ontological emplacement. This helps to explain Derrida's contention that there is something "rather violent" and "rather dogmatic" about Heidegger's discussion of the status of Christianity in Trakl (GIII: 108; see also 111).

Heidegger assumes that poetry, properly speaking, falls on the side of thinking, not faith. If Trakl is a proper poet—and for Heidegger he is—then his work should be amenable to thoughtful dialogue. But this would mean that Trakl, like Hölderlin, was committed to the project of "instituting being" (GA 4: 41):

> For Luther, Paul's Letter to the Romans was a revelation from the beginning; in it he heard the word of God. When the thinker hears a poet such as Hölderlin, this is something completely different; it is a hearing within a different realm of "revealability," in the grounding of which the poet, in contrast to the revelation of the word of God, which is always already decided, essentially takes part.³⁷

Why, however, is Trakl not more like Luther, to whom the poet Else Lasker-Schüler once compared him?

> Seine Augen standen ganz fern.
> Er war als Knabe einmal schon im Himmel.
>
> Darum kamen seine Worte hervor
> Auf blauen und weißen Wolken.
>
> Wir stritten über Religion,
> Aber immer wie zwei Spielgefährten,
>
> Und bereiteten Gott von Mund zu Mund.
> Im Anfang war das Wort.
>
> Des Dichters Herz, eine feste Burg,
> Seine Gedichte: Singende Thesen.

Er war wohl Martin Luther.

Seine dreifaltige Seele trug er in der Hand,
Als er in den heiligen Krieg zog.

—Dann wußte ich, er war gestorben—

Sein Schatten weilte unbegreiflich
Auf dem Abend meines Zimmers.[38]

*

His eyes were quite distant.
As a boy he had once been in heaven.

Thus, his words came forth
On blue and white clouds.

We quarreled over religion,
But always as two playmates,

And prepared God from mouth to mouth.
In the beginning was the Word.

The poet's heart, a mighty fortress,
His poems: singing theses.

He must have been Martin Luther.

He bore his triune soul in his hand,
When he went to holy war.

—Then I knew, he had died—

His shadow lingered incomprehensibly
On the evening of my room.

Or like Milton?

> [. . .] I thence
> Invoke thy aid to my advent'rous song,
> That with no middle flight intends to soar
> Above th'Aonian mount, while it pursues
> Things unattempted yet in prose or rhyme.
> And chiefly thou O Spirit, that dost prefer
> Before all temples th'upright heart and pure,
> Instruct me, for thou know'st; thou from the first
> Wast present, and with mighty wings outspread
> Dove-like sat'st brooding on the vast abyss
> And mad'st it pregnant; what in me is dark
> Illumine, what is low raise and support;
> That to the highth of this great argument
> I may assert Eternal Providence,
> And justify the ways of God to men.[39]

What if faith—however fraught and despairing—defined Trakl's work, and not the claim of being? Should we not consider such questions in advance of, or at least concomitantly with, all *Erörterung*?

These questions become more pressing once we are confronted with Trakl's own statements about his poetic activity. Perhaps not all of these statements belong to Trakl's authentic *Dichtung*. But Heidegger, for his part, does not hesitate to draw on putative parerga such as letters and marginalia when interpreting his master poet Hölderlin, and it is not as though the thinker were ignorant of Trakl's life. Even at the time of "Language" in 1950, he had already read far more about the poet than his summary dismissal of biographical relevance might lead one to suspect. In the original version of the lecture, for example, Heidegger acknowledges that "[t]he Christian world unequivocally factors into the poem ['A Winter Evening']. The poet belonged to the Protestant enclave of his Salzburg homeland" (GA 80: 988). While it may not matter, as Heidegger goes on to suggest, that Trakl was raised Protestant in arch-Catholic Salzburg (although with an Alsatian-Catholic governess), Trakl's own comments on the Christian character of his poetry are not so easy to ignore, and they should not, without further ado, be relegated to a mere "worldview [*Weltansicht*]" (GA 80: 989).

In chapter 1, I discussed a report about Trakl's 1914 exchange with Carl Dallago, which Heidegger annotated with numerous markings in his personal copy of Trakl's poems. Trakl allegedly avowed his Christianity, indeed, his Protestantism, and claimed that he, unlike Jesus, had "no right to escape from Hell." Aesthetic satisfaction is pernicious. Faced with "the deepest questions of humanity," we must, Trakl stressed, turn to "Christ," who "solves" them "with every simple word" (DD: 211–212). To Christ, nota bene—not to philosophy, not even to poetry, Trakl's own calling.

A different report, from a year and a half earlier, corroborates Trakl's commitments. In a standing beer hall one evening, Trakl contrasted Mörike and Liliencron with Goethe. Whereas the first two "gave themselves" wholeheartedly to their art and "bled" for their material, Goethe remained "at the surface level," never having composed "neurasthenically." Trakl continues:

> All writing of poems is nothing; what does one need poems and the world as will and representation [read: Schopenhauer] for when one has the Gospel? A few words of the Gospel have more life and world and judgement of character than all these poems: "Blessed are the poor in spirit, for theirs is the kingdom of heaven" [Matthew 5:3]. Next to this, the poets are so superfluous, so foolish [. . .]. All poets are vain and vanity is repulsive.[40]

While it might seem as though Trakl were dismissing poetry as such here, I believe he is instead highlighting his Christian priorities by way of hyperbolic negation. Otherwise, the contrast he draws between Goethe and the other poets would be otiose. Otherwise, he would not have provided an answer to what appears to be nothing more than a rhetorical question in this quotation: *Wozu Gedichte?* What are poems for? Trakl's answer, which comes in the form of a rare programmatic statement, written in Trakl's own hand, situates—I use this word intentionally—it *situates* Trakl's own poetic activity in the religious context of iniquity and redemption. Just before departing for war against Russia, Trakl presented his mentor with the following lines, which Ficker published posthumously in *Der Brenner* in 1915: "Feeling in the moments of death-like being: all humans are worthy of love. Awaking, you feel the bitterness of the world; therein is all your unresolved guilt [*Schuld*]; your poem an imperfect atonement [*Sühne*]" (HKA 1: 256).[41] For Trakl, poetry was partial expiation for sin, in his case the cardinal sin of incest. (I should note that I am not concerned with whether Trakl actually slept with his sister, as a variety of evidence suggests, or whether he merely imagined and lusted after doing so; the theme—and its disastrous consequences—pervades his poetry, as we will see in later chapters.[42] Franz Fühmann puts it well: "the forbidden love between brother and sister that is such a peremptory presence in the poems represents the actual reality, above and beyond the facts of a biography, the reality of such urgent concern to the readers that they would have to face it even if the biography spoke against an incestuous relationship."[43]) What Trakl is dealing with is accordingly not the existential guilt of *Being and Time*. Nor is it the tragic guilt of antiquity. "*Omnia mea culpa*," confessed Trakl's close friend Karl Borromäus Heinrich in a 1913 article for *Der Brenner*, one year before Kierkegaard and Trakl's beloved novelist Dostoevsky would appear in translation in the journal's pages and begin to exercise great influence on its ideological trajectory. Heinrich explains:

> No wrong [*Schuld*] has been done to me except what I have done myself. [. . .] Only by completely and unquestioningly taking responsibility for all the wrong done to me and all the wrong done by me can I find the cross that, according to the severity of my guilt, God has determined for me. And only by finding this cross and carrying it with good will can I find peace.[44]

Incidentally, the novel we know as *Crime and Punishment* was, in Trakl's milieu, known as *Schuld und Sühne*, Guilt and Atonement. Trakl's guilt stems from sin, and the poet, by his own testimony, writes to make amends.[45]

I will not belabor the point, as the above quotations should suffice to justify a consideration of the primacy of Christian elements in at least some of Trakl's poetry.[46] I agree with Heidegger that Trakl's poetry is not a matter of expressing inner feelings. It is not a matter of aesthetic escapism or *l'art pour l'art*. Trakl is not a latter-day Orpheus, whose lyricism would transform sorrow into song. But this does not mean that Trakl's "one single poem" (GA 12: 33) sings only of being. To illustrate this, I would like to return to "A Winter Evening." After providing some background to the poem and its genesis, I will endeavor to read it in a manner that does not depend on Heidegger's interpretation but instead takes the Bible as its point of departure. My intention is not to fill the empty pews of the Trakl church. Rather, I will strive, for my part, to take Trakl at his word.

§4. Language of Body and Blood

On the evening of December 10, 1913, in the Innsbruck Musikvereins-Saal, Trakl gave the one and only poetry reading of his life. The event had been organized by *Der Brenner* and also featured the novelist Robert Michel, who opened the evening with a reading of his short story "Vom Podvelež" (HKA 2: 719), which likely served as inspiration for "A Winter Evening." In the story, a man makes an arduous journey through a blizzard only to witness, looking in through the window of his snowed-in home, his wife *in flagrante delicto* with his friend; rather than crying out or knocking on the pane for entrance, the man "dug his nails into the beam [. . .] and bit his teeth into the wood," freezing to death shortly thereafter.[47]

Eleven days after the reading,[48] Trakl wrote from a local inn to Kraus, whom he had befriended in the summer of the previous year: "In these days of raving drunkenness and criminal melancholy," he explained, "a few verses have emerged that I ask you to accept as an expression of admiration for a man who, like no other, sets an example for the world" (HKA 1: 311). In increasingly sloppy handwriting, Trakl copied out an early version of "A Winter Evening," offering it as a tribute to the famous author of *Die Fackel* (*The Torch*). Shortly thereafter, Trakl prepared the final version, which would not appear in print until after his death, as a part of the cycle "Der Herbst des Einsamen" ("Autumn of the Solitary One") in his second collection of poetry *Sebastian im Traum* (*Sebastian in Dream*) (HKA 2: 174–175).

Of Kraus, I will remark only that, although he left little room for religious redemption—to this extent, Trakl's tribute can also be read as a critical delineation—Kraus's unrelenting commitment to honest language and his uncompromising scorn for everything that fell short of it served as an ethical model for Trakl and his contemporaries. Despite Kraus's secularism, Trakl wrote of him as of a belated Old Testament prophet, fulminating against the injustices, obfuscation, and hypocrisy of his age. Earlier in 1913, *Der Brenner* sent out a questionnaire aimed at defending Kraus against his opponents. (Kraus, for his part had called *Der Brenner* "the only honest journal in Austria," which, incidentally, led the young Wittgenstein to donate a large sum of money to the journal to support its authors, especially Trakl, and even to try—in vain—to publish the *Tractatus* in the journal's pages.[49]) Trakl joined the ranks of Arnold Schoenberg, Thomas Mann, Oskar Kokoschka, Adolf Loos, and many other luminaries of the day in providing an answer to the questionnaire.⁵⁰ Trakl's appeared in the form of a four-line poem, which I here cite from the slightly different version he prepared for publication in *Sebastian in Dream*:

> Weißer Hohepriester der Wahrheit,
> Kristallne Stimme, in der Gottes eisiger Odem wohnt,
> Zürnender Magier,
> Dem unter flammendem Mantel der blaue Panzer des Kriegers
>   klirrt. (HKA 1: 68)

*

> White high priest of truth,
> Crystalline voice, wherein God's icy breath dwells,
> Raging magician,
> Under whose flaming cloak the blue armor of the warrior
>   clangs.

The ending of Trakl's 1912 poem "Psalm," which Trakl dedicated to Kraus, goes further. The poem's penultimate line alludes to Kraus's spellbinding, white-magical powers:

> In seinem Grab spielt der weiße Magier mit seinen
>   Schlangen.

*

> In his grave the white magician plays with his snakes.

Its final line, however, offers a glimmer of religious hope on the far side of critique, even if God should remain silent:

> Schweigsam über der Schädelstätte öffnen sich Gottes
>   goldene Augen. (HKA 1: 32)

*

Silently over Golgotha open the golden eyes of God.⁵¹

I remarked earlier that Heidegger was conscious enough of context to mention not just an earlier version of "A Winter Evening" but also the fact that it had appeared in a letter to Kraus. Oddly, Heidegger does nothing else with it, and even when he discusses Trakl's "Psalm" in "Language in the Poem" and elsewhere, he is silent about the poem's dedicatee, as he is about Kraus in general.[52] Heidegger's omission—or rather, in "Language," his preterition—of Kraus's significance for Trakl is of a piece with his general strategy when it comes to religion: to refer to it, but only as derivative and therefore inessential. However, Trakl's *poetic* response to Kraus, and not merely his personal relation to the celebrated polemicist, shows that matters are not so simple. To complicate them further, let us now turn back to "A Winter Evening," bearing in mind Trakl's comments on the Gospel and the Krausian background to this poem. Like Heidegger, I will refrain from referring to other poems in my interpretation.[53]

∼

Wenn der Schnee ans Fenster fällt,
Lang die Abendglocke läutet,
Vielen ist der Tisch bereitet
Und das Haus ist wohlbestellt.

*

When the snow falls on the window,
And the evening bell tolls long,
There's a table prepped for many
And the house arranged just so.

The poem begins with a common setting. The narrator is inside a building, looking through a window blurred by snow. It is a winter evening, like many others. The opening conjunction *wenn*, "when," suggests familiarity, that this has happened before or happens regularly, even as it creates a sense of expectation: when—or "if," another translation for *wenn*—x, then y. Trakl, incidentally, never gives the consequent. This absence is more evident in the original. German syntax requires that the verb of the consequent be either in the first position or preceded by *dann*, neither of which occurs in the poem. Instead, Trakl provides another antecedent, "And the evening bell tolls long," and shifts to normal sentence structure for verses 3–4, with the verb in second position.[54] Thus, already at the level of syntax, our sense of stability is shaken by the end of the first stanza. We seem to be in the realm of dream or fable, where one thing does not always follow another. Perhaps this is no ordinary winter evening after all.

With the tolling of the bell, we move from the visual to the auditory and are taken farther outside, beyond the snow directly falling against the window and to a church that is inviting its community to evening prayers, to Vespers. Realistically, the narrator may be noticing the way sound travels differently in colder, snowy conditions, which would, however, affect clarity rather than duration. But the length of the bell's sound is mainly figurative: its call, like the liquid *l*'s and the long vowels of the verse—*Lang die Abendglocke läutet*—its call lingers, beckoning.[55]

Verses 3–4 suddenly transport us into the church, or at least into a recollection of its services. Or perhaps we realize that we were inside it all along. The table is prepared for many, not just a few. The building, verse 5 states, has a gate (*Tor*), not merely a door (*Tür*). Although verse 4 speaks of a house, the biblical allusions suggest that this well-prepared—*wohlbestellte*—home is a *Gotteshaus*, a "house of God": "Bestelle dein Haus," Isaiah warns in a passage famously set to music by Bach, "denn du wirst sterben." "Set thy house in order: for thou shalt die" (38:1). In Luke's Gospel, Jesus explains that God will have his blessed servants "sit down to meat [*zu Tisch setzen*]"; they "shall sit down [*zu Tische sitzen*] in the kingdom of God" (12:37, 13:29). For Jesus will go "to prepare [*bereiten*] a place" for them (John 14:2).

>
> Mancher auf der Wanderschaft
> Kommt ans Tor auf dunklen Pfaden.
> Seine Wunde voller Gnaden
> Pflegt der Liebe sanfte Kraft.
>
> *
>
> Several in their pilgrimage
> Come on dark paths to the gate.
> His wound so full of grace is
> Tended by love's gentle might.

The second stanza, especially in the earlier version I have cited here, confirms these Christian connotations. It is at once general and particular, progressive and perfect. Ever since the Fall, humans have wandered in darkness. Ever since the Passion and Resurrection, they have been given access to salvation by way of grace. "I am the door: by me if any man enter in, he shall be saved" (John 10:9). The seventh and eighth verses of the earlier version refer to Jesus, whose gentle charity suffered countless wounds as recompense for others' sins. But his grace-filled wound or wound-filled grace is also a possible synecdoche or paradigm for God's power to have mercy and heal all wounds. ("Wound-filled" if one hears *wundevoll<u>en</u> Gnaden*, which also opens the possibility of *wunde<u>r</u>vollen Gnaden*, "wonderful grace.") At one point, Trakl considered the variant: "*Every* grace-filled wound / Is *healed* by love's gentle might" (HKA 2: 176; emphases added).

> Golden blüht der Baum der Gnaden
> Aus der Erde kühlem Saft.
>
> *
>
> Golden blooms the tree of grace
> Rising from the earth's cool sap.

The second version of verses 7–8 retains elements of the original, although, in keeping with Trakl's compositional practice of de-personalization and de-contextualization (HKA 1: 273–274), its referent and import are more elusive. Trakl does, to be sure, refer to a specific object, namely a tree, but its associations are atypical and hard to place. I mentioned earlier that the color gold might call to mind the Tabernacle or New Jerusalem. The golden statue of Christ that hangs on the trefoil cross of the Evangelische Christuskirche evokes the tree of Calvary and therefore suffering and redemption, and in the poem "Psalm," it is God's golden eyes that lift over Golgotha. But why does Trakl mention the tree's *earthly* source? Why, in general, has Trakl taken the narrator and reader back outside? To recall, I believe, our prelapsarian state, where there was another tree, one that provided eternal life. But also, to look ahead to a time when the faithful will again eat of its fruit:

> and the street of the city was pure gold [. . .] and on either side of the river was there the tree of life [*Holz des Lebens*]

[. . .] and the leaves of the tree were for the healing of the nations. And there shall be no more curse [. . .]. Blessed are they that do his commandments, that they may have right to the tree of life, and may enter in through the gates [*Toren*] into the city. (Revelation 21:21, 22:2–3; see also 2:7).

These ideas are echoed in the apocryphal *Vita Adami et Evae*. Eve goes with Seth to the garden of paradise to ask God for oil from the tree of life so as to be able to relieve Adam's pains (*dolores*). Here the tree of life is called *arbor misericordie*, the "tree of grace or mercy," which could readily be translated into German with *Baum der Gnade(n)*. The archangel Michael refuses their request, explaining that only in the last days will one be able to anoint oneself with the tree's oil.[56] I do not know whether Trakl was acquainted with this text, but its lexical and thematic parallels with "A Winter Evening" are striking, and Trakl would have certainly found Eve's version of the Fall interesting.[57]

O! des Menschen bloße Pein.
Der mit Engeln stumm gerungen,
Langt von heiligem Schmerz bezwungen
Still nach Gottes Brot und Wein.

*

Oh! sheer agony of man.
He who strove with angels mutely,
Reaches, vanquished by holy pain,
So still, for God's bread and wine.

In any case, until those last days, Jesus has prepared a different sort of meal: not the fruit of the tree of life, let alone the bread and wine of earth and sky, but the bread and wine of his body and blood, which he gave for the redemption of sinners—even of those who, like Jacob, fought with angels. "And Jacob was left alone; and there wrestled [*rang*] a man with him until the breaking of day" (Genesis 32:24). "Jacob," admittedly, "had power over the angel [*Engel*], and prevailed" (Hosea 12:4), but only the holy (or "sweet," as one variant has it[58]) pain of Christ overcomes death. In the German, one might pronounce *heiligem* as a trochee (*heil'gem*); however, as written, it is the poem's only dactyl and thus a prominent interruption of the otherwise steady meter. Trakl does not depict arrival, but the marked holiness of verse 11 and the peaceful adverb of verse 12 suggest that the wanderers have not just identified their true home; they already have one foot in the door and are illumined by the glow within.

> Wanderer tritt still herein;
> Schmerz versteinerte die Schwelle.
> Da erglänzt in reiner Helle
> Auf dem Tische Brot und Wein.
>
> *
>
> Wanderer steps in, so still;
> Pain has petrified the threshold.
> There in purest brightness gleam
> On the table bread and wine.

The second version of the final stanza combines both the internal and the external perspective: an inside awareness of the saving power of grace, but also the need to accept it, to let it transform one. The German verbs *tritt* and *versteinerte* in verses 9–10 capture this tension. The wanderer *steps in* (indicative). But the wanderer is also quietly *called on to step in* (imperative without exclamation, direct address without comma). Pain *petrified* the threshold (simple past), turning it into a stumbling block, a *skandalon* to all systems and philosophies. But pain *would petrify* the threshold (subjunctive) further or even, at the threshold of death, completely, if one were to persist in one's selfish pride.[59]

Like nearly everything Dostoevsky ever wrote,[60] Trakl's poem brings the reader before the threshold of a decision. With its traditional trochaic tetrameter and enclosed-rhyme scheme ("masculine" outer rhymes embracing "feminine" inner ones), the form of "A Winter Evening" intimates what it would be like to partake in Holy Communion and all it stands for. The content stops short of portraying it, however, thereby preventing vicarious, thus inauthentic experience. Words may well be deeds, as Dostoevsky once put it.[61] But, in the best case, they can only partly atone. They do not suffice for salvation. Bread and wine may, for a moment, gleam like Pindar's gold or stand still like the commonplace objects of a *nature morte*. But this is a moment that must be acted on. It is not enough just to observe. You must either take part or turn back. You are the wanderer, and it is up to you to complete the story.

∽

Just because the ending of "A Winter Evening" is uncertain does not mean it is hopeless, as several scholars have argued.[62] To this extent Heidegger is right. But, as I have tried to show, the hope the poem offers cannot be secularized or ontologized so easily. At one point in "Language," Heidegger cites the Bible in order to clarify how he uses the word *befehlen*: not as "to command," but as "to commit" and "to commend." "We," Heidegger writes, "are still familiar with this sense from the saying: *Befiehl dem Herrn deine Wege*" (GA 12: 26). Heidegger does not state that this is Luther's translation of Psalm 37:5. In the King James Version: "Commit thy way unto the Lord." On what basis, however, may we turn to the Bible in order to understand words properly when we ought not to turn to it in order to understand a poem's sense? Did not language speak itself in the song of King David? Or did a sixteenth-century translation supplant the original, to the point of contextual irrelevance? Heidegger wants it both ways: to refer to the Bible when it suits him, and to ignore it or relegate any attempt to understand it to metaphysics when it does not.[63] Yet, in doing so, he overhears, or rather drowns out, crucial voices in Trakl's compositions, not just those that chant the *communio* but also those that sing the great lamentations for the sin and suffering of the world. As Ficker once wrote, contrasting Trakl and Kraus:

> Trakl's consciousness of his own forlornness was deeply rooted in a faith that made him a far-sighted realist. [. . .] In contrast, Kraus should be regarded as the last idealist of the times—he who grappled with the most terrifying reality [. . .] but was able to come to terms with it only by vivisecting what was lethal about it and revivifying it for posterity in the laboratory of his spirit, which was invariably intent on conservation. Trakl, however, looked straight through the hell of his life (never beyond it!) into the actuality of the distant heaven [*Himmels*]. That is the difference, the vast [*himmelweite*] difference, that separates the two, even in the nature of their self-sacrifice.[64]

Chapter 3

For the Love of Detachment

> Das echte Bild mag alt sein, aber der echte Gedanke ist neu. Er ist von heute. Dies Heute mag dürftig sein, zugegeben. Aber es mag sein wie es will, man muß es fest bei den Hörnern haben, um die Vergangenheit befragen zu können. Es ist der Stier, dessen Blut die Grube erfüllen muß, wenn an ihrem Rande die Geister der Abgeschiedenen erscheinen sollen.[1]
>
> —Walter Benjamin

What does it mean to place a word of which the thing tends to resist all place? What, moreover, does it mean to restrict the meaning of a word of which the thing, and the word, tends to thwart all restriction? I am asking here not just about how to manage polysemy, about how to shelter it from dispersion and dissemination, about how to prevent one of the valences of a word from detaching itself and taking on a life of its own. I am also, and in particular, asking how to delimit a word such as "detachment." In his second lecture on Trakl, Heidegger identifies this word, or rather its German counterpart, *Abgeschiedenheit*, as the point at which Trakl's entire body of poetic work is gathered together. Indeed, Heidegger defines "detachment" as a sort of gathering, as though nothing were oxymoronic about a detached gathering or a detachment that gathers, as though nothing were in need of further explanation or justification. Far from needing to detach ourselves from space, time, and language, as one might expect from the word and its history, Heidegger instead exhorts us to attach ourselves to the specific spatial, temporal, and linguistic senses he ascribes to detachment. In keeping with his linguistic modus operandi, he subjects nearly every key term in his lecture to etymological scrutiny (*Ort, fremd, Geschlecht, Wahnsinn, Geist*); about the origins of detachment, however, he remains silent. What is Heidegger avoiding? What is haunting him?

Jacques Derrida's work on Heidegger, especially his seminar sessions on *Geschlecht* from *Le fantôme de l'autre* (*The Phantom of the Other*), is, among other things, a work of exorcism: an exercise in not exactly driving away Heidegger's ghosts but driving them out into the open for investigation, no matter how ghastly they may be.[2] Derrida has summoned many such specters, and not just those haunting Heidegger's reading of Trakl. The latter include, to name but a few: sexual difference, animality, the idiom, *Geist*, and even the ghostly sense of *Geist* itself (GIII: 82). We, too, will have occasion to summon and interrogate these specters, especially in later chapters, but here I want to focus on a term that Derrida does not, as such, deconstruct, but that preoccupies him in his marginalia to, and interpretation of, "Language in the Poem," namely, *Abgeschiedenheit* ("detachment," "departedness"), especially as it is connected to the problem of gathering.[3] I will argue that detachment is one of the most problematic, most deconstructible concepts in Heidegger's text. And yet it is not, for all that, an exclusively problematic concept. Rather, when loosed from the strictures that Heidegger places on it, detachment will prove to be a helpful way to heed Trakl's song and even to think about the very work and love of deconstruction.

§1. The Problem of Polysemy

Derrida points out that Heidegger sees only two options when it comes to polysemy: either it is gathered together into a unique point of unification, or it succumbs to lax and sloppy imprecision—*tertium non datur* (GIII: 96–97; cf. GA 12: 71). If the polysemy of poetic speech is to be properly poetic, surely it cannot be a product of slapdash wordplay. If it were, poetry would hardly merit its equal status with thought. The polysemy of poetic speech must therefore spring from a single source, or, to use Heidegger's metaphor, poetic polyphony must resound from a tonic (*Grundton*) (GIII: 97; GA 12: 35, 74). There can be dissonance, perhaps even modulation, but the music of poetry will always be rooted in a home key. Poetry, at least any poetry deserving of the name, is never atonal.

Nor is thought. Rather, all thinking, for Heidegger, if it is to be authentic, must gather in language what being has already gathered in deed. On this view, Derrida writes, "there can be no rigorous thought or poetic writing of dissemination" (GIII: 97). We might have to resort to Old High German, but no meaning as such will escape us. Only the bad poet and the bad thinker go essentially astray. Only they are condemned to wander without a home. Only they lack a destination.

Heidegger also likes the language of detours, byways, and timber tracks. The role of these apparent digressions is, nevertheless, different. While they may seem useless, they actually help Heidegger on his way. Heidegger may have blundered about in the dark at times, but there was always "one star" guiding him (GA 13: 76), however faintly, however much it may have seemed like a foolish fire.

A similar star guides Trakl's poetry. Indeed, if Derrida is right that Heidegger's reading of Trakl is marked by Heidegger's own situation, his own signature, and the sense of his own path (GIII: 86–89), then perhaps Heidegger sees it as the same star. At any rate, Heidegger takes great pains throughout his reading to situate Trakl's body of work properly, to put it in its proper place. This place is detachment.

I will now turn to the circuitous course Heidegger takes, or leads us on, to arrive at this place. One major question guiding my analysis will be whether detachment is in fact beholden to the binary of gathering/carelessness, or whether, in this case, a third is not given after all.

§2. Heidegger's Placement of Detachment

From its first word (namely, *Erörtern*) on, Heidegger's lecture confronts us with problems of translation and of how to hear the proper sense of the self-speaking of language. The subtitle tells us that Heidegger will be attempting an *Erörterung* of Trakl's *Gedicht*: a discussion, we might think, of Trakl's poem. But Heidegger declares from the outset that *erörtern* will instead mean to indicate, to guide toward the *Ort*, the place. To discuss is to situ-ate or em-place. And what Heidegger intends to put in its proper place is not just a particular poem by Trakl but everything that Trakl has gathered and condensed (*ge-dichtet*) into song.[4] We thus have a gathering in place of what has already been gathered in language, a condensation of a condensation. Like the tip of a spear, which, Heidegger explains, *Ort* meant "originally" (GA 12: 33), the place is where everything in the *Gedicht* comes together—sharply and to the point. Heidegger asserts that there can be only one *Gedicht* from which the poet precipitates his song. (Heidegger's poets, by the way, are all men, with the possible exception of Sappho.⁵) Likewise, the place in and from which all of this occurs and the tone in which it resounds are *singular* (GA 12: 35).

We could at this point begin questioning Heidegger's authoritative, even authoritarian tone here, his confidence in the singularity of the place and of the poetry. I would, instead, like to take a different approach and turn to Heidegger's development of the place of Trakl's *Gedicht*. The questions of singularity and gathering will not leave us, however. Rather, the singular place of gathering will be exposed and shaken by the very situation of Heidegger's reading.

Where to begin? Which poem or line will provide the measure? In order to find the place of the poetry as a whole, we must elucidate (*erläutern*) certain poems. But in order to draw out the limpid (*lauter*) light that shines through these poems we must already have some sense for the place in which they are situated and from which such light comes. Emplacing and elucidating are therefore interdependent (GA 12: 34) or, as Heidegger would have put it earlier in his career, hermeneutically circular (SZ: §§32, 63).⁶ Any selection will inevitably seem arbitrary at the outset. Nonetheless, Heidegger already has the place in view, however he came to see it. Like the supposed wandering of the stranger that we are soon to learn about, Heidegger's discourse has a determinate and already determined destination. Even if, like on the crest of a wave, any of the poems would ultimately guide us there—provided that for every "great poet" (GA 12: 33) there is but one unspoken source from which the billows arise and into which they again fall—Heidegger knows in advance which poem will work best or, to shift the simile with him, which will "bring our attention to the place of the poem, almost as through a saccade or leap of our gaze [*Blicksprung*]" (GA 12: 35).

Whatever the case may be for Heidegger's initial selection, the path we will end up following will not be *leise*, soft and quiet. Nor will we glide along smoothly (*gelisian, gleiten*), which, according to Heidegger's declaration, is what *leise* means (or, perhaps, calls for, *heißt*) in Trakl's *Gedicht* (GA 12: 39; cf. 59). Rather, our trajectory will be filled with leaps and bounds from one poem to the next, concatenated only by what

Derrida identifies as a loose metonymy whose explanations go unheard (GIII: 64–65 et passim).

It seems, from Heidegger's perspective, that the fastest way to the place of Trakl's poetry is to begin not with a poem, nor even with a line from a poem, but with a portion of a line from the 1914 poem "Frühling der Seele" ("Springtime of the Soul"). Trakl writes, using one of his favorite grammatical constructions, "Es ist die Seele ein Fremdes auf Erden." The reader might hear this initially as, "The soul is something strange on earth" or, more literally, "There is the soul, something strange on earth." The soul belongs elsewhere. It is not at home here on earth. Even in its body the soul is more like a prisoner than a master chariocer (Plato).[7] Recall Trakl's letter to Ficker from June 1913, which I quoted at the end of chapter 1:

> I yearn for the day when the soul will no longer want and be able to dwell in this unholy, soulless body that is tainted with melancholy; when the soul will leave behind this figure of derision that is made of excrement and putrefaction and is but an all-too-faithful reflection of a godless, accursed century. (HKA 1: 301)

But, in Heidegger's eyes, the reader (and, we might ask, Trakl himself?) would be mistaken. Having just begun, we must therefore immediately backtrack. *Fremd*, Heidegger says, does not "authentically [*eigentlich*]" mean alien, foreign, or strange, "what we are not familiar with, what does not appeal to us, something that instead burdens and disquiets us" (GA 12: 36–37). *Fremd* authentically and—strangely—still means the same as its Old High German radical *fram*, "forward toward somewhere else, on the way to . . . , on toward what is already held in store for one" (GA 12: 37). It is not entirely clear how. Nor, for instance, is it clear how Trakl would have had much time to study Old High German in his short and troubled lifespan.[8]

Pace Heidegger, I suspect that Trakl adapted the phrase *Es ist die Seele ein Fremdes auf Erden* not from archaic German but from a Hebrew book that Heidegger ignores (or is willfully deaf to) in his interpretation of the Austrian poet. The psalmist sings, in Luther's translation:

> Ich bin ein Gast auf Erden; verbirg deine Gebote nicht vor mir. [. . .] Deine Rechte sind mein Lied im Hause meiner Wallfahrt. (119:19, 54)[9]

> I am a guest on earth; do not conceal your commands from me. [. . .] Your commands are a song in the house in which I am a stranger.

Compare, further, the following New Testament commentary on the Psalm (Hebrews 11:13–16):

> These all [namely, the faithful prior to the Incarnation, such as Abraham] died in faith, not having received the promises, but having seen them afar off, and were persuaded of them, and embraced them, and confessed that they were strangers and pilgrims on the earth [*Gäste und Fremdlinge auf Erden*]. For they that say such things declare plainly that they seek a country [*Vaterland*]. And truly, if they had been mindful of that country from whence they came out, they might have had opportunity to have returned. But now they desire a better country, that is, an heavenly: wherefore God is not ashamed to be called their God: for he hath prepared for them a city.

Just as strangers must learn the laws of the land in order to survive, so the psalmist beseeches God for statutes to live by in a formidable world. Even if Trakl did not seek solutions in rules and regulations, he would have identified with the psalmist's feeling of earthly estrangement after the Fall.

Furthermore, whatever the historical-critical status of this psalm, many have read it in a Platonic spirit and advanced its sense of terrestrial alienation—including, on my interpretation, not just Trakl but several of the great "German thinkers" to whom one might have expected Heidegger to turn in his lecture.[10] For example, the medieval Dominican theologian Meister Eckhart, with whom Trakl was familiar (HKA 2: 756), preached that:

> *here*, the body is bold and strong, for here it is at home, [. . .] the earth is its fatherland, and all its relatives are helpful to it here: food, drink, leisureliness. This is all contrary to the

spirit [*Geist*]. Here, the spirit is in the foreign [*in der Fremde*]; its relatives, its entire kind [*Geschlecht*], are in *heaven*.[11]

In "Der Geist des Christentums und sein Schicksal" ("The Spirit of Christianity and Its Fate")—a text that became available in 1907 and would have certainly resonated with Trakl's own interest in the fate of Christianity—Hegel spoke of Abraham becoming "ein Fremdling auf Erden" the moment the future patriarch cut ties with Haran and placed his hopes in an otherworldly deity.[12] Finally, the theme of the stranger was also especially important for Novalis, whom Trakl thrice calls a "heiliger Fremdling" (HKA 1: 182–183), and who was the only poet, apart from Hölderlin, whom Trakl honored with an eponymous title ("An Novalis," "To Novalis"). After the death of his beloved, Novalis started to see himself, in the words of his brother Karl von Hardenberg, as "ein Fremdling auf Erden." Novalis himself explained: "Strangers in the world [*Fremdlinge auf der Welt*] are those who bear within themselves the recollection of a past time of harmony [*Eintracht*] and have faith in its return."[13] Although the romantic poet occasionally described this return as a new golden age, he also, and in particular in the *Hymnen an die Nacht* (*Hymns to the Night*), believed that only a Christ-mediated dissolution into the night would restore the serenity of old. Novalis, speculative geologist as he was, certainly did not neglect the earth. But his soul was hardly filled with the desire that, in Heidegger's reading, animated Trakl: "to save the earth *as* the earth" (GA 12: 37).

With Heidegger's remarks and these historical resonances in our ear, let us listen to Trakl's "Springtime of the Soul." I am particularly interested in whether the poem as a whole supports Heidegger's reading or whether, on the contrary, it suggests redemption *from* the earth (cf. Revelation 14:3) or, at best, a redemption, not of the earth *as earth*, but of the earth *as suffused with divine spirit*. Notice that the poem begins with the scream of a nightmare and ends with a gentle song at evening. In between, the poet invokes paradise and death, purity and incest:

> Aufschrei im Schlaf; durch schwarze Gassen stürzt der Wind,
> Das Blau des Frühlings winkt durch brechendes Geäst,
> Purpurner Nachttau und es erlöschen rings die Sterne.
> Grünlich dämmert der Fluß, silbern die alten Alleen

Und die Türme der Stadt. O sanfte Trunkenheit
Im gleitenden Kahn und die dunklen Rufe der Amsel
In kindlichen Gärten. Schon lichtet sich der rosige Flor.

Feierlich rauschen die Wasser. O die feuchten Schatten der Au,
Das schreitende Tier; Grünendes, Blütengezweig
Rührt die kristallene Stirne; schimmernder Schaukelkahn.
Leise tönt die Sonne im Rosengewölk am Hügel.
Groß ist die Stille des Tannenwalds, die ernsten Schatten am Fluß.

Reinheit! Reinheit! Wo sind die furchtbaren Pfade des Todes,
Des grauen steinernen Schweigens, die Felsen der Nacht
Und die friedlosen Schatten? Strahlender Sonnenabgrund.

Schwester, da ich dich fand an einsamer Lichtung
Des Waldes und Mittag war und groß das Schweigen des Tiers;
Weiße unter wilder Eiche, und es blühte silbern der Dorn.
Gewaltiges Sterben und die singende Flamme im Herzen.

Dunkler umfließen die Wasser die schönen Spiele der Fische.
Stunde der Trauer, schweigender Anblick der Sonne;
Es ist die Seele ein Fremdes auf Erden. Geistlich dämmert
Bläue über dem verhauenen Wald und es läutet
Lange eine dunkle Glocke im Dorf; friedlich Geleit.
Stille blüht die Myrthe über den weißen Lidern des Toten.

Leise tönen die Wasser im sinkenden Nachmittag
Und es grünet dunkler die Wildnis am Ufer, Freude im rosigen Wind;
Der sanfte Gesang des Bruders am Abendhügel. (HKA 1: 77–78)

*

Outcry in sleep; the wind tumbles through black alleys,
The blue of spring beckons through breaking branches,
Crimson night-dew and all around the stars go out.
Greenish, the river dawns, silver, the old avenues

And the towers of the city. Oh, gentle drunkenness
In the gliding skiff and the dark calls of the blackbird
In the gardens of childhood. Already the rosy blossom becomes
    clearer.

Solemnly rush the waters. Oh, the damp shadows of the
    meadow,
The striding animal; greenery, flowering branches
Touch the crystalline brow; shimmering, swaying skiff.
Quietly the sun resounds in the rose-cloud by the hill.
Great is the stillness of the fir forest, the stern shadows at
    the river.

Purity! Purity! Where are the terrible paths of death,
Of gray, stony silence, the cliffs of night
And the peaceless shadows? Radiant sun-abyss.

Sister, when I found you in a lonesome clearing
Of the forest and it was noon and great was the silence of
    the animal;
White one, under a wild oak, and silver bloomed the thorn.
Violent dying and the singing flame in the heart.

More darkly did the waters flow about the lovely games of
    the fish.
Hour of grief, silent spectacle of the sun;
The soul is something strange on earth. Spiritually,
Blueness dawns over the thrashed forest and long
A dark bell tolls in the village; peaceful convoy.
In stillness the myrtle blooms over the white eyelids of the
    dead one.

Quietly the waters resound in the sinking afternoon
And the wilderness greens more darkly on the bank, joy in
    the rosy wind;
The gentle song of the brother on the evening hill.

   After the brutal awakening of the poem's opening, the first two
stanzas conjure images of dawning tranquility: the blueness of spring,

mild intoxication, roseate clouds and flowers. The crystalline brow and swaying boat recall Trakl's figure of Elis, an innocent child of God who died young and whose historical or mythological precedence—if there even is one—has mystified commentators.[14] Here, plant, animal, and human are in harmony. This is a time, the third stanza suggests, before the wages of sin (cf. Romans 6:23; 1 Corinthians 15:55).

But innocence is fleeing. As in Trakl's Elis poems, purity becomes tainted, and paradise is lost. The paradoxical compound of abyss and sun at the end of the third stanza prepares the shift in status (from perfection to corruption), in time (from eternity to a before and after), and in quantity (from universal to particular) that marks the fourth stanza. Here, the narrator, presumably a brother speaking to his dead sister, recounts the misdeed that brought about her demise and estranged his soul. He seems to speak of incest and murder. A thorn blossomed, becoming silver like a knife or the head of a phallic spear. The fire of his passion consumed her purity (metaphorical whiteness) and perhaps literally turned her white (her color fading in death). Then, in the fifth stanza, we learn that, with the descent of the sun, which had witnessed this transgression, everything began to darken. The brother grew full of sorrow and remorse.

Strikingly, the narrator now switches back to the present. Only, this is not the eternal present of paradise, but the brother's present state of despair, which, like the expulsion from Eden, he extends to all of humankind. The soul is no longer at home on earth; it is something apart, something cut off (*abgeschieden*) from the prior unity of nature.

This is not the end of the story, however. In contrast to the Elis poems, sacred blueness begins to spread over the landscape. A church bell calls the brother to repentance and ultimately back to peace. Recall the bell in "Ein Winterabend" ("A Winter Evening"). Yet this is not a return to prelapsarian innocence. It is a *geistliche* restoration with religious overtones. (The adjectives *geistlich* and *geistig* both mean "spiritual," but the former has an ecclesiastical connotation: a *Geistlicher* is a clergyman. Luther, incidentally, also uses *geistlich*, as opposed to *geistig* or *im Geiste*, in his translation of Matthew 5:3, which Trakl was fond of quoting: *Selig sind, die da geistlich arm sind*. Heidegger, for his part, will provide a radically different interpretation of the word.) I hear Isaiah 55:12–13 in Trakl's lines, where the prophet calls on the exiles to abandon Babylonia and "to be guided in peace" (*im Frieden geleitet werden*). Compare Trakl's *friedlich Geleit*, "peaceful convoy." The "hills will shout for joy," and the thrashed forest[15] will be transformed: there will be "cypresses instead of thorns," "myrtles instead of nettles." "And it shall redound to the glory of the Lord, as an eternal sign that shall not perish."

The myrtle is not just a sign for the fulfillment of God's promise to the Jews or, by extension, to all Christians. It also signifies marriage, whether pagan (Virgil: "dearest is the myrtle to beautiful Venus") or Judeo-Christian.[16] Recall Trakl's conversation with Dallago and other members of the Brenner Circle, which I discussed at the end of chapter 1. After proclaiming his faith, Trakl turned to the problem of sexual difference:

> It is unheard of [. . .] how Christ solves the deepest questions of humanity with every simple word! Can the questions regarding the community between man and woman be solved more completely than through the command: *They shall become One Flesh* [E i n   F l e i s c h]? (DD: 212)

I do not take Trakl to mean religiously institutionalized marriage here, not even the three-strand variety of Ecclesiastes (4:12). Rather, he is referring to an eschatological redemption and reunification of the sexes, which, if we recall Trakl's earlier poem "Abendländisches Lied" ("Song of the Occident"), may serve as a synecdoche for humankind or even all of nature. In that poem's final stanza, Trakl had also sung of despair and salvation:

> O, die bittere Stunde des Untergangs,
> Da wir ein steinernes Antlitz in schwarzen Wassern beschaun.
> Aber strahlend heben die silbernen Lider die Liebenden:
> E i n Geschlecht. Weihrauch strömt von rosigen Kissen
> Und der süße Gesang der Auferstandenen. (HKA 1: 66)

*

> Oh, the bitter hour of downfall,
> When we behold a stony countenance in black waters.
> But radiantly the lovers raise their silver eyelids:
> O n e *Geschlecht*. Incense streams from rosy pillows,
> And the sweet song of the resurrected ones.

The word I have left untranslated here, *Geschlecht*, has a wider scope than man and woman. Translators of the poem have rendered it in at least eight different ways: not just with "sex" and "gender" but also with "flesh," "body," "kin," "kind," "race," and "House."[17] "Lineage" might work, too, as in the poem "Gesang des Abgeschiedenen" ("Song of the Departed One"):

> Liebend auch umfängt das Schweigen im Zimmer die
>   Schatten der Alten,
> Die purpurnen Martern, Klage eines großen Geschlechts,
> Das fromm nun hingeht im einsamen Enkel.

*

> Silence in the room also lovingly embraces the shadows of
>   the ancestors,
> The crimson torments, lamentation of a great lineage
> That now piously passes on in the solitary grandson.

The only English word that seems to capture all of these senses is "being." In any case, given the lovers, and given Trakl's own plagued preoccupations with the figure of sister (to say nothing of his own sister), sexual difference seems to be the primary sense of *Geschlecht* in "Song of the Occident." In death and resurrection, the lovers see and sing their union. Secondarily, at least in order of implication if not of time, they may also be celebrating the ultimate union, when God will have become "all in all" (1 Corinthians 15:28). In chapter 6, I will examine the extent to which difference, and in particular sexual difference, is dissolved in such oneness. Trakl's emphatic spacing of "O n e" should in any case give us pause.

In "Springtime of the Soul," there is also higher union in death, at least for those who heed the call of spirit. "In stillness," we hear in the penultimate stanza, "the myrtle blooms over the white eyelids of the dead one." Here, the gender of the *Tote*, the dead one, is ambiguous. It is either masculine—perhaps the brother has suffered a sort of *Liebestod*—or neuter—the sister has become a corpse, spiritual redemption has neutralized the sin and the gendered marks of temptation, and the siblings are now not (*ne*) either (*uter*) man or woman, et cetera. In any case, the brother—whether the brother in the poem, now resurrected or redeemed, or the poetic brother in general (Hölderlin, Novalis, Trakl himself)—has become gentle, and the scream a song.

By no means do I wish to settle on a single reading of "Springtime of the Soul." Others are no doubt possible. But Heidegger's neglect of context, which as I have tried to show is largely coherent irrespective of the poet's biography, is problematic. Throughout his lecture, Heidegger cites the line, *Es ist die Seele ein Fremdes auf Erden*, nine times, as though glossing the day's reading in a homily. Although he does refer to other verses of the poem on two occasions, he never situates them within the whole, and he does not hesitate to declare early on that, in the poem, "not a single word is uttered about a supra-terrestrial homeland for the immortal soul" (GA 12: 36). None, I would counter, other than the very word about the *strange* and *foreign* soul, which both internal and external considerations have helped us to see as sinful and in search of spiritual salvation.[18]

Heidegger, however, is not burdened or disquieted by concerns about Trakl's supposed acquaintance with archaic German or by the figures and traditions with which Trakl overtly affiliated himself, let alone by the particular poem from which he takes Trakl's line. Heidegger knows the true meaning of the word *fremd* and believes we should too.

But where, we might now ask, does Heidegger himself get his etymology? How does he know that *fremd* means *fram*, not "foreign" or "strange," but "forward toward somewhere else [*anderswohin vorwärts*], on the way to . . . , on toward what is already held in store for one" (GA 12: 37)? Did he derive it from a study of the medieval canon? Or is he simply drawing on a lexicon, as he did for the word *Geschlecht* in the notes he took in preparation for his Trakl lecture? In their dictionaries, Hermann, Kluge, and Schade all trace *fremd* back to *fram*, for which, like Heidegger, they give *vorwärts* ("forward"), but there is no indication that this direction implies destination, that the *Fremdes* would be moving toward what is held in store for it.[19]

Without citing any examples from Old High German literature, let alone a dictionary, Heidegger next assures the reader—declaratively and without hesitation—that the path is not one that the essentially foreign soul must first forge. Rather, the soul's path already lies out ahead of it. It therefore need not err aimlessly along the way. Wandering, properly understood, is *not* without a reason why. The way is *not* the goal. Only the *Geschlecht* of decaying and degenerate humans has no course to follow (GA 12: 43, 46, 70).[20] The soul, in contrast, has left such people behind. It has died to their corruption. It has even separated from its loved ones, who have become other to it. As Trakl writes in the poem "Herbstseele"

("Autumn Soul"), with words reminiscent of Jesus's requirements for discipleship (cf. Luke 14:26):

> Jägerruf und Blutgebell;
> Hinter Kreuz und braunem Hügel
> Blindet sacht der Weiherspiegel,
> Schreit der Habicht hart und hell.
>
> Über Stoppelfeld und Pfad
> Banget schon ein schwarzes Schweigen;
> Reiner Himmel in den Zweigen;
> Nur der Bach rinnt still und stad.
>
> Bald entgleitet Fisch und Wild.
> Blaue Seele, dunkles Wandern
> Schied uns bald von Lieben, Andern.
> Abend wechselt Sinn und Bild.
>
> Rechten Lebens Brot und Wein,
> Gott in deine milden Hände
> Legt der Mensch das dunkle Ende,
> Alle Schuld und rote Pein. (HKA 1: 60)

*

> Cry of hunters, bloodhounds' bay;
> Mirror-pond, behind the cross
> And brown hill, is softly blinding,
> Harsh and bright the hawk is screaming.
>
> Over stubble field and path
> A black silence trembles now;
> Purest heaven in the boughs;
> Just the brook runs still and quiet.
>
> Fish and game soon slip away.
> Blue soul, darksome wand'ring, soon did
> Sever us from loved ones, others.
> Evening changes sense and image.

Bread and wine of proper living,
God into your mild hands
Layeth man the darksome ending,
All the guilt and scarlet torment.

One might hear in Trakl's words a call to leave this wicked, wayward world behind and to commend oneself to God. This call need not entail indifference to the damned. Rather, there is much in Trakl's poetry to suggest deep sorrow and sympathy for the degenerate *Geschlecht*, even if he wishes to part from it. Recall the aphorism he gave to Ficker before leaving for war: "Feeling in the moments of death-like being: all humans are worthy of love. Awaking, you feel the bitterness of the world; therein is all your unresolved guilt; your poem an imperfect atonement" (HKA 1: 256).

Heidegger, however, would have us believe the opposite. He deploys numerous strategies in his earthbound, asocial interpretation. I will mention just three. First, he reads selectively. For instance, in his lecture, he only ever cites from the penultimate, less clearly religious stanza of "Autumn Soul" (GA 12: 45, 47, 73), with no regard for its place within the poem as a whole. Indeed, contrary to the final stanza ("God into your mild hands / layeth man the darksome ending"), he even says that the day's decline into evening is "not an ending," but rather only an inclination to prepare the beginning of the soul's journey (GA 12: 47). It is thus less a departure in the sense of death, which the German *Abgeschiedenheit* suggests, than a point of departure for something new.

Second, as we saw in previous chapters, Heidegger downplays or recasts the Christian elements of bread and wine, spirit and resurrection (GA 12: 72). Recall that, even when Heidegger did bring up the final stanza of "Autumn Soul" the day after delivering "Language in the Poem," he claimed that it pertains only to the "others," thus not to the detached soul in search of the earth. *They* still pray. *They*, not the stranger, still need transcendence. Just as Trakl's *Gedicht* has a univocal sense, so do Christianity, Platonism, metaphysics, and science, and not necessarily independently, for they are all ultimately of a piece. Only, in the case of the former (Trakl's *Gedicht*), Heidegger sees a "good univocity," as Derrida puts it, whereas in that of the latter (Christiano-Platonico-metaphysico-science) the univocity is "bad" (GIII: 98, 109).

Third, Heidegger resorts to German etymology or reinterprets words according to a putatively more original sense. We have already seen this with *fremd*. The soul is not moving *away* from the earth; it is on the way *to* the earth. It must, moreover, go under (*untergehen*), but "going under" does not mean "downfall" or "deterioration," or even anything "catastrophic," as one might expect (GA 12: 38; cf. 67). It is the course the soul must follow, or rather rediscover, before the metaphysical interpretation of it had gone astray. This course leads to the tranquility of the dead (GA 12: 38). But, Heidegger explains, again in tension with the last stanza of "Autumn Soul," death does not signal the "ending of earthly life" (GA 12: 42; cf. 51, 63), let alone the death to sin that is the life in Christ (Romans 6:11). Death is instead the very course of the stranger's going under. Provided we follow this stranger, we too will become strangers to the putrid *Geschlecht* and find what is most properly and essentially our own (GA 12: 37, 45, 57).

Heidegger's radical rereading continues. By going under, the soul comes to experience the earth not as a material counterpart to the soul, not as a realm of accident and corruption, but as a "more serene homeland for the *Geschlecht* that is returning home" (GA 12: 45, 76). Here the soul does not eliminate or overcome difference—be it between the sexes, the tribes, the generations, or the species (and, remember, *Geschlecht* can mean all of these things)—but twists the outcome of the discordant blow of difference into a softer and more tranquil mark of gentleness.[21] Or rather it twists the dissonant difference *back* into a gentleness of old, where the *Geschlechter* were not at war, where there was no dissension, but only the gathering of a more tender, more consonant double. Gentleness, *das Sanfte*, just is, in fact, this "peaceful gathering," "according to the literal sense of the word," as Heidegger decrees in another attempt at clarification through etymologization (GA 12: 41).[22]

This gathering of gentleness is not without multiplicity, or, better, duplicity, in both senses of the word. Gentleness is a gathering, or enfolding, of two folds. But there is something double-dealing about this. For, we might ask, how did or does the peaceful gathering of gentleness end up striking us with the curse of dissension, shattering the double into conflicting singles (GA 12: 46)?[23] Why, as Heidegger indicates in a marginal note of his personal copy of Trakl, does *Aufruhr* ("insurgency," "upheaval") belong together, not only with gentleness, but with *Gelassenheit* ("releasement") as essential, even if opposed, components of *Geist*, which Heidegger does not want to read as "spirit," but rather as Gothic *gheis*, to be "outside oneself"? And how does the peaceful gathering of gentleness let itself be overpowered by such an insurrection?

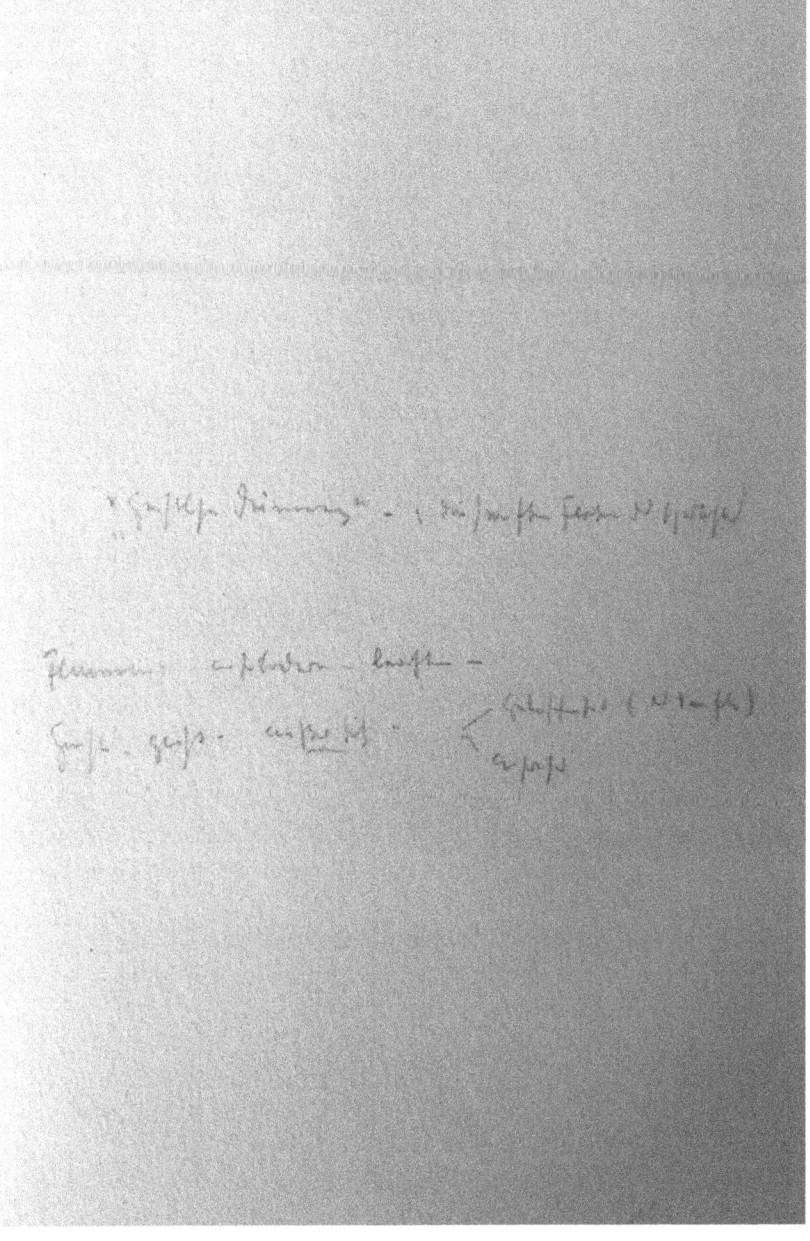

Image 5. Heidegger's marginal note following Trakl's "Grodek," in his personal copy of *Die Dichtungen*, ed. Horwitz, located in the Martin-Heidegger-Archiv der Stadt Meßkirch.

Additionally, Heidegger sees the harmonious double as so tightly plied that he is beckoned or compelled to describe it oxymoronically, as a "onefold twofold" (GA 12: 46), or, in Latinate terms he would not allow,[24] as a simple duplicity. Heidegger's oxymoronic rendering may be a result of his desire to preempt dispersion, while at the same time avoiding a static monism. Heidegger clearly thinks there has been and can still be dissension. But is his alternative sufficient? Will the plies of this fantastically folded fabric never come undone? Ought they never to come undone?

These questions, which we will return to in chapter 7, are especially pertinent to what Heidegger identifies as the place to which we have apparently been wandering all along. The place of Trakl's *Gedicht*, he says at the end of the first section of his lecture, is *Abgeschiedenheit*. Here too we must be cautious, for Heidegger is going to understand this word differently from what one might take to be its primary meanings. *Abgeschiedenheit*, in its current sense, refers to seclusion or solitude, for example, that of a monastic life or of a hermitage on a mountain. We can find a similar, though more metaphorical, use of the term in a recollection by Erwin Mahrholdt with which Heidegger was familiar, where Mahrholdt speaks of his friend Trakl's "Christian resignation" and "cloistral, inner *Abgeschiedenheit*" (DD: 203). The word also has the valence of having departed, not just from worldly concerns, but from the world as such. Thus, *die Abgeschiedenen* are the deceased. This sense can be heard in the work of another friend of Trakl, Karl Borromäus Heinrich, who composed two texts from the perspective of a departed one, both titled "Briefe aus der Abgeschiedenheit," before attempting suicide himself.[25]

For Heidegger, there is, admittedly, a stroke of departure in *Abgeschiedenheit*, although, as we have seen, it has nothing to do with death in the customary sense. The soul must sever itself (*sich scheiden*) from the corrupt and corrupting *Geschlecht* (GA 12: 46, 55, 64–65, 67–68). But the separation is not merely negative. The soul has both a guide and a destination. It can and must follow the stranger, who has already departed elsewhere, who is, in Heidegger's eyes, the *Ab-geschiedener* (GA 12: 46), the one who has cut himself off from lovers and mundane others, the one who, in losing himself, has not been destroyed but has slid into the evening that "changes sense and image" ("Autumn Soul"). In Heidegger's reading, there is accordingly not only detachment *from*, but detachment *toward* (GA 12: 68). And that toward which the stranger and soul have and are becoming detached has a singular *Sinn*, which means not just "sense," but also "direction," in connection with the Old High German *sinnan*, "to journey, strive after . . . , strike out a path" (GA 12: 49). Heidegger says that everything Trakl sings is "gathered" together into "a single song," namely, that of "the detached, departed one [*Abgeschiedenen*]" (GA 12: 48); indeed, he says that it is detachment itself that is doing the gathering (GA 12: 54). Likewise, Heidegger will say in the third and final section of his lecture that this entire complex of detachment, which is none other than the place of Trakl's *Gedicht*, is itself gathered by what Heidegger calls the *Ortschaft des Ortes*, not the abstract "placeness of the place," but a specific locale that serves as the center of support, something like the "shaft" (*Schaft*) of the "tip" (*Ort*) of the spear (to take Heidegger's etymology one step further). This *Ortschaft*, namely, the "concealed essence of *Abgeschiedenheit*," is, Heidegger declares, the *Abendland* (GA 12: 73; cf. 33).

Abgeschiedenheit therefore has (1) a singularly spatial *Sinn* ("sense," "direction") in Heidegger's interpretation. It also, as we will see, has (2) a singularly linguistic *Sinn*.

(1) In the final portion of his lecture, Heidegger again returns to the third stanza of "Autumn Soul," this time tying it to a line from "Song of the Departed (or Detached) One," where Trakl sighs:

O das Wohnen in der beseelten Bläue der Nacht. (HKA 1: 79)

*

Oh, dwelling in the besouled blueness of night.

Heidegger claims that what grants dwelling is, "in our language, the 'land' [*das 'Land'*]" (GA 12: 73). And since, according to "Autumn Soul," it is the "evening [*Abend*]" that "changes sense and image," the entire place of Trakl's *Gedicht*, its *Abgeschiedenheit*, must be embedded in the *Abendland*. We might follow convention and translate this word with the Germanic "West." The problem, however, is that we thereby lose the sense of place, of a particular locality or land, which the everyday use of *Ortschaft* indicates. "West" stems from the same root as *hesperos* and *vesper*, meaning "evening," not "land." The Latinate "Occident" will not do, either, as Derrida recognizes, but whose French does not allow a ready way out (GIII: 132; GA 71: 98–99). For, among other reasons,

"Occident" connotes only going down. But, as we have seen, there is always a path to the *Untergang*. And this path must lead somewhere. Moreover, Heidegger notes that the *Abendland* does not itself go under, but rather awaits those who do (GA 12: 73). If, therefore, we care about etymology—and, in Heidegger's view, as in that of his grammarian predecessor Dionysius Thrax, we must[26]—the best it seems we can do in English is to render it with the cognate "evening-land" or "land of evening."

Whence this appeal to land? Readers of "Song of the Departed One," as of "Autumn Soul," might hear a reference to a possible homeland in God. The whole stanza, of which Heidegger cites only the last line in his lecture, reads:

> Und es leuchtet ein Lämpchen, das Gute, in seinem Herzen
> Und der Frieden des Mahls; denn geheiligt ist Brot und Wein
> Von Gottes Händen, und es schaut aus nächtigen Augen
> Stille dich der Bruder an, daß er ruhe von dorniger Wanderschaft.
> O das Wohnen in der beseelten Bläue der Nacht. (HKA 1: 79)

*

> And a little lamp, the good, shines in his heart
> And the peace of the meal; for sanctified are bread and wine
> By the hands of God, and from night-like eyes
> In stillness the brother beholds you, that he may find rest from thorny wandering.
> Oh, dwelling in the besouled blueness of night.

It is, at any rate, hard to see how Trakl's poem would amount to an allusion to Germany—a land in which one says *Abendland*—or to any earthly place at all, for that matter. Heidegger is nevertheless insistent that *Abgeschiedenheit* must lead the soul to the land of evening, as he is insistent there must be a path thereto.

There is an exclusionary, even nationalistic character to this land of evening. Not just anyone can follow the stranger's going under. The transition into what Heidegger now calls a land of beginning, of ascent or dawn, is rather only possible for the "elect," for those who have been "separated out [*ausgeschieden*], i.e., gathered into a gathering that gathers more gently and more quietly beckons" (GA 12: 64). (Heidegger poses this sentence as a question, but there is little doubt that we are meant to take it rhetorically.) Heidegger does, admittedly, speak of a transformation of the Menschengeschlecht, which suggests the whole human race. The resurrected "One Geschlecht" of which Trakl sings in "Song of the Occident" might therefore refer to humanity as a whole, and not just to the lovers that had appeared in the preceding line, which Heidegger ignores.[27] But Heidegger also claims that Trakl would have celebrated the very deaths in Gródek that likely drove him to suicide, if that is indeed what Trakl is referring to in his late eponymous poem (GA 12: 61–62). In any case, it is the Germans, the Swabians in particular, who will lead the way, and where they are going is certainly not heaven, it is certainly not Europe, and it is not at all clear that everyone will be given passports.[28]

(2) If there is indeed a nationalist strand in Heidegger's appeal to the Abendland, we should not be surprised to find that it has one official language (or maybe two, but the second would be permitted only in its ancient form). Heidegger is, admittedly, dialoguing with a German poet, and, as Derrida notes, a certain "irreducible tether to the German language" cannot be denied in his lecture, especially at its crucial moments (GIII: 36n1). Heidegger's thought, and our attempt to think after him, is so bound up with language that we must not fail to heed its idiom and tongue. But to think after Heidegger means not just thinking according to Heidegger or in the wake of Heidegger. It means not just thinking in or with his German. It also means to think against Heidegger, against the unnecessary or unjustified restrictions he imposes on the language. As Derrida writes, "we will have to multiply the drafts [of the attempt at translation], harass the German word, and analyze it according to several waves of touches, caresses, or blows" (GIII: 36n1).

There are, in other words, not just nationalist themes or motifs in Heidegger's lecture, such as the appeal to come full circle, to turn back home in the manner of Odysseus. Even the language itself, at least in its tendency, bears an idiomatic, properly nationalist character. The idiom of Heidegger's dialogue with Trakl, more than just its themes, fascinates Derrida (GIII: 153). It makes Heidegger's text of particular relevance to a seminar dealing with "philosophical nationality and nationalism."[29] Derrida therefore frequently interrogates the moments when Heidegger appeals to German, both old and modern—to words spoken *in unserer Sprache*—in order to clarify seeming ambiguities between Trakl's poetic language and Heidegger's interpretation of it (e.g., GIII: 127–128). We are in turn compelled to ask about the idiom of language and the idiom of property, about the *idios* of Heidegger's reading. Whose language? To whom does the possessive adjective refer? Who owns German? Anyone who speaks it? Or only those who grew up speaking it, the native Germans? Would the Plautdietsch of the Mexican Mennonite count? Or must one be a part of the homeland? Is it enough to have been born there? But what would *its* boundaries be? Who would draw them? And what to make of regional idioms, such as the Austrian-German *stad* ("quiet") in Trakl's "Autumn Soul"?

Perhaps we could say it is enough to just read Heidegger in the original. But when I do so is German mine? And what is the original? Is it the modern German that I presume to understand? Or is it the Old German that still resounds for those able to hear it (or for those with a good dictionary)? Or is the original older yet? The Protogermanic? Or the *Indo*-Germanic that Heidegger seems to have no qualms invoking (GA 12: 43, 49)? But is that even German any longer, however secret? And why does he not say Indo-*European* like "we" do?

These questions expose some of the difficulties surrounding what Derrida identifies as Heidegger's insistence on an "absolute univocity of tongue" (GIII: 98):

> What [Heidegger's] text is signaling and opening up toward, what it is appealing to, cannot be separated from this German possibility, [i.e.,] not the possibility of Germany in general, but a possibility that is unthinkable without the destiny of something like the German tongue and German poeticity [*la langue et la poéticité allemande*], and of its relation, of its *Gespräch* [dialogue] with thought, if not with philosophy. (GIII: 155)

Now, while it may be plausible to focus on German—such as when confronted with the idea that the place of Trakl's poetry is inseparable from the poems themselves, which were, after all, written in German—to insist absolutely on it marks the height of linguistic hubris, and hubris, as we learn from the Greeks, is bound to fall. The collapse of such a regime need not be provoked from without, however, for example from a language foreign to the mother tongue. Rather, as we will see, *Abgeschiedenheit*, the very term under which Heidegger places Trakl's *Gedicht*, undermines the center of power from within. Language, as Derrida reminds us, is never our own.[30]

§3. *Abgeschiedenheit* in (Our?) Middle High German

To show this, I will return to a tradition Heidegger disavows in his reading of Trakl, namely, Christianity, but this time in one of its medieval mystical guises. Derrida, for his part, does not so much seek to ascertain whether and in what way Trakl's work is Christian as to problematize Heidegger's denial and preterition of it (see especially GIII: 108–117). Here, I too am not so interested in answering one way or the other, although some of the material I quoted and interpreted above and in the previous chapters suggests that it would not be so easy to dam up the Christian current as Heidegger thinks. I would, instead, like to show how *Abgeschiedenheit* itself has a heritage—a predominately Christian heritage—that undermines the interpretation Heidegger gives it.

The word *Abgeschiedenheit* stems from the Middle High German *abegescheidenheit*, itself a combination of the verb *scheiden*, "to cut," "to separate," and the prefix *abe-*, "away." Meister Eckhart, who was extremely influential on Heidegger, appears to have been the first to use the noun form in his late-thirteenth-century text *Die rede der underscheidunge* (*Counsels on Discernment*), where, incidentally, one also finds the first appearance of *Gelassenheit*, or rather the Middle High German *gelâzenheit*, which Eckhart employs as a synonym of *abegescheidenheit*.[31] Heidegger not only quotes from Eckhart's tractate on several occasions but also marked it up extensively in his personal copies of the Middle High German and of a modern German translation.[32] *Abegescheidenheit* would go on to become one of the most important words in Eckhart's corpus, even becoming the topic of a self-standing treatise titled *Von abegescheidenheit*. As Eckhart himself explains: "When I preach, I am accustomed to speak about *abegescheidenheit* and the fact that the human must become empty of himself and of all things."[33] Here I will briefly discuss how the term relates to (1) language, (2) space and time, and (3) teleology in Eckhart.

(1) The first thing to note is that *abegescheidenheit* does not have a linguistic or nationalist precedence for Eckhart. Not only did he spend a significant portion of his career abroad in Paris, where he held the chair once occupied by Thomas Aquinas; he is the only medieval theologian of rank whose body of work survives substantially in both Latin and the vernacular, and it is not easy to sort out which language expresses which ideas, at least not when it comes to terms such as *abescheiden*, which also appears in Latin under the guise of *abstrahere* and *separare*. In fact, rather than relegating Latin to the realm of corruption, Eckhart often

does the opposite, using Latin terms to help his audience understand a new or challenging word in Middle High German. From an Eckhartian perspective, it would therefore be absurd to restrict Latinate terms in German to a pejorative function, as Heidegger himself frequently does.[34] This is because, for Eckhart, the language is not what is important, whether it be German or Latin; rather, language is itself something from which we must detach ourselves.

(2) In both Latin and German, Eckhart frequently exhorts his audience to detach themselves from space and time, from the here and now, so they may recognize and live in accordance with the highest powers of their soul. These powers, for their part, are already "detached [*abegescheiden*] from time and place"; they are where "the human being is of God's *Geschlecht* [*geslehte*]."[35] But even this is insufficient. For the danger looms that we could still interpret the *One Geschlecht* of God and the detached human being as located somewhere, at some point in time, as a gathering of two. Despite his love of paradox, Eckhart would not settle for such a reading. What Eckhart is after is not a gathering or unification. Rather, he is advocating an implicit, always operative oneness so abyssal that it is beyond any power of the soul to realize— indeed it is even beyond God to realize. For this oneness, which we can appropriate only if we have left behind all notions of power and multiplicity, including that of God as Father or Person of the Trinity, itself transcends the categories of the understanding. It is beyond articulation, in both senses of the word.

(3) Although Eckhart's exhortations to detachment initially suggest a complete retreat *from* the world, the implications of detachment ultimately suggest a complete return *to* the world. Drawing on Aristotle's *De anima*, Eckhart preaches:

> Take away the now of time, and then you will [. . .] have all time. [. . .] Detach yourself [*Scheit abe*] from being either this or that or having either this or that, and you will be all things and have all things; and thus, if you are neither here nor there, then you are everywhere.[36]

At this point, we will be able to live anywhere in the world, seeing all things as divine, without needing a reason why. We will, in short, become like the rose of Silesius:

Ohne warumb.

Die Ros' ist ohn warumb / sie blühet, weil sie blühet /
Sie achtt nicht jhrer selbst / fragt nicht ob man sie sihet.³⁷

*

Without Why.

The rose is without why / it blooms because it blooms /
It does not heed itself / asks not if one does see it.

Heidegger was familiar with this distich (GA 10: 53–63), as well as its source in Eckhart's appeal to live without why (GA 81: 187). Heidegger even recognized, without pursuing it, that "what is unsaid in [Silesius's] saying—and everything depends on this—[. . .] says that the human being, in the most concealed ground of his essence, first truly is only when in his own way he is like the rose—without why" (GA 10: 57–58). Moreover, although he does not indicate this in his Trakl lecture, Heidegger was also aware of how this idea of a life without why connects to the German mystical tradition of detachment.

§4. Heidegger's Early Acquaintance with Detachment

Perhaps the best example of this acquaintance comes from what appears to be the conclusion of Heidegger's very first lecture course, held in Winter Semester 1915–1916, of which only unpublished notes survive. The theme of this conclusion is *Abgeschiedenheit*. In it, Heidegger notes that the detached individual has little regard for their city and its customs. Heidegger mentions Nicholas of Cusa's notion of the coincidence of opposites and then speaks of the need for detachment from both self and world. Finally, he invokes Matthew 18:3 and Genesis 1:2: at the peak of detachment, we return to our origins, we become like little children, and the spirit of God again hovers over the waters.³⁸

Our whole relationship to the world changes as a result of such detachment. We no longer view things as disconnected but are able to see them as an unfolding of the unified contraries in God. Indeed, we are able to see them *as* God. At this point, teleology no longer reigns, our knowledge becomes a learned ignorance (Cusa), and our comportment toward God becomes overtly playful. As Heidegger wrote in 1916, quoting an author whom he believed to be Meister Eckhart: "'The Father thus conveys His word to the soul and the soul, again in the word, conveys itself to the Father. Let us nurture this eternal play in God, so help us God.'"[39]

The last thing I want to highlight in the conclusion of this 1915–1916 lecture course is that it contains a rare reference to spirit as the Hebrew *ruach* of God, where God was not yet the creator God, where the beginning was not yet *the* beginning, but something more original than the creation of the world.[40] We will return to the issue of spirit in chapter 7.

I could discuss many other passages throughout Heidegger's corpus, including, a few months before his death, a conversation he had with a priest about Eckhart's understanding of *Abgeschiedenheit*, but suffice it to say here that Heidegger was by no means unaware of the Eckhartian strain of detachment.[41] Why, then, does he suppress it in his reading of the very place of Trakl's poetry?

§5. Deconstructing Detachment

At the beginning of this chapter, I asked whether the dichotomy Heidegger draws between a polysemy that gathers and an imprecision that scatters is exhaustive. In other words, if "the center cannot hold," is it really the case that "Things fall apart," as Yeats put it in the aftermath of World War I? Is "Mere anarchy [. . .] loosed upon the world" ("The Second Coming")? We may well be unable to conceive of *archic* dissemination, for dissemination, as Derrida writes, "means anything but a move toward the center [*dit tout sauf le recentrement*]" (GIII: 92). But this does not necessarily mean that a de-centered, *an-archic* dissemination is pernicious or a product of carelessness, as Heidegger suggests.[42] Rather, a detached life of wandering without reason or why, without gathering into a particular place, time, or tongue, may be the most "proper," most joyful way to be, and it may require utmost cultivation and care. My concern here is not to determine whether this is so but to point it out as a possibility suggested by the German word *Abgeschiedenheit*. Why are we justified in hearing *fremd* as *fram*, *leise* as *gelisian*, and *Sinn* as *sinnan*, but not *Abgeschiedenheit* as *abegescheidenheit*? It is one thing to question whether a valence of a word has relevance. It is another to silence it.

The thing called detachment cannot be readily contained either. Once we begin to detach ourselves, at what point should we stop? When we are no longer within the problematic domain of metaphysics, perhaps. But how can Heidegger be so sure that what the soul does not detach itself from is not itself metaphysical? As Derrida points out, Heidegger had used the term *geistig* positively earlier on in his career,[43] but in the Trakl lecture he relegates this word to metaphysics, where, "put in terms of Plato and the *Abendland* [*platonisch-abendländisch gesprochen*]," there is a separation between the sensible and supersensible realms (GA 12: 55).[44] Here, too, there is a problem. Note that Heidegger uses the adjectival form of *Abendland* pejoratively. I would have expected Heidegger to say *europäisch* or *okzidental*. But why ought we to hear *Abendland* as metaphysical at the beginning of his lecture but as our hidden non-metaphysical destiny in the third and final section of it? If there is some secret power to the words themselves, why should *geistig* and *Abendland* be acceptable in one text or passage or time period but unacceptable in another?

Many years before *Geschlecht III*, Derrida interpreted the metaphysics of presence as "the demanding, powerful, systematic, and irrepressible desire" for a "transcendental signified," for a term that would stop the chain of signification and would not, itself, be subject to dissemination.[45] Such a desire guides Heidegger's placement of detachment, despite, or perhaps even because of, his varied attempts to safeguard it against metaphysical incursion. Heidegger's desire to cordon off detachment, to turn it into a site of gathering rather than a comportment of releasement, remains plagued by what he is trying to purge. His thinking of detachment remains metaphysical.

But the word suggests other possibilities. Earlier, I quoted Derrida's claim that, for Heidegger, "there can be no rigorous thought or poetic writing of dissemination" (GIII: 97). Whatever the case may be as such—and Derrida's own work is nothing if not an attempt to think dissemination rigorously—a rigorous *practice* of detachment might nevertheless save us from becoming fixated on one particular meaning or aspect of a word or thing. Even if we cannot fully comprehend dissemination, in detaching ourselves, we may yet learn to love it.

§6. *Pour l'amour de l'Abgeschiedenheit*

In April 1960, Heidegger gave a short, improvised speech at a banquet in celebration of the eightieth birthday and honorary doctorate of "Trakl's great friend" (GA 16: 812), the editor of *Der Brenner*, Ludwig von Ficker, whom by this point Heidegger had befriended as well. Although Heidegger had already prepared a text, he decided to change course after hearing Ficker himself speak a word of thanks.[46] For, Ficker's word, which among other things spoke of love, of the "immortalized seer" Georg Trakl, and of the insufficiency of the scientific worldview (MH/LF: 123–135), had reminded Heidegger of a line, not from a Greek or German poet, but from, of all authors, Antoine de Saint-Exupéry, an icon and hero of France who had died fighting the Germans in 1944.[47] Heidegger even quotes the line, which comes from Saint-Exupéry's posthumous *Citadelle*, in the original French, before providing what appears to be his own translation: "'Fonde l'amour des tours qui dominent les sables,' 'Stifte die Liebe zu den Türmen, denn sie beherrschen die Wüste'" (GA 16: 563). Or in English: "Establish the love of towers, which dominate the desert." Heidegger goes on to claim that, today, we live in an age of desolation, where everything is subject to calculation and where language is increasingly becoming a mere instrument of information transfer. But the desert is not yet completely naked. Even if dilapidated, towers still stand whose bells sound the "peal of stillness: that saying in which poets and thinkers attempt to speak" (GA 16: 563). In order to hear such stillness through the cacophony of contemporary life, we must, Heidegger says, *love*. But what is love? To whom will we turn for guidance? Heidegger responds: "Probably the deepest interpretation of what love is comes from Augustine, when he says 'amo volo ut sis,' I love, that is, I want what is loved to be what it is. Love is letting-be [*Sein-lassen*] in a deeper sense, according to which it calls forth essence" (GA 16: 563).[48]

The guiding figures, indeed the only figures who are named in Heidegger's speech, are thus a twentieth-century Frenchman from Lyon and an early medieval bishop from what is today Algeria. In contrast, Heidegger refers solely, indeed with seeming obstinacy, to German and ancient Greek authors in his two lectures on Trakl. Moreover, other than the negative comment about detachment from "loved ones, others" that I discussed above, Heidegger has nothing to say on the subject of love in either "Language in the Poem" or "Language," and only once does he mention letting-be, although even there it is not a matter of letting-be as such (GA 12: 58). In his personal copy of Trakl, there is, as mentioned, a marginal note on *Gelassenheit*, a term that Heidegger himself ties to *Seinlassen* and love on several occasions elsewhere (GA 73: 693, 699, 711; GA 97: 52; GA 98: 16). But *Gelassenheit*, both the word and the thing, did not make its way into the Trakl lectures. In his speech for Ficker, however, everything comes down to letting be.

It is unlikely Heidegger would go so far as to say, with Trakl, that "all human beings are worthy of love" (HKA 1: 256). One would, additionally, have to interrogate what Heidegger means by "essence" in his claim that letting-be calls it forth. But his appeals—in French and Latin—to love and let be at least *suggest* a different way of reading Trakl and the placement of his *Gedicht*.

What would such a reading look like? What would happen if we started from Trakl's aforementioned letter to Ficker, where, like a voice crying out in the wilderness, he declaims: "God, only a tiny spark of pure joy—and one would be rescued; love—and one would be redeemed" (HKA 1: 301)? Or with Mahrholdt's interpretation that Trakl's *Losungswort*, his password—his *parole*—for humankind was "to purify and bear yourself up to God," and that Trakl's aims were "to tell people what they no longer knew: that their soul is something foreign on earth, is something divine, worthy of the highest care, and to sing to them of its golden stillness" (DD 202–203)? Would we remember, if not Trakl's love for all people or for the decaying *Geschlecht*, then at least Georg's for sister Grete? Would we remember that the siblings spoke French growing up? That Rimbaud was, for a time, as important a poet for Trakl as Hölderlin was?[49] Even sticking with *Abgeschiedenheit* as the proper place of the poetry, would we, would Heidegger, recall that Eckhart uses this term synonymously with *Gelassenheit*, and that Heidegger himself brought these terms together on at least two occasions (GA 14: 20n6; GA 60: 309)? That the Middle High German words *gelâzenheit*, *abegescheidenheit*, and their cognates are, paradoxically, ways in which we are enjoined to liberate us ourselves from any and all attachment to place, to words, and even to these very ways themselves? That we truly *are* only when we live like Silesius's rose, without determination, destination, or a reason why, when everything becomes divine to us, when we see all human beings, indeed all things, as worthy of love? That "love," in Derrida's words, "means [. . .] to respect the Other, to pay attention to the Other, not to destroy the otherness of the Other"?[50]

Chapter 4

Pain Is Being Itself

Werner Hamacher in memoriam

Much Gesture, from the Pulpit—
Strong Hallelujahs roll—
Narcotics cannot still the Tooth
That nibbles at the soul.

—Emily Dickinson[1]

[Trakl] zwingt uns damit zur Brüderlichkeit, mit jenem Zwang, der Dichtung eigen: eine offene Wunde, ein unstillbarer Schmerz.[2]

—Franz Fühmann

Among the many words Heidegger explores in order to elucidate his primary matter for thought—*Sein/Seyn, Ereignis, Lichtung, a-lētheia, logos*[3]—one would not likely expect *Schmerz* ("pain") to play a prominent role. And yet, in a selection of notes published in a limited German edition under the title *Über den Schmerz* (*On Pain*), Heidegger goes so far as to claim that pain is being itself. Pain, for the later Heidegger, is not *merely* ontological, although this idea already differs markedly from the traditional physiological and psychological interpretations of pain; rather, pain belongs to the very sense and structure of being. Accordingly, in order to understand Heidegger's later thinking of being, one cannot neglect his thinking of pain. To anticipate Heidegger's argument: pain (*algos*) cares for (*alegei*), indeed just *is*, the articulation (*legein*)—that is, both the gathering and saying—of being. The gathering of being is thus the gathering of pain, and to study being is to study pain. Ontology is algology.

Heidegger does, to be sure, highlight the importance of pain in his lectures on Trakl. For example, we read that pain separates, but (like Hölderlinian *Innigkeit*) it also intimately holds together what it has separated; searing pain leads some to storm heaven (like the egotistical angels of *Paradise Lost* or the spherical doubles of Aristophanes's encomium), but pain can also become gentle and let all things shine in their essence; pain produces not gloomy isolation but gleaming community; pain sustains the difference between things and world; pain is the source of life (cf. GA 12: 24–25, 27, 41, 57–62, 68). Provocative as these claims are, they are nevertheless undeveloped and at times seem to come from nowhere, which has led to a variety of scholarly responses, from outright rejection to pious recapitulation; many have ignored the theme altogether. To modify a claim made by Robert Bernasconi about Heidegger's remarks on evil in the "Letter on 'Humanism,'" it is as though Heidegger did not intend for his audience to understand, at the time, what he meant by pain in his Trakl commentaries.[4]

In this chapter, I would like to situate Heidegger's peculiar comments within the broader framework of *On Pain*, which provides his most extensive treatment of pain now available and serves as the basis for much of the Trakl material. Since many scholars will be unfamiliar with *On Pain* or unable to access it, I will begin with a brief discussion of its source and status (§1). Readers less interested in Heidegger philology might consider starting with the next section, where I will briefly examine Heidegger's critical relation to the author whose work provided the basis for *On Pain*, namely Ernst Jünger (§2). Thereafter I will turn to Heidegger's modus operandi in *On Pain* (§3) and to his critique of traditional interpretations of pain in this text and in other writings (§4), before moving on to his own affirmative position on the matter (§5) and to the etymology of the Greek word for it, *algos* (§6). Last, I will raise some lexical and philosophical objections to Heidegger's treatment, asking whether he does not end up anesthetizing his readers to pain's most rending effects (§7) and to the very pain that Trakl suffered and sang (§8).

§1. Heidegger's *On Pain*

Every year or two, the Martin-Heidegger-Gesellschaft publishes a short, limited-edition book containing a previously unavailable text by, or closely related to, Heidegger. The society prints approximately one thousand copies and distributes them exclusively to its members. While not all of these volumes are of great importance to Heidegger scholarship or to philosophy more broadly, the 2017–2018 volume, *On Pain*, is pathbreaking.

The editors of this recent volume, Dietmar Koch and Klaus Neugebauer, explain that the twenty-five pages of material published in this text come from a slipcase in Heidegger's literary remains titled "Über den Schmerz. Vgl. zu E. J. 'Der Arbeiter.'" They relate that, in total, the slipcase contains around 570 pages of notes on pain that Heidegger composed within the timeframe of 1942 to 1959 and organized into numerous bundles. Although all of the notes will eventually be published as a supplementary volume to Heidegger's *Gesamtausgabe*,[5] the volume currently available reproduces only a portion of one of the bundles and a single sheet from another. The editors state that their "selection was oriented around interrelated textual passages whose level of elaboration allowed a publication within the framework of the present yearbook to appear sensible" (ÜdS: 56).

The selections from the first bundle are organized as follows:

"Der Schmerz" ("Pain"), one page.

"Der Anschein des Schmerzes" ("The Semblance of Pain"), five pages.

"Der Schmerz" ("Pain"), five pages.

An unpaginated slip of paper with quotes from and references to Thomas Aquinas and Aristotle.

"Die Metaphysik des Schmerzes" ("The Metaphysics of Pain"), six pages.

"xxx," six pages.

Due to an internal reference to Schopenhauer in "The Semblance of Pain," the editors decided to include the following sheet from the second bundle:

"Schopenhauer über den Schmerz" ("Schopenhauer on Pain"), one page, with excerpts from and notes on Schopenhauer.

The online catalogue of the German Literary Archive in Marbach provides additional information about the content of the second bundle,[6] which I will reproduce here so as to provide the most comprehensive picture of the materials possible at present:

"Der Schmerz und der Tod" ("Pain and Death").

"Die Physik und die Meta-Physik des Schmerzes" ("The Physics and the Meta-Physics of Pain").

"Der erste Steg. Der Schmerz" ("The First Footbridge. Pain").

"Über den Schmerz" ("On Pain").

"Der Schmerz selbst" ("Pain Itself").

"Die 'Gegebenheit' des Schmerzes" ("The 'Givenness' of Pain").

"Der Schmerz als das Widrige und Negative" ("Pain as the Adverse and Negative").

"Der Schmerz und das animal rationale" ("Pain and the *Animal Rationale*").[7]

These lists should give one an initial sense for the scope of Heidegger's appreciation of pain, which would seem to be more than physical, and indeed more than metaphysical.

As for the title, "Über den Schmerz. Vgl. zu E. J. 'Der Arbeiter,'" "E. J." refers to the twentieth-century soldier and author Ernst Jünger, and "Der Arbeiter" to one of his most important nonfictional works: *Der Arbeiter: Herrschaft und Gestalt* (*The Worker: Dominion and Form*) (1932). For those familiar with this text, it might seem surprising that Heidegger would connect his treatment of pain so explicitly to it (and, in the title, *only* to it), as pain is hardly one of the book's overt themes—indeed, the noun is altogether absent from Jünger's opus. Why, then, does Heidegger mention Jünger? What, moreover, does Jünger have to do with this topic, and why does Heidegger give him such a prominent role in his consideration of it?

§2. Ernst Jünger: On or beyond Pain?

In 1934, just two years after the appearance of *The Worker*, Jünger published an essay bearing the very same title as Heidegger's notes on pain. This essay appeared in a collection of Jünger's writings titled *Blätter und Steine* (*Leaves and Stones*), which also included Jünger's influential essay from 1930, "Die totale Mobilmachung" ("Total Mobilization"). In the foreword to this collection, Jünger explains how these two essays relate to *The Worker*:

> the terminology introduced in *The Worker* as an optic expedient is once again applied in the reflection "On Pain." "Total Mobilization" depicts the great process, *The Worker* the form whose historical task consists in carrying out the process. The present reflection [namely, "On Pain"] advances the investigation one step further; it demonstrates that the touchstone of this procedure is to be sought, not in *values*, but in *pain*.[8]

The process to which Jünger is referring is the increasing transformation of individual life into mass energy through technological, industrial, political, economic, and military mobilization. Rather than protest against this trend, Jünger prophesies and promotes a new form or breed (a *Geschlecht*) of human existence called the worker, which is wholly in accord with the epochal shift.[9] In the eponymous treatise, Jünger describes the worker as cold, functional, and merciless, hardly different from a machine. In Jünger's later essay, workers are marked by their ability to steel themselves against pain.

Heidegger was well aware of these connections among Jünger's three texts. He cites a portion of the above block quote in a presentation on Jünger from January 1940 (GA 90: 257), and in notes from 1934–1940, he advances the argument that "the treatise on pain" in Jünger's "last publication (*Leaves and Stones*)" is a continuation of what had preceded it (GA 90: 33). Given the considerable attention Heidegger devotes to Jünger's "On Pain"—he mentions it on numerous occasions and annotated it extensively in his personal copy of *Leaves and Stones*[10]—and given that Heidegger did not begin to develop his own unique views on pain until the 1941–1942 manuscript *Das Ereignis* (*The Appropriative Event*) (see §5, below), thus *after* his encounter with Jünger's essay,[11] it is reasonable to identify this essay as the point of departure for Heidegger's own work on pain. The ample secondary literature on the Jünger/Heidegger connection has largely neglected this work, tending to focus instead on Heidegger's reading of "Total Mobilization," *The Worker*, or Jünger's contribution to the Festschrift for Heidegger's sixtieth birthday, titled "Über die Linie" ("Beyond the Line").[12] While it would be advantageous for future research to study Jünger's influence on Heidegger's appreciation of pain more closely, here I would just like to take note of Heidegger's critique:

> What "pain" itself is, is neither interrogated nor stated, but is only presupposed as a physiological fact of the "body." The "description" simply follows the manner in which this "pain," which is "in itself" present at hand, is *objectified*. Jünger does not see that the inner presupposition of this objectification is the meaninglessness of beings. Hence the leftover stock of all dying metaphysics comes in at the end: the *"bestowing of meaning."* The "objectification" itself is of a piece with the securing of standing reserve that is proper to the will to power. (GA 90: 437)

In other words, Jünger, like Spengler and Nietzsche before him, remains trapped within a presupposition-laden metaphysics that fails to ask after the meaning of being itself or the meaning of pain itself. In response to Jünger's declamation, "Tell me your relation to pain, and I will tell you who you are!,"[13] Heidegger writes: "Tell me your relation to being—should you have any sense for it at all—and I will tell you *how* you are and whether you will 'occupy' yourself with 'pain' or whether you can *think* in accordance with it [*ihm nach*denken]" (GA 90: 439). We could thus translate the title of Jünger's essay, not as "On Pain" (*über* qua *de*), but as an attempt to go "Beyond Pain" (*über* qua *trans*). Heidegger makes a similar point regarding Jünger's "Über die Linie," namely, the line of metaphysics (GA 9: 386 et passim); however, in the case of pain, meditating *on* it does not lead us elsewhere, i.e., to being itself as subtending metaphysics; for, as we will soon see, to contemplate pain is already to contemplate being. Before moving on to Heidegger's own position on pain, it should prove helpful to examine how he prepares for it.

§3. *Via doloris heideggeriana*

As published in *On Pain*, Heidegger's notes begin with a paradox. Pain is at once utterly familiar and unspeakably obscure. Without further ado, we can all list off the things that ail us: back pain, headaches, the loss of loved ones, nightmares, anxiety, alienation, despair, evil. But what unifies them? What makes it possible for us to say that things as disparate as betrayal and a mosquito bite are both painful? How, to use Hegel's terminology, do we in this case raise what we are all acquainted with (*das Bekannte*) to the level of cognition (*das Erkannte*)? Not, to be sure, by way of Hegel's own phenomenology, which, as I will discuss in the next section, takes the painful path of negative experience only to arrive at the painless state of absolute knowing. The goal is to understand pain in itself, not for another; it is to understand pain in terms of what Heidegger calls the "simplicity of its still hardly thought essence" (ÜdS: 30). For this we would need a different sort of experience and a different sort of phenomenology. Heidegger claims that such an experience would not occur within the domain of beings, *Seiendes* (physics); it accordingly would not be of something particular, whether physiological or psychological. Nor, moreover, would it occur within the domain of the being, *Sein*, of beings (metaphysics); it accordingly would not be of something common to all entities, both physiological and psychological. Rather, a proper experience of pain would be an experience on the order of being itself, which Heidegger sometimes designates with the archaic spelling *Seyn* ("beyng" in premodern English). This is an experience that would "unsettle metaphysics at its core" and "transform the human being's relation to truth" (ÜdS: 39). Heidegger endeavors to prepare (us) for this experience in his notes, even as he articulates a distinctive sense of pain that only such an experience could have made possible. I will not delve into a discussion of the apparent hermeneutic circularity at work here; instead, I will simply leap into the circle with Heidegger (SZ: 315) and work from there.

Although Heidegger does not use this language, we can, at least provisionally, view his notes in *On Pain* as deploying several strategies or methodologies to prime and elucidate the genuine experience of pain. First, to use terminology from the late Husserl and the earlier Heidegger, there is a genetic or deconstructive phenomenology, whereby Heidegger traces the genesis and standardization of common approaches to pain. By de-sedimenting our interpretive foundations and dismantling the edifice we have built on them, Heidegger frees us up for a direct encounter with pain.

This liberation is terrifying, at least initially. We must nevertheless first experience the emergency of exposure and the paralysis of impasse if we are truly to allow a transformation to transpire, rather than carrying on in our ignorance and complacency. As Kierkegaard put it in a passage published in one of the 1914 issues of *Der Brenner*: "Woe to the person who wants to build up without knowing the terror; indeed, he does not know what he himself wants!"[14] This transformation may do nothing to alleviate our pain and suffering. Indeed, practically speaking, it might be altogether useless. It is not, for all that, unnecessary. Recalling Meister Eckhart and the Taoist classic *The Zhuangzi*, Heidegger contends that this uselessness is actually what is most needed (ÜdS: 40, 53).[15] Heidegger tries to awaken us to this necessity in his notes, or, if you prefer, "to provoke [the requisite] terror in our Dasein," as he put it many years prior (GA 29/30: 255). There is thus a second, hortatory or provocative strategy at play in *On Pain*.

Finally, in his positive account of pain, Heidegger is conducting what he later calls a "phenomenology of the inapparent" (GA 15: 417). Pain, at this level, does not show itself to the senses or show up in consciousness. It, together with its transformative truth, actually hides behind what it appears to be (ÜdS: 35). As with being itself, there is something essentially concealed about it. The task, however, is not to tear the truth out of pain but to learn to correspond in language to what the pain of being gives to be said, however darkly (ÜdS: 49, 51). We must learn to stop thinking *about* pain, thus from a perspective outside of it. We must instead learn to start "thinking 'painfully'—from the side of pain as the assertion of beyng [*vom Schmerz her als dem Zuspruch des Seyns*], which ad-sertion [*Zu-Spruch*] is the appropriative event [*Ereignis*] as the truth of beyng itself" (ÜdS: 51).[16] In other words, our thinking must not claim to apprehend pain, let alone declaim against it; it must instead hold itself *open* to and then hold itself *to* the claim or address of pain itself: *Denken an den Schmerz als den An-spruch* (ÜdS: 53; cf. 51). What we are dealing with is thus not a treatise "*über*" pain—whether "on" it or, with Jünger, "beyond" it—but a thinking that is, in German, "*an*" pain, which in this context might best be rendered as a thinking that is *aligned* with pain: *iacet ad dolorem*.

Yet we must work our way there. Or better: we must work off the common misconceptions of pain so as to let pain be as it always already implicitly is. If pain really is the matter for thought and the matter of thought (ÜdS: 51), if pain is *die Sache selbst*, then this preliminary work might go by a different title; it could just as well be a reformulation of Husserl's motto for phenomenology: *Back to pain itself!*

§4 Zum Schmerz selbst!

Among the advantages of the recently published *On Pain* is that it provides not only Heidegger's most developed treatment of pain but also a distinctive deconstructive-phenomenological analysis of some of the standard ways in which it has been interpreted. I will discuss several of these approaches in this section and draw out their implications for understanding pain and for understanding in general.

When we think about pain, we tend to treat it as some *thing* to be explained (ÜdS: 46, 48). *What is pain?*, we ask, *ti esti algos?*, as though pain were no different from a triangle, a horse, or virtue. There are many ways to answer this question, all with their own set of aporias. Perhaps the most common response is to locate pain within the domain of sensation and feeling. Excessive force is applied to one of my sense organs, and I cringe or cry out. Pain, whether provoked from within (an erupting tooth, a heart attack) or from without (a bee sting, a blinding light), is something that befalls me and causes a reaction, or rather multiple reactions. Physiologically, the affected organ itself responds to the assault (with inflammation, for example). Psychologically, I interpret the pain as something to be resisted (with Ibuprofen) or tolerated (when the Ibuprofen fails and I do not want to take anything stronger for fear of dependency). Heidegger notes that this active/reactive paradigm of pain remains firmly "within the ken of body and soul" (ÜdS: 31).

A third reaction is possible. Let us call it metaphysical. Although pain seems to present itself initially and for the most part within the psychosomatic framework—I say *seems*, because Heidegger does not state whether this presentation is essential to all human experience or already the product of a wrong state of affairs—it is only in *interpreting* pain accordingly that the domains of the physical and the psychological become fixed as the domains of being as such. In other words, Heidegger is contending that metaphysics, which he defines as the "distinction between the physical and the non-physical, between the sensuous and the super-sensuous" (ÜdS: 43), emerges precisely from a mistaken, albeit phenomenologically understandable interpretation of pain. Heidegger develops this contention in a long passage from the group of notes titled "The Semblance of Pain." The first half traces the conceptual genesis of the physical domain:

> The mode of cognitive comportment toward pain is also reactive. It is an explaining and a construing. The explaining moves within the series of cause and effect, which the realm of the physical and physiological showcases. Thought rigorously and seen truly, it is in pursuing the presentification of the adverse incursion that this realm is first thought as that which it is. Pain first showcases the physiological and the physical, and, therefore, the explaining that clearly goes back to this from the givenness of the incursion is taken to be satisfying and intelligible. (ÜdS: 32)

The second half of the passage points to the genesis of a psychological domain of resistance that nevertheless remains essentially dependent on the physical:

> The construing goes beyond the physical, but into a region that for its part is already given together with the incursive character of the adverse as that from which pain can be countered willfully and by means of comportment and bearing [*Verhaltung und Haltung*]. (ÜdS: 32)

If for no other reason—though there is much more to come—this striking derivation of metaphysics from the misreading of pain should provide sufficient impetus to examine Heidegger's work on the topic.

Pain, like no other, exposes the fragility of the barrier erected between body and soul, even if it does not always break that barrier down completely. Cancer changes a person, and stress can cause otherwise unaccountable chest pain. Despite this, pain affords ample opportunity to reestablish the divide. Heidegger's discussion considers several of these dissociative techniques (ÜdS: 33–34, 37–38, 43–44), which I will arrange under the headings of (1) denial, (2) development, (3) reduction, and (4) biological construal.

(1) One can deliberately deny the relevance of pain for one's psychological well-being (*I won't let pain stop me from leading a fulfilled life*).

(2) Or one can give pain meaning for one's development. Pain is, after all, crucial for athletes (no pain no gain), artists ("knowledge," Trakl writes, "comes only to those who despise happiness"), and all sorts of spiritual seekers ("tribulation worketh patience," Romans 5:3).[17]

Both of these approaches, denial and development, emphasize human willpower (ÜdS: 33). But if Heidegger is right that the will is not merely something that *can* be perverted, but is *itself* a perverted determination of our proper relation to being (ÜdS: 47), then neither approach can suffice to explain the nature of pain (GA 7: 97–98). It is no accident that Heidegger traces the will to a time before its rigorous thematization in Christianity. The will, he maintains, is already at work in the very inauguration of metaphysics in Ancient Greece.[18]

(3) Another way to reinforce the barrier between body and soul, or in this case between body and self, is to diminish pain's significance by placing it within the broader context of beings as a whole (ÜdS: 34), that is, by reducing its status to that which it putatively shares with the totality of what is. For example, one might say that pain, like everything else, is nothing more than material in motion. This approach could provide consolation. Or it could provoke a desire to dominate pain as one dominates nature, à la Claude Bernard or Francis Bacon. Either way, if one abstracts oneself from such a totality, one by definition remains trapped within an unquestioned metaphysical inheritance. But even if one does not treat oneself as any different from the totality (however it may be interpreted), one still fails to ask after the grounds for the conceptualization of that totality. One treats only of beings as such, not of the truth of being. Starting around the mid-1930s, Heidegger uses the same pejorative term "metaphysics" to characterize this limited approach.

(4) Another possibility is to interpret pain more narrowly, as pertaining solely to the lived experience (*Erleben*) of living entities (*Lebewesen*), and in particular, even if not exclusively, the human being. This biological or organismic interpretation of pain has the same metaphysical drawbacks as the earlier approaches: it first presupposes a distinction between physical disturbance ("actual or potential tissue damage") and psychical apprehension ("an unpleasant sensory and

emotional experience associated with, or resembling that associated with" it);[19] it then construes pain as a signal to reestablish security by fight or flight. Additionally, the very focus on life and lived experience is already metaphysical for Heidegger. He suggests as much in *On Pain* when he speaks critically of the predominance of "metaphysical 'lived experience,'" which blocks access to an experience that would transform our relation to truth and to being as such (ÜdS: 39–40). Heidegger typically reserves the term *Erfahrung* for this latter sort of experience.

In sum, all of these approaches presuppose a problematic rationalist—and therefore humanist—methodology. In Heidegger's words:

> To experience [—here, curiously, Heidegger uses the German *erfahren*—] and think pain metaphysically means to represent it "rationally," as a fact that is explainable and in need of explanation; it means to think pain in human terms, whereby the human being remains the inexhaustible *animal rationale* and that at which the "sense" of pain is aimed. (ÜdS: 51; see also 43)

The task, as mentioned above, will not be to think of pain in human terms, but to think of the human being, and indeed of being as such, in terms of pain. To this end, it will be necessary to ask, not *what* pain is, but *how* it holds sway beneath or before definable objects.

Before we turn to painful thought or thinking painfully, there is one final way of interpreting pain I should mention, which Heidegger does not as such address in *On Pain*, but which is important for an appreciation of his understanding of this topic. I am referring to Hegel's position on pain, which Heidegger names explicitly on several occasions elsewhere throughout his corpus. This alone is significant, as Heidegger rarely mentions other philosophers when discussing pain. They are absent in the material on pain in the Trakl lectures, for example, and in *On Pain*, the only references are to Aquinas and Aristotle on the primacy of the sense of touch (ÜdS: 41) and to Schopenhauer on the notion that pain is positive and pleasure negative, that is to say, devoid of pain (ÜdS: 33, 54).[20]

(5) Pain, for Hegel, is characteristic of finitude, otherness, and alienation. Rather than avoiding these, however, or taking refuge in a self-subsisting and ever-selfsame God, we must, if we are to attain the satisfaction of absolute knowledge, take "the path of despair" and

undertake the "labor of the negative." That is, we must work through the particular shapes that consciousness assumes and suffers during its scientific formation so as to reach a universal self-consciousness that does not abandon these earlier shapes but elevates and preserves them as essential moments of its genesis. Or, in religious terms, we must endure the dark night of the soul before the dawn of reunification, the Cross before the Resurrection, Good Friday before Easter. Pain is thus put into its proper, ultimately pleasurable perspective: "The pain that the finite senses in its sublation," Hegel writes, "is not painful, since it is thereby raised up to a moment in the process of the divine."[21] Or, in Goethe's words, which Hegel adduces in summary:

Sollte jene Qual uns quälen,
da sie unsre Lust vermehrt?

*

Should this torture, torture us,
since it does increase our pleasure?

Heidegger attacks Hegel's position from three sides. First, Hegel treats pain as a matter for consciousness, not for being itself (GA 68: 103). It is accordingly subjective. Second, the pain of negativity is "swallowed up" in the positivity of absolute knowledge (GA 68: 15). It is accordingly temporary, instrumental. Third, seen from the perspective of the end, pain is thereby deprived of its genuinely disruptive potential. Conceptually, even if not experientially, "everything," in Heidegger's gloss, "*is* already *reconciled*" (GA 86: 269). While Heidegger's own interpretation of pain can, without much difficulty, escape the first two charges he levels against Hegel, we will have to ask whether the same can be said of the third, that is, whether Heidegger does not end up viewing pain *sub specie aeternitatis et reconciliationis*. Before doing so, let us turn to Heidegger's affirmative treatment in *On Pain* and in the Trakl lectures.

§5. The Gentle Gathering of Pain

In *On Pain*, Heidegger draws heavily on etymology to describe the non-metaphysical structure of pain. He primarily uses two sets of terms.

The first set draws on the root word *reißen*, "to rend," and should be familiar to readers of Heidegger's lectures on Trakl, where, as we have seen, etymology is also key (ÜdS: 34; GA 12: 24, 57). The second set plays on the connection between the verb *zeigen*, "to show," and the noun *Zeichen*, usually rendered as "sign" (ÜdS: 35).[22]

(1) *Reißen*. Initially, we see that pain rips away (*entreißt*) our sense of well-being. Far from opening our eyes to the sense of being itself, however, pain tends to eclipse itself and blind us to its truth. It sweeps us along (*fortreißt*, literally "tears us forth") in the belief that pain is merely a matter for sensation and subsequent sense-*making*. It seduces us into metaphysics. Pain, like the *phusis* of Heraclitus, hides what is most proper to it behind that *as* which it shows itself. A complete account of pain cannot neglect this non-phenomenal domain. Heidegger again uses the language of *reißen*. Pain, properly speaking, is a certain type of *Riß*, which means "tear" or "rift," even as its etymology also points toward the seemingly opposite sense of inscription. (Compare the English "write" and German's own *Aufriß* or "outline.") Since, as we will see, Heidegger develops the philosophical implications of this contronym, *Riß* would, in Hegel's language, be a speculative word on the order of *aufheben*: it marks the unification of opposition, the identity of difference.[23] We could translate the auto-antonymy of *reißen* in English with the verb "to cleave," meaning both to sever and to stick fast. In *On Pain*, Heidegger describes, albeit elliptically and idiosyncratically, the various aspects of cleaving pain as follows:

> in this sweeping along [*Fortriß*], a cleaving [*Riß*] properly takes place [*sich . . . ereignet*] that shrouds itself in the semblance of the incursion and the adverse. / The cleaving holds itself within the ambiguity between, on the one hand, the ripping away and sweeping along [*entreißenden Fortrisses*] and, on the other, the cleaving that conceals itself as the difference [between beyng and beings]. / The cleaving as the outline [*Aufriß*]. That is, the clearing and joining bringing of the difference into its own [*die lichtende fügende Ereignung des Unterschieds*]. (ÜdS: 34)

Since the other references to the *Riß* of pain in *On Pain* provide little clarification of its connection to the terms of the final sentence of this quotation (see ÜdS: 36, 40, 50), it should prove helpful to recall Heidegger's development of the *Riß* of pain in his reading of Trakl.[24]

In chapter 2, I quoted a portion of the following passage from Heidegger's lecture "Language":

> Pain cleaves [reißt]. It is the cleaving [Riß]. Only, it does not cleave asunder [zerreißt] into splinters that drive apart. To be sure, pain does cleave apart, it cises, but it does so in such a way that it at the same time draws [zieht] everything to itself, gathers everything in itself. Its cleaving, as the gathering cising, is at the same time the drawing that, like the delineation [Vorriß] and outline [Aufriß], sketches [zeichnet] and joins what is held apart in the scission. Pain is what joins in the cising-gathering cleaving. Pain is the jointure of the cleaving. It is the threshold. It bears out the between, the middle of the two that have been cised into it [in sie Geschiedenen]. Pain joins the cleaving of the inter-scission [Unter-Schiedes]. Pain is the inter-scission itself. (GA 12: 24; cf. GA 80: 998)

In other words, and in line with how Heidegger interprets the final stanza of Trakl's "Ein Winterabend" ("A Winter Evening"), pain holds things and world apart even as it holds them together. Their separation is the condition for their articulation, by which I mean both jointure and (self-)expression. *Analogically*, we could say that pain at once isolates individuals and calls them to community: I feel that no one can relate to my pain, and yet I call out for comfort and connection; upon parting from the mother, the newborn cries out in a first attempt at conversation.[25] But we must be careful not to let the analogue become the thing itself; indeed we might need to forget it altogether if the task truly is to think of being and of the human being in terms of pain and not of pain in terms of the human. Moreover, it is not as though things and world were once wholly unified and only subsequently disconnected or once wholly disconnected and only subsequently unified. Their articulation is *also* the condition for their separation. Primordial pain just is this co-constitutive interplay, or in the terms of the passage from *On Pain* cited above: pain clears, that is, opens up, *lichtet*, the difference even as it joins, *fügt*, things and world.

For things and world, we could, as Heidegger suggests in his notes, substitute beings and being, but we would need to take these in a non-metaphysical sense. Even so, Heidegger is not always terminologically consistent: sometimes he uses *Seyn* to refer to one side of the difference (ÜdS: 36); sometimes he reserves it for pain in its primordial enabling and sustaining, *Ereignung*, of the difference (ÜdS: 48). The point is that Heidegger's way of thinking of pain is a way of thinking that goes deeper than the entire tradition of Western metaphysics. Indeed, in *On Pain*, we learn, remarkably, that pain is the *sine qua non* of Heidegger's longstanding project to think otherwise: "The human being and pain otherwise, and *only therein* is the Other Thinking [*das Andere Denken*] determined" (ÜdS: 51; emphasis added).

If it is true that, with our discussion of difference, we have already begun to think painfully and thus otherwise, our relation to truth itself must have also been transformed (see ÜdS: 39), or rather we must have already begun to think in accordance with our "essential, albeit long concealed relation to the truth of beyng" (ÜdS: 40). That is to say, we must have already let ourselves be claimed by the truth of the pain of beyng and let it speak. The second set of terms Heidegger develops in *On Pain* will help us further articulate this connection to truth.

(2) *Zeichen, Zeigen, Zeichnen*. In his 1927 magnum opus, Heidegger provides a formal definition of phenomenology in accordance with its radical etymological sense. Phenomenology engages in "letting that which shows itself [*sich zeigt*], just as it shows itself from itself or of its own accord, be seen from itself or of its own accord" (SZ: 34). De-formalized, or in terms of content, phenomenology would pertain to that which initially and for the most part does not show itself, yet is nevertheless foundational for that which does; phenomenology would deal with the hidden, if not altogether forgotten, being of beings.

Although, for various reasons outlined above, this phenomenological-ontological approach will not work for pain itself (if it ever could for being), Heidegger nevertheless retains some of its language, even as he reinterprets this language to suit his later ends. I mean the language of letting and the language of showing. I will return to that of letting later. For now, let us listen to how Heidegger once again draws on etymological connections to reconfigure the truth of a word, and indeed to reconfigure truth itself. I will first cite a couple passages and then provide an interpretation. These passages, like so many in Heidegger's treatment of pain, defy ready translation. The first passage reads:

> Pain *is* signing [*Zeichen*]. What does this mean, that it is a sign [*ein Zeichen*]? The essence of signing is determined on the basis of self-showing [*Sichzeigen*], and its essential constitution emerges from the necessity that includes self-

showing. This, however, is the appropriative event. Pain is not merely "signing" in the vague and indefinite sense that something points to something only in some respect. Pain is the signing of that which essentially is in the sign. Pain is a sign of the appropriative event. In properly taking place, pain is as signing, that is, as the self-showing appropriative event. (ÜdS: 35).

Later in the manuscript, Heidegger writes:

> pain is not merely something that is [etwas Seiendes], (a datum), but rather beyng itself—this in its self-showing—not, for instance, a sign that would point [zeigte] to being (thus again a being in relation to being), but rather beyng itself in its truth (clearing) as showing [Zeigung]. It is in this manner that pain essentially holds sway [west]. (ÜdS: 48)

First of all, it is important to recognize that the German Zeichen ("sign") is related to sich zeigen ("to show oneself"). Both date back to the Proto-Indo-European deyk- ("to point out"). Given the discussion of the Riß of pain as both pulling apart and joining together in an outline or sketch (Aufriß), Heidegger might also be thinking of the derivative German word zeichnen ("to draw," "to sketch"), which we saw him use in the above block quotation from the first Trakl lecture. In any event, we are not dealing here with a sign pointing elsewhere, be it to other beings (such as my hand and the boiling water I just touched) or to being as the whole or essence of all that is (such as one who takes pain to be the origin of philosophizing might imagine) (see ÜdS: 49). This referential reading of pain's Zeichen is either non-ontological (remaining solely on the plane of beings, what Heidegger calls "ontic" in Being and Time) or superficially ontological (failing to heed the source of the difference between being and beings, a failure that the later Heidegger often, as in the second quote above, designates by his use of the term Sein or "being" without a y).

But if pain does not point elsewhere, is pain therefore meaningless? Could we not then say, with Cicero, that it is nothing to us—*nihil est plane dolor*[26]—or at least to that part of us which is itself meaningful and for which things can have a meaning, namely our reason? Could we not perhaps go further by doubting meaning altogether and taking some perverse shred of solace in the sheer nihilism of body and soul? Could we not celebrate what Hölderlin laments at the start of "Mnemosyne" (also titled "Das Zeichen" in one of its versions)?

> Ein Zeichen sind wir, deutungslos
> Schmerzlos sind wir und haben fast
> Die Sprache in der Fremde verloren.[27]

*

> We are a sign, without meaning
> We are without pain and have almost
> Lost language in the foreign.

Before abandoning all hope, we should see that such a meaningless, painless sign is but a sign of modern alienation, as Heidegger frequently remarks in his interpretation of this poem.[28] Just because pain is not a sign in its customary sense does not mean it has no significance. What we need is a different sort of sign, a sign in the fullest sense of the word. Again, Hölderlin, this time from "Der Ister":

> Ein Zeichen braucht es,
> Nichts anderes, schlecht und recht.[29]

*
> A sign is needed,
> Nothing else, pure and simple.

Pain, as such a sign, would be the very self-showing of the eventuating of beyng. Such self-showing, however, would not be without its own self-restraint and self-concealment. As Heidegger writes in a note on Hölderlin's river-poem: "Supreme showing [*Zeigen*] in restraint [*Verhaltenheit*]" (GA 73: 739). Or, in the language of *On Pain*: "Especially by unveiling and concealing itself in such a way that the apparent itself veils the inapparent, pain is in itself already different from what it appears as in the semblance. Pain *is* signing" (ÜdS: 35). In short, pain would be truth as primordial *a-lētheia*, a meaningful configuration of "un-concealment" in which *lēthe*, "concealment," never wholly gives way. It would, moreover, be truth in its Germanic sense of sheltering:

> Pain is the sign of the clearing harbor, in which the departive [*abschiedliche*] inception is retained [*gewahrt*] and the truthful keeping [*Wahr-heit*] holds sway. In the experience of pain as the cleaving, the transformation of the essence of truth [*Wahrheit*] properly takes place. (ÜdS: 40)

Heidegger is here alluding to themes he had developed in the 1941–1942 manuscript *The Appropriative Event*, where he speaks not just of pain as the essence of the ontological difference (GA 71: 129), but of the pain of parting (*Abschied*, literally "cutting away") from the hegemony of beings (GA 71: 137) and, most importantly, of the pain of indwelling another, non-metaphysical inception (GA 71: 28, 184; see also ÜdS: 46–50).[30] Perhaps, given how far we have come from our initial appreciation of the topic, it will not be surprising to hear that, on Heidegger's account, this is also a pain that bears its own "delight" (GA 73: 724; GA 97: 447).

In Heidegger's reading, pain not only furnishes us with a new way—perhaps the only way—to experience truth itself and understand beyng itself. Pain also furnishes our dwelling (*Wohnen*) with delight (*Wonne*) and serenity (see GA 98: 407 for the wordplay). Or better: pain, properly experienced, is this dwelling. Heidegger has moved from the truth of pain as the self-showing sheltering of thing and world to pain as our proper abode.

In other places, Heidegger does, admittedly, ascribe a twofold, even duplicitous, tendency to pain, especially when he is discussing the flame of spirit in Trakl's work. Like the Old High German *gheis*, pain can break out into insurrection or gather into gentle releasement (*Gelassenheit*). It can, as Heidegger glosses Trakl, "tear the wandering soul forth [*reißt . . . fort*] and inscribe it [*zeichnet . . . ein*] into the jointure of storming and hunting, which, storming heaven, would like to hunt down God," but it can also "reach mildness" and "bestow what is essential" (GA 12: 57–58, 60). In terms of *On Pain*, however, the insurrectionary trait would seem to be merely metaphysical, and in any case, even on the twofold reading, disruptive pain can be essentially contained.[31]

Heidegger does not redeem pain by making it serviceable for life. He does not provide us with coping mechanisms. But that is precisely the point. We must learn to heed the pain of beyng, beyond or before all programs and praxis. Only in doing so will we discover a gentleness beyond or before all physical and psychological consolation:

> Thinking which has been transformed, as thinking which is aligned with pain [*an den Schmerz*] as the claim or ad-dress [*An-spruch*] (no longer thinking about pain as a fact and occurrence), is of *no use* in the effort to make progress and improvements in combatting pain, *not even in the elimination of sorrow* [*Leides*]. What is it for, then? But in it [this thinking that is aligned with pain] a softening properly takes place [*ereignet sich die Be-sänftigung*], in the sense of bringing the gentle into its own [*Ereignung des Sanften*]. Not only use*less*—but [the fact] that use and the useful are not the most valuable and the most necessary. The most necessary is the "*unnecessary*." (ÜdS: 53)

Yet why, one might ask, has the truth of pain not forced its way into our purview after all these millennia of reckoning and tampering with it? *Because*, Heidegger answers, *pain itself has nothing to do with compulsion. Because everything comes down to letting be and letting be said, not to apprehension and appellation.* "Because," he exclaims,

> it [the essence of pain] is beyng itself! Because this is, inceptively, grace [*Huld*] and the gentle—the never-urging—but rather always only serene, consensual in beings, what speaks assuringly [*Zu-sprechende*], hence the gathering of releasement [*Ge-lassenheit*]: indwelling is not "work" ["*Arbeit*," contra Jünger] and action, but rather the wholly other—namely, the *determinative attunedness* [*Be-stimmtheit*] of the human being into his inceptive essence. (ÜdS: 50)

Even if Heidegger's treatment of pain provides little comfort for our everyday cares, and even if it does little to explain why pain was misconstrued and thereby exacerbated to begin with, Heidegger has, in his way, justified pain's ultimate purport. Pain is the meaning of being. Heidegger's algontology is an algontodicy.

Elsewhere, Heidegger even tries to save the word "pain"—or to be more accurate, he tries to save only *one* word for pain in *one* particular language: not the English, not the German, but the Greek *algos*.

§6. *Algos*: An Etymological Excursus

In an anonymously compiled Byzantine Greek–Greek lexicon known under the Latin title *Etymologicum Magnum* (where, incidentally, a possible source for Heidegger's oft-contested understanding of *alētheia*, "truth," as *a-lēthē*, "un-concealment," can be found[32]), one reads:

> Pain, distress: along the lines of "care about," "worry about"; [along the lines of] what we value highly and worry about. For, things involving much suffering merit worrying about. Or, [pain is] the kind of thing one does not speak of or name.

❋

Ἄλγος, ἡ λύπη · παρὰ τὸ ἀλέγω τὸ φροντίζω · ὃ περὶ πολλοῦ ποιούμεθα καὶ φροντίζομεν. τὰ γὰρ πολυπαθῆ, φροντίδος ἄξια. ἢ ἃ μὴ λέγει τὶς καὶ ὀνομάζει.[33]

Here, pain is understood in two or possibly three senses. First, to worry is to suffer. The things I care about (*alegō*) are precisely the things that bring me pain (*algos*). Second, and somewhat speculatively, we might read *para*, not as "along the lines of," but as "contrary to." (*Speculatively*, because *para* does not have this sense when used in the same position in other entries in the lexicon.) Be it physiological or psychological, from within the body or without, pain would then be an incursion into my everyday concerns and values. Pain would be what throws my cares into disarray. Indeed, according to this interpretation, the very word for pain in Greek would embody and inscribe its jumbling activity: *algos*—both the word and the thing—is a distortion of *alegō*—both the word and the thing. Finally, pain belongs in the realm of the inarticulable or of the precariously articulable. It is among those things about which (*ha*) one just does *not* speak (*legei*). Although the anonymous lexicographer uses the negative particle *mē* here, thereby suggesting typification of a class or disquiet, what seems to be implied is an alpha privative. *Algos* would then be the *unsaid* (*a-legomenon*) or at least what ought to remain unsaid, lest, like the Northern European bear, uttering it should summon it. Perhaps, taking the power of the privative further, we could even say that pain rends all language asunder, just as certain anarchists are not merely without government, but actively seek to destroy it.

In contrast, Heidegger does not correlate pain with quotidian cares and ontic affairs. Pain has a deeper sense, and it is to pain itself that I should turn my attention; it is precisely of pain that I should speak or let be spoken. Heidegger's etymology also differs from the lexicon's. In a long letter to Ernst Jünger published during Heidegger's lifetime under the titles "Über 'Die Linie'" ("On/Beyond 'The Line'") and "Zur Seinsfrage" ("On the Question of Being"), Heidegger writes:

> If one were to venture to think through the relations between "work" as the basic feature of beings and "pain," going back through and beyond Hegel's *Logic*, then the Greek word for pain, namely *algos*, would first come to speak for us. *Algos* is presumably related to *alegō*, which, as an intensifier of *legō*, means intimate gathering [*innige Versammeln*]. Pain would then be what gathers into utmost intimacy [*das ins Innigste Versammelnde*]. (GA 9: 404; cf. GA 7: 214)

Although the connection between *algos* and *alegō* is tenuous, it seems Heidegger is correct in deriving *alegō* from *a + legō*.[34] However, we can easily see here that Heidegger, like Hegel, does not interpret pain privatively, as what cannot be said or as what undoes all saying. Instead, he takes the alpha to be an *alpha intensivum*, strengthening the *legō*, which, for its part, does not, in Heidegger's reading, have its most common meaning of "I say," but rather has the radical sense of "I gather." Heidegger often associates being (*on*) with *legein* qua gathering: ontology is the gathering of being, in both senses of the genitive. Pain, then, as intense, intimate gathering, is like being, only more so. Might *algos*, as intensified *legein*, therefore be even more important than the other Greek words by which Heidegger tries to think being itself?

§7. In the Name of *Schmerz*

But what of the German word *Schmerz*? Why does Heidegger not trace *its* origins, especially given its possible connection with burning (*verbrennen*, *cremare*),[35] which he easily could have harnessed for his interpretation of the flame of spirit in Trakl's work? This is all the more surprising, since he dissects the etymology of almost every key term in his reading of Trakl. As I argued in chapter 3, one of the major exceptions is the term *Abgeschiedenheit*, whose history Heidegger ignores altogether, despite claiming that Trakl's entire body of poetic work is situated around it. The second major exception, I would now like to argue, is *Schmerz*. If Heidegger avoids the etymology of *Abgeschiedenheit* because of its universalist implications, he avoids the etymology of *Schmerz* because of its singular and scattering effects. The history of the word *Schmerz* hardly supports the sense of gathering Heidegger wants to locate in it. Its roots refer to hurting, chafing, and stinging, and its cognates are comparably resistant: the Greek *smerdnos/smerdaleos* suggests something dreadful, the Sanskrit *marditum* suggests crushing destruction, the Latin *mordere* suggests biting, and the English "smart" suggests sharp pain: "Then raging with intolerable smart, / He writhes his body, and extracts the dart."[36]

Heidegger's thought is undoubtedly (and notoriously) guided by what he once called the *"force of the most elementary words"* (SZ: 220). The tricky thing, of course, is to discern which words qualify. While many may not, Heidegger never suggests that *Schmerz* would be included among the excluded. He does, at one point in *On Pain*, offer a genealogy of pain:

> Yet in this process [of experiencing pain properly] pain must set aside the semblance that has everywhere and for a long time dominated its appearance, according to which it is such as to assail the human being, to do something to him (affection). Something that presses in on [him] is inflicted. What is inflicted is suffered as what is adverse. Pain comes forth "in" the human being as a bodily and psychic manifestation. The metaphysical name for this is the title "sensation" and "lived experience" and "feeling"—*aisthēton* and *aisthēsis* would correspond to this. But pain is *lupē*, and before this and actually [it is] *algos*. (ÜdS: 36)

But *Schmerz*, the *word*, is not in play here. Heidegger does not treat it as he does all those bastardized Latin translations of the Greek *Urwörter*. It is as though, uncharacteristically, he wanted to separate the thing from the word, being from language. Yet is not *Schmerz* a primal German word if ever there was one? One might reply that all Heidegger is doing is simply prioritizing Greek over German, *algos* over *Schmerz*. But on what basis? And how to account for his opposite maneuver in his reading of Trakl, where *Geist* means, not *pneuma*—let alone *spiritus*—but being outside of oneself, a sort of ontological ec-stasy? Even granting the primacy of *algos* over *Schmerz*, how to discern (*legein*) its true sense (*etymon*) among the plethora of possibilities? Why, finally, should it outstrip the pain of *lupē*, which, for its part, might call to mind the *loo*sening, dissolution, and destruction of Greek *luein*, or the shattering and rending asunder of Sanskrit *loptum*, thus precisely not the gathering Heidegger finds in *algos*?[37]

Leaving etymology aside—if this is even possible—what of the thing called pain? Heidegger deserves credit for thinking seriously about pain, and it is remarkable that, in *On Pain*, he places it at least on the same fundamental level as his notions of the clearing, the appropriative event, and truth as sheltering unconcealment. In the future, every scholar of Heidegger's thought will need to address his treatment of pain. But they will also need to question it. For, Heidegger's treatment, at least in the material available to scholars at present, fails to heed and account for the profound significance of irreparable ontic pain—the pain, for example, that rends the body asunder, not the pain that mends all wounds; the pain of personal loss and alienation, not the pain that gathers into community. Heidegger, for his part, dismisses this searing pain of particularity as derivative, as the product of a failure to heed the gentle call of being.

One might contend that, on a deeper level, Heidegger has already accounted for it: there is, after all, a moment of rending, of cleaving apart, in his ontological conception of pain. And yet, as we have seen, such separation is always brought back together by a higher mending. In gathering, pain ultimately sublates its own scattering. The wounds of being—to modify Hegel—always heal, even if scars should remain. When it comes to pain, Heidegger thus does not escape the final charge he levels against his German predecessor: "everything *is* already *reconciled*." While this might be a saving grace for some, it hardly saves the phenomenon of pain. For the sake of all those who have suffered, for the sake of the truth, and, dare I say, for the sake of being itself, we owe more fidelity to this phenomenon than Heidegger allows. Heidegger's algontology is doubtless an analgesic. Whether it is a tranquilizing act of bad faith is another matter.

§8. "ein gewaltiger Schmerz": Trakl's "Grodek"

On March 29, 1953, five months after the delivery of "Language in the Poem" at Bühlerhöhe, Heidegger traveled to Mühlau to see Ludwig von Ficker and visit Trakl's gravesite for the first time. Of this trip, Heidegger wrote, in a letter to the poet's erstwhile patron:

> Everything, [Trakl's] saying and his pain, the most concealed, still confidence and the beauty of his essence, moved me into a

new present. / Since this visit, something completely different from what can be merely represented historiographically and biographically came closer to me and flows into the ever more reflective, still dialogues with the poet. / Precisely in these weeks, in which I am again [. . .] toiling away on Nietzsche's *Thus Spoke Zarathustra*, I experience *what* a step Georg Trakl had to take in twisting free [*Verwindung*, "convalescing"] from the Dionysian, despite all the pain [*bei allem Schmerz*]. (MH/LF: 53)

Heidegger is right to recognize Trakl's struggle with, even his triumph over, the Nietzschean-Dionysian element of his earlier poetry, especially that of the collection from 1909, which was published posthumously in a volume, owned by Heidegger, bearing the title *Aus goldenem Kelch: Die Jugenddichtungen* (*From a Golden Chalice: Poems of His Youth*). The priest Alfred Focke, who attended the Bühlerhöhe Trakl celebration, made the same point already in 1951.[38] But this triumph is not necessarily a triumph over what Heidegger also seems to recognize here: ontic pain. I say this because, if Heidegger were using the word as he uses it in his lectures on Trakl, he would have written "because" or "on account of" all the pain. That is to say, Trakl would have twisted free from the culmination of metaphysics in the will to power as the will to will, from active nihilism and the eternal return, precisely *because* he would have been attuned to the fundamental, non-metaphysical, gentle gathering of pain. One might object that Heidegger's comment appears in a letter, and that I should not hold Heidegger to the terminological standards of his published writings. But it had been only five months since Heidegger had written about pain in "Language in the Poem" and only two since he had published the lecture in *Merkur*, and he was writing about Trakl to Trakl's most ardent supporter, who by that point was quite familiar with Heidegger's overall interpretation of the poet. Moreover, in an earlier letter to Ficker, from November 16, 1952, Heidegger expresses the hope that they would someday be able to discuss what Trakl "suffered in advance"—*vorausgelitten*, a rare word with religious overtones (cf. *propaschein*, 1 Thessalonians 2:2) that also suggests trial *in vita*, thus a matter for biography.

Trakl does, to be sure, sing of a more tender, less rending pain in some of his poetry, such as in the final stanza of "Heiterer Frühling" ("Bright Spring"):

> So schmerzlich gut und wahrhaft ist, was lebt;
> Und leise rührt dich an ein alter Stein:
> Wahrlich! Ich werde immer bei euch sein.
> O Mund! der durch die Silberweide bebt.
>
> *
>
> So painfully good and true is what lives;
> And quietly an ancient stone touches you:
> Truly! I will always be with you.
> Oh, mouth! which trembles through the white willow.
>   (HKA 1: 28)

However, as I have been arguing throughout the book, this pain is mediated by the passion of the tortured Christ, whom Trakl follows in faith as he takes up his own cross, and whom the poet even cites in this stanza. "Go ye therefore," Jesus commends his disciples,

> and teach all nations, baptizing them in the name of the Father and of the Son and of the Holy Ghost: / Teaching them to observe all things whatsoever I have commended you: and, lo, I am with you always [*ich bin bei euch alle Tage*], even unto the end of the world. (Matthew 28:19–20; see also 1 Peter 2:4–6).

Even setting the Christian elements to the side, why, in his lectures, does Heidegger not address the moments of ontic suffering and pain that pervade Trakl's poetry and that would seem to be necessary for its "great success" (GA 12: 15)? Why, for example—and most poignantly—does Heidegger not just discount the traumatic history of Trakl's "Grodek" but mock the notion that it would have any bearing on poem? "Pain," Heidegger contends, and here I quote at length,

> is truly pain only when it serves the flame of spirit. Trakl's last poem is called "Grodek." One praises it as a war poem. But it is infinitely more, because other. Its last verses read [. . .]:
>
> Die heiße Flamme des Geistes nährt heute ein gewaltiger
>   Schmerz,
> Die ungebornen Enkel.

*

The searing flame of spirit is nourished today by a mighty pain,
The unborn grandchildren.

Under no circumstances are the "grandchildren" who are named here the sons who remained unbegotten, the sons of the fallen sons who stemmed from the decaying *Geschlecht*. Were it only a matter of that, of the breaking off of the further begetting of the prior *Geschlechter* [plural], then this poet would have to jubilate over such an end. But he is in mourning, albeit a "prouder mourning," which, flaming, beholds the repose of the unborn one.

The unborn are called grandchildren, because they cannot be sons, i.e., direct descendents of the lapsed [*verfallenen*] *Geschlecht*. Another generation [*Generation*] lives between them and this *Geschlecht*. This generation is different, because of a different kind [*andersartig*] in accordance with its different essential provenance from the earliness of the unborn one. The "mighty pain" is the beholding that flames over everything and has foresight into the earliness, which is still withdrawing, of that dead one for the sake of whom the "spirits" ["*Geister*"] of those who fell early died [*früh Gefallenen entgegenstarben*]. (GA 12: 61–62)

Decades ago, David Krell wrote that this passage was "the most unnerving of [Heidegger's] entire corpus, even more disconcerting than all his silences."[39] It would be one thing if Heidegger had simply ignored the implications of a comment, made in his personal copy of the Collected Poems, about Trakl's "most terrible fear that his beloved human race [*Menschengeschlecht*] could at some point completely perish" (DD: 203), or even Trakl's own declaration, made right before leaving for war, that "all humans are worthy of love" (HKA 1: 256). But to claim that Trakl would *jubeln*—from the Latin *jubilare*, which Christian authors in particular used in the sense of shouting for joy—to claim that Trakl would jubilate over the sterilizing death of his fellow soldiers is monstrously tone deaf.

In conclusion, I would like to help us hear, not the gentle pain of being, but the pain of the human being Georg Trakl in his final days. We must, I believe, heed this pain; we must tarry, for a time beyond reckoning, on the thresholds that this pain has turned to stone, if we are ever to cross over.

At Bühlerhöhe, the day after delivering "Language in the Poem," Heidegger listened to Ficker give an extemporaneous speech based on a text he had written about his last encounter with Trakl. Confined, in October 1914, to a military hospital in Krakow under suspicion of psychosis, Trakl told Ficker, who had come to visit him, about the travails of war that had brought him to such a state. It is worth quoting Ficker at length, not just because Ficker's speech, which included a recitation of "Grodek," moved Heidegger to tears,[40] but because, in spite of this, it did not compel Heidegger to revise his interpretation when he decided to publish it in 1953 and again in 1959:

> The medical column to which [Trakl] belonged had been deployed for the first time during the battle of Gródek, shortly before the turning point, and already in the backlash of a panic breaking out on the front. In a barn near the town's central plaza, he had, without any medical assistance, taken over the care of ninety severely wounded men; powerless, even helpless, he had to endure this torture [*Marter*] for two days. The groans of the tormented and their pleas to bring an end to their suffering still ring in his ears. Suddenly, and barely audible amid their wailing, there was a faint explosion: someone who had been shot in the bladder had put a bullet through his head, and all at once there were bloody brain particles sticking to the wall. Trakl had to get out of there. But, whenever he stepped outside, a different image of horror would always draw his attention and make him freeze. [. . .] A group of trees eerily motionless, each with a hanged person dangling from it. Ruthenians, executed locals. One of them, the one strung up last, had, as Trakl learned (or did he witness it himself?), put the rope around his own neck. The sight was branded on his memory: the *complete* misery of humanity, here it had taken hold of one! Never could he forget that, nor the retreat; nothing is so terrifying as a retreat in disarray.[41]

Ficker goes on to relate Trakl's report of how, one evening, the horror of it all brought the poet to the brink of suicide, which his comrades prevented by forcefully taking away his pistol. A couple of weeks later,

Trakl was transferred to the military hospital, initially under the impression he would be serving as a pharmacist, only to discover he was a patient and prisoner, now fearing he might be tried and executed for cowardice.

Ficker went to see Trakl again the following day, at which time he learned of the little Trakl had managed to write over the preceding months.

> And now Trakl read me two poems softly, in the simple, casual voice that was unique to him: "Klage" ["Lamentation"] and "Grodek"—the latter, which was to remain his last, still in a version in which the outlook on the fate of the unborn grandchildren was a bit more broadly laid out and did not yet demonstrate that sudden narrowing of perspective into which Trakl's gaze then seemed to have plainly broken off and lifted out of the world. I was shaken and, despite the fact that the snoring of the person next to us sawed loudly and embarrassingly through the stillness, was for a long time embraced by my friend's sorrowful reticence as though by an arm that had fallen asleep. — "Would you like it for the 'Brenner'?" he said at last. "Gladly," I replied and thanked him. — "When will you bring it out?" — "In the spring, I hope, as a yearbook . . . It will also depend on whether the war is over soon and whether I will be enlisted and have to leave." — "God forbid," Trakl murmured.[42]

Trakl next asked Ficker whether he had heard of the baroque poet Johann Christian Günther. Ficker had not. Trakl said that, until recently, he hadn't either, but that this was a poet who had penned "the bitterest verses that a German poet ever wrote" and who, "you must know, died young, at the age of twenty seven." (Trakl himself had turned twenty-seven in February.) Trakl proceeded to read aloud from a couple of Günther's poems, including his last, "Bußgedanken" ("Thoughts of Repentance"), which Trakl found to be "the most beautiful and significant" of them all. Ficker reports that, after Trakl had read the final stanza aloud—

> Soll ja mein jäher Fall den Körper niederstürzen,
> So laß mir Zeit und Schmerz auf deine Brust verkürzen
>   Und nimm den freien Geist mit Arm und Mitleid auf!
> Wem irgend noch von mir ein Aergerniß geblieben,

> Dem sei der Spruch ans Herz, wie mir an Sarg, geschrieben:
>   Oft ist ein guter Tod der beste Lebenslauf.

*

> Should my sudden fall topple my body,
> Let my time and pain pass more quickly on your breast
>   And take my free spirit in your arms with compassion!
> Should anyone remain angry with me,
> Let this saying be written on his heart, as on my coffin:
>   Often a good death is the best course of life.

—after Trakl had read this stanza, "he appeared exhausted and in need of rest. He closed his eyes."[43] One week later, Trakl would be found dead, having overdosed on cocaine.

In the meantime, Trakl had sent Ficker a letter in which the poet anticipates his imminent demise:

> Since your visit to the hospital I have been doubly sad [*traurig*]. I feel I am almost already beyond the world [*jenseits der Welt*]. / In conclusion, I would like to add that, in the event of my death, it is my wish and will that my dear sister Grete should have everything I own in terms of money and other items.[44]

Included with the letter was the one and only copy of "Grodek." Trakl began the poem with Roman script, only to break off, after the first sentence, into Gothic, as though it had been too much of a pain to produce a readily legible version,[45] as though Trakl's pain would not allow him to steady his hand. Trakl is not looking forward to a new birth for the West here, as Heidegger claims. Trakl is lamenting a painful miscarriage, a tragedy of spirit that will soon drive him not to the poetic sounding of silence but to the irrevocable silence of suicide.

> At evening the autumn woods issue tones
> Of deadly weapons, the golden plains
> And blue lakes, over which the sun
> Rolls on more gloomily; the night envelops
> Dying warriors, the wild lamentation
> Of their shattered mouths.

Yet quietly in the pasture red clouds,
In which a raging god dwells,
gather up the blood that was shed, lunar chill;
All streets enter the mouth of black decay.
Under golden boughs of night and stars
The shadow of the sister sways through the silent grove,
To greet the spirits of heroes, the bleeding heads;
And softly in the reeds the dark flutes of autumn resound.
Oh, prouder mourning! you brazen altars,
The hot flame of spirit is nourished today by a mighty pain,
The unborn grandchildren.

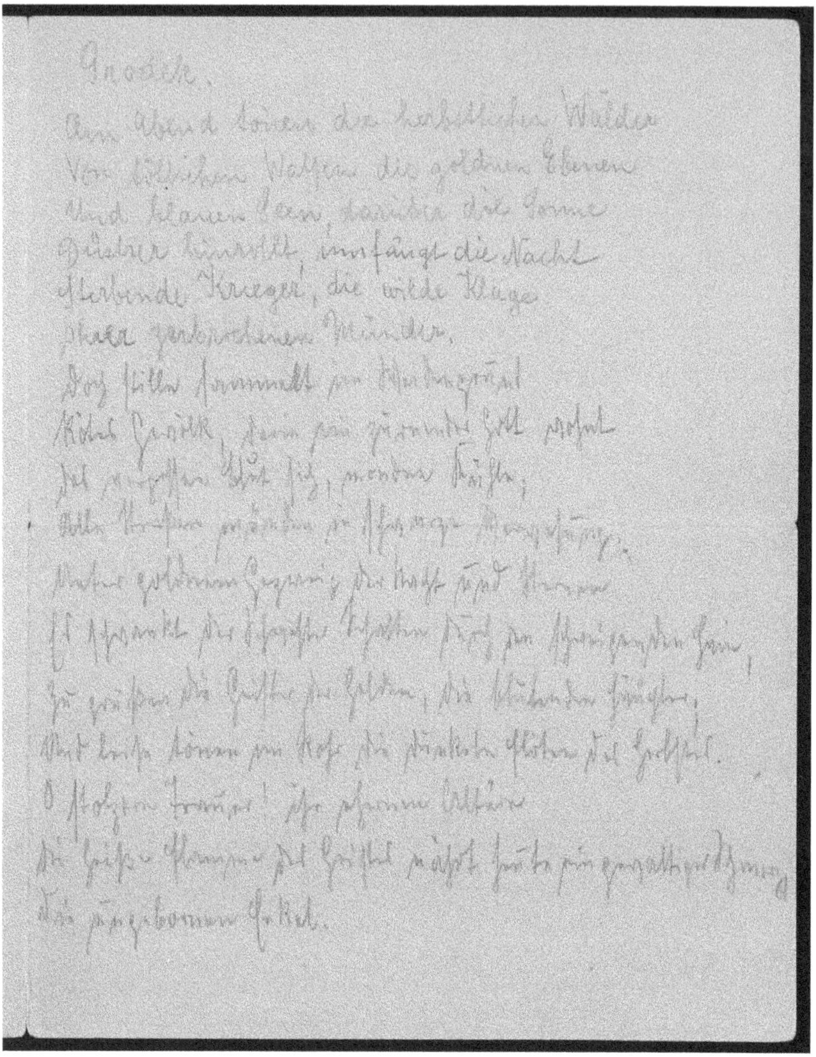

Image 6. Manuscript of Trakl's "Grodek."

Chapter 5

Poetic Colors of the Holy

Trakl with Pindar

> They're out of the dark's ragbag, these two
> Moles dead in the pebbled rut,
> Shapeless as flung gloves, a few feet apart—
> Blue suede a dog or fox has chewed.[1]
>
> —Sylvia Plath

In the epigraph to one of the most formative books for Heidegger's education, *Vom Sein: Abriß zur Ontologie* (*On Being: An Outline of Ontology*), the theologian Carl Braig cites the medieval Franciscan St. Bonaventure:

> Strange, then, is the blindness of the intellect which does not consider that which it sees before all others and without which it can recognize nothing. But just as the eye, intent on the various differences of color, does not see the light through which it sees other things, or if it does see, does not notice it, so our mind's eye, intent on particular and universal beings, does not notice that being which is beyond all categories, even though it comes first to the mind, and through it, all other things.[2]

Bonaventure's analogy is clear enough. Color is to light as beings are to being. Just as we do not pay attention to the light that makes the perception of color possible, neither do we pay attention to being, despite presupposing it in all of our thoughts and actions. Yet how are we to understand the analogy when the terms are switched and being is compared not just to light but to color, thus to what would seem to be merely *a* being or, at best, a finite set of beings? What, moreover, is going on when being is not just compared to particular colors but equated with them?

In this chapter, I want to return to a topic broached in chapter 2 and to examine the work of two poets who, on Heidegger's interpretation, use particular colors to characterize being and the related concept of the holy. Although separated by two and a half millennia, Heidegger finds that the victory odes of the Ancient Greek lyricist Pindar and the melancholic poetry of the twentieth-century Austrian expressionist Trakl were both written under a "holy compulsion" (GA 78: 67). Through them, being spoke itself—synesthetically—in colors: gold in the case of Pindar, and blue (along with gold) in the case of Trakl. Trakl, who flunked Greek in high school, may never have read Pindar. But, if there is really such a thing as "poetic dialogue between poets," then, odd as it may sound, and perhaps even unbeknownst to him or in spite of himself, Trakl was, on Heidegger's interpretation, engaged in an "authentic dialogue" with Pindar (GA 12: 34)—not, to be sure, the Pindar of classics departments, but a Pindar whose voice Heidegger endeavors to make out amid millennia of cacophonous and stifling commentary.

I will first try to listen for this voice in Heidegger's extensive excursus on Pindar's 5th Isthmian in the undelivered lecture course *Der Spruch des Anaximander* (*Anaximander's Verdict*) (§1). Then, I will show how many of the motifs Heidegger identifies, including their timbre or "color," are reprised in his discussion of Trakl's "Ein Winterabend" ("A Winter Evening"), "Abendländisches Lied" ("Song of the Occident"), and "Sommersneige" ("Summer's Decline") in his two lectures on Trakl (§2). While it might seem that, at the ontological level, golden shining is proper exclusively to the ancients and bluish twilight to the post-Hölderlinian moderns, I will argue that, in his respective analyses, Heidegger is drawing out different aspects of being and the holy that belong to all epochs, even if they cannot always be seen as such, and even if different gods show up in them. Next, I will offer some thoughts on the possibility of what might be called, following Goethe, a Heideggerian *Farbenlehre*, or "color theory," and on whether such a theory can accommodate poetic responses to sacrilege (§3). I will conclude with commentary on the topic of madness and its putative holiness in Trakl's oeuvre (§4).

Before I begin, three caveats. First, I focus on material from Heidegger's late thought, starting in the 1940s. In the late 1910s and early 1920s, Heidegger, like many of his contemporaries (Ernst Troeltsch, Wilhelm Windelband), was interested in the significance of the holy, especially in the wake of Rudolf Otto's pathbreaking quasi-phenomenological study *Das Heilige* (*The Holy*) (1917), where Otto famously coined the term "the numinous" to characterize the incomprehensible, mysterious, simultaneously threatening and enticing aspects of the holy,[3] Husserl, on whom Otto's analysis had, in the words of the founder of phenomenology, "a stronger effect [. . .] than almost any other book in years," once expressed disappointment that Heidegger did "not have time to write a (thoroughgoing) critique" of it.[4] While it would be worthwhile to compare what Heidegger did manage to write on Otto in this time period (GA 60: 332–334) with his later treatment of being and the holy in Pindar and Trakl, for reasons of space I cannot do so here, especially since neither Otto nor the early Heidegger examines the holy's chromatic manifestations. Second, after Heidegger's interest shifted away from medieval mysticism and primal Christianity to phenomenological ontology in the mid-1920s, comments on the holy nearly disappeared from his writings (the word is absent in *Being and Time*, for example), only to resurface in 1934–1935 with his first lecture course on Hölderlin. However, despite Hölderlin's overwhelming importance for the topic in Heidegger and for Heidegger's general appreciation of Pindar, the only times, of which I am aware, when Heidegger links the holy to color (in this case, gold) in his writings on Hölderlin are when he is drawing on Pindar, whose work accordingly remains the primary source for Heidegger's appreciation of the colored aspects of the holy.[5] (I will nevertheless turn to Hölderlin, briefly, in §4, when I analyze Trakl's recently discovered poem on Hölderlin's madness.) Third, I will bracket the question of whether and to what extent Heidegger's articulation of the holy overlaps with, or can assist in the understanding of, holiness in Biblical faith. In the "Brief über den 'Humanismus'" ("Letter on 'Humanism'"), Heidegger is clear that, by being, he means neither the holy, nor divinity/godhead (*Gottheit*), nor God (*Gott*) (GA 9: 351). Instead, being is that on the basis of which the others may be understood. And yet, in a later discussion with a group of philosophers and theologians, Heidegger clarifies that, in the "Letter," "God" is meant to refer "only to the god of the poet, not to the god of revelation."[6] This clarification would, presumably, also hold for the holy, although that need not concern us here.

§1. Chrusology, Ontology, Hierology

Heidegger's most extensive engagement with Pindar's 5th Isthmian—indeed his most extensive engagement with Pindar as such—can be found in a long introduction he wrote for a lecture course (never delivered) on Anaximander, which would later serve as the basis for the final chapter of Holzwege (Logging Paths). Although the manuscript is undated, it appears to have been written in 1942, thus as the first in a series of lecture courses on the pre-Socratics, followed by the treatment of Parmenides in 1942–1943 and that of Heraclitus in 1943–1944 (GA 78: 340–344; GA 54; GA 55). In this important manuscript, which has yet to be translated into English or discussed in extenso in the secondary literature, Heidegger turns to Pindar in order to elucidate the Greek experience of being, which he then uses to interpret ta onta ("beings") in Anaximander's only extant fragment.[7] The manuscript contains two versions of Heidegger's commentary on Pindar: a first, shorter version, which draws heavily on the gold of the poet's earlier 1st Olympian (GA 78: 284–296), and a later, more elaborate version, which focuses almost exclusively on the 5th Isthmian (GA 78: 65–98). My remarks will center on the second version.

Heidegger's translation and interpretation of the first eighteen verses of the Isthmian victory ode are as remarkable and creative as his translation and interpretation of the first stasimon of Sophocles's Antigone (in, for example, GA 40 and GA 53)—and they are just as liable to draw criticism from classicists the world over. Like his rendering of Sophocles's choral ode, Heidegger returned to and revised his rendering of Pindar on numerous occasions later in his career, including, as we saw in chapter 2, in his first lecture on Trakl. To gain a sense for the radicality of Heidegger's reading of Pindar's poem, let us begin by comparing his translation of just its opening three verses with two conventional approaches. Here, first, is Pindar's Greek, along with my attempt at a literal, lexicological rendering:

Μᾶτερ Ἀελίου πολυώνυμε Θεία,
σέο ἕκατι καὶ μεγασθενῆ νόμισαν
χρυσὸν ἄνθρωποι περιώσιον ἄλλων.[8]

*

Mother of Sun, many-named Theia,
on your account humans judge gold
mighty far beyond other things.

Next, a translation into German that Heidegger consults—and criticizes—
in his excursus on Pindar:

Mutter des Helios, vielnamige Theia,
deinetwillen glauben die Menschen
großmächtig das Gold, überschwänglich vor allem andern.⁹

Compare, finally, Heidegger's version:

Mutter des Helios, reichnamige, (die) Gottheit (selber den
   Göttern),
dich in der Acht, denn auch weitwaltend erachten
das Gold die Menschen, (das) anwesender rings um anderes
   alles. (GA 78: 65–66; Heidegger's parentheses)

*

Mother of Helios, richly named, (the) godhead (even to the
   gods),
you, in consideration, because humans also consider gold
far-prevailing, (which) [is] more present around everything
   else.¹⁰

At the grammatical-lexical level, Heidegger reads the last phrase of Pindar's invocation, *periōsion allōn*, independently from *megasthenē* ("mighty"), he takes *allōn* together with *peri-* ("around [all] others"), and he exploits the derivation of *-ōsion* from *einai* ("to be [present]"). Gold is not just *exceedingly* mighty in comparison with everything else (*periōsion* as adverb, *allōn* as genitive of comparison). Gold is *more in being, more present*, amid all else (*periōsion* as adjective, *allōn* as object of an implied prepositional phrase). How might Heidegger justify these idiosyncratic linguistic decisions, beyond simply claiming that all genuine translation first requires that *we* be trans-lated, carried across, into the realm in which a poet or thinker speaks (GA 78: 55; GA 54: 17–18)?

On Heidegger's interpretation, Pindar's poem is not simply about the heroes it names, whether it be Phylakidas of Aegina, who won the all-in boxing and wrestling contest at the Isthmian Games, probably in 478 BCE (verses 17–19); the Greek sailors who had recently defeated the Persians at the battle of Salamis (verses 48–50); or Achilles, son of the local Aiakidai (verses 39–42). The poem is, accordingly, not simply an encomium or "the fitting boast, mixed with song, about toils" (κόμπον τὸν ἐοικότ' ἀοιδᾷ / κιρνάμεν ἀντὶ πόνων), as Pindar himself sings in the second strophe (verses 24–25).[11] The 5th Isthmian also—and more fundamentally—names the holy and lets being appear. To cite Heidegger's conclusion right away (before working our way up to it):

> because the poetizing saying, in itself, brings the being of beings to shine [*zum Scheinen*], everything that is said in the truly saying song "is" "more in being" ["*seiender*"], which is to say, however, more shining, more gleaming [*glänzender*]. For the saying of the songs names the holiness [*das Heilige*] of *Theia*. They are therefore called *hierai aodai*, "holy songs." [. . . The] "ground," on the basis of which the poet says [such things], can [. . .] be called the "ground" of the pure gleaming forth [*Erglänzens*], the "gold-ground." (GA 78: 96–97, in reference to Pindar Fragment no. 194[12])

To appreciate the foundational role that gold plays in Heidegger's analysis of Pindar, we must first shift our commonplace impressions of it, whether it be as (1) a color, (2) an element, or (3) currency. (1) Gold is not, fundamentally, the property of an object that causes ocular sensation through the reflection or emission of light. It is not the perception of a particular wavelength within the visible spectrum. If it were, gold would not shine most among the colors, and we would have to wonder whether, as the product of perception, it would even be a being at all, let alone being itself. (2) Might Pindar be referring to the metal, then, which, unlike color, has chemical properties that explain its existence independently of human sensation? This brings us closer, but even the polished element is not the brightest of all. (3) Should we therefore return to the subjective standpoint and consider how people, and the ancient Greeks in particular, have tended to view it, namely, as valuable and thus as useful for exchange? Since, from this standpoint, gold has a greater purchasing power than other things—since it is greater in acquiring wealth (*ousia*) than they are—it is "mighty far beyond [*periōsion*] other things" (verses 2–3). Yet Heidegger does not, primarily, hear *ousia* in this sense. He is instead thinking about the word and its ontological roots (*einai*, *on*) before it becomes the guiding concept of substance metaphysics and before gold becomes little else than a quantifiable medium of exchange (see, however, GA 78: 60, 62, 93).

In Heidegger's reading, *einai*, "to be," has the sense of "to be present"—"present," not as an object among others or as a resource to be exploited, but as a being that rises up into unconcealment, shining in its finite splendor. We might think of the Athenian sculptor Phidias's chryselephantine statues of Athena in the Parthenon and of Zeus in the sanctuary of Olympia, which, surely, were *periōsios* in relation to everything around them; surely, these statues "out-gleamed and gleamed around and gleamed through" everything around them (GA 78: 73). Heidegger does not mention these works of art specifically, but, with their references to Victory and the most famous of the Panhellenic Games, they are fitting material counterparts to the epinician ode.

But even these artistic wonders do not do justice to Pindar's gold. We have to imagine something other than individual beings or even all beings as a whole, however glorious they may be. For the gold of the 5th Isthmian is such that its mightiness first lets all beings gleam forth. We therefore cannot understand its own gleam solely in terms of that which it makes possible. Exceeding each and every particular being, gold is of being itself. In Heidegger's words:

> Gold is thus in no way named only as one gleaming thing among others, a thing that would, gradually by degrees, exceed these others in the intensity of its gleam. Rather, gold is named because, thought in Greek terms, the essence of being consists in shining, so that this being that we call "gold" is in a certain way the being of beings. In gold, the essence of being has gathered itself in such a peculiar way that, in the being of this being, being can appear [*erscheinen*] as itself. (GA 78: 73–74)

We are accordingly beyond the realm of bodily sensation, despite the seemingly fundamental ocular terminology (appearing, shining, gleaming). Indeed, we cannot even take these terms as metaphors or analogically, since the shining of particular things is possible only on the basis of the prior, prevalent shining of golden being itself, and there is no way from the former to the latter. We are not subjectively "deeming" gold great (*nomizein*, verse 2, in one of its derivative senses); we are letting it show itself as it is in itself and accordingly giving it its due: "letting what belongs to it belong to it," "heeding it in such a way that it comes into its own [*Er-achten*]" (*nomizein* in the more primordial sense Heidegger identifies in the word) (GA 78: 75, 292–293).[13] In order to have such a regard for gold—a regard that, notably, Heidegger contends is proper to our very essence (GA 78: 80–82, 86, 91–92, 94, 291, 295)—we must not interpret the shining of golden being in traditional causal terms. It is neither mechanistic nor teleological. It is, instead, more like the blooming of Silesius's rose, *ohn warumb*, "without a reason why."[14] Its strength (*sthenos*, verse 2) is not the exercise of violence (*Gewalt*), but a gathered and gathering (*Ge-*) radiance that gently prevails (*waltet*) over all things, letting them appear and thereby letting them be (GA 78: 73–74).[15] If gold, at this level, is holy—and, judging from some of Heidegger's later commentaries on the poem (GA 12: 21; GA 80: 994, 1016), it is—then, for all its uncanniness, it has lost one of the key characteristics that Otto located in the numinous: fearsomeness. By this point in his career, Heidegger is much closer, not just temporally but also philosophically, to the releasement of the first *Feldweggespräch* ("Country Path Conversation") than to the violence of *Einführung in die Metaphysik* (*Introduction to Metaphysics*), where, incidentally, Pindar also appears as one of the great representatives of Greek poetry (GA 40: 108, 121).

We must, furthermore, not interpret the middle-voiced letting of ontological gold as the activity of yet another being, such as Helios, Selene, or any of the other Greek gods, to say nothing of God as *causa prima* or the maker god of metaphysics and monotheism. The gods, *theoi*, on Heidegger's interpretation, are so many ways of looking, *theasthai*, into beings, which is to say, bringing them to light (compare the formative imagination, *Ein-Bildung*, of the German theosophists). In the other direction, these gods are also so many names for and perspectives on Theia (GA 78: 77–79).

But is Theia not also a goddess? Does not Pindar, following Hesiod (*Theogony*, verse 371), describe her as the *mother* of Helios, the sun god (verse 1)? And—we could imagine Socrates asking here—are not the parents of gods also gods? Heidegger, who takes the Greek suffix *-ia* literally, as forming an abstract noun, interprets Theia as the essence of *theos*; "she"—if gender is even appropriate here—is, in Heidegger's rendering, *(die) Gottheit (selber den Göttern)*, "(the) divinity or godhead (even to the gods)" (GA 78: 65; cf. 76).[16] Theia is, therefore, not *a* god or *a* being. We now need to consider whether she would then in a certain way be the same as being, and, if so, how she would relate to gold as in a certain way the same as being.

It makes sense that Heidegger would identify Helios, god of the sun, as "pure shining." But, interestingly, he also describes the god's mother, who "shelters [*birgt*] pure shining in her womb," as "even more shining" than the sun. Shining, at its deepest level, is not what shows up to the animal eye; it is what "first bestows the luminous [*das Lichte*] and open" (GA 78: 77). In this respect, as the most shining, Theia most makes room for other things—nay, for all things—to shine. Heidegger therefore equates her with one of his most important ontological terms: Theia is the *Lichtung*, the "clearing," for the manifestation of beings:

> The mother of light is the one who is invoked, insofar as she is *Theia*. As the latter, she grants, looking ahead to the brightness [*Helle*] of shining—before the brightness and always—the widely resounding [*weithallende*] open of the clearing. In this clearing, what comes to light is capable of first appearing and, as what is present, of shining. (GA 78: 78)

Although this is not his main focus, which lies, rather, on the shining of being, Heidegger also uses the language of sheltering to describe Theia's essence, thereby anticipating the more nocturnal, "bluer" dimension of the holy in the Trakl lectures. (This, in spite of her different lineage from that of Night in the *Theogony*, verses 123–124, 132–135.) "The maternal essence of the godhead," Heidegger writes, "consists *im hütenden Hervorgehenlassen*"; rendered periphrastically: "in a letting emerge that, at the same time, tends and keeps watch over that which emerges" (GA 78: 79). Theia is the "womb and protection of what pertains to the gods [*des Gotthaften*]" (GA 78: 77). More than a god, she is also more abyssal than any god. She is like—or perhaps she just *is*—the *Geborgenheit* ("sheltering") and *lēthē* ("concealment") that lie at the heart of all truth, manifestation, and unconcealment (*alētheia, Unverborgenheit*).

In his commentary on Pindar, Heidegger does not delineate the fourfold order of implication "being–the holy–the godhead/divinity–gods" as clearly as he does in the "Letter on 'Humanism.'" It is obvious that the gods come last in both cases. But, in the Pindar material, it is not so easy to distinguish being, the holy, and the godhead from one another. On the one hand, Heidegger implicitly links being and the godhead (Theia) by describing the latter as shining, clearing, sheltering, and, through its/her connection to gold, gathering. He also explicitly associates them in an overview of verses 2–17, which he calls "the pure poem of the godhead of the gods, and nothing else besides": "in the poetizing of the godhead of the gods, the essence of being is thought. For this reason, and only for this reason, is gold named" (GA 78: 78). On the other hand, toward the end of his commentary, Heidegger situates the godhead *within* what seems to be the deeper dimension of being: "The Unifying One, which brings what appears to shine, is, as the gathering, as *ho Logos*, being itself, wherein the godhead of the gods [. . .] rests" (GA 78: 96). To resolve this tension, I am inclined to interpret Theia and gold as poetic articulations of different aspects of being, rather than as lower members in a hierarchy. In Pindar's ode, which, Heidegger clearly states, "poetizes the essence of being" (GA 78: 290; see also 64, 286), Theia stands for a more chthonic, lethic, even *choro*-logical aspect of being, whereas gold is more ouranic, a-lethic, *phainomeno*-logical—despite Theia's own oxymoronically obscure shining. Through the mouth of the poet, being approaches us in the gleam of gold and in the *musterion* of Mother Theia.

There is, furthermore, something holy about this golden mystery. Pindar's poetry is not, on Heidegger's interpretation, about making things last longer by preserving them for posterity with compelling and beautiful words. Pindar's poetry is compelling, but this is because he, like few others, assented to "the holy compulsion" to sing of gold and "forge the 'gold-ground'" into a language in which things are "'more in being,' which is to say, however, more shining, more gleaming" (GA 78: 67, 96–97). To name this shining and all it involves is to name the "holiness of *Theia*." Pindar's chrusology is, at the same time, a hierology. His theology is—*sit venia verbo*—a theialogy. And his poetry, like any work deserving of the name, is an unspoken ontology.

§2. Sacré bleu

In the early 1950s, as Heidegger begins to write about Trakl, he returns to many of the ideas he had developed in his commentary on Pindar, including the synesthetic etymological link between *Helle* ("brightness") and *hallen* ("to resound") (GA 78: 78, 86, 88; GA 12: 40); the ability of poetry "to let the unspoken [dimension of being] be in all its fullness and, in such letting, to bring it 'to' language and thereby bring it close to us" (GA 78: 283; cf. GA 12: 33–35); the proper meaning of jewelry (GA 78: 73; GA 12: 51); and, most importantly for the present chapter, the way in which holy being manifests itself in particular colors. In the first Trakl lecture, which, as we saw in chapter 2, examines the poem "A Winter Evening" in order to let language speak (itself) beyond or before human expression, Heidegger even returns explicitly to the gold of Pindar's 5th Isthmian. Here, it is a matter of understanding a peculiar couplet from the second stanza of Trakl's poem:

> Golden blüht der Baum der Gnaden
> Aus der Erde kühlem Saft. (GA 12: 20)

*

> Golden blooms the tree of grace
> Rising from the earth's cool sap.

Recall that Heidegger disregards the Christian connotations of these verses, preferring instead to interpret them in terms of the fourfold:

> The tree is rooted solidly in the earth. Thus, it thrives to the point of blooming, which opens itself to the blessing of the sky. [. . .] The poem names the tree of grace. Its solid blooming shelters the fruit that falls unearned: the salvific holiness [*das rettend Heilige*] that is propitious [*hold*] to mortals. In the golden, blooming tree, earth and sky, divinities and mortals prevail. Their united fourfold is the world. (GA 12: 21)

As in his reading of Pindar, Heidegger here associates gold with the holy; only, this time, the holy (*das Heilige*) is tied more explicitly to salvation (*Rettung, Heil*). Not, to be sure, the salvation of the soul and its promise of eternal bliss in the beyond, but the salvation that comes with accepting "death" as "the highest concealment of being" (GA 12: 20) or "of beyng" (GA 80: 1016)—salvation, not from the earth, but from the fantasy of everlasting life on the far side of it. Holy gold enables us to dwell authentically on the earth, accepting the gifts of being even as we accept being's insuperable concealment.

To develop the connection between the golden holy and being—the latter of which Heidegger names, as such, only once in his lecture, but to which, by this point in its trajectory, he has already alluded with his reference to the fourfold of the world (see GA 79: 74)—Heidegger now invokes Pindar. In the recently published first version of "Language" (1950), Heidegger claims that, if we are to hear the color of Trakl's "A Winter Evening" "rightly," that is to say, the color of a poem penned by a drug-addled twentieth-century Austrian, then it is necessary to draw on, of all things, the ancient Greek of a Theban lyricist (GA 80: 994). The second and final versions of the lecture (1951, 1959) are hardly less abrupt, although they not quite as assertive: the turn to Pindar is more an issue of expediency, helping the audience to hear Trakl's gold "more clearly" (GA 80: 1017, GA 12: 21). In any case, it is plain that Heidegger simply imports his earlier analysis of the 5th Isthmian into his interpretation of Trakl. Here, I am interested less in the legitimacy of this approach as a reading of Trakl than in what it reveals about Heidegger's own color theory when it comes to the holy. In the first, more overtly ontological version of the lecture, Heidegger writes:

> At the beginning of this poem [sc., Isthmian 5], Pindar names gold[,] *chruson*[,] [. . .] *periōsion allōn*, that which gleams above all and through all: all *ousia*, every instance of presencing, every shining forth [*Erscheinen*] into unconcealment. The word "golden" summons the luminous letting-gleam-forth, which brings everything forth into serene cheerfulness and shelters it therein. (GA 80: 994; Heidegger's bracketed ellipsis)

The final version, with its development of the prefix *peri-*, is even more reminiscent of the 1942 analysis:

> At the beginning of this ode, the poet names gold *periōsion pantōn*, that which, like a ring around everything that is present [*jegliches Anwesende ringsum*], gleams above all through all, *panta*. The gleam of the gold shelters everything present, bringing it into the unconcealment of its appearing [*birgt alles Anwesende in das Unverborgene seines Erscheinens*]. (GA 12: 21)[17]

These quotations suggest that Pindar's gold pertains as much to Trakl's world—and thus to our world—as it did to that of the pre-Platonic Greek world, even if we might need a different language for becoming attuned to it (German rather than Greek) or a different attunement altogether (Hölderlin's holy mourning rather than wonder) (GA 78: 85; GA 39: §8). For, to modify a famous term for humans in Pindar's 8th Pythian, daylight may well have passed in the interim, making us *Nachtwesen*, "creatures of the night."[18]

The suggestion of subterranean continuity between Pindar's and Trakl's gold finds support in another reference to the invocation of Pindar's ode, this time in notes for a 1955 lecture on two poems by Mörike. Regarding the latter's "September-Morgen" ("September Morning") and in particular its final verse, which sings of "warm gold," Heidegger writes that one should compare it with the 5th Isthmian, whose first three verses Heidegger cites and translates anew (GA 74: 177). Moreover, in his exchange with Emil Staiger, discussed in chapter 2, Heidegger argues that the word *scheint* in the final verse of Mörike's "Auf eine Lampe" ("On a Lamp") does not mean "seems," *videtur*, but rather "shines," *lucet*, in the precise ontological sense he finds in Pindar's ode.[19] Thus, if Trakl's and Mörike's concerns line up with those of Pindar, then the Greek *chrusos* and all it entails do not belong solely to the Greek experience of being, as one might be led to expect from a study of the earlier treatment in the Pindar commentary alone. They also belong—or more accurately, could and ought to belong, if only we were to pay heed to them—to our experience as well.

What, however, should we make of the fact that, in Heidegger's second lecture on Trakl, it is not gold but blue that characterizes the holy? Has Heidegger's position changed? Might this, moreover, mark a shift in his primary matter for thought? Has he, as Vincent Blanchet argues, moved beyond or before, not only the Greek understanding of being—even in its most primordial form—but also beyond or before being altogether? Has *alētheia* become irrelevant? Does, *horribile dictu*, even Hölderlin no longer have anything to say?

Blanchet, the only scholar I know of to bring Heidegger together with Pindar and Trakl, sets up what I believe is a false dichotomy in his otherwise noteworthy study:

> if Trakl surveyed the same dimension as Pindar, why did the holy [*le sacré*] open up around him in blue rather than through

the radiance of gold? Does this ultimately mean that, in Pindar, gold was not itself the holy? Or is it, rather, a sign that the Pindaric Occident is not yet, or no longer, that of Trakl? The alternative, therefore, is as follows: either gold—thought in the most Greek way possible—is not the holy, or blue itself is no longer Greek at all. In this sense, what blue and gold fundamentally expose to us is the question of the difference between the site of *Ereignis* and that of *alētheia*.[20]

As I see it, and as I will attempt to demonstrate in the following, Heidegger is not suspending gold, being, Hölderlin, and Grecian unconcealment in favor of blue, the appropriative event, Trakl, and Germanic *Wahr-heit* ("sheltering"). It is, rather, a matter of emphasis, of highlighting different aspects of being or, better, of letting being show its true colors, which we can take literally as both gold and blue. Heidegger does, admittedly, associate *polemos* with *alētheia* in the *Beiträge* and elsewhere (GA 65: §233; GA 54: passim), and, in a 1969 seminar, he claims that, with *Ereignis*, he is "no longer thinking in a Greek fashion" (GA 15: 366). But this does not necessarily mean that he is thinking in a Greek fashion when he is rethinking Pindar's gold, that *Ereignis* is incompatible with being (or, more properly, with ~~being~~ or beyng), or that, just because Trakl sings of a gentle twofold (*Zwiefalt*) beyond all polemical discord (*Zwietracht*) (GA 12: 41, 46, 63, 74), *alētheia* and the Greek language would have fallen to the wayside. To cite just one example among many: one of the last things Heidegger ever wrote, he wrote in Greek, in a manuscript for a never-completed introduction to the *Gesamtausgabe* titled "Vermächtnis der Seinsfrage" ("Legacy of the Being-Question"). Here, it is precisely a question of how to think *alētheia* and therefore of how to think as such:

> When you attempt to think, heed beforehand and incessantly the state of affairs that the following word ventures to name: *en tēi archēi ēn kai menei hē Lēthē—tēs A-lētheiēs pēgē*. "In the beginning concealment [*Verbergung*] (the sheltering [*die bergende*]) was and remains the source of unconcealment."[21]

Further, the Pindar material, which Blanchet references only in passing, anticipates the very treatment of the holy in Heidegger's second Trakl lecture.

In this 1952 lecture on the *poète maudit*, Heidegger, unlike many commentators, concentrates not just on the pain and putrefaction, the agony and lamentation, that pervade Trakl's poetry but also on the rarer moments in which the poet prophesies redemption for the West and the possibility of what Trakl in his poem "Song of the Occident" calls, following Boehme and Novalis, "*One Geschlecht*"—a gentle unification, without abolishing difference, of race, sex, generation, species, and even, if we take the dependence on Novalis seriously, color. (Novalis: "Humans, animals, plants, stones and stars, elements, tones, colors, come together like One Family, act and speak like One Geschlecht.")[1] In the meantime, Trakl, like his poetic precursor Arthur Rimbaud and his painter friend Oskar Kokoschka, uses colors in the oddest of ways. At times, these colors border on—or, as some commentators see it, even cross over into—meaninglessness. Trakl lifts color adjectives from their corresponding nouns and places them beside words to which they otherwise do not belong ("the red stillness of your mouth"). There are syntagms impossible to perceive ("black minutes of madness") and *contradictiones in adiecto* ("black snow"). Colors become adverbs ("The sun will shine blackly") or transform into substantives with radically distinct senses ("Out of derelict blueness steps something deceased," "Spiritually, / Blueness dawns over the thrashed forest").[23]

Heidegger, for his part, acknowledges the ambiguity of Trakl's discourse, which is essentially on the way to a new language and locale (*Ortschaft*), or rather to a language and locale that have always been held in store for it, if only in the pauses between everyday chatter and in the cracks of metaphysical, Christian architechtonics. On the one hand, Trakl's poetry must draw on the language from which it is detaching itself. On the other hand, it speaks, full of intimation, of what is to come, namely, the "holiness of blueness" or "the blueness of the holy" (GA 12: 61, 70). "The language of [Trakl's] poetic work," Heidegger explains, "is essentially polysemous, and this in its own way. We will hear nothing of the saying of the poetry so long as we bring to our encounter with it some dull sense of a univocal meaning" (GA 12: 70–71).[24] Heidegger proceeds to adduce examples for such ambiguity, with particular emphasis on Trakl's colors:

> Twilight and night, downgoing and death, madness and wild game, pond and stone, bird-flight and skiff, stranger and brother, spirit and God, likewise the words for color: blue

and green, white and black, red and silver, golden and dark, in each case say something manifold.

"Green" is decaying and blossoming, "white" is pale and pure, "black" is gloomily [*finster*] closing off and darkly [*dunkel*] sheltering, "red" is crimsonly fleshy and rosily gentle. "Silver" is the pallor of death and the sparkle of the stars. "Gold" is the gleam of the true and the "hideous laughter of gold." (GA 12: 71, citing Trakl's "An die Verstummten," "To the Muted")

Heidegger is quick to clarify, however, that the ubiquitous, supposedly dissonant ambiguity of Trakl's vocabulary is not the result of "lax impression." Rather, "ambiguity" is itself ambiguous, and Trakl's comes from the "rigor" of "letting" language and being speak as they give themselves to be spoken. Trakl, like Pindar before him, is hearkening unto a peculiar consonance whose intervals are not, as such, specified, but which—if only we had ears to hear it—has already gathered all the disparate tones into an *Einklang*, not exactly a "unison" in the literal sense of the word, but more like the state of being of a "single accord" (GA 12: 71). We might expect Heidegger to shift registers here and to speak of a color—imperceivable by the senses, but also incapable of depiction in the present state of the world or perhaps even as such—in which all colors are gathered together into an *Einfarbigkeit*, not, for example, white as the totality of wavelengths of visible light or black as the absence of light, but a gathering of color (*Farbe*) into the One (*Ein*). Instead, and despite his overt acknowledgment of its ambiguity, Heidegger seems to except the color blue, along with blue's "darkness," and make it an essential aspect of holy being and of the authentic human response to it. It is noteworthy that, of all the colors Heidegger mentions, he does not provide examples for the bivalent usage of blue in Trakl's oeuvre, although this would not have been hard to do;[25] "dark," for its part, appears only on the gentler, purer, side of "black."

In the poem "Summer's Decline," Trakl sings of a "blue quarry" or "wild blue game" that, he hopes, will "commemorate the path of the stranger" and "the consonance of his spiritual years":

Der grüne Sommer ist so leise
Geworden und es läutet der Schritt

Des Fremdlings durch die silberne Nacht.
Gedächte ein blaues Wild seines Pfads,

Des Wohllauts seiner geistlichen Jahre! (HKA 1: 75)

*

The green summer has become
So quiet and there sounds the step
Of the stranger through the silver night.
Would that a wild blue game commemorate his path,

The consonance of his spiritual years!

On Heidegger's interpretation, the stranger is the one who treads the path away from the corrupt race of contemporary humanity and toward a new, more proper way of dwelling upon the earth. The wild blue game represents those humans who are willing to follow the stranger thoughtfully into this new homeland. To this end, they must heed (related to the German *hüten*, "tend," thus as "shepherds of being" [GA 9: 331, 342]) the holy blue. Glossing a verse from Trakl's "Song of the Occident," which refers to "the gentle cornflower cluster of night" (*das sanfte Zyanenbündel der Nacht*) (HKA 1: 66)—interestingly, unlike the English "cornflower," the German *Zyane*, from Ancient Greek *kuanos*, "cyan," bears a reference to the color of the flower's petals, although the English recalls the golden fields of wheat in which cornflowers grow as weeds (see Van Gogh's *Wheat Field with Cornflowers*)—Heidegger writes:

> The night is a cluster of corn flowers, something gentle. [. . .] The cluster of blueness gathers, in the ground of its spray, the depth of the holy. From out of the blueness, the holy glows [*leuchtet*], even as it veils itself through the blueness's own darkness. The holy holds together [*verhält*] while it withdraws. It confers its arrival by preserving itself in its holding withdrawal. The brightness that is sheltered in darkness is blueness.[26] Bright [*Helle*], i.e., resounding [*hallend*], is originally the tone that calls from out of the sheltering domain of stillness and thus lights up [*sich lichtet*]. Blueness resounds in its brightness

by pealing. In its resounding brightness, the darkness of blueness glows. [. . .] Blue is not an image for the sense of the holy. Blueness itself is the holy, on account of blueness's gathering depth, which only first shines in its veiling. (GA 12: 40; see also 61)

There are numerous parallels between this passage and what we saw Heidegger develop in his Pindar commentary. Blue, like Pindaric gold, is not a mere sign for the holy; it *is* the holy in one of its essential moments. In the Pindar material, Heidegger emphasizes the luminous side of holy being, without, however, ignoring its sheltering concealment (poetized as Theia). Here, he emphasizes withdrawal, even darkness, without, however, ignoring the brightness that it safeguards (poetized, in the spirit of Novalis's hymns, as night). At the ontological, hieratic level—or, in the language of the Trakl lecture, at the level of *Geist*—words indexed to sight intermix with those indexed to sound: we hear the brightness of blueness and see its paradoxically glowing darkness. Furthermore, just as it was crucial for Greek existence, in order to have the requisite regard for gold, to be "caught sight of [*erblickt*], i.e., shined on [*beschienen*] in the pure shining of the godhead" (GA 78: 82), so do modern humans require a colorful illumination in order to "become," to reference Pindar once again, "who they are":[27]

In the poetic name "wild blue game," Trakl calls upon that human essence whose countenance, i.e., counter-gaze, is, in thinking of the steps of the stranger, caught sight of by [*er-blickt*, perhaps: "brought into being through the glimpse of," cf. GA 49: 125–129] the blueness of night and thus is shined on by the holy. The name "wild blue game" names mortals who commemoratively think of the stranger and would like, with him, to wander out to attain the native element [*das Einheimische*] of the human essence. (GA 12: 42)

The poet, above all, is receptive to the resonant illumination of holy blueness, just as the poets of Greece were especially receptive to the shining peal of holy gold: "The lunar coolness of the spiritual night's holy blueness rings and shines throughout all gazing and saying. The language of the latter thus becomes something that speaks after and in accordance with this [*nachsagenden*], it becomes: *poetry*" (GA 12: 67; see also 70).

Heidegger cites numerous poems in support of his interpretation, none perhaps more beautiful than Trakl's "Gesang des Abgeschiedenen" ("Song of the Departed One"), with its blending of sight and sound, light and darkness; its palette of blue and crimson, green and black; its call for Hölderlinian measure and for the *Heiligung*, the "hallowing" or "sanctification," of bread and wine. Heidegger's entire interpretation of Trakl is an effort to understand, to sanctify, and to safeguard the ontological import of what this poem refers to as "the blueness of night" and its sheltering "embrace." Only with efforts of this sort might we, in our current situation of global calamity (*Unheil*), find healing (*Heilung*) and salvation (*Heil*). Only then might we develop a genuine regard for the holy (*das Heilige*).[28]

Voll Harmonien ist der Flug der Vögel. Es haben die
　grünen Wälder
Am Abend sich zu stilleren Hütten versammelt;
Die kristallenen Weiden des Rehs.
Dunkles besänftigt das Plätschern des Bachs, die feuchten
　Schatten

Und die Blumen des Sommers, die schön im Winde läuten.
Schon dämmert die Stirne dem sinnenden Menschen.

Und es leuchtet ein Lämpchen, das Gute, in seinem Herzen
Und der Frieden des Mahls; denn geheiligt ist Brot und Wein
Von Gottes Händen, und es schaut aus nächtigen Augen
Stille dich der Bruder an, daß er ruhe von dorniger Wanderschaft.
O das Wohnen in der beseelten Bläue der Nacht.

Liebend auch umfängt das Schweigen im Zimmer die Schatten
　der Alten,
Die purpurnen Martern, Klage eines großen Geschlechts,
Das fromm nun hingeht im einsamen Enkel.

Denn strahlender immer erwacht aus schwarzen Minuten des
　Wahnsinns
Der Duldende an versteinerter Schwelle
Und es umfängt ihn gewaltig die kühle Bläue und die leuchtende
　Neige des Herbstes,

Das stille Haus und die Sagen des Waldes,
Maß und Gesetz und die mondenen Pfade der Abgeschiedenen.

*

The flight of birds is full of harmonies. The green woods have
Gathered at evening to form lodges of greater stillness;
The crystalline pastures of the roe deer.
The dark makes gentle the splashing of the brook, the moist shadows

And the flowers of summer, which ring out beautifully in the wind.
Already the brow of meditative man enters into twilight.

And a little lamp, the good, shines in his heart
And the peace of the meal; for hallowed are bread and wine
By the hands of God, and from night-like eyes
In stillness the brother beholds you, that he may find rest from thorny wandering.
Oh, dwelling in the besouled blueness of night.

Silence in the room also lovingly embraces the shades of the elderly,
The crimson torments, lamentation of a great lineage,
Which now piously passes on in the solitary grandson.

For ever more radiantly does the tolerant one awaken
From black minutes of madness on a petrified threshold
And embracing him mightily is the cool blueness and the luminous decline of autumn,

The still house and the sayings of the forest,
Measure and law and the lunar paths of the departed ones.
  (HKA 1: 78–79)

§3. A Heideggerian *Farbenlehre*?

To the many well-known words for "being" in Heidegger's oeuvre—*Ereignis*, *Lichtung*, *alētheia*—we must now, after our consideration of Heidegger's interpretation of the holy in Pindar and Trakl, add the colors gold and blue. These colors, to be sure, are not reflections or emissions of light. Nor are they what we perceive, however we may perceive it, on the surface of beings. We are far from optics, or even Goethe's alternative to Newton. Rather, gold and blue *are* being insofar as being shines in truth and shelters in withdrawal. Colors, on Heidegger's theory, are ontological before they are aesthetic.

What, however, would happen to this theory, or at least to the ontological results it arrives at, if we were to consider other poets and other colors, or even if we were to take seriously the *unholiness* of blue in some of Trakl's poems? Perhaps Hölderlin's "yellow pears" and the gentle law of Stifter's *Bunte Steine* would be compatible, but what of Sappho's "more greenish-yellow than grass," Dickinson's "slash of Blue," or Celan's "suppurating gorselight" and yellow-starred "arnica"? What would Heidegger do with the post-Holocaust poet's appeal for a "'grayer' language, a language that, among other things, wants to know that even its 'musicality' is situated in a place where it no longer has anything in common with that 'euphony' which, in a more or less carefree manner, continued to resound in the midst of the most terrible"?[29] Putting Celan's later poetry to the side, what would the *Meister des Denkens* do with the "ashen hair of Shulamite"? Are there colors for the unholy?

Heidegger's poetics of the holy calls for a poetics of sacrilege.

§4. (Un)holy Madness: Trakl with Hölderlin and Celan

In lieu of such a poetology—which, admittedly, would go beyond the scope of this book—I would like, in conclusion, to address a topic that is surely connected with it, if not one of its essential moments: madness. In his translation of Sophocles's *Antigone*, Hölderlin distinctively renders the Greek *atē* ("delusion," "ruin") with the German *Wahnsinn*, a common word for madness. Yet, in his accompanying remarks on the tragedy, Hölderlin also refers to Antigone's "sublime scorn" as a moment of "holy madness [*heiliger Wahnsinn*]" that marks the "highest human manifestation [*Erscheinung*]."[30] Trakl's poetic response to madness, for its part, contains something of this tension between insane destruction and noble estrangement.

In 2015, Trakl's personal copy of Hölderlin's translation was discovered. It was in the third of a three-volume collection of Hölderlin's writings that Wilhelm Böhm edited for the publishing house Eugen

Diederichs.³¹ The paste-down contains Trakl's famous ex libris, designed by painter Max von Esterle. On the facing page is a handwritten poem by Trakl from 1911, previously unknown, bearing the title "Hölderlin." One of the remarkable things about this poem is that it gives us an opportunity to see how Trakl directly responds to his Swabian predecessor. Decades ago, Klaus Mann remarked that Trakl "picked up the lyre that Hölderlin had let sink down."³² Allusions to Hölderlin do abound, but, until this recent discovery, Hölderlin's name did not appear once in Trakl's corpus, and there was only one noteworthy biographical report about Trakl's relation to him: according to Trakl's friend and patron Ludwig von Ficker, Trakl would frequently refer to the idea that Hölderlin "gave the impression of wearing his quiet madness [*stillen Wahnsinn*] like a mask against the world."³³

More importantly, for my present concerns, is the poem's own focus on madness, or *Wahnsinn* in German, which Trakl (mis)spells with three *n*'s (three *s*'s in the translation):

Der Wald liegt herbstlich ausgebreitet
Die Winde ruhn, ihn nicht zu wecken
Das Wild schläft friedlich in Verstecken,
Indes der Bach ganz leise gleitet.

So ward ein edles Haupt verdüstert
In seiner Schönheit Glanz und Trauer
Von Wahnsinnn, den ein frommer Schauer
Am Abend durch die Kräuter flüstert.

*

The forest lies spread out in autumn
The winds repose, as not to wake it
The game sleeps hid away in peace,
The brook so softly glides along.

A noble head was thereby clouded
In shine and sadness of its beauty
By madnesss, which a pious shudder
At evening whispers through the herbs.

The immediate context here is Hölderlin's so-called "period of insanity [*Zeit des Irrsinns*]," the title given by the editor of a different volume of the Böhm edition to the poems Hölderlin composed mainly during the second half of his life, when he was living under the care of a carpenter in a Tübingen tower overlooking the Neckar River.[34] As Trakl biographer Hans Weichselbaum demonstrates, Trakl is doubtless drawing on one of these late poems, titled "Der Frühling ("Spring").[35] But we should not think that Trakl considers madness to be merely negative. The fact that he is carefully reading these putatively insane, supposedly "inane"[36] poems is already telling. Moreover, Trakl frequently associates madness with harmony and insight. "The golden, the true, often shows itself to gentle madness," he writes in the poem "Winkel am Wald" ("Nook in the Forest"), which itself plays on Hölderlin's "Der Winkel von Hahrdt" ("The Nook at Hahrdt") (HKA 1: 21). Elsewhere, the "the holy brother"—Hölderlin, perhaps—is "sunk in the gentle string music of his madness" ("Helian," HKA 1: 40; compare the first and third stanza of Hölderlin's elegy "Brod und Wein," "Bread and Wine"). In another poem reminiscent of "Hölderlin," namely, "In den Nachmittag geflüstert" ("Whispered in the Afternoon"), which Heidegger annotated in his copy of the Salzburg edition of Trakl's poems, Trakl writes:

> Stirne Gottes Farben träumt,
> Spürt des Wahnsinns sanfte Flügel. (HKA 1: 30)

*

> The brow dreams God's colors,
> Feels the gentle wings of madness.

According to literary scholar Ingrid Strohschneider-Kohrs, whose work Heidegger greatly admired, "[i]n Trakl, the word 'madness' does not signify a state of mental illness [*kranken Seelenzustand*], but rather immersion in an incomprehensibly powerful and true reality."[37]

Heidegger, who shows particular interest in this theme—not just in his interpretations of Hölderlin and Trakl, but also, as we saw in chapter 1, in his marginalia to the testimonials and recollections in the Zurich edition[38]—comes to a similar conclusion. Of Hölderlin, he writes:

> Hölderlin's poems from the period between 1800 and 1806 are obscure [*dunkel*, "dark"]; the inner connections seem to be missing. On the other hand, one knows of the approaching madness [*Wahnsinns*] in these years. The case of Hölderlin is therefore clear. No. Taken in this way, it is not at all clear, since, with the fixation of one's gaze on the evident psychological-biological explanation of the work as the "product" of someone "deranged" [*"Verrückten"*], the work, indeed, does not at all come to word, but only the presumptuous all-knowingness of those who are supposedly "normal" and not deranged. To be sure, the poet was deranged, in the sense of a de-ranging [*Ver-rückung*] of his essence, which had been ranged out [*herausgerückt*] of the night of his time. This essential deranging then had, as a result, a "derangement" [*"Verrücktheit"*] that was certainly also one of a kind. But from the result the ground can never be grasped. (GA 52: 43)

In "Language in the Poem," Heidegger goes further, claiming that Trakl's figure of the *Wahnsinniger* actually has nothing to do with madness in the way we typically understand this word. Heidegger again tries to resolve the paradox with recourse to etymology:

> Does [the *Wahnsinniger*] signify someone who is mentally ill [*Geisteskranken*, "sick in spirit"]? No. *Wahnsinn* does not mean the pondering [*Sinnen*] that imagines what is nonsensical [*Unsinniges wähnt*]. "*Wahn*" belongs to the Old High German *wana* and means: without. The *Wahnsinniger* ponders, and he even ponders like no one else. But he thereby remains without the sense [*Sinn*] of the others [namely, of those who belong to the degenerate *Geschlecht*]. He is of another sense. "*Sinnan*" means originally: to travel, to strive after . . . , to strike a direction; the Indo-Germanic root *sent* and *set* means path. The detached or departed one [*Der Abgeschiedene*] is the *Wahnsinniger*, because he is on the way to elsewhere. From there, his *Wahnsinn* may be called "gentle"; for he ponders after [*sinnt . . . nach*] what is stiller. (GA 12: 49, citing Trakl's "Helian")[39]

However, there are unmistakable moments in Trakl's corpus when madness becomes gruesome, malicious, and incestuous, characteristic of the decaying *Geschlecht* from which, in Heidegger's reading, the *Wahnsinniger* is supposedly detaching himself. Trakl sings of a "countenance full of insane ferocity [*Grausamkeit und Irrsinn*]" and laments "the madness of the metropolis" with its "spirit of evil." "Woe," he writes in the prose poem "Traum und Umnachtung" ("Dream and Lunacy"), "woe, the stony eyes of the sister, when at table her madness trod the nocturnal brow of the brother, under the mother's suffering hands the bread became stone."⁴⁰ Here, we are confronted with an anti-miracle, a surrender to temptation, an unholy madness that leads not to redemption but to ruin (*atē*) (cf. Matthew 4:3, Luke 4:3).

Heidegger, like Strohschneider-Kohrs, largely ignores such moments in his interpretation, moments that Heidegger would in any case view as transfigured in the higher unity of the "O n e *Geschlecht*": the new race, species, or gender to come. Even if Trakl's emphatic spacing allows for the difference of derangement, whether mental or otherwise, this would, for Heidegger, be a difference that makes little difference to the single *logos* under which it is gathered.⁴¹

But, to return to Trakl's "Hölderlin," what of the word or mark *Wahnsinnn*, with its three *n*'s? Is the last *n* merely a slip of the pen? If you look at the facsimile, you will notice that there are no crossed-out words or corrections. This is not a poem hastily jotted down on whatever paper happened to be at hand. It is a tribute to one of Trakl's masters, neatly arranged at the beginning of his personal copy of that master's works. Whatever the case may be—and how could we ever know, unless other versions of the poem were to emerge?—the three-*n*-ed *Wahnsinnn* resists the sort of sense that Heidegger locates in Trakl's poetry and therefore in Hölderlin and his madness. The supernumerary *n* draws attention away from the meaning to the mark, from the signified to a letter that either does not signify or is, conversely, perhaps the only way to signify madness, provided that there is something irredeemably sense-less (*wana sin*) about it. *Wahnsinn*, madness, would then *have* to be misspelled. Of course, the moment I write it anew, the word regains graphic and semantic stability, and I am forced (by madness, the "thing"?) to alter the mark once again, this time with a fourth *n*, for instance. Trakl's *Wahnsinnn*, or *Wahnsinnñ . . .*, this recursive +n, would accordingly stand on the side of dissemination in the gigantomachia over gathering between Derrida and Heidegger.

Image 7. Trakl's ex libris and manuscript of the poem "Hölderlin," in his personal copy of Hölderlin's *Dramen und Übersetzungen*.

In 1911, Trakl had an eye—"perhaps," like Oedipus and Hölderlin himself, "one eye too many"[42]—not just for the horrifying truth of his and Hölderlin's times but for the truth of the horrors to come. To stay true to these truths, one must struggle with and against language; one must slacken syntax and subvert logical sequence, hold out consonants, for example, until they become senseless sounds (see HKA 1: 274). Colors must take on new meanings or even, as Trakl editor Walther Killy has argued, lose symbolic value altogether. In these respects, Trakl is a precursor of Paul Celan, who, for his part, saw Trakl's colors as subversive "counter-words" rather than, like Heidegger, as aspects of the holy (at least regarding gold and blue).[43]

Celan was also moved by Hölderlin's *Wahnsinn(n)*. I do not just mean the night Celan drowned himself in the River Seine, when he left behind on his desk a copy of Wilhelm Michel's biography of Hölderlin, open to a page on which Celan had underlined the following portion of a citation from Clemens Brentano: "Sometimes this genius becomes dark and sinks into the bitter wells of his heart."⁴⁴ I also mean Celan's poem "Tübingen, Jänner" ("Tübingen, January"), written in response to Hölderlin's *Wahnsinn*, to the aftermath of the January 1942 *Wannsee* Conference, and to the "thousand darknesses [*Finsternisse*, 'eclipses'] of death-bringing discourse."⁴⁵ It is with this poem, with its reference to Hölderlin's idiolectic (non)word *Pallaksch* (at once "yes" and "no"), that I will bring this chapter to a close. Celan, too, knows something of the incessancy of madnesss . . .

    Zur Blindheit über-
    redete Augen.
    Ihre—"ein
    Rätsel ist Rein-
    entsprungenes"—, ihre
    Erinnerung an
    schwimmende Hölderlintürme, möven-
    umschwirrt.

    Besuche ertrunkener Schreiner bei
    diesen
    tauchenden Worten:

    Käme,
    käme ein Mensch,
    käme ein Mensch zur Welt, heute, mit
    dem Lichtbart der
    Patriarchen: er dürfte,
    spräch er von dieser
    Zeit, er
    dürfte
    nur lallen und lallen,
    immer-, immer-
    zuzu.

    ("Pallaksch. Pallaksch.")

    *

    Into blindness out-
    talked eyes.

Their—"an
enigma is what has purely
sprung forth"—their
recollection of
swimming Hölderlin-towers, gull-
engulfed.

Visits from drowned carpenters to
these
diving words:

Come,
if a human were to come,
if a human were to come into the world, today, with
the beard of light of the
Patriarchs: he'd dare,
if he were to speak of this
time, he'd
dare
only babble and babble,
in-, in-
cesscessantly.

("Pallaksch. Pallaksch.")[46]

Chapter 6

Geschlecht

Nicht der Mann oder das Weib soll Gottes Reich besitzen, sondern die Jungfrau, die aus des Mannes und Weibes Tode ausgeboren wird, soll Königin der Himmel sein. Ein Geschlecht, nicht zwei, ein Baum, nicht viele! Christus war der Stamm, weil er die Wurzel des neuen Leibes war, der aus dem Tode gründete, der die verstorbene Jungfrau wieder als einen schönen Zweig aus dem Tode ausführte. Und wir alle sind die Äste und stehen alle auf einem Stamme, der ist Christus.[1]

—Jakob Boehme

Menschen, Thiere, Pflanzen, Steine und Gestirne, Elemente, Töne, Farben kommen zusammen wie Eine Familie, handeln und sprechen wie Ein Geschlecht.[2]

—Novalis

Einst ist alles Leib,
E i n Leib,
In himmlischem Blute
Schwimmt das selige Paar.[3]

—Novalis

In his personal copy of the Salzburg edition of Trakl's *Die Dichtungen*, Heidegger wrote in lead pencil, at the top of the poem "In ein altes Stammbuch" ("Into an Old Family Album"): "Das Buch des Geschlechts u. seines Wesens!" "The book of the *Geschlecht* and its essence!" For the moment, I will leave this most enigmatic of German words untranslated. Let us listen, first, to Trakl's poem, which initially bore the title "An die Melancholie" ("To Melancholy"):

> Immer wieder kehrst du Melancholie,
> O Sanftmut der einsamen Seele
> Zu Ende glüht ein goldener Tag.
>
> Demutsvoll beugt sich dem Schmerz der Geduldige
> Tönend von Wohllaut und weichem Wahnsinn.
> Siehe! es dämmert schon.
>
> Wieder kehrt die Nacht und klagt ein Sterbliches
> Und es leidet ein anderes mit.
>
> Schaudernd unter herbstlichen Sternen
> Neigt sich jährlich tiefer das Haupt. (HKA 1: 22–23)

*

> Again and again you return, melancholy,
> Oh, gentleness of the solitary soul.
> A golden day gleams and comes to an end.
>
> Humbly the patient one bends before pain
> Ringing with sounds of harmony and soft madness.
> Look! already it is twilight.
>
> Again the night returns and something mortal laments
> And another thing suffers in sympathy.
>
> Shuddering under autumnal stars
> Each year the head declines more deeply.

Here, in contrast to Nietzsche's eternal recurrence, the return of the days and seasons brings, not the same, but further decline. We are not moving in a circle; we are moving down a spiral, away from any center that would hold. After Wagner's *Götterdämmerung* comes a *Menschheitsdämmerung*, a "twilight of humanity," as Kurt Pinthus titled his celebrated compilation of

German expressionist poetry (1920). One might also call this crepuscule a *Menschengeschlechtsdämmerung*, a "twilight of the human race."

It is in this sense that Heidegger primarily understands the word *Geschlecht* in "Language in the Poem." Drawing on its cognates *Schlag* ("blow," "stroke," "type") and *verschlagen* ("to strike," often in a fatal or fateful sense), Heidegger explains:

> Our [German] language names the human essence that is stamped on the basis of a stroke [*aus einem Schlag geprägte*] and struck into this type [*in diesen Schlag verschlagene*] the "*Geschlecht.*" [. . .] The poet names the *Geschlecht* of the "decayed shape" [. . .] of the human the "decaying" *Geschlecht* [. . .]. It is set out [*herausgesetzt*] from the manner of its essence [*Art seines Wesens*] and for this reason is the "displaced" [*"entsetzte,"* less literally, "horrified"] *Geschlecht*. (GA 12: 45–46, quoting "Siebengesang des Todes," "Der Abend," and "Traum und Umnachtung"; "Sevensong of Death," "The Evening," and "Dream and Lunacy")

But we must be careful. For twilight occurs not only at evening but also at dawn, as both Pinthus and Heidegger stress.[4] Even if "Into an Old Family Album" ends sadly, its gentle music of forbearance and sympathy is in accord with the promise of what another poem names the "*One Geschlecht*" (HKA 1: 66): not just one race, but also, in Heidegger's words, a unification of "the *Geschlechter* [plural] in the sense of tribes, clans, and families, all of this in turn stamped into the double [*Zwiefache*] of the *Geschlechter* ["sexes" or "genders" presumably, words that Heidegger, in any case, does not distinguish]" (GA 12: 46).

One might wonder whether a word with so many disparate senses—alongside gender, tribe, clan, family, and race (of humans, gods, etc.), *Geschlecht* can signify lineage, dynasty, species, generation, and genitals—should even be called a word, provided that words always have some unifying referent, some Aristotelian *pros-hen* relation, in cases of polysemy.[5] Here, the human species might serve as such a referent, although, in the passage above, Heidegger says the *Menschengeschlecht* is "in turn" affected by what comes after it in the order of implications, that is to say, by sexual difference, be it the first stroke of gentle twofoldness or the second of raging dissension. Later in "Language in the Poem," Heidegger completes a similar taxonomy with the claim that "the word

'Geschlecht' everywhere names the twofold of the Geschlechter," which, again, seems like it must refer to the male and female sex (GA 12: 75; emphasis added). Geschlecht as race or Geschlecht as sex? Even Heidegger, it appears, cannot decide on a focal meaning or core-dependent homonymy. Perhaps it will not be so easy to prevent dissemination, after all. Perhaps the book of the Geschlecht narrates the downfall not just of "Man" but also of "Geschlecht" itself. Perhaps Geschlecht is, then, more a marker of discontinuity than a word properly speaking, especially when we consider that the mark Geschlecht is actually a re-marking of the Schlag, the "strike of coinage," that stands at its origin. (Note that my very attempt to demarcate the meaning of Schlag presupposes the ability to mark it out; it presupposes the Schlag it is trying to define. Hence Heidegger's use of the cognate nominative phrase der Schlag schlägt, "the strike strikes," GA 12: 46; cf. GIII: 150.)

Furthermore, in an etymological dictionary that Heidegger consulted while taking as-yet-unpublished notes on Trakl's use of Geschlecht, the philologist Friedrich Kluge speculates that one of the Old Teutonic roots of Geschlecht probably had the sense of "begetting," which, together with sex in all its senses, would complicate Heidegger's effort to keep Sein and the human free of biological and animal contamination. It is worth citing extensively from this entry, if only to appreciate better how, as Derrida puts it in the first of his four texts devoted to the problem of Geschlecht in Heidegger, "one will not so easily clear away the mark of the word ('Geschlecht') that blocks our access to the thing itself (the Geschlecht)":

> GESCHLACHT, adj., "of good quality, soft, tender, shapely," from MidHG. geslaht, OHG. gislaht, "well brought up, noble, well behaved" ["*wohlgeartet, edel, geartet*"]; UNGESCHLACHT, "uncouth, unwieldy, boorish," even in MidHG. ungeslaht, OHG. ungislaht, "ignoble, base." Allied to ModHG. GESCHLECHT, n., "species, race, extraction, family," from MidHG. geshlehte, n., "race, tribe, family, quality" ["*Geschlecht, Stamm, Familie, Eigenschaft*"], OHG. gislahti; comp. OHG. slahta, f., "race [Geschlecht], family," MidHG. slahte, "manner, relation" ["*Art, Verwandtschaft*"]; akin also to SCHLAG (e.g., MENSCHENSCHLAG, "race of men"), foreign to OHG. and MidHG. It is difficult to determine the relation of these cognates to SCHLAGEN ["to strike"]; even in OHG. slahan itself means "to take after, resemble" ["*nacharten, nachschlagen*"]

(e.g., *nâh dên fordôrôn slahan*, "to resemble one's ancestors"), for which in late MidHG. *nâch-slahen* occurs, ModHG. NACHSCHLAGEN. Probably the str. vb. in OTeut. once had the meaning "to beget," which cannot now be authenticated.[6]

Throughout the book, we have seen many instances in which Trakl's poetry prompts Heidegger to reflect on issues that would otherwise seem to come within the purview of regional ontologies, the positive sciences, or the altogether separate domain of faith, issues such as pain, color, and Christianity. In this chapter, I would like to explore two more of these, both bearing marks of "*Geschlecht*."

The first issue, sexual difference, might seem to be a matter of indifference to the thinker of being, who in any case has little to say about it apart from an appendix to a lecture course on Leibniz and from his commentary on Trakl. Yet Heidegger's engagement with the Austrian poet leads him—inadvertently perhaps, or even despite himself—to compose, in Derrida's words again, "a grand discourse on sexual difference" (GIII: 49), one that will in turn lead us to a host of questions about other underrepresented matters such as maternity and sorority, eros and androgyny.

The second issue, animality, appears throughout Heidegger's corpus, but, with one notable exception (GA 29/30), precisely as a *non*-issue for thought. Heidegger takes pains to hold the human essence apart from its "abyssal bodily affinity to the animal" (GA 9: 326). Indeed, Agamben has called him, without qualification, "the philosopher of the twentieth century who more than any other strove to separate man from the living being."[7] Even in his comments on *Geschlecht*, Heidegger, like Kluge before him, neglects to mention that the word names, not just "humankind [*Menschheit*] as opposed to the other living beings (plant and animal)" (GA 12: 74–75), but any species (*Art*) or genus, "the *Geschlecht* of cats," for example.[8] Yet, if there was a time when Heidegger could interpret the animal only as dazed, unthinking, inarticulate, incapable of genuine death, and unable to see beings for what they are—in short, as "poor in world" (GA 29/30: 263 et passim)—in his commentary on Trakl, Heidegger will strike a different path (*einen anderen Weg einschlagen*) on which to contemplate, as Andrew Mitchell puts it, "a new relation between mortality and animality, problematizing the distinction between the two."[9] We will have to see how far he goes along this path, and whether he does not end up turning back to familiar territory.

§1. "A Grand Discourse on Sexual Difference"

To begin, I would like to approach the question of sexual difference by way of Heidegger's marginalia to Trakl's "Gesang des Abgeschiedenen" ("Song of the Departed One"). Judging from a page reference in his annotations to "Grodek," Heidegger initially turned to "Song of the Departed One" because of the latter's reference to an *Enkel* ("grandson" or "descendant") in the last verse of the fourth stanza.[10] Using the symbols ">" and "<," Heidegger marked off this verse, together with the next two verses in the fifth. For orientation, here are these stanzas, as well as the sixth, final one, with Heidegger's symbols interpolated:

> Liebend auch umfängt das Schweigen im Zimmer die
>   Schatten der Alten,
> Die purpurnen Martern, Klage eines großen Geschlechts,
> > Das fromm nun hingeht im einsamen Enkel.
>
> Denn strahlender immer erwacht aus schwarzen Minuten des
>   Wahnsinns
> Der Duldende an versteinerter Schwelle <
> Und es umfängt ihn gewaltig die kühle Bläue und die
>   leuchtende Neige des Herbstes,
>
> Das stille Haus und die Sagen des Waldes,
> Maß und Gesetz und die mondenen Pfade der Abgeschiedenen.
>   (DD: 171–172)

*

> Silence in the room also lovingly embraces the shades of
>   the elderly,
> The crimson torments, lamentation of a great lineage,
> > Which now piously passes on in the solitary grandson.
>
> For ever more radiantly does the tolerant one awaken
> From black minutes of madness on a petrified threshold, <
> And embracing him mightily is the cool blueness and the
>   luminous decline of autumn,

The still house and the sayings of the forest,
Measure and law and the lunar paths of the departed ones.

There are many moments in these stanzas that could have struck Heidegger and led him to make connections to his reading of Trakl in his two lectures on the poet. These moments include the petrified threshold, which appears also in "Ein Winterabend" ("A Winter Evening"); *Wahnsinn*, which means "madness," but which Heidegger interprets as *wana sin*, "lacking the sensibility" of the putrescent *Geschlecht*; and, of course, *Geschlecht* itself, which I have rendered here as "lineage." What I would like to focus on, however, are two additional annotations Heidegger made, which will bring us to other connotations of *Geschlecht*: (1) he partially underlined the word *fromm*, "piously," and (2) he crossed out the *r* in the plural genitive article of the final syntagm *der Abgeschiedenen*, "of the departed *ones*," and replaced it with an *s* in the margin, thus making it *des Abgeschiedenen*, "of the departed *one*."[11]

(1) Why, of all the words in the poem, might Heidegger have shown particular interest in the word *fromm*? Two explanations come to mind. First, *fromm* might have made Heidegger think of *fremd* ("foreign" or "strange") and of its obsolete etonym *fram*, "on the way to." *Fromm* and *fram* are, after all, not just morphologically similar but derive from the same roots.[12] This reading finds support in the verb from the verse, "That now piously passes on [*fromm nun hingeht*] in the solitary grandson." *Hingehen* suggests death—Trakl at one point considered the verb *hinstirbt* (HKA 2: 263)—but literally means "going thither." Whether Trakl understands this to mean that a great *Geschlecht* is on the way toward the earth, going forth toward a new birth that would bring reconciliation once and for all, is another matter, as we saw in chapter 3 and will return to in the final chapter.

Second, and relatedly, Heidegger could be thinking of his occasional association of *fromm*, "pious," with *fügsam*, "compliant." As he puts it in "Language in the Poem":

> Detachment pulls hearing into its harmonious sound beforehand, in order that this sound might resound throughout the saying in which it echoes. The lunar coolness of the spiritual night's holy blueness rings and shines throughout all gazing and saying. The language of the latter thus becomes something

that speaks after and in accordance with this [*nachsagenden*], it becomes: *poetry.* [. . .] The saying that is called into hearing, the saying that is after and in accordance, thereby becomes "more pious" ["*frömmer*"], i.e., more compliant [*fügsamer*] with the exhortation of the path on which the stranger goes out in advance, [moving] from the darkness of childhood into the stiller, brighter earliness. (GA 12: 67, quoting "Kindheit," "Childhood"; see also GA 7: 35; GA 55: 145)

Although *fromm* and *fügsam* are unrelated etymologically, there is a semantic overlap. For instance, in German one can speak of a *frommes Pferd*, "a compliant horse," and the modern German verb *frommen* has the sense of "being of use." As Herman Büttner once rendered a famous apocryphal saying by Meister Eckhart, "Ein Lebemeister frommte mehr denn tausend Lesemeister," "A master of life would be of greater benefit than a thousand masters of letters."[13] Heidegger can accordingly understand the piety of thought as compliantly serving the exhortation of being, even before all questioning (GA 12: 165).[14] Unsurprisingly, he finds a similar piety, a companion piety of poetizing, in Trakl's *Gedicht*, where we are called to compliance not only with being, but with the stranger *himself*.

(2) This particular *Gedicht* bears the title "Song of the Departed One," although it ends with a reference to the "lunar paths of the departed *ones*," perhaps joining the speaker with the ubiquitous figure of the sister or with Trakl's brother-in-spirit Karl Borromäus Heinrich. Heidegger, as mentioned, changed the phrase in his personal copy to read, "lunar paths of the departed *one*." It is doubtful he believed he was correcting the editor, as the Salzburg edition, which he mainly used, also has the plural, and Heidegger even cites the phrase in the plural in "Language in the Poem" (GA 12: 48). Perhaps Heidegger wanted to note the inconsistency between, on the one hand, the title of the poem (and of the grouping in which the poem appears) and, on the other, the poem's final verse. Or perhaps he was marking the fact that, in earlier versions of the poem, Trakl had the singular article *des* (HKA 2: 263).[15] Whatever the case may be on the factual level, philosophically and exegetically Heidegger is interested in a certain type of singularity: not, to be sure, the scattered splinters of accursed dissension (GA 12: 24, 46), but something more akin to the authentic individuation that is afforded by anxiety (SZ: 39, 187–191). The poem names the departed *ones*, and

yet, Heidegger claims, it "aims specifically at the 'departed *one*' [*eigens dem 'Abgeschiedenen' gilt*]" (GA 12: 48; emphasis added). The stranger may have followers, who may in turn become detached and strange, too (GA 12: 64, 66). Nonetheless, in Heidegger's reading, it is *he*, the masculine singular one, who leads the way. The sister, the feminine as such, remains secondary—when, that is, she is not silenced altogether.

Heidegger does not often mention the figure of the sister in "Language in the Poem," despite her frequent appearance as a sign of guilt, torment, protection, or transfiguration throughout Trakl's oeuvre, from beginning to end. But when Heidegger does mention her (GA 12: 45, 66, 72), "one cannot," as David Krell puts it, "get over the feeling that the sister is being manhandled."[16] For example, Heidegger explains, with extreme amphiboly, that,

> insofar as the hearkening friend sings the "Song of the Departed One" and thus becomes the brother of the latter [i.e., of the departed one, who is also the stranger], the brother [i.e., the now-fraternized friend] of the stranger becomes, only first by means of the latter [i.e., the stranger], the brother of his sister [*wird der Bruder des Fremdlings durch diesen erst zum Bruder seiner Schwester*], the sister whose "lunar voice sounds through the spiritual night," as the final verses of the poem "Geistliche Dämmerung" ["Spiritual Twilight"] [. . .] say. (GA 12: 66)

It is unclear whose sister Heidegger has in mind. The friend's? Or the stranger's? The German is ambiguous. If the masculine possessive pronoun refers to the friend, it would mean that he, the friend—and therefore everyone (everyman?) who wishes to abandon the corrupt *Geschlecht*— must become a brother to the stranger in order to be a proper brother to his, the friend's, own sister or to whatever this figure stands for. Calamitous incest will cease only when the discord between the sexes, which *Geschlecht* typically signifies in the plural, becomes a gentle twofold: "As the spirit of the gentle, that which gathers [. . .] stills the spirit of evil [*Bösen*]. The latter's insurrection reaches its most extreme maliciousness [*Bösartigkeit*] where it even breaks out of the discord of the sexes [*Geschlechter*] and breaks into the sibling realm [*das Geschwisterliche*]" (GA 12: 63). If, however, the masculine possessive pronoun refers to the stranger, it would mean that the friend's own sister, or whatever this figure stands for, is irrelevant to his, the friend's, spiritual journey.

Little wonder that Grete Langen, née Trakl, never appears in Heidegger's emplacement of Trakl's poetry.

Based on an earlier passage in the lecture, Heidegger appears to mean the latter, that is to say, the sister of the stranger, a sister whom Heidegger metonymically associates with the moon and dissociates from any ties to blood, whether lineal, menstrual, or that of *Blutschuld*, a word that Trakl uses for "incest" (cf. *Blutschande*) but that literally means "blood guilt" or "blood crime" (see the early poem by that name in HKA 1: 146). Commenting on the final stanzas of "Spiritual Twilight"—

> Auf schwarzer Wolke
> Befährst du trunken von Mohn
> Den nächtigen Weiher,
>
> Den Sternenhimmel.
> Immer tönt der Schwester mondene Stimme
> Durch die geistliche Nacht. (HKA 1: 65)

*

> On a black cloud
> Your ride, drunken with poppy,
> The nocturnal pond,
>
> The spangled sky.
> Ever the lunar voice of the sister sounds
> Through the spiritual night.

—Heidegger writes:

> In the nocturnal pond of the spangled sky [. . .] the twilit blueness of the spiritual night appears. Its gleam is cool. / The cool light stems from the shining of the mooness [*Möndin*] (*selanna*). All around her luminosity, even the stars become pale and cool, as ancient Greek verses say [verses by Sappho, to be exact, whom Heidegger neglects to mention].[17] Everything becomes "lunar" ["*monden*"]. (GA 12: 44–45)

But is the sister also irrelevant to the stranger's journey? It might seem, at this point, that the sister leads the way, even if the stranger stands next in line. However, Heidegger immediately shifts his focus to the stranger himself, whose own luminosity supplants that of the sister as celestial body and beacon. First the stranger is lunar, then golden like the sun. The stranger may, at the outset, seem to share in the lunar light. But, in the following passage, as in physics, the brightness of the moon turns out to be nothing more than his own projection:

> The foreign/strange man [Der . . . Fremde], treading through the night, is called "the lunar one" ["der Mondene"] [in Trakl's poem "Anif"]. The "lunar voice" of the sister, which always sounds through the spiritual night, is heard by the brother when, in his skiff, which is still "black" and barely lit by the golden [color, vom Goldenen] of the stranger [Fremdlings], he [i.e., the brother] attempts to follow the latter [i.e., the stranger] on the nocturnal pond-journey.
>
> When mortals wander in pursuit of and in accordance with [nachwandern] the "strange thing" [dem . . . "Fremden"], and that means now the stranger [Fremdling], who is called into downgoing, they themselves reach the foreign/strange [gelangen . . . ins Fremde], themselves become strangers [Fremdlinge] and solitary ones (64, 87 et alibi). (GA 12: 45)[18]

And that means now the stranger. Trakl does, to be sure, speak in many poems of *der Fremdling*, the *male* stranger. Yet the sister is also strange and often has a guiding power all her own. We can hear this in Trakl's "Psalm," which Heidegger discreetly refers to at the end of the block quote (p. 64 of the Salzburg edition), but which, as with his discreet reference to Sappho's *selanna*, he never develops:

> Die fremde Schwester erscheint wieder in jemands bösen Träumen.
> Ruhend im Haselgebüsch spielt sie mit seinen Sternen.
>
> *
>
> The strange sister appears again in someone's evil dreams.
> Resting in the hazel bushes, she plays with his stars. (HKA 1: 31)

Trakl, like Hölderlin before him, even speaks of a *Fremdlingin*, or "strangeress," a figure Heidegger never mentions in "Language in the

Poem" and mentions only once, to my knowledge, in his readings of Hölderlin (GA 75: 205), where, however, he does nothing with the gender.[19] Trakl writes:

> Seltsam sind die nächtigen Pfade des Menschen. Da ich nachtwandelnd an steinernen Zimmern hinging und es brannte in jedem ein stilles Lämpchen, ein kupferner Leuchter, und da ich frierend aufs Lager hinsank, stand zu Häupten wieder der schwarze Schatten der Fremdlingin und schweigend verbarg ich das Antlitz in den langsamen Händen. (HKA 1: 95, "Offenbarung und Untergang," "Revelation and Downfall")

*

> Peculiar are the human's nocturnal paths. When, sleepwalking, I went past stone rooms and there burned in each a still little lamp, a copper candlestick, and when, freezing, I sank down on the bed, at the head again stood the black shadow of the strangeress and silently I buried my countenance in languid hands.

In Heidegger's reading, however, the sister is not strange by nature, as it were, but only by grace of her male counterpart. She *becomes* a stranger, she *reaches* this state, only in his wake. The sister, in short, remains subordinate to what is colloquially called *das starke Geschlecht*, "the stronger sex." Or, in Simone de Beauvoir's terminology, she is always of "the other sex" (*das andere Geschlecht*, as Beauvoir's opus magnum is titled in German translation).

This stereotypical subordination is present even when Heidegger is describing the gentle confluence of the sexes in the first stroke of spirit, before it has broken out into discord and corrupted the innocence of youth. Not the sister, but Trakl's mysterious figure of the pure, dead boy Elis, whom Heidegger links with the stranger, stands at the forefront:

> In the figure of the boy Elis, the boyish [*Knabenhafte*] does not consist in an opposition to the girlish [*Mädchenhaften*]. The boyish is the appearance [*Erscheinung*] of the stiller childhood. The latter shelters and keeps within itself the gentle twofold of the sexes [*Geschlechter*], of the youth [*Jünglings*] as well as the "golden figure of the youthess [*Jünglingin*]." (GA 12: 51)

Why, after referencing the girlish—which he never does elsewhere—does Heidegger leave this figure behind in the transition to stiller childhood? Do girls fail to give the appearance of pacification? Or, taking *Erscheinung* literally, as "shining forth," does the promise of a concordant difference between brother and sister not manifest itself in the *Mädchen*, who, however, almost always appears in the plural in Trakl's poems? Why does Heidegger not develop the rare word *Jünglingin* (which is modeled on *Fremdlingin* and, as we will see, the similarly rare word *Mönchin* or "monkess")[20] in Trakl's poem "Das Herz" ("The Heart"), especially since it is she who marks the shift to spiritual restoration after blazing, gruesome battle?

> Aus dunklem Hausflur trat
> Die goldne Gestalt
> Der Jünglingin
> Umgeben von bleichen Monden,
> Herbstlicher Hofstaat,
> Zerknickten schwarze Tannen
> Im Nachtsturm,
> Die steile Festung.
> O Herz
> Hinüberschimmernd in schneeige Kühle. (HKA 1: 87–88)
>
> *
>
> From the dark hallway stepped
> The golden figure
> Of the youthess
> Surrounded by pale moons,
> Autumnal entourage,
> Black firs snapped
> In the nocturnal storm,
> The steep fortress.
> O heart
> Shimmering across into snowy coolness.

Why, furthermore, does Heidegger neglect to consider other relationships between male and female, be they familial, amicable, professional, or erotic? Would none of these belong to the serener twosome? And what of same-sex, intersex, and queer relationships?

It is, to be sure, remarkable that Heidegger does not try to erase difference, even sexual difference, from the origin. Indeed, if we take seriously comments Heidegger makes elsewhere on the non-primordiality of counting and on the possibility of a "potency [*Mächtigkeit*] of essence" (GA 26: 172) that, as Derrida interprets it, is not necessarily asexual even though it neutrally precedes the fixed dyad (which, one could argue, inevitably ends up in service of the masculine sex), then even the gentle twofold of the *Geschlechter* need not be bound by dichotomy, let alone the dichotomy of girls and boys. Such a reading would, I admit, require a level of interpretive generosity parallel to that of Derrida's own attempt to think a positive and non-dual sexual difference in Heidegger's earlier work.[21] For all its eclipses—the obfuscation of the lovers, for instance—Heidegger's reading of Trakl's "Abendländisches Lied" ("Song of the Occident") nevertheless invites the consideration. Here, again, is the poem's final stanza, which I discussed back in chapter 3:

> O, die bittere Stunde des Untergangs,
> Da wir ein steinernes Antlitz in schwarzen Wassern beschaun.
> Aber strahlend heben die silbernen Lider die Liebenden:
> E i n Geschlecht. Weihrauch strömt von rosigen Kissen
> Und der süße Gesang der Auferstandenen. (HKA 1: 66)

*

> Oh, the bitter hour of downfall,
> When we behold a stony countenance in black waters.
> But radiantly the lovers raise their silver eyelids:
> O n e *Geschlecht*. Incense streams from rosy pillows,
> And the sweet song of the resurrected ones.

Concentrating on the word *Geschlecht*—which certainly refers to sex or gender, but, given the earlier stanzas, also connotes both diachronic generations and synchronic tribes, nations, and peoples—Heidegger writes:

> The "One" is emphasized. It is, so far as I see, the only word in Trakl's poems that is written *gesperrt* ["spaced out for emphasis"].[22] This emphasized "*One Geschlecht*" shelters the fundamental tone from which the *Gedicht* of this poet

safeguards the mystery in silence [*das Geheimnis schweigt*]. The unity of the *one Geschlecht* wells up from the blow [*Schlag*] that—on the basis of detachment, of the stiller stillness prevailing in it, of its "sayings of the forest," of its "measure and law"—simply [*einfältig*, "artlessly"] gathers the discord of the *Geschlechter* into the gentler twofold [*Zwiefalt*] by way of the "lunar paths of the departed ones." (GA 12: 74, quoting "Song of the Departed One")

Heidegger proceeds to make three qualifications: he does not mean number in the sense of arithmetical value or quantity, he is not talking about biology, and *Geschlecht* means more than sexual difference, even if the latter is always in play:

> The "*One*" in the word "*One Geschlecht*" does not mean [the number] "one" ["*eins*"] instead of "two." Nor does the "*One*" signify the monotonous one-and-the-same-ness of a vapid equality [*Einerlei einer faden Gleichheit*]. The word "*One Geschlecht*" here does not name any factual finding in biology at all, be it "unisexualism" ["*Eingeschlechtlichkeit*"] or "asexuality" ["*Gleichgeschlechtlichkeit*"]. (GA 12: 74)

Since the last two are supposed to be examples from biology, I take it Heidegger is referring to gonochorism and asexual reproduction, although *Gleichgeschlechtlichkeit* also means "homosexuality." Heidegger continues:

> In the emphasized "*One* Geschlecht," there is concealed the unifying that unifies on the basis of the gathering blueness of the spiritual night. The word speaks from the song in which the land of evening is sung. Accordingly, the word "*Geschlecht*" retains here its full [. . .] manifold meaning. To begin with [*einmal*], it names the historical *Geschlecht* of the human, humankind [*Menschheit*] as opposed to the other living beings (plant and animal). The word "*Geschlecht*" then names the *Geschlechter*, the tribes, clans, families of this *Menschengeschlecht*. At the same time, the word "*Geschlecht*" everywhere names the twofold of the *Geschlechter*. (GA 12: 74–75; see also 45–46, 63)

Despite the secondariness of the selenic sister, and despite the stated ubiquity of the twofold, Heidegger's "grand discourse on sexual difference" (GIII: 49) invites contemplation of other possibilities, beyond bifurcation, rejuvenation, and subordination.

First, we might consider how Heidegger's own ontological language bears maternal and feminine traits that invert and subvert patriarchic hierarchy, especially when it is a matter of describing difference:[23]

austragen, "to carry out," but also "to carry a child to full term";

Scheide, "separation," but also and more commonly "vagina" (not used explicitly by Heideger, but suggested by the proximity to *Unter-Schied,* "dif-ference" or "inter-scission," and other words built on *scheiden;* this is an ambiguity important in Schelling, for example);

stillen, "to still or pacify," but also "to breastfeed" (German *Sein* as French *sein*);

Theia, not just abstract "god-hood," but also as distinctly feminine.

Might <u>die</u> *Sprache* (the feminine noun for language) be speaking *herself* in Heidegger's emplacement?

Second, we might look more carefully at instances in which Trakl complicates gender roles through the use of neuter articles or the addition of suffixes or umlauts. In a couple of the many versions of Trakl's late metric poem "Nachtergebung" ("Surrender to the Night"), for example, the narrator oxymoronically invokes a female monk, a *Mönchin,* and beseeches her to embrace him. The final, published version of the poem, which Heidegger never refers to in his published writings, but which he annotated in his personal copy of the Zurich edition of Trakl's poems, reads:

> Mönchin! schließ mich in dein Dunkel,
> Ihr Gebirge kühl und blau!
> Niederblutet dunkler Tau;
> Kreuz ragt steil im Sterngefunkel.

Purpurn brachen Mund und Lüge
In verfallner Kammer kühl;
Scheint noch Lachen, golden Spiel,
Einer Glocke letzte Züge.

Mondeswolke! Schwärzlich fallen
Wilde Früchte nachts vom Baum
Und zum Grabe wird der Raum
Und zum Traum dies Erdenwallen. (DD: 187)

*

Monkess! close me in your darkness,
Oh, you mountains cool and blue!
Downward bleeds the darksome dew
Cross doth rise in astral glitter.

Crimson, broke both mouth and lie
Coolly in the ruined room;
Laughter, golden play, yet shines,
Final tolling of a bell.

Mooncloud! Wild fruits fall blackly
From the tree while it is night.
All of space becomes a grave
And this earthly pilgrimage a dream.

At the outset, it would seem that, again, a strange sort of woman takes the lead. She is the all-encompassing, deathlike night into which the narrator would like to dissolve. Her mountains (*Gebirge*) are less a range of large elevations of the earth than a primordial gathering (*Ge-*) and harboring (*Bergen*) of all that is—the dark background of concealment against which anything can come to stand out as bright and manifest (see GA 12: 40–41; GA 79: 56). However, given Trakl's frequent self-identification as a monk (*Mönch*), which he sometimes distorts into *Münch*, possibly signifying epicenity or a transformation of gender,[24] the figure of the monkess is not so much a celibate woman as an androgynous, gently sexualized being. They—and here the singular "they" is especially apt—bear the mark of the dream of the "O n e *Geschlecht*."[25]

Image 8. Trakl's self-portrait.

Third, we might return to the questions raised in chapter 2 about the strange amalgamation of Christ and the sister in some of Trakl's poetry, especially the first version of "Passion." Trakl's Christianity was certainly unorthodox. But his invocation of the figure of the sister in his final two poems does not, ipso facto, demonstrate his unbelief, as Heidegger contends (GA 12: 72). Might not the sister, at least in "Klage" ("Lamentation") and "Grodek," instead represent the other side of Christ as brother, where, in Derrida's words, one could envisage a "tender desire, a relation to the other as double homosexuality, a reflection without appropriation of the desire of the other" (GIII: 114–115)?

The sister, in any case, clearly merges with another *Geschlecht* in Trakl's poetry: the *Geschlecht* of animals, and in particular wild prey (*das Wild* in German). Heidegger's confrontation with Trakl does not just compel and complicate his consideration of sexual difference; Heidegger's confrontation also compels and complicates his reconsideration of the separation between human and animal in "Language in the Poem."

§2. The Wild Blue Game

The German word *Wild* appears frequently in Trakl's poetry.[26] It can be used as a collective noun to refer either to hunted wild animals (more clearly indicated by *Jagdwild*), what in English one would call "game" or "quarry," or to the meat so obtained, as in the description, "the wine pairs well with game." But the word can also be used for a single one of these animals, *ein Wild*, "a game animal" or "a quarry." Kluge records the possibility that the word might be connected to *Wald* ("forest"), just as the French *sauvage* derives from the Latin *silva*, although he finds this etymology improbable since *Wild* "seems to be used only of living beings," albeit "senseless, irrational [*verstandlos, unvernünftig*]" ones.[27] *Wild* can also mean a specific animal, namely, a deer, or its meat, although this would be more clearly indicated by *Rotwild*, and Trakl himself uses other words for deer such as *Hirschkuh* and *Reh* when he wants to refer to this animal. As an adjective, *wild* overlaps in meaning with its English cognate "wild." Kluge notes that the related Old Icelandic *villr* "usually signifies 'going astray, confused [*irre gehend, verirrt*].'" Finally, the nominalization *Wildheit*, literally "wildness," has the sense of "ferocity" or "savagery."

Hunted, irrational, errant, ferocious—all stereotypes that would seem to place the *Wild* firmly on the less favored side of the human/animal split. Trakl does, to be sure, use cognates of the word in this stereotypical fashion. In "Sevensong of Death," for instance, Trakl not only associates the animal (*Tier*) with pernicious wilderness (*Wildnis*) but also links humanity, in its contemporaneous state of corruption, with searing bestiality:

> O des Menschen verweste Gestalt: gefügt aus kalten
>   Metallen,
> Nacht und Schrecken versunkener Wälder
> Und der sengenden Wildnis des Tiers. (HKA 1: 70)

*

> Oh, the decayed shape of man: joined from cold metals,
> Night and terror of sunken forests
> And of the scorching wilderness of the animal.

However, there are several memorable instances in which the wild game animal, transformed into blueness, takes on traditionally human attributes and even becomes a figure for the promise of a life free from malice and malediction. In one of the more serene sister poems, titled simply "An die Schwester" ("To the Sister," originally "An meine Schwester," "To My Sister"), Trakl calls the sister a "wild blue game, ringing out under trees [Blaues Wild, das unter Bäumen tönt]," and gives her the aura of a sacred commission:

> Gott hat deine Lider verbogen.
> Sterne suchen nachts, Karfreitagskind,
> Deinen Stirnenbogen. (HKA 1: 32)

*

> God has bent your eyelids.
> Stars seek at night, Good Friday child,
> The arch of your brow.[28]

The *Wild*, like Christ, must suffer, but, again like Christ, it does so with gentle forbearance, even with a certain musicality, that of Bach's *Matthäus-Passion*, perhaps. We can hear this in the poem "Elis," which, among other possibilities (Elisha, Endymion from the Greek region Elis, Elis Fröbom, and Novalis), calls to mind Jesus's lamentation on the cross: "Eli, Eli, lama asabtani?" (Matthew 27:46, Mark 15:34), cited in the original Hebrew in both the Lutherbibel and Bach's sacred oratorio. The second section of the poem begins:

> Ein sanftes Glockenspiel tönt in Elis' Brust
> Am Abend,
> Da sein Haupt ins schwarze Kissen sinkt.
>
> Ein blaues Wild
> Blutet leise im Dornengestrüpp. (HKA 1: 49)

*

> A gentle glockenspiel sounds in Elis's breast
> At evening,
> When his head sinks into the black pillow.

A wild blue game
Bleeds quietly in the scrub of thorns.

Trakl, as mentioned above, even has a poem titled "Passion," which plays—transgressively—on the transgression of forbidden love and on what, in German and in English, one calls *the* Passion. In this poem, too, Trakl draws a contrast between perverted cognates (*wild*, *Wildnis*) and pristine or recovered innocence (*Wild*). After invoking "the shadow of the sister," the first stanza declaims the

Dunkle Liebe
Eines wilden Geschlechts,
Dem auf goldenen Rädern der Tag davonrauscht. (HKA 1: 68–69)

*

Dark love
Of a wild *Geschlecht*,
From which the day rushes away on golden wheels.

The second stanza gives the reason for the narrator's grief. As with "Frühling der Seele" ("Springtime of the Soul"), the proximate cause is incest, although we should remember that incest serves as the prime synecdoche for sin in Trakl's poetic world. Unlike "Springtime of the Soul," the narrator of "Passion" describes this sin as bestial, lupine. Trakl is probably thinking, critically, of the incestuous union of the wolflike Volsungs Siegmund and Sieglinde as depicted in Wagner's *Die Walküre*. Here, at any rate, is the final version of the second stanza of "Passion":

Unter finsteren Tannen
Mischten zwei Wölfe ihr Blut
In steinerner Umarmung; ein Goldnes
Verlor sich die Wolke über dem Steg,
Geduld und Schweigen der Kindheit.
Wieder begegnet der zarte Leichnam
Am Tritonsteich

Schlummernd in seinem hyazinthenen Haar.
Daß endlich zerbräche das kühle Haupt!

*

Under gloomy firs
Two wolves mixed their blood
In stony embrace; something golden
Got lost, the cloud over the footbridge,
Patience and silence of childhood.
Again the delicate corpse is met
At Triton pond
Slumbering in its hyacinthine hair.
Would that the cool head shatter at last!

The first, much longer version of the poem, which Heidegger may not have known at the time of composing "Language in the Poem," more explicitly pairs incestuous passion with Christ's crucifixion. Here I will cite just eight lines, which overlap in part with those of the final version. Note the inclusion of the first-person plural pronoun, the biblical language (1 Corinthians 15:55–57), and the introduction of the word *Wildnis*:

Zwei Wölfe im finsteren Wald
Mischten wir unser Blut in steinerner Umarmung
Und die Sterne unseres Geschlechts fielen auf uns.

O, der Stachel des Todes.
Verblichene schauen wir uns am Kreuzweg
Und in silbernen Augen
Spiegeln sich die schwarzen Schatten unserer Wildnis,
Gräßliches Lachen, das unsere Münder zerbrach. (HKA 1: 216)

*

Two wolves in the gloomy forest
We mixed our blood in stony embrace
And the stars of our *Geschlecht* fell upon us.

Oh, the sting of death.
Deceased, we behold ourselves at the crossroads [or "on the
    Way of the Cross"]
And in silver eyes
The black shadows of our wilderness are mirrored,
Hideous laughter that shattered our mouths.²⁹

The final stanza of "Passion" seems either to depict the transformation of discordant bestiality into consonant animal blueness, of *wild* into *Wild*, or to suggest that, no matter how horrendous the situation, there is always the possibility, however remote, of penitence and redemption, promised by the ever-attendant wild blue game:

Denn immer folgt, ein blaues Wild,
Ein Äugendes unter dämmernden Bäumen,
Dieser dunkleren Pfaden
Wachend und bewegt von nächtigem Wohllaut,
Sanftem Wahnsinn.
Oder es tönte dunkler Verzückung
Voll das Seitenspiel
Zu den kühlen Füßen der Büßerin
In der steinernen Stadt.

*

For always a wild blue game follows,
An eyeing one, under twilit trees,
Over these darker paths
Keeping vigil and moved by nocturnal consonance,
Gentle madness.
Or there sounded, replete with dark
Rapture, the string music
At the cool feet of the penitent woman
In the stony city.

Heidegger will follow Trakl in dissociating the gentleness of the wild blue game from the "scorching wilderness of the animal." He will even—for a moment—suggest that the former is more than a metaphor for a humanity to come.

§3. Humanimality

Heidegger arrives at the question of the animal as though by accident. Early on in "Language in the Poem," he attempts to demonstrate that twilight, in Trakl's poetry, refers not just to the dusk and dawn of a day but also to the course of a year. The demonstration proceeds by way of metonymic association, as do most of the transitions in "Language in the Poem." In Heidegger's reading of "Springtime of the Soul," the stranger makes his way (*fremd* as *fram*) through the spiritual twilight:

> Es ist die Seele ein Fremdes auf Erden. Geistlich dämmert
> Bläue über dem verhauenen Wald. (HKA 1: 78)

*

> The soul is something strange on earth. Spiritually,
> Blueness dawns over the thrashed forest.

In order to show that twilight has an annual—and eventually by further extension, an epochal—significance, Heidegger next cites the final lines of "Sommersneige" ("Summer's Decline"):

> Der grüne Sommer ist so leise
> Geworden und es läutet der Schritt
> Des Fremdlings durch die silberne Nacht.
> Gedächte ein blaues Wild seines Pfads,
>
> Des Wohllauts seiner geistlichen Jahre! (HKA 1: 75)

*

> The green summer has become
> So quiet and there sounds the step
> Of the stranger through the silver night.
> Would that a wild blue game commemorate his path,
>
> The consonance of his spiritual years!

In short, if twilight and years are both spiritual or capable of spiritual transformation, then twilight is connected with the year and years, not only night and day. The stranger is making his way through the "night" of two and a half millennia of metaphysics toward the "dawn" of a new age beyond calculation.

The shift from "Springtime of the Soul" to "Summer's Decline" may seem abrupt, but Heidegger goes on to provide further support by linking the wild blue game back to the blueness that dawns spiritually over the thrashed forest (*Wald*). Furthermore, *Wild* and *Wald*, only one letter apart, have topological and tropological connections in Trakl's poetry, whether or not they trace back to the same root. In any event, at issue now, for Heidegger, is how to understand blueness and the role that the wild blue game plays in it.

In the previous chapter we saw how blueness served as a manifestation of salvific holiness and as an aspect of being itself. Yet what exactly is this wild blue game? Is it an animal? What role does it play on the path to the land of evening?

At first, Heidegger blurs the human/animal divide with his interpretation of the wild blue game. He says that the latter is not just an animal, but a "gentle animal," a *sanftes Tier*, that *thinks* (GA 12: 39–40, quoting "An den Knaben Elis," "To the Boy Elis"). The German verb *gedenken* ("to recall," "to commemorate") from "Summer's Decline" contains the root *denken* ("to think"). What is more, Heidegger writes that the wild blue game *nachdenkt*, that is, "ponders" or, more literally, "thinks in the wake and direction of" the stranger, who, like the setting sun, goes down toward a new dawn. This is noteworthy because, typically, Heidegger draws a strict line of demarcation between animals as such and the thinking or pondering that is proper to humans or to what Heidegger, after the Greeks, names "the mortals." The human is not an animal plus some specific difference. Indeed, based on many of his writings, it would be questionable even to call the human an animal. "Nonhuman animals"—a preferred phrase today—would be a pleonasm, and, since animals are "unable to experience death as death" (GA 12: 203), the phrase "mortal animals" would be an oxymoron. Yet, contrary to all expectation, the wild blue game is said, here, to be a thinking animal.

But the divide comes back into focus as Heidegger describes the emergence of the wild game from out of "mere" animality (GA 12: 40–41). In reference to a sentence from "Nachtlied" ("Nightsong")—

> Ein Tiergesicht
> Erstarrt vor Bläue, ihrer Heiligkeit. (HKA 1: 39)

*

> An animal face
> Rigidifies before blueness, its holiness.

—Heidegger correlates the development of the wild game with the development of a particular type of face, one capable of beholding the holy with a cold stare (*Starren*). He thereby privileges not the face as such, not sight as such, but a countenance and a way of seeing that belong to a particular *Geschlecht* alone, that of the *Wild*. Despite a chasm of differences, we are not so far from Levinas's humanism of the face here.[30] Nor are we far from Heidegger's blatant denial of the hand to animals (GA 54: 118–119). Playing on the literal and figurative senses of *zusammenfahren* ("to come together," "to recoil" [in fear, for example]), Heidegger writes, in "Language in the Poem":

> The rigid character of the animal face is not that of something that has died off. In rigidifying, the face of the animal recoils/comes together. Its look gathers itself, so that, keeping to itself, it may, vis-à-vis the holy, gaze into the "mirror of truth." (GA 12: 41, citing "Nightsong")

It might seem that, in this passage, Heidegger is presenting an account of evolution, one that, however idiosyncratic, would certainly be a blow (*Kränkung*, or better: *Schlag*) against "the naïve self-love of men," even that of Heidegger.[31] Yet, as Heidegger's discussion goes on to indicate, what we have instead is a harmonious *re-volution*, a return to a gentler state before the twofold became duplicitous and scattered into countless bits, before *Wild* became *wild*, thus before "mere" animality. The wild game's peculiar prosopogenesis is actually, on Heidegger's account, more a self-administered plastic surgery than the result of random genetic mutations. The contraction of the animal's countenance corresponds to the original gathering of gentleness, to which the *Wild* must go *back*:

> In the face of blueness, the countenance of the *Wild* takes itself back into *das Sanfte* ["gentleness"]. For *das Sanfte* is, literally, that which peacefully gathers.[32] It transforms the discord by

twisting [*verwinden*] the injurious and scorching elements of wilderness [*Wildnis*] into tranquilized pain. (GA 12: 41).

Five pages later, Heidegger describes the nature of the beast, again casting it in terms precariously close to the *Wild* that is supposed to mark a departure from brute animality. Notice that the latter itself becomes a mark of the degenerate, scattered *Geschlecht*:

> With what is this *Geschlecht* struck [*geschlagen*], i.e., cursed? Curse means, in Greek, *plēgē*, our [German] word *Schlag* ["blow, strike"]. The curse of the decaying *Geschlecht* consists in this old *Geschlecht* being struck apart [*auseinandergeschlagen*] into the discord of the *Geschlechter*. As a result of this discord, each of the *Geschlechter* strives into the unleashed insurrection of the each-time individuated and mere wildness of the wild game [*bloßen Wildheit des Wildes*]. Not the double as such, but discord is the curse. As a result of the insurrection of blind wildness, discord carries the *Geschlecht* into divisiveness and thus strikes [*verschlägt*] it into unleashed individuation. Thus divided and struck asunder [*zerschlagen*], the "fallen *Geschlecht*" can no longer, of its own accord, find its way into the right *Schlag*. (GA 12: 46, possibly paraphrasing "Unterwegs," "Underway")

In the next chapter, I will examine the reasons (or rather, lack of reasons) for the insurrectionary curse of discord. Here, I want to concentrate on what it implies about animality. The animal, *Tier*, must become the wild game, *Wild*. But the wild game must twist free from the uncollected wilderness of sheer wildness. Is, then, animality as such concomitant with wildness unbound? Is animality the curse? Would this, in turn, make the accursed *Geschlecht* no more than a beast?

What is strange about Heidegger's (and Trakl's) use of the noun *Wild* is that one cannot fail to hear the adjective *wild* in it, which is why I have translated the former as "wild game" and not merely as "game." The wild game may be blue, that is to say, transfigured by the holy; it cannot, for all that, erase the trace of its *animal* face, just as we cannot erase our "abyssal bodily affinity to the animal" (GA 9: 326), despite all our manners, clothing, and makeup. Heidegger's discussion displays an ambivalence, even an anxiety, in the face of this abyss. On the one hand, he tries to hold the wild blue game, and by extension the humankind that is on the way to a new homeland, apart from both mere animality and the corrupt *Geschlecht*, which, given the tropes of zoomorphism in rationalizations for human slaughter, are thereby brought into dangerous proximity:

> In the poetic name "wild blue game," Trakl calls upon that *human* essence whose countenance, i.e., counter-gaze, is, in thinking of the steps of the stranger, caught sight of by the blueness of night and thus is shined on by the holy. The name "wild blue game" names mortals who commemoratively think [*gedenken*] of the stranger and would like, with him, to wander out to attain the native element [*das Einheimische*] of the *human* essence. [. . .] The wild blue game has, where and when it essentially holds sway [*west*], left behind the hitherto essential shape of the human. The human hitherto falls insofar as he loses his essence [*Wesen verliert*], i.e., he decays [*verwest*]. [. . .] The decayed shape of the human is delivered over to the agony of the scorching and to the pricking of the thorn. Its wildness [*Wildheit*] is not shined through by blueness. (GA 12: 42–43; emphases added)

On the other hand, there are several aspects of "Language in the Poem" that shake the boundaries between human and animal and provide new openings in which to contemplate their kinship.

As I suggested, the near-identity of *wild* and *Wild*, which are distinguishable only at the level of orthography or through the addition of a grammatical article, implies that *Wild* cannot leave behind *wild* entirely. Of the "dark *Wild*" that appears in Trakl's poem "Spiritual Twilight," Heidegger writes: "Its wild character [*Sein Wildes*] has at once the pull into gloominess and the inclination toward still blueness" (GA 12: 43). Even if the *Wild* does not break out into wild individuation, it has an innate *tendency* to do so, just as spirit has an innate tendency toward insurrection. The *Wild* cannot be purified of potentiality. Further, if the *Wild* is supposed to return to a prior state of collected gentleness, it will bear the traces of its traumatic history. Replication entails difference. Rather than flee animal corruption, Heidegger, who insists that Trakl offers an alternative to Platonism, should accept it as an insuperable trait of humankind.[33]

There are, indeed, moments when Heidegger moves in the direction of a universal mortality of exposure, a mark of finitude shared by humans and animals. "The name 'wild blue game,'" writes Heidegger, "names mortals" (GA 12: 42). A metaphor, perhaps. Yet, when, in "Spiritual Twilight," Trakl places the nocturnal pond and the spangled sky in apposition, Heidegger contends that the poet is not merely using some "poetic image" for the heavens. Rather, "the nocturnal sky is, in the truth of its essence, this pond" (GA 12: 44). Might we not say the same for the *Wild*? This animal *is* the human.

Andrew Mitchell has argued that this is in fact Heidegger's new position.[34] I would maintain, instead, that Heidegger only approaches the threshold to "humanimality." When he sees what is inside, he does not focus his gaze and enter, but jumps back and looks to familiar surroundings. Even in later texts and publications, including the collection in which "Language in the Poem" appears, Heidegger's actual position—or what he believes to be such—is fully on display: "Mortals are those who are able to experience death as death. The animal is not capable of this. But the animal cannot speak either" (GA 12: 203; see also GA 7: 152, 180, 200; GA 10: 188).

As for Trakl, Heidegger is right to locate an eschatological thrust in his poetry. Trakl fears the "animal drives [*animalischen Triebe*] that toss life through the ages" (HKA 1: 261). But, if Novalis is the source for Trakl's hope of "*One Geschlecht*," then, in the messianic end, humans *and* animals will "come together like One Family, act and speak like One *Geschlecht*."[35] Remarkably, there is more than a trace of animality in Heidegger's own version of the *eschaton* of the Evening-Land, even if, in his vision, it belongs only to the purified *Menschengeschlecht*. Heidegger, for a moment, is in search of an animality to come:

> The wild blue game is an animal [*Tier*] whose animality [*Tierheit*] is presumably based, not in the animalistic or bestial [*Tierischen*], but in that gazing commemorative thinking for which the poet calls. This animality is still distant and barely to be caught sight of. Thus, the animality of the animal that is meant here wavers in the indeterminate. It is not yet brought into its essence. This animal, namely the thinking one, the *animal rationale*, the human, is, according to a saying by Nietzsche, not yet *fest gestellt*.[36]
>
> This statement in no way means that the human is not yet "established" as a fact [the typical meaning of *feststellen*]. He is indeed established as a fact, only all too decidedly. The

saying means: the animality of this animal is not yet brought into what is firm [ins Feste], i.e., "home," into the native element of its veiled essence. (GA 12: 41)

Yet, as with the sister, Heidegger does not have the wild blue game lead the way, despite the guiding role of both of these figures in Trakl's poetry. If some sense of animality is to be salvaged, it will come after the work on the human, an "after" that, in the texts available to us, never arrives. Like the sister, the wild blue game *follows* the stranger in Heidegger's interpretation. To the extent that it merges with the sister in Trakl's poetry (although not in Heidegger's interpretation), this should not be surprising. However, the subordination of the animal becomes tenuous as soon as we realize that Heidegger, for his part, conflates the stranger with the boy Elis (GA 12: 50), who, in the eponymous poem cited in the previous section, himself merges with the wild blue game. (Heidegger provides the pagination for this poem, together with that of "Passion," immediately after referring to the wild blue game, proving he was aware of these connections, GA 12: 39).

Derrida titled one of his books *L'animal que donc je suis*: the animal that therefore I am, the animal that therefore I follow. I propose, in conclusion, that, if Heidegger had followed the tracks of the animal more closely in Trakl's poetry—if, for instance, he had paid closer attention to the thrush in "Sebastian im Traum" ("Sebastian in Dream"), which does not follow *ein Fremdes* (neuter), but *calls* the latter to go down—then he may not have been so quick to subordinate the animal, whether *wild* or *Wild*, to the stranger (or strange *thing*), a gesture that, incidentally, but not accidentally, synchronizes with the subordination of the sister and that of the feminine more broadly. The fact that Heidegger, the sexagenarian philosophy professor from Meßkirch, the self-proclaimed thinker of being (and not of beings), nevertheless begins to push the conventional limits of sexual difference and (hum)animality in "Language in the Poem," the fact that he begins to recognize the sexed animals that we are, is, even if he ultimately sets these limits back in place, nothing short of astounding. The book of the *Geschlecht* did not end with Trakl.

Chapter 7

Spirit in Tatters

Spiritus ubi vult spirat et vocem eius audis sed non scis unde veniat et quo vadat.

der geist geistet wo er wil. du hörest sin stÿme. du enweist aber nit wenn er komet. oder war erfert.[1]

—John 3:8, in the Vulgate, and a translation thereof by Meister Eckhart

Several times in *Geschlecht III*, as well as in the volume *De l'esprit*, Derrida notes the following peculiar feature about Heidegger's reading of Trakl: Heidegger insists that the core of Trakl's work is more original, more essential, and more promising than anything on offer in the metaphysical and Christian traditions; however, Heidegger's description of that core, which Heidegger himself signs on to, does little more than repeat the very same content of these traditions. Heidegger's discourse, in other words, remains caught up in what it is trying to escape. And yet, for all that—and at times despite itself—his reading of Trakl provides a fertile re-reading of the nature of being and of our beleaguered relation to it.

In this final chapter, I want to focus on a possibility Heidegger opens up but just as soon forecloses: namely, the idea that spirit is inherently and insuperably riven. Rather than allowing for the inevitability of discord, distress, and dissemination in this life—as his own logic demands—Heidegger tranquilizes the pain of being, turning it into a force of gathering and an actor in a conventional three-part drama about ontological history.

§1. The Promise

On several occasions throughout the book, I have retold Heidegger's story of the land of evening. Here, I want to reiterate that, temporally, this *Abend-Land* is more originary (*ursprünglich*) and hence more futural or "to-come" (*zukünftig*) than anything available in the West (*Abendland*, no hyphen, *das Westliche*) (GA 12: 63, 73; GA 71: 98–99). Spatially, it is the destination of the wanderer and his followers. As the place in which, and only in which, it makes sense to talk properly about demarcated space, this land of evening may not be identifiable by the borders of Adenauer's Germany. But, if and when it emerges, it will not be from non-German-speaking territory. Judging from comments Heidegger made in 1945, it appears that Swabia—the homeland of Schelling, Hölderlin, and Heidegger—is alone fit to summon its spirit, or rather its *Geist*, which, at bottom, in Heidegger's reading, has nothing to with Latin *spiritus* or even the breath of Greek *pneuma*, let alone Anglophone derivatives or the Hebrew *ruah*.[2] Should this *Geist* emerge for those who are deaf to German, it would only be because those who are capable of hearing the hidden force of the elementary German words have in fact listened to and preserved them and thereby saved the promised land of evening.

In Heidegger's drama, we begin Act I in an imagined paradise. But paradise is soon lost, not on account of Satanic pride or envy, but owing to an inflammatory impulse at the heart of being, to a sort of ontological autoimmunity or asthma of the spirit. Act II recounts this lapsarian attack, even as it prophesies purgation for the elect and promises a homecoming. Act III imagines a paradise permanently regained, where pain does not rend the folds of the one *Geschlecht* but more firmly mends them together. For all his silence about the genre, Heidegger's *agon* is essentially a comedy.

But what of an epilogue? Would it close the circle with a Dantean presentation of our will and desire "turning with / the Love that moves the sun and all the other stars" (*Paradiso* XXXIII, 142–145)—or might it instead suggest a sequel?

§2. The Promise, Painfully Broken

Heidegger allows for no sequel in his reading of Trakl. To be sure, he never explicitly says the arrival will be permanent, but his promissory, even messianic, language readily suggests as much. Before questioning this eschatological thrust in Heidegger's text, I should pause for a moment to consider an alternative advanced by Derrida toward the end of *Geschlecht III*. On Derrida's reading, what Heidegger promises is not merely a long-awaited return to our proper abode; additionally, Heidegger's promise of a return is "necessarily and irreducibly the return of the promise. [. . .] [T]he promise is already the salvation" (GIII: 171–172). The show, in other words, must go on, and it must continue to go on, as such and evermore. The best we can do is to learn to be at home with not being at home (cf. GA 53: §13).

While valuable in its own right, this interpretation stands in tension with Heidegger's own text, which frequently points to arrival at specific destinations, and thus to the fulfillment of the promise. Take a few examples from the third and final section of "Language in the Poem," and note the peculiar usage of the German preposition *in* with accusative objects ("into" in English):

—"die Zwietracht der Geschlechter einfältig *in* die sanftere Zwiefalt versammelt";

—"die Flamme des Geistes *ins* Sanfte spricht";

—"*in* die Frühe aufersteht";

—"das Menschengeschlecht *in* sein noch vorbehaltenes Wesen verschlägt, d. h. rettet." (GA 12: 74–76; emphases added)

*

—"simply gathers the discord of the *Geschlechter into* the gentler twofoldness";

—"speaks the flame of *Geist into* gentleness";

—"resurrects *into* earliness";

—"strikes, i.e., saves, the human *Geschlecht into* its essence still held in reserve."

In either case, however, whether it be as Heidegger develops it or as Derrida deconstructs it, I will argue in this section that the promissory structure of spirit necessitates that such promises be broken, and that they ought never to have been made in the first place.

Let us begin with a classic question from the annals of speculative philosophy: why does the One become Many? We can imagine Heidegger's response: *first, you need to see that there is no One to begin with, or if there is, it's not the One as you understand it. I'm no Neoplatonist. The One I'm speaking about is always already a gathering of two. Its very nature is twofold. But I'm not some sort of Binitarian either; I'm not advocating two Persons instead of three. As much as my remarks on the onefold/twofold of Geist might be helpful to Christians trying to understand the interrelation of the three hypostases in the one substance, my Geist is fire, and fire is not, or at least not in the first place, the purifying fire of Baptism or the cloven tongues of Pentecost; my flames may just as well flare up into evil as radiate goodness. You wish to know my spiritual fathers? Then put down your Plato, Paul, and Plotinus, and pick up some German theosophy. Here, as with so much else in my text, Boehme, Baader, and Schelling are my guides.*[3]

Still, though, how is it that Heidegger's duplicitous *Geist* comes to be discordant? Heidegger has no answer. He simply describes:

> what is *Geist*? Trakl speaks, in his last poem "Grodek," of the "hot flame of *Geist*" [. . .]. *Geist* is the flaming and, only first as flaming, perhaps something blowing. In the first place, Trakl understands *Geist*, not as *pneuma*, nor as spiritual [*spirituell*], but rather as flame that inflames, rouses, horrifies [*entsetzt*, literally "dis-places"], compels a loss of composure [*außer Fassung bringt*]. [. . .] Trakl beholds "*Geist*" from out of that essence which is named in the original meaning of the word "*Geist*"; for *gheis* means: upset, horrified, outside of oneself.[4]
>
> *Geist*, understood in this way, essentially holds sway within the possibility of the gentle *and* the destructive. The gentle in no way strikes down that outside-itself of the inflaming, but rather holds it gathered in the tranquility of the amicable. The destructive comes from the unbridled, which consumes itself in its own insurrection and thus drives on the malicious [*Bösartige*]. Evil [*Das Böse*] is always the evil of a *Geist*." (GA 12: 56)

The gentle (or the good of spirit) holds the destructive in check, even as the destructive (or the evil of spirit) threatens to break out "into the ungatheredness of calamity or perdition [*das Ungesammelte des Unheilen*]" (GA 12: 56). Yet why does it break out? Based on Heidegger's text, the only answer that can be given is tautological: it breaks out because it breaks out. Evil lies in the nature of being, and, like being, evil is without a reason why.

While this may be unsatisfying to the intellect, it at least takes evil outside the domains of divine and human agency—or, to put it more cautiously: evil, on this account, is not primarily of a theological or anthropological nature. This theoanthropodicy is, incidentally, consistent with earlier treatments of evil in Heidegger's corpus.[5] Here I do not wish to question it per se. Nor do I wish here, in any detail, to question its legitimacy as a reading of Trakl, for whom evil cannot be so easily dissociated from sin, and for whom *Geist* cannot be so easily dissociated from one of his favorite Bible verses: "Selig sind, die da geistlich arm sind; denn das Himmelreich ist ihr," "Blessed are the poor in spirit: for theirs is the kingdom of heaven" (Matthew 5:3).[6] Rather, what I would like to question is the role Heidegger assigns evil in his history of being, particularly the possibility that it could be contained as such.

Before the possibility of such containment, another possibility is haunting the origin. It is the possibility that the tender doubling of spirit might become accursed dissension. It is the possibility that pain might not merely gather, but instead shatter and scatter. It is, in short, the possibility of insurrection. Listen to Derrida on the implications of such a possibility:

> The fact, the *factum*, or the fatality of division *being able* to arrive, the fact of this possibility (which, after all, Heidegger recognizes) implies that the structure of that to which this can happen is such that it can happen to it. It thus happens to its structure enough for one to say that this structure is essentially not indivisible but divisible. Besides, in order for it to gather or tend toward gathering, it is necessary that it be divisible and that this divisibility not just be an accident. At bottom, an accident does not happen if the essence cannot be affected by such an accident. If the essence is accidentable, it is a priori accidented [*Si l'essence est accidentable, elle est a priori accidentée*]. (GIII: 106)

Derrida is not simply arguing, with Aquinas, that whatever is capable of not being, at some point is not.[7] Negativity must in fact always already affect the origin. If the origin can be affected by insurrection, insurrection has already affected it. The source (*pēgē*) is already the curse (*plēgē*).

Since, moreover, we are talking about auto-affection, and not calamity from without, this accidented status of *Geist* is hardly superable. On a dualist model, we could also say that one of the two principles must at some point be affected by the other and is therefore on some level always already affected. But this need not exclude the possibility of an ultimate triumph of one over the other. Think, here, of Gnosticism in its various guises. Such will not work for Heidegger's model, however. For, despite its many folds, it is still a monism of spirit.

We might compare Heidegger's model with the similarly complicated monism of theosophy, then. Take Schelling, whom Heidegger certainly knew better than Boehme or Baader, and whose influence can be felt throughout Heidegger's reading of Trakl.[8] In the *Freiheitsschrift*, Schelling shows how, in God, being qua ground (darkness) is inseparably subordinate to being qua existence (light). God, however, in order that he may be revealed as the spirit in which these two non-dualistic principles are thus united, allows for the possibility of their separation and perversion through the freedom of the human being, who, like God, but unlike animals, is also of spirit. Evil occurs as a result of the human being's freely chosen negation of the divine order and the human being's assertion of the predominance of the ground in its stead, thus as a sort of insurrection. But this is only temporary. As Scripture prophesies,

> The last enemy that shall be destroyed is death. [. . .] And when all things shall be subdued unto him [namely, Jesus], then shall the Son also himself be subject unto him [namely, God] that put all things under him, that God may be all in all [*ta panta en pasin*]. (1 Corinthians 15:26–28)

Or, in Schelling's terms,

> spirit [*Geist*] is the first being which unified the world of darkness with that of the light and subordinates both principles to its realization and personality. Yet, the ground reacts against this unity and asserts the initial duality, but only toward ever greater increase and toward the final separation of good from

evil. The will of the ground must remain in its freedom until all this may be fulfilled and become actual. [. . .] [T]he end of revelation is casting out evil from the good, the explanation of evil as complete unreality.[9]

For Heidegger, however, evil does not serve as revelation. There is no spiritual God permitting it or gaining anything from it, since, on Heidegger's model, evil comes before God or gods (at least on the order of principles, see GA 12: 56). Heidegger's eschatology no doubt resembles Schelling's. But what justifies it? Heidegger, unlike Schelling, has no God or principle of revelation to rely on. Heidegger wants resurrection to follow insurrection, but without a savior being foreordained.[10] Why this would follow, and why another fall would not in turn follow it, remain questions without adequate answer.

Heidegger's analysis of evil is at once distinctive and conventional. Importantly, evil becomes a matter for ontology, but Heidegger's ontology of evil smacks of the very metaphysics of substance that he had striven to dismantle. Rather than conceding and articulating the inevitability of insurrection, Heidegger tries to purify the being of spirit and its one *Geschlecht*—he quarantines a strain for a future free from contamination. Or, in Derrida's words, he still adheres to "the most continuous grand logic philosophy, which supposes an exteriority between essence and accident, the pure and the impure, the proper and the improper, good and evil" (GIII: 107).

Heidegger's analysis of pain, as we saw in chapter 4, bears a similar status. On the one hand, he endeavors to understand pain on a level deeper than physiology or psychology (GA 12: 24–25, 58; ÜdS), in terms of what Werner Hamacher has called "Other Pains." On the other hand, Heidegger's treatment of pain renders it innocuous. All harm is illusory or merely temporary. Pain, properly understood, always serves the higher end of gathering. There may be scars, and we may not be dealing here with absolute knowing, but the wounds of pain, like those of Hegel's *Geist*, always heal. If, however, insurrection is inevitable on Heidegger's model, so too is shattering pain. Not the pain that "bestows what is essential"—but precisely the pain that Heidegger denigrates as superficial semblance: "[w]hat is disturbed, inhibited, calamitous and without the possibility for salvation, all the suffering in what is decaying [*Das Gestörte, Verhemmte, Unheile und Heillose, alles Leidvolle des Verfallenden*]" (GA 12: 60).

§3. "Grodek" Redux

Earlier, I mentioned a tone-deafness in Heidegger's appreciation of Trakl's "Grodek." Where others hear a compassionate lament for the soldiers who died at the Battle of Gródek and for their unborn descendants, Heidegger hears hope for a race yet to come. Where others hear a rending pain that would soon drive Trakl to a lethal overdose, Heidegger hears a gentle pain that would serve the spirit of gathering. Heidegger's marginalia to the poem in his personal copy of the Zurich edition, which I would like to discuss now, nevertheless delineate an alternative to this hermeneutic anodyne and provide further insight into Heidegger's onto-historical interpretation of Trakl's poetry.

Regarding the line, "And softly in the reeds the dark flutes of autumn resound," Heidegger wrote on the blank space of facing page of his copy (DD: 195): "'Geistliche Dämmerung'—: die sanften Flöten des Herbstes." This is a reference to Trakl's poem "Spiritual Twilight," where Trakl sings not of the dark, but of "the gentle flutes of autumn," which "keep silent in the reeds" (DD: 131). Although, in "Grodek," the dark flutes resound softly, Heidegger seems to want to mark a contrast between darkness and gentleness, between plaintive foreboding and collected silence.

Whatever the case may be, Heidegger's next marginal note demarcates an even more fundamental opposition. At the center of spirit—nay, not at the center, for there is no center; *Geist*, like fire, is inherently "outside of itself" (*gheis, ek-statikon*)—in the eccentric, ecstatic movement of spirit, there is, as we have seen, a tendency toward gentleness, but there is also a tendency toward uprising and upheaval. Remarkably, Heidegger's annotation links gentleness with the key word of his later thought, *Gelassenheit* ("releasement"), a word that Heidegger seems at pains to avoid in "Language in the Poem," even though Eckhart used it as a synonym of *Abgeschiedenheit*, as Heidegger well knew. Across from Trakl's line, "The hot flame of spirit is nourished today by a mighty pain," Heidegger wrote (see image 5 in chapter 3 for the original):

To flame: flare up—shine—

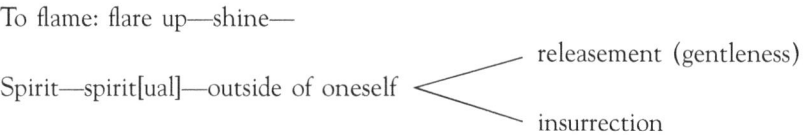

Spirit—spirit[ual]—outside of oneself

*

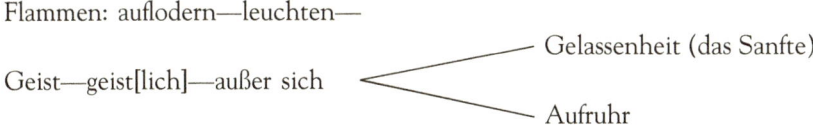

Around the time when he composed his second text on Trakl, Heidegger was elsewhere trying to understand being and the appropriative event in terms of releasement (GA 99: passim); later, he would even say that "the deepest meaning of being is *letting* [Lassen]" (GA 15: 363). What is interesting about the marginal note, however, is its suggestion that insurrection is *intrinsic* to the sway of spirit. If we were to speak of a self-purging or self-containment, of spiritual progress on the part of *Geist*, then it would be hard to make sense of the claim that spirit is, *as such*, outside of itself, and that being-outside-of-oneself entails revolt. Heidegger attempts to insulate his interpretation against the metaphysics of Platonism and Christianity, but his annotation compels us to ask whether there is not something metaphysical about his aspirations for a purified homeland and a purified *Geschlecht*. How much gathering can there be before the incalculable freedom of being is rendered null? The quelling of its rage and the softening of its pain may sound appealing, but is this not ultimately a fantasy on par with the grandest of the metaphysical tradition? Do not such fantasies blind us to indomitable malice and thereby only fuel its flames?

Heidegger would have us read all of Trakl's work under the aegis of triumph—not, to be sure, the triumph of the tortured Christ, which Trakl also sings, but the triumph of a *Land* and a *Geschlecht* long held in store for the favored. I have, however, argued that the promise of such triumph hardly follows from Heidegger's own account of spirit. Furthermore, it hardly follows from the tortured song of Trakl's "Grodek." Yet, by recognizing an intractable impulse toward insurrection in the searing flame of *Geist*, Heidegger's annotation embodies the spirit of the poem more faithfully than his lecture does.

In a different marginal note, this time to Trakl's poem "Nachtergebung" ("Surrender to the Night"), Heidegger copied out a variation on the final two verses provided in Walter Killy's *Merkur*-essay "Gedichte im Gedicht" ("Poems in the Poem"). Instead of

Und zum Grabe wird der Raum
Und zum Traum dies Erdenwallen.

*

All of space becomes a grave
And this earthly pilgrimage a dream. (HKA 1: 93),

Trakl considered the lines:

Einer Stadt verfallner Saum
Loht, die Feuerglocken hallen.

*

Derelict seam of a city
Blazes, and the fire bells resound.[11]

Heidegger had long been interested in the serene mystery of old town bells (GA 13: 113–116; GA 81: 88; GA 98: 191). We can readily hear this in his reading of the first stanza of Trakl's "Ein Winterabend" ("A Winter Evening") (GA 12: 18–19). This manuscript variation on "Surrender to the Night" is especially striking, however, because it evokes the sound of alarm. Trakl's bells do not just embody the gentle spirit of *Gelassenheit*. They also signal the all-consuming fire.

Postscript

Le souci de la *seule* Allemagne ne l'aura jamais quitté.[1]

—Philippe Lacoue-Labarthe

Despite all the twists and turns of his path of thinking, Heidegger never gave up on the idea that he was headed toward a secret Germany, as promulgated by the very "voice of beyng," Friedrich Hölderlin (GA 70: 167; see also GA 16: 290, GA 84.1: 337, GA 94: 155). Or, rather, as promulgated by members of the circle that formed around the poet Stefan George such as Norbert von Hellingrath, who wrote, in a 1915 lecture titled "Hölderlin und die Deutschen":

> I call us "the *Volk* of Hölderlin" because it is of the very essence of the Germans that their innermost, fervid core (which lies infinitely deep beneath the veneer of its dross-covered crust) can only come to light in a *secret* Germany [geheimen *Deutschland*]. This innermost core expresses itself through human beings who, at the very least, must be long dead before they are recognized and find a response; and works that will always impart their secret only to the very few, saying nothing to most, and wholly inaccessible to non-Germans. Indeed, this is true because this secret Germany is so certain of its inner value [. . .] that it makes no effort to be heard or seen. [. . .] Hölderlin is the greatest example of this hidden fire, of this secret Reich, of the still unrecognized coming into being of the divine burning core.[2]

In Heidegger's words, from 1934, which comment on a fragment by Hölderlin: "The fatherland, our fatherland Germania—most forbidden, withdrawn from quotidian haste and the bustling racket. The highest and hence most difficult, the last, because at bottom the first—the origin kept secret [*verschwiegen*]" (GA 39: 4).

Whatever the merit of this Germano-nationalist mythos about Hölderlin—and there is much in it to be wary of, even as a matter of exegesis—it is more astounding that Heidegger would also hear the promise of the *geheimes Deutschland*, or its coded *noch verborgenes Abend-Land*, in the poetry of Trakl. Trakl, seemingly the second great example of this "secret Reich" in the thinker's corpus, is at least as pure as Hölderlin: never does a critical word about the Austrian expressionist come from Heidegger's mouth or pen.[3]

Austrian expressionist—a phrase that Heidegger never used, and never would have used, for Trakl, but one that points to a tension in Heidegger's Hölderlin-inspired engagement with the poet. Trakl does, to be sure, have much in common with his "brother" Hölderlin. Yet Trakl is less hopeful than his predecessor, and the hope he does offer comes, not from remembrance of the absconded gods of Greece, but from a tortured, idiosyncratic imitation of Christ. Furthermore, *enfant terrible* of the Austro-Hungarian Empire though he was, Trakl fiercely opposed Germany and German culture, particularly in the years leading up to World War I. "I wish every German would die by the executioner's axe," he is reported to have said. "Nothing great could come from the Germans anymore."[4] In place of Hölderlin's famous concluding words, "there follows German song" ("Patmos"), Trakl put, "there follow dark years" ("Afra").[5] There is no "Germania" or "Der Rhein" in this poet's oeuvre. Russia, if anywhere, was his dreamland.

As for the label of expressionism, although Trakl differs formally from his expressionist contemporaries such as Gottfried Benn and August Stramm, he shares their thematic interests in death, decadence, and decay, in the trauma of history and in history as trauma, in the experience of profound alienation from society and its idols. Moreover, Trakl's two books of poetry appeared alongside Benn's, Brod's, Kafka's, and Kokoschka's in the principal organ for literary expressionism of the time, Kurt Wolff's series *Der jüngste Tag* (*Judgement Day*). Trakl was, in short, a poet of 1910, "the year when all scaffolds began to crack" (Benn).[6] Just four years later, anticipating the outcome of the so-called "war to end all wars," he would himself collapse in a psychiatric ward of a military hospital, one thousand kilometers from home—surely a peculiar author to place in the poetic, Greco-German pantheon of "Being."

Heidegger's Hölderlinian and Hölderlinizing reading of Trakl is the most violent ever offered of the Austrian poet and perhaps the most violent reading Heidegger ever offered as such—and that is saying a lot of a man who, on many occasions, underscored the necessity of violence in all authentic interpretation (GA 3: XVII, 202; GA 40: 171; SZ: 327). Throughout this study, we have seen that, ultimately, in Heidegger's reading, bread and wine signify not body and blood, but earth and sky; detachment and pain are sources not of anarchy and dissolution, but of collected strength; madness results not in ruinous nonsense, but in supreme insight; colors, when they are properly poetic, are words not for sacrilege, but for being itself; the voice of the sister does not sing from the place of the promised land, but merely provides accompaniment to the music of the masculine stranger; the wild blue game is just another word for the humanity to come, not a cipher for the merging of the sexes and species; and the searing flame of spirit does not warn of the wrath of God but rather, phoenix-like, announces a new birth from the ashes of destruction.

In the foregoing chapters, I have criticized Heidegger's efforts to commandeer Trakl's poetry for the cause of the coming land of evening, even as I have tried to show how Heidegger himself was, at times, taken by the poetry. This led Heidegger to take up such underrepresented themes in his corpus as madness and maternity, pain and Christianity, sexual difference and color theory. He even made strides toward a new thinking of the human/animal relation. Theodor Adorno once wrote that "philosophy, if it grasped its idea of the poetic in a binding way, would flee precisely from contamination with the material of thought in the poetic work."[7] Although, in the end, Heidegger shrank back from the implications of his encounter with Trakl's poetry, although he repurposed the work for the sake of the secret Germany, Heidegger, to his credit, did not circumvent the Austrian expressionist altogether. For a time, Heidegger's corpus was touched by a pained, perverse, peculiarly Christian author whom Heidegger would, remarkably, come to call the poet of his generation.

A larger framework for this picture of Heidegger's confrontation with Trakl can be found in Reiner Schürmann's *Broken Hegemonies*, which contains one of the most important, if underappreciated, interpretations of the later Heidegger. Schürmann analyzes Heidegger's *Beiträge zur Philosophie*

(1936–1938) not as the latter's oft-touted second magnum opus, but as a "monstrous site" riven by opposing forces. On the one hand, a centrifugal force pulls Heidegger's discourse away from all arch-referents. Philosophy—or what replaces it at the end of metaphysics—need no longer "console the soul and consolidate the city."[8] Philosophy or "thinking" becomes a matter of an-archic *Gelassenheit*, of letting being be in its internal strife, even in its tragic condition. On the other hand, a centripetal force simultaneously pulls Heidegger's thinking in the *Beiträge* toward the prioritization of a particular language (German), a particular people (the German *Volk*), their particular leaders (Germans, no doubt), and a particular place (Germany). Heidegger blinds himself to his own insights by "contributing," once again, to philosophy as machinational metaphysics.

We should read Heidegger precisely because of this extreme tension in his thought, a tension from which we have by no means extricated ourselves. Of the *Beiträge*, Schürmann writes:

> I know of no other text that offers so painfully, to our thinking, the great repression of the tradition of tragic being. Heidegger lends his voice both to the forces of repression and to those of the return. The pain remains unabated, for the same adversity traverses, from within, both the site of the text and the thought that echoes there. The distress of the site and the pathos of thinking indicate one and the same epochal monstrosity. The agonistic dissension in terms of which Heidegger from then on understood being, in turn, becomes manifest in this monstrosity. [. . .] To speak only of philosophy, where [if not to the *Beiträge*] is one to turn, since the 1930s, to find a thought that raises even so much as the question of the conditions of what has befallen us?[9]

What Schürmann says here of the *Beiträge* of the second half of the 1930s can be said of Heidegger's engagement with Trakl in the early 1950s: Heidegger once again lends his voice to the repressed even as he struggles to silence the impact that their return would have on his thinking. With due respect to Schürmann, Heidegger did not, therefore, learn his lesson.[10] Both the centripetal and the centrifugal forces only grew stronger. Heidegger's reading of Trakl marks at once the most extreme flight from the confines of his philosophy theretofore and the most extreme search for confinement to centralized authority. Heidegger's reading of Trakl is an exemplary site for thinking today.

Appendix 1
Heidegger's Trakl Marginalia

Tucked away in a locked, secluded library of the Meßkirch Castle, with no label to distinguish it, is a precious item that only a few people have set eyes on: Heidegger's personal, annotated copy of Trakl's *Die Dichtungen: Gesamtausgabe, mit einem Anhang Zeugnisse und Erinnerungen* (*The Poems: Collected Works, with an Appendix: Testimonials and Recollections*) (Zurich: Die Arche, 1946) (= DD). Although Heidegger's marginalia in this volume are not extensive, they provide, as I have argued throughout the book, valuable insight into his reading of the spirit of Trakl's poetic work and into the place in which Heidegger situates it. In the process, they also shed light on Heidegger's understanding of topics such as biography, Christianity, sexual difference, and the relation between being and language. Additionally, his markings in the volume's appendix reveal his acquaintance with—and aversion to—traditional ways of reading Trakl, especially by the authors affiliated with the journal *Der Brenner*, in which many of Trakl's poems first appeared. In this appendix, I will first consider the history of Heidegger's copy and the dating of his marginalia (§1). I will then provide a transcription and translation of the annotations (§2). In the last section (§3), I will provide details about Heidegger's extensive marginalia to "In ein altes Stammbuch" ("Into an Old Family Album") in his personal copy of a different edition of Trakl's work.

§1. Background

Admittedly, Heidegger never cites from the Zurich edition of his personal copy of Trakl's poems, which the actor and theater director Kurt Horwitz edited and published with the press Die Arche in 1946. Heidegger preferred instead to cite from his "workshop volume" (MH/LF: 49), namely, the first of a three-volume edition published in Salzburg by Otto Müller Press. (Incidentally, this latter volume also bears the title *Die Dichtungen* and, with the exceptions of a preface and no appendix, seems to be identical to the Zurich version.) It is nevertheless noteworthy that, in both of his lectures on Trakl, Heidegger mentions the Zurich edition (GA 12: 15, 36n1; GA 80: 987, 1011). While this does not necessarily prove that he owned or even consulted a copy while composing his lectures, on both occasions he tells the reader to compare the Zurich edition, which would be surprising had he not done so himself. Also, Heidegger used several writing utensils (blue pen, black pen, and lead pencil) in his marginalia, suggesting he may have returned to the Zurich edition multiple times. Unfortunately, unlike in some of his other volumes, Heidegger's personal copy bears no date of acquisition.

Inside this copy is a loose, typewritten sheet folded into quarters. In addition to containing a partial, conjectural transcription of the marginalia with emendations in blue pen, at the top of the page is an explanation that the copy was "bei Thomas gefunden (Sept. 2011)" ("found at the home of Thomas [Sept. 2011]"), and contains "schriftliche Anmerkungen von MH" ("handwritten annotations by MH"). "MH" stands for Martin Heidegger, and "Thomas" refers to Heidegger's nephew. As a different nephew of the philosopher, Heinrich Heidegger, explained to me in a letter, he (Heinrich H.) is the author of the typewritten transcription. I have made use of this typewritten transcription in §2, below, although I have deviated from it or supplemented it when appropriate. Heinrich H. provided further details about the possible history of the volume in a letter to me from December 12, 2019:

> You write that the name "Heidegger" is on the cover page, evidently without any further information. / My suspicion: because Medard Boss, in Zurich, had been in contact with my uncle [Martin H.] [. . .], he had the book sent to him; shortly after the war it was difficult for us to get anything from Switzerland.
>
> How did the book come to Meßkirch? [. . .] [E]ver since 1938, my father [Fritz Heidegger] had transcribed many of his brother's [Martin H.'s] manuscripts [. . .]. I suspect that my uncle gave him the Trakl-book as a token of thanks; because

there is no dedication, it was presumably delivered personally, perhaps during one of their meetings in Hüfingen, where their sister Maria Oschwald lived, and where they would meet regularly around the 11th and 12th of November (St. Martin's Day on November 11, and November 12 was the birthday of my aunt Marie [* 1891–† 1956]).

After the death of my father († June 26, 1980), we rented the house; only the so-called "Study Room" remained untouched. Yet my brother [Thomas H.] took the most important books regarding Heidegger with him to Bonndorf i. Schw. [. . .]; he had more room than I did (at the time in St. Blasien). Around 2010–2011, he moved with his wife into a smaller place in Neustadt i. Schw.; thus, it was necessary to clear things out again. Because, after my retirement, I had moved into my relatively small family home [in Meßkirch], we decided—because of how little room we had; I, after all, had my own books—to give the valuable books to the Heidegger-Archive.

*

Sie schreiben, dass auf dem Cover "Heidegger" steht, offenbar keine weiteren Angaben. / Meine Vermutung: weil Medard Boss, Zürich, [. . .] in Kontakt stand mit meinem Onkel, hat er ihm das Buch zukommen lassen; kurz nach dem Krieg war es für uns schwer, etwas von der Schweiz zu bekommen.

Wie kommt das Buch nach Meßkirch? [. . .] mein Vater hatte seit 1938 viele der Manuscripte seines Bruders transcripiert [. . .]. Ich vermute, dass mein Onkel das Trakl-Buch zum Dank ihm übereignet hat; weil keine Widmung, vermutlich persönlich übergeben, vielleicht beim Treffen in Hüfingen, wo ihre Schwester Maria Oschwald wohnte, wo regelmäßig um den 11. und 12. November ein Treffen stattfand (Martinstag am 11.11. und der 12.11 war der Geburtstag der Tante Marie [* 1891–† 1956]).

Nach dem Tod meines Vaters († 26.6.1980) vermieteten wir das Haus; nur das sog. "Studierzimmer" blieb unangetastet. Doch die wichtigsten Bücher, was Heidegger betraf, nahm mein Bruder zu sich nach Bonndorf i. Schw. [. . .]; er hatte mehr

Platz als ich (damals in St. Blasien). Um 2010/11 zog er mit seiner Frau nach Neustadt i. Schw. in eine kleinere Wohnung; also mußte wieder geräumt werden. Weil ich nach meiner Pensionierung nach hier in mein relativ kleines Elternhaus zog, beschlossen wir,—zu wenig Platz, ich hatte ja auch meine eigenen Bücher—die wertvollen Bücher ins Heidegger-Archiv zu geben.

As for the dating of the marginalia, the annotations to "Nachtergebung" ("Surrender to the Night") must, if I am not mistaken, stem from 1958 or later, since this is the year in which some of the manuscript variations of the different versions of the poem—variations that Heidegger reproduces in his marginalia—first became available to the public in an essay by Walther Killy titled "Gedichte im Gedicht" ("Poems in the Poem") (pp. 1114–1115). Heidegger is doubtless drawing on this essay, since the editors of HKA 2, from 1969, read Trakl's handwriting in the variations differently: rather than *Gottes Rose* ("rose of God"), one finds *Gottes Rosen* ("roses of God"); rather than *stets* ("always"), one finds *stumm* ("mutely") (308–309). Because Heidegger mentions Killy's essay in December 1958 (MH/LF: 65), it seems likely that he made his annotations to "Surrender to the Night" around this time. One annotation in "Gesang des Abgeschiedenen" ("Song of the Departed One") might also point to Heidegger's reading of variations in this poem, which, to my knowledge, were made public only in 1969 (HKA 2: 262–263), although it should be noted that Killy did share some Trakl manuscripts with Heidegger in 1959. Regarding the other marginalia, all I can say definitively is that they were composed in or after 1946, when the Zurich edition appeared in print. In any case, it does not necessarily follow that Heidegger gave his brother his personal copy after 1958 or 1969, since he would make use of his brother's library when visiting him in Meßkirch over the years, including in the late 1960s and early 1970s.

§2. Marginalia in the Zurich Edition

Cover page:

—Heidegger wrote his name in black pen.

Pages 171–172:

GESANG DES ABGESCHIEDENEN

[. . .]

Liebend auch umfängt das Schweigen im Zimmer die Schatten der Alten,
Die purpurnen Martern, Klage eines großen Geschlechts,
Das fromm nun hingeht im einsamen Enkel.

Denn strahlender immer erwacht aus schwarzen Minuten des Wahnsinns
Der Duldende an versteinerter Schwelle
Und es umfängt ihn gewaltig die kühle Bläue und die leuchtende Neige des Herbstes,

Das stille Haus und die Sagen des Waldes,
Maß und Gesetz und die mondenen Pfade der Abgeschiedenen.

SONG OF THE DEPARTED ONE

[. . .]

Silence in the room also lovingly embraces the shadows of the ancestors,
The crimson torments, lamentation of a great lineage
That now piously passes on in the solitary grandson.

For ever more radiantly does the tolerant one awaken
From black minutes of madness on a petrified threshold,
And embracing him mightily is the cool blueness and the luminous decline of autumn,

The still house and the sayings of the forest,
Measure and law and the lunar paths of the departed ones.

—In lead pencil, Heidegger underlined *fromm* ("piously") in the third verse listed here. In the lefthand margin, next to that verse, he drew the symbol ">."

—In lead pencil, to the right of *Schwelle* ("threshold") in the penultimate stanza, Heidegger drew the symbol "<."

—In blue pen, in the final verse of the poem, Heidegger drew a vertical line through the "r" of *der*. In the lefthand margin, he drew another vertical line, to the right of which he wrote the letter "s," thereby suggesting the singular masculine genitive definite article ("of the departed *one*") instead of the plural ("of the departed *ones*"). Compare HKA 2: 263.

Page 187:

NACHTERGEBUNG

Mönchin! schließ mich in dein Dunkel,
Ihr Gebirge kühl und blau!
Niederblutet dunkler Tau;
Kreuz ragt steil im Sterngefunkel.

Purpurn brachen Mund und Lüge
In verfallner Kammer kühl;
Scheint noch Lachen, golden Spiel,
Einer Glocke letzte Züge.

Mondeswolke! Schwärzlich fallen
Wilde Früchte nachts vom Baum
Und zum Grabe wird der Raum
Und zum Traum dies Erdenwallen.

SURRENDER TO THE NIGHT

Monkess! close me in your darkness,
Oh, you mountains cool and blue!
Downward bleeds the darksome dew
Cross doth rise in astral glitter.

Crimson, broke both mouth and lie
Coolly in the ruined room;

Laughter, golden play, yet shines,
Final tolling of a bell.

Mooncloud! Wild fruits fall blackly
From the tree when it is night.
All of space becomes a grave
And this earthly pilgrimage a dream.

—In the righthand margin next to the first verse, Heidegger drew an "x." Below the poem, he wrote, in reference to this first verse: "zuerst: 'Nymphe zieh mich in dein Dunkel" ("initially: 'Nymph, draw me into your darkness"). See Killy, "Gedichte im Gedicht," 1114, and the first verse of what Killy and Szklenar refer to as the fourth version of "Surrender to the Night" (titled "An die Nacht" ["To the Night"]), in HKA 1: 230.

—Above and to the right of the exclamation point after *Mondeswolke* ("Mooncloud") in the first verse of the final stanza, Heidegger drew an "x" with a circle around it. Below the poem, he reproduced this symbol and wrote: "zuerst: 'Blaue Wolke!' und: 'Gottes Rose'" ("initially: 'Blue cloud!' and: 'Rose of God'"). For *Blaue Wolke!*, see Killy, "Gedichte im Gedicht," 1115, and the first verse of the third stanza of what Killy and Szklenar refer to as the fourth version of "Surrender to the Night" (titled "An die Nacht" ["To the Night"]), in HKA 1: 230. For *Gottes Rose*, see Killy, "Gedichte im Gedicht," 1115, and the variant on *Blaue Wolke!* (as *Gottes Rosen* ["Roses of God"]) in HKA 2: 309.

—In the righthand margin bracing the final two verses, Heidegger drew a close bracket, to the right of which he drew a symbol that looks like two "u"s connected by a horizontal line. Below the poem, he reproduced this symbol and wrote: "zuerst: 'Kind an deinem blauen Saum / Muß ich stets vorüber wallen.' // u. // 'Einer Stadt verfallner Saum / Loht, die Feuerglocken hallen.'" ("initially: 'Child, at your blue seam / I must always make my pilgrimage.' // and // 'Derelict seam of a city / blazes, the fire bells resound.'") See Killy, "Gedichte im Gedicht," 1115, and the variants on what Killy and Szklenar refer to as the second version of "Surrender to the Night" (titled "Anblick" ["Spectacle"]), in HKA 2: 308, where one finds *stumm* ("mutely") instead of *stets* ("always").

Pages 194–195:

GRODEK

Am Abend tönen die herbstlichen Wälder
Von tödlichen Waffen, die goldnen Ebenen
Und blauen Seen, darüber die Sonne
Düstrer hinrollt; umfängt die Nacht
Sterbende Krieger, die wilde Klage
Ihrer zerbrochenen Münder.
Doch stille sammelt im Weidengrund
Rotes Gewölk, darin ein zürnender Gott wohnt,
Das vergossne Blut sich, mondne Kühle;
Alle Straßen münden in schwarze Verwesung.
Unter goldnem Gezweig der Nacht und Sternen
Es schwankt der Schwester Schatten durch den schweigenden Hain,
Zu grüßen die Geister der Helden, die blutenden Häupter;
Und leise tönen im Rohr die dunkeln Flöten des Herbstes.
O stolzere Trauer! ihr ehernen Altäre,
Die heiße Flamme des Geistes nährt heute ein gewaltiger Schmerz,
Die ungebornen Enkel.

GRÓDEK

At evening the autumn woods issue tones
Of deadly weapons, the golden plains
And blue lakes, over which the sun
Rolls on more gloomily; the night envelops
Dying warriors, the wild lamentation
Of their shattered mouths.
Yet quietly in the pasture red clouds,
In which a raging god dwells,
gather up the blood that was shed, lunar chill;
All streets enter the mouth of black decay.
Under golden boughs of night and stars
The shadow of the sister sways through the silent grove,
To greet the spirits of heroes, the bleeding heads;

And softly in the reeds the dark flutes of autumn resound.
Oh, prouder mourning! you brazen altars,
The hot flame of spirit is nourished today by a mighty pain,
The unborn grandchildren.

—In lead pencil, in the lefthand margin, Heidegger put open brackets around the first six verses, the next four, the four after that, and the final three. To the left of each of the brackets, he wrote, respectively, "6," "4," "4," and "3."

—In lead pencil, in the righthand margin next to verse 14, *Und leise tönen im Rohr die dunkeln Flöten des Herbstes* ("And softly in the reeds the dark flutes of autumn resound"), Heidegger drew an "x." On a blank portion of the facing recto (p. 195), Heidegger drew an "x," underlined it, and wrote: " 'Geistliche Dämmerung'—: die sanften Flöten des Herbstes" (" 'Spiritual Twilight'—: the gentle flutes of autumn"). See DD: 131.

—In lead pencil, after *Enkel* ("grandchildren") in the final verse of the poem, Heidegger drew a line and then wrote "Gesang des Abgeschiedenen, 171" ("Song of the Departed One, 171"). See DD: 171 ("Klage eines großen Geschlechts, / Das fromm nun hingeht im einsamen Enkel" ["lamentation of a great lineage / That now piously passes on in the solitary grandson"]).

—In lead pencil, on blank space of the facing recto (DD: 195), across from the final three verses of the poem, Heidegger wrote:

Flammen: auflodern—leuchten—

Geist—geist[lich]—außer sich ⟨ Gelassenheit (das Sanfte)
                                Aufruhr

[To flame: flare up—shine—

Spirit—spirit[ual]—outside of oneself ⟨ releasement (gentleness)
                                        insurrection]

One might expect here the Gothic *gheis* rather than *geist[lich]* (see GA 12: 56); however, Heidegger typically does not use Sütterlinschrift, in which the word in the annotation seems to be written, for foreign or archaic German terms, and in either case it is difficult to discern how the letters could form *gheis*. I am therefore inclined to read it as shorthand for *geistlich*, even though Heidegger clearly has the etymon in mind. See image 5 in chapter 3.

Pages 200–203 (text by Erwin Mahrholdt, "Aus einer Studie über Georg Trakl" ["From a Study on Georg Trakl"]):

> Man darf sich Trakl nicht als weltfremden Jüngling oder als verfallenden grosstädtischen [sic] Schwächling vorstellen, wie es manche taten. Seine ungeheure Widerstandskraft, das Leibliche und Böse, trat in krassen Gegensatz zur Veranlagung seiner Seele, der Schwermut. Der zähe und starke Körper verdoppelte sein Leiden, da kaum ein Betäubungsmittel ihn niederzwang und dadurch auch dem Geist Ruhe gab. Bestimmt und gerade ging Trakl dahin, nur sein Haupt war etwas gebeugt durch die Qual des blendenden Bewusstseins. Manchmal trieb ihn seine Körperkraft zu Auswüchsen, die er nachher bitter bereute.
>
> [One should not imagine Trakl as a youth who was a stranger to the world or as a decadent urban weakling, as some people did. His tremendous resilience, the corporeal and vicious side, stood in stark contrast to the disposition of his soul, his melancholia. His robust and vigorous body doubled his suffering, since there was scarcely a narcotic that could numb him and thereby also provide rest for his spirit. Trakl went along with determination and an upright posture, only his head was somewhat bent by the torture of his blinding consciousness. Sometimes his bodily strength led him to excesses that he later regretted bitterly.]

—In lead pencil, Heidegger drew a vertical line to the left of *blendenden Bewusstseins* ("blinding consciousness").

> [. . .] Trakl trug beide Gefahren des Genies, von denen Weininger spricht, die des Verbrechens und des Wahnsinns,

in sich: das Verbrecherische bezwang er früh, wenn es sich auch oft noch aufbäumte in seinem herben Gesichte, gleichsam versteinert die Menschen abschreckte; bis zum Tode aber fürchtete er sich vor dem gänzlichen Verfall in den Wahnsinn, der den unendlich Schwermütigen schon manchmal angefasst hatte. Hinter diesen Schlacken blühte ein wahrhaft gütiger und gläubiger Mensch, in seiner Milde und Reinheit erst durch das ungetrübte Abbild seines Wesens, die Dichtung, erkennbar.

[Trakl bore within himself both of the dangers of genius that Weininger speaks of, those of crime and madness: he subdued the criminal element early on, even if it often reared up in his severe and, as it were, petrified face and scared people off; to the death, however, he feared falling entirely into madness, which had already at times grabbed hold of the infinitely melancholic one. Blooming behind this slag was a truly benevolent and faithful human being, recognizable in his mildness and purity only through the untarnished reflection of his essence, the poetry.]

—In lead pencil, Heidegger underlined *ungetrübte Abbild seines Wesens* ("untarnished reflection of his essence") and drew a question mark next to it in the lefthand margin.

[. . .] FREMD WAR IHM der sinnlose Macht- und Handelsgeist, der Deutschland zerrüttete, samt dem Sportidealismus und der Glücksgier des Abendlandes.

[The senseless spirit of power and commerce that wrecked Germany was foreign to him, together with the West's idealism about sports and its craving for happiness.]

—In lead pencil, in the righthand margin, Heidegger drew a vertical line next to the lines beginning with *FREMD* ("foreign") and ending with *Glücks-* ("happiness").

[. . .] Sich zu reinigen und zu Gott emporzutragen war sein Losungswort ("Die Nacht"). Den Menschen zu sagen, was sie nicht mehr wussten: dass ihre Seele ein Fremdes auf Erden,

> ein Göttliches sei, wert der höchsten Pflege, und von ihrer goldenen Stille ihnen zu singen (in der Handschrift der "Verwandlung des Bösen").

> [His watchword was to purify oneself and bear oneself up to God ("The Night"). To tell people what they no longer knew: that their soul is something foreign on earth, is something divine, worthy of the highest care, and to sing to them of its golden stillness (in the manuscript of "Transformation of Evil").]

—In lead pencil, in the righthand margin, Heidegger drew a vertical line next to the lines beginning with *wussten* ("knew") and ending with *ihnen* ("to them").

Page 207 (text by Karl Borromäus Heinrich, "Die Erscheinung Georg Trakls" ["The Phenomenon of Georg Trakl"]):

> SO WEISS NUN wohl jeder (was Sie und ich wissen), dass aus dem Antlitz nicht Trüb- oder Wahnsinn gesprochen, sondern Liebe, Mitleid, unsägliches Leid, dazu gewaltige Stille des schauenden Menschen.

> [So now everyone should know (what you and I know) that gloom and madness did not speak from his countenance, but rather love, compassion, unspeakable suffering, in addition the mighty stillness of the gazing human being.]

—In lead pencil, in the lefthand margin, Heidegger drew a vertical line next to this passage.

Pages 210–212 (text by Hans Limbach, "Begegnung mit Georg Trakl" ["Encounter with Georg Trakl"], in which he talks about meeting Trakl for the first time at the home of Ludwig von Ficker ["F."]; "D." refers to Carl Dallago):

> Gleich bestürmte ihn D. in seiner unbefangenen Art mit Fragen; aber Trakl gab nur kurz und wie unwillig Antwort, und wenn ihm eine der Fragen zu nahe zu kommen schien, wich er scheu und fast feindselig zurück.

[Right away D. bombarded him with questions in his uninhibited manner, but Trakl responded only briefly and seemingly unwillingly, and when one of the questions appeared to come too close, he shrank back in a timid and almost hostile way.]

—In lead pencil, Heidegger drew a vertical line in the lefthand margin along the text beginning with *wenn* ("when") and ending with *zurück* ("back"). To the left of the vertical line, he drew a circle.

[. . .] D.s offene, etwas kindliche Natur schien Trakl zu reizen und herauszufordern. Denn es war ihm, allem Anschein nach, peinlich, Rede und Antwort stehen zu müssen, und jener schien dies nicht genügend zu beachten. Trakls Wesen war tiefste Verschlossenheit. "Ich bin ja erst halb geboren!" sagte er einmal und behauptete, bis zu seinem zwanzigsten Lebensjahr überhaupt nichts von seiner Umwelt bemerkt zu haben, ausser *dem Wasser*.

[D.'s open, somewhat childlike nature appeared to irritate and provoke Trakl. For, by all appearances, it was embarrassing for him to have to justify himself, and the former did not seem to heed this sufficiently. Trakl's essence was characterized by the profoundest reticence. He once said, "I'm only half-born!," and claimed to have up until his twentieth year noticed nothing at all of his environment except *water*.]

—In lead pencil, Heidegger drew a vertical line in the lefthand margin along the text beginning with *herauszufordern* ("provoke") and ending with *nicht* ("not"). To the left of the vertical line, he drew a circle. He also underlined the word *peinlich* ("embarrassing"), and drew an arrow in the lefthand margin pointing to the sentence, *Trakls Wesen war tiefste Verschlossenheit* ("Trakl's essence was characterized by the profoundest reticence").

[. . .] Aber D. mochte nun einmal kein Organ für seine Art haben und rückte ihm immer näher auf den Leib.

[But D. had no sense for his way of being and laid into him more and more.]

—In lead pencil, Heidegger drew an arrow in the lefthand margin pointing to this sentence (which is also a self-standing paragraph).

> / "Kennen Sie eigentlich Walt Whitman?" fragte er ihn plötzlich. / Trakl bejahte es, fügte aber bei, dass er ihn für verderblich halte. / "Wieso?"—fuhr D. auf—"Wieso verderblich? Schätzen Sie ihn denn nicht? Sie haben doch gewiss in Ihrer Art manches Verwandte mit ihm?![″] / F. bemerkte, dass doch wohl eher ein tiefer Gegensatz zwischen den beiden zu erkennen sei, indem Whitman das Leben einfach in allen seinen Erscheinungsformen bejahe, während Trakl durch und durch Pessimist sei. Ja, ob er denn gar keine Freude am Leben habe?—bohrte D. weiter. Ob ihm denn z. B. sein Schaffen gar keine Befriedigung verleihe? / "Doch"—gab Trakl zu—, "aber man muss gegen diese Befriedigung misstrauisch sein." / D. lehnte sich vor masslosem Erstaunen in seinem Stuhl zurück. / "Ja, warum gehen Sie dann nicht einfach in ein Kloster?" fragte er endlich nach kurzem Schweigen. / "Ich bin Protestant," antwortete Trakl dumpf.

[Are you in fact familiar with Walt Whitman?," he asked him suddenly. / Trakl answered that he was, but added that he found him to be pernicious. / "How so?"—D. bridled up—"How so, pernicious? Do you not admire him, then? After all, you certainly have in your manner much in common with him?![″] / F. remarked that more of a contrast between them should really be recognized, insofar as Whitman simply affirms life in all its manifestations, while Trakl is a pessimist through and through. Okay, then doesn't he have any joy in life?—D. bored further. Doesn't his creative work afford him any satisfaction? / "Certainly"—Trakl admitted—"it's just that one must be mistrustful of such satisfaction." / Extremely astonished, D. leaned back in his chair. / "Why don't you simply enter a cloister, then?," he asked finally, after a short silence. / "I'm a Protestant," Trakl answered in a muffled tone.]

—In lead pencil, Heidegger underlined the last word (*dumpf*, "in a muffled tone"). In the righthand margin next to it, he drew an exclamation point.

/ "Pro-te-stant?" fragte D. gedehnt—"das hätte ich allerdings nicht gedacht!—So sollten Sie doch wenigstens nicht in der Stadt, sondern auf dem Lande leben, wo Sie dem wüsten Treiben der Menschen ferner und der Natur näher gerückt sind!" / "Ich habe kein Recht, mich der Hölle zu entziehen," gab Trakl zurück. / "Aber Christus hat sich ihr doch auch entzogen." / "Christus ist Gottes Sohn!" antwortete jener. / D. wusste sich kaum zu fassen. / "So glauben Sie also auch, dass alles Heil von ihm komme? Sie verstehen das Wort 'Gottes Sohn' im eigentlichen Sinne?" / "Ich bin Christ"—antwortete Trakl. / "Ja,"—fuhr jener fort, "wie erklären Sie sich denn solche unchristlichen Erscheinungen wie Buddha oder die chinesischen Weisen?" / "Auch die haben ihr Licht von Christus bekommen."

["Pro-te-stant?," asked D. slowly—"I certainly wouldn't have thought that!—You should at least not live in the city, then, but in the country, where you would be farther removed from the hustle and bustle of people and closer to nature!" / "I have no right to escape from Hell," Trakl retorted. / "But Christ also escaped from it." / "Christ is God's Son!," answered the former. / D. hardly knew how to contain himself. / "So then you also believe that all salvation comes from him? You understand 'God's son' in the proper sense of the word?" / "I'm a Christian"—answered Trakl. / "Okay,"—continued the former—"then how do you explain such non-Christian phenomena as the Buddha or the Chinese sages?" / "They, too, received their light from Christ."]

—In lead pencil, to the right of the last sentence, in the margin, Heidegger drew an arrow pointing upward.

/ Wir verstummten, über die Tiefe dieses Paradoxes nachsinnend. Doch D. konnte sich noch nicht zufrieden geben. / "Und die Griechen? Glauben Sie denn nicht auch, dass die Menschheit seitdem viel tiefer gesunken ist?" / "Nie war die Menschheit so tief gesunken, wie jetzt nach der Erscheinung Christi"—versetzte Trakl. "Sie *konnte* gar nicht so tief sinken!," fügte er nach kurzer Pause hinzu. / D. schien nicht wahrhaben zu wollen, dass Trakl immer mehr sich in sich zurückzog und verschloss, und brachte als letzten Trumpf Nietzsche vor.

[We fell silent, meditating on the profundity of this paradox. Yet D. couldn't let it rest. / "And the Greeks? Don't you also believe that humanity has sunk much lower since then?" / "Humanity never sank so low as now, after the appearance of Christ"—retorted Trakl. "It was not at all *able* to sink so low!," he added after a short pause. / D. did not seem to want to perceive that Trakl withdrew into himself more and more and closed himself off, and [D.] brought up Nietzsche as a final trump.]

—In lead pencil, Heidegger drew two vertical lines in the righthand margin along the last sentence about Nietzsche.

/ "Nietzsche war wahnsinnig!" warf Trakl barsch hin, indem seine Augen unheimlich funkelten. / "Wie verstehen Sie das?" / "Ich verstehe das"—grollte jener—"dass Nietzsche die selbe Krankheit hatte wie Maupassant!" / Grauenvoll war sein Antlitz, als er dies sagte: der Dämon der Lüge schien aus seinen Augen zu funkeln. / Das dürfe man nicht sagen, wies ihn D. streng und mit der ganzen moralischen Autorität dessen, der die Wahrheit vertritt, zurück.—Das dürfe man nicht sagen! "Sie müssen wissen, dass der Wahnsinn seelische Ursachen hat!" / Trakl, der das Haupt gesenkt hatte, sah auf, mass sein Gegenüber mit einem seltsamen Blick und schwieg. Aber nach einer Weile schien er sich seines Wortes über Christus zu besinnen. / "Es ist unerhört"—begann er—"wie Christus mit jedem einfachen Wort die tiefsten Fragen der Menschheit löst! Kann man die Fragen der Gemeinschaft zwischen Mann und Weib restloser lösen, als durch das Gebot: *Sie sollen Ein Fleisch sein?*" [. . .] Der Rest des Abends verlief ruhig. Trakl hatte mich schon vordem mehrere Male betrachtet. Jetzt fragte er mich über Russland, und seine tiefe Sympathie für dieses Volk trat offen zutage. / Besonders lieb war ihm Dostojewski. Von einigen seiner Gestalten, wie

Aljoscha Karamasoff und Sonja aus "Schuld und Sühne," redete er mit tiefer Ergriffenheit. / So viel ich mich erinnere, sprach er aus Anlass von Sonja das schöne Wort aus—wieder mit wild funkelnden Augen—: "Totschlagen sollte man die Hunde, die behaupten, das Weib suche nur Sinnenlust! Das Weib sucht *ihre Gerechtigkeit,* so gut, wie jeder von uns!"

["Nietzsche was mad!," Trakl fired off gruffly, with his eyes uncannily glistening. / "How do you understand that?" / "I understand that"—the former grumbled—"in the sense that Nietzsche had the same sickness as Maupassant!" / His countenance was grim as he said this: the demon of falsehood seemed to glisten in his eyes. / One should not say that, D. rebuffed him severely and with all the moral authority of one who represents the truth.—One should not say that! "You must know that madness has psychic causes!" / Trakl, who had sunk his head down, looked up, measured his opponent with a strange gaze, and kept silent. But after a while he appeared to be reflecting on his words about Christ. / "It is unheard of"—he began—"how Christ solves the deepest questions of humanity with every simple word! Can the questions regarding the community between man and woman be solved more completely than through the command: *They shall be One Flesh?*" [. . .] The remainder of the evening passed quietly. Trakl had already observed me previously several times. Now he asked me about Russia, and his deep sympathy for this people became quite manifest. / He was especially fond of Dostoyevsky. He spoke with deep emotion about several of his figures, such as Alyosha Karamazov and Sonja from *Crime and Punishment.* / As far as I remember, the mention of Sonja induced Trakl to utter the beautiful words—again with wildly glistening eyes—"The hounds who assert that woman only seeks sensual pleasure should be struck dead! Woman seeks *her justice* as well as each of us do!"]

—In lead pencil, Heidegger drew two vertical lines in the lefthand margin along the last sentence. To the left of these lines, he drew the symbol ">."

Page 229 ("Nachwort" ["Afterword"], by the editor Kurt Horwitz):

> Er [Trakl] hat die entscheidende Frage des Evangeliums: "Was haltet ihr von Christus? Wessen Sohn ist Er?" eindeutig und klar beantwortet. In seinen Gedichten erscheinen Brot und Wein und die Engel nicht nur als schöne und süsse Bilder. Seine Schwermut, seine Einsamkeit und seine Verzweiflung sind absolut christlich bedingt.

> [He [Trakl] has answered the decisive question of the Gospel clearly and distinctly: "What do you all hold about Christ? Whose son is He?" [Matthew 22:42] In his poems bread and wine and the angels do not merely show up as sweet and beautiful images. His melancholy, his solitude, and his despair are absolutely conditioned by Christianity.]

—In blue pen, Heidegger underlined the word *bedingt* ("conditioned") and to the right of this passage in the margin, he drew a large question mark.

§3. Marginalia to "Into an Old Family Album"

Heidegger's personal copy of the sixth Salzburg edition was, in 2016, on display in the Literaturmuseum der Moderne in Marbach, Germany. It was locked in a glass case along with several other books Heidegger owned and annotated. The volume was open to the poems "In den Nachmittag geflüstert" ("Whispered in the Afternoon") and "Into an Old Family Album" on pages 54–55. For the sake of space, and because of its greater relevance to this study, I provide information only about Heidegger's marginalia to the latter poem. I have not been successful in obtaining access to the entire volume; however, Heidegger's annotations to "Into an Old Family Album" should give readers a good sense of how carefully Heidegger read and cross-referenced Trakl's poems.

INTO AN OLD FAMILY ALBUM

> Again and again you return, melancholy,
> Oh, gentleness of the solitary soul.
> A golden day gleams and comes to an end.

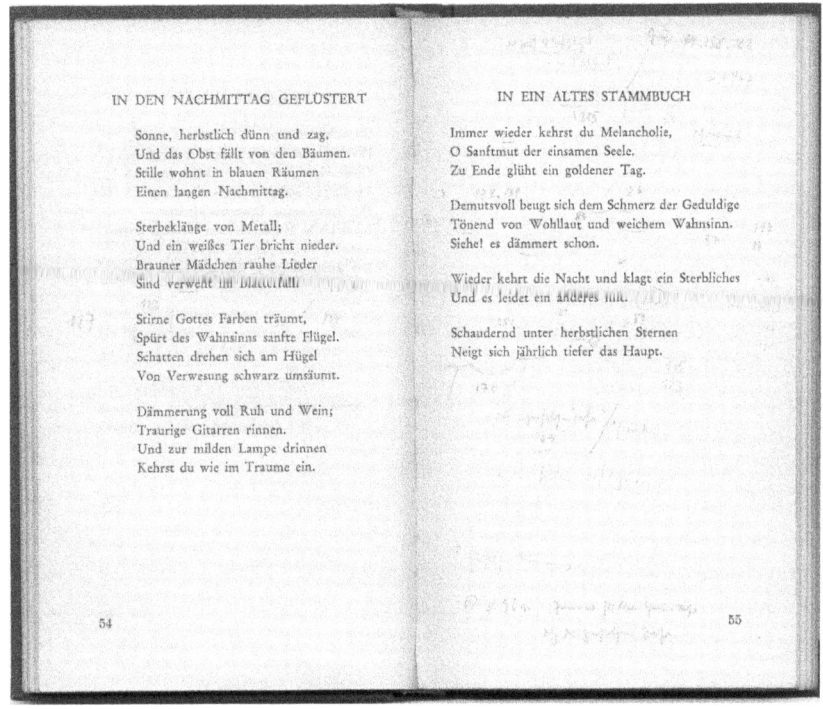

Image 9. Heidegger's marginalia to Trakl's "Into an Old Family Album," in his personal copy of *Die Dichtungen*, ed. Schneditz.

Humbly the patient one bends before pain
Ringing with sounds of harmony and soft madness.
Look! already it is twilight.

Again the night returns and something mortal laments
And another thing suffers in sympathy.

Shuddering under autumnal stars
Each year the head declines more deeply.

—At the top of the page, Heidegger wrote "das <u>Buch des Geschlechts</u> u. seines <u>Wesens</u>!" ("the <u>book of the Geschlecht</u> and of its <u>essence</u>!").

—Regarding the title, Heidegger underlined the word ALTES ("OLD") and wrote "105" under it, which refers to the first section of "Sebastian im Traum" ("Sebastian in Dream") ("altes Hausgerät / Der Väter / Lag im Verfall" ["old household articles / of the fathers / lay in decay"]). Above STAMMBUCH ("FAMILY ALBUM," literally "stem- or trunk-book"; the word is also used for German friendship books), he wrote "Geäst ["branches"], 149, 158, 162," which refer, respectively, to "Frühling der Seele" ("Springtime of the Soul") ("Das Blau des Frühlings winkt durch brechendes Geäst" ["The blue of spring beckons through breaking branches"]) and the first and fourth paragraphs of "Traum und Umnachtung" ("Dream and Lunacy") ("Früchte, die von verkrüppelten Bäumen fielen" ["fruit, which fell from stunted trees"]; "in dem braunen Geäst des Stammes zerfielen grinsend die irdenen Gesichter" ["in the brown branches of the stem, grinning, the earthen faces fell to ruin"]). To the right, he wrote "146f," which refers to the poem "Passion" (see especially the verses: "Dunkle Liebe / Eines wilden Geschlechts, / Dem auf goldenen Rädern der Tag davonrauscht" ["Dark love / Of a wild *Geschlecht,* / From which the day rushes away on golden wheels"]). Heidegger also partially underlined BUCH ("BOOK") and drew a line connecting STAMM to Melancholie in verse 1.

—Regarding the first stanza, Heidegger underlined *wieder* ("again") and wrote "53" and "Schwermut" (a Germanic word for melancholy, more literally "heavy disposition") above and next to Melancholie. The number refers to Trakl's poem "Melancholie."

—Regarding the second stanza, Heidegger wrote an "x" above and to the left of it. This is possibly tied to a comment at the bottom of the page, where he wrote, after an "x," "Geistliche Dämmerung" ("Spiritual Twilight") (see Trakl's poem of the same name, especially the verses "Immer tönt der Schwester mondene Stimme / Durch die geistliche Nacht" ["Ever the lunar voice of the sister sounds / Through the spiritual night"]). Above Demutsvoll, he wrote "174, 139," which refer, respectively, to "Gesang einer gefangenen Amsel" ("So leise blutet Demut" ["So quietly does humility bleed"]) and "Abendländisches Lied" ("Hirten gingen wir einst an dämmernden Wäldern hin / Und es folgte das rote Wild, die grüne Blume und der lallende Quell / Demutsvoll" ["Shepherds, we once walked along twilit forests / And there followed the wild red game, the green flower, and the babbling source / Humbly"]). He underlined *dem Schmerz* ("before pain") and wrote "26" above it, which refers to the third section of "Heiterer Frühling" ("So schmerzlich gut und wahrhaft ist, was lebt" ["So painfully good and true is what lives"]). He underlined *Tönend* ("Ringing"), to the left of which he wrote "114," which refers to "Hohenburg" ("Umfängt den Tönenden mit purpurnen Armen sein Stern" ["His star embraces the sounding one with crimson arms"]). Above *Wohllaut* ("sounds of harmony"), he wrote "83," which refers to "Abendlied" ("Evening Song") ("Doch wenn dunkler Wohllaut die Seele heimsucht, / Erscheinst du Weiße in des Freundes herbstlicher Landschaft" ["Yet when dark sounds of harmony overtake the soul, / You, white one, appear in the autumnal landscape of the friend"]). He underlined *weichem* ("soft"), to the right of which he wrote "147," "54," and "87," which refer, respectively, to "Passion" ("bewegt von nächtigem Wohllaut, / Sanftem Wahnsinn" ["moved by nocturnal harmony, / Gentle madness"]), to "In den Nachmittag geflüstert" ("Whispered in the Afternoon") ("Stirne Gottes Farben träumt, / Spürt des Wahnsinns sanfte Flügel" ["The brow dreams God's colors, / Feels the gentle wings of madness"]), and to the second section of "Helian" ("Wo vordem der heilige Bruder gegangen, / Versunken in das sanfte Saitenspiel seines Wahnsinns" ["Where previously the holy brother had gone, / Sunk in the gentle string music of his madness"]). He underlined *dämmert* ("is twilight").

—Regarding the third stanza, Heidegger underlined *wieder* ("again") and drew an "x" above *und klagt* ("and [. . .] laments"). Below the poem, after an "x," he wrote: "(wieder)?" ("(again)?"), although the "x" might also refer to his comment/the poem "Geistliche Dämmerung" ("Spiritual Twilight") (see especially the verses: "Immer tönt der Schwester mondene Stimme / Durch die geistliche Nacht" ["Ever the lunar voice of the sister sounds / Through the spiritual night"]). To the right of the stanza, he wrote "66," which refers to the poem "Verwandlung" ("Transformation"). Below *Sterbliches* ("mortal"), he wrote "ein Menschliches ["a human thing"] / 114 / 141"; these numbers refer, respectively, to "Hohenburg" ("Also zittert im Dunkel der Fremdling, / Da er leise die Lider über ein Menschliches aufhebt" ["Thus the stranger trembles in the dark, / When quietly he lifts his eyelids over a human thing"]) and to "Siebengesang des Todes" ("Sevensong of Death") (see, for example, the verses "Daß jener leise die bleichen Lider aufhob / Über sein schneeiges Antlitz" ["That that one quietly lifted his pale eyelids / over his snowy countenance"]).

At the end of the stanza, he wrote and circled "113," which refers to "Am Mönchsberg" ("At the Mönchsberg") (perhaps especially the verse: "Näher rauscht der blaue Quell die Klage der Frauen" ["Closer the blue source rustles the women's lament"]). Below *anderes* ("another thing"), he appears to have written "164," which refers to the end of "Traum und Umnachtung" ("Dream and Lunacy") (see the lines: "da in zerbrochenem Spiegel, ein sterbender Jüngling, die Schwester erschien; die Nacht das verfluchte Geschlecht verschlang" ["when in a broken mirror a dying youth, the sister, appeared; the night devoured the accursed *Geschlecht*]). In the middle of the blank space after the poem, Heidegger wrote "Mit-Leiden u. | Schmerz |" ("sym-pathizing and | pain |").

—Regarding the final stanza, Heidegger wrote "151" above *Schaudernd* ("Shuddering"), which refers to "Im Dunkel" ("In the Dark") ("Unter feuchtem Abendgezweig / Sank in Schauern die Stirne den Liebenden" ["Under damp evening branches / the brow of the lovers sank in shudders"]). He underlined *herbstlichen* ("autumnal") and wrote "83" above it, which refers to "Abendlied" ("Evening Song") ("Doch wenn dunkler Wohllaut die Seele heimsucht, / Erscheinst du Weiße in des Freundes herbstlicher Landschaft" ["Yet when dark sounds of harmony overtake the soul, / You, white one, appear in the autumnal landscape of the friend"]). He underlined *Neigt* ("declines") and *jährlich* ("Each year"), and drew a curved line connecting them, under which he wrote "170," which refers to "Jahr" ("Year") (see especially the verses: "im Hasellaub wölbt sich ein purpurner Mund, / Männliches rot über schweigende Wasser geneigt"; "Neige in steinernem Zimmer" ["in the hazel foliage a purple mouth arches, / Manly red bowed over silent waters"; "decline in the stony room"]). Below *jährlich*, he wrote: "die 'geistlichen Jahre' [the 'spiritual years'] / <u>169</u>," which is a quotation from "Sommersneige" ("Summer's Decline"). Above *tiefer* ("more deeply") he drew an "x" with a circle around it. At the bottom of the page, he reproduced the same figure and then appears to have written: "vgl. 169: Immer stillere Heimkehr / durch die geistlichen Jahre" ("cf. 169: Ever stiller homecoming / through the spiritual years"). The first part comes from "Herbstliche Heimkehr" ("Autumnal Homecoming"), which Heidegger would have been able to access in Trakl, *Nachlass und Biographie*, 12. The second seems to be a variation on Trakl's line in "Summer's Decline": "Des Wohllauts seiner geistlichen Jahre!" ("The consonance of his spiritual years!"). Below and to the right of the stanza he wrote "115," which refers to "Kaspar Hauser

Lied" ("Kaspar Hauser Song") ("Silbern sank des Ungebornen Haupt hin" ["Silvery the head of the unborn one sank down"]), and "123," which refers to "Der Herbst des Einsamen" ("Autumn of the Solitary One") ("Bald nisten Sterne in des Müden Brauen; In kühle Stuben kehrt ein still Bescheiden / Und Engel treten leise aus den blauen / Augen der Liebenden, die sanfter leiden" ["Soon stars nest in the brow of the weary one; / Into cool rooms returns a still modesty / And angels quietly emerge from the blue / Eyes of the lovers, who suffer more gently"]).

Appendix 2
Heidegger's Occasional References to Trakl

Below I reproduce most of Heidegger's occasional references to Trakl. I accordingly do not include material from his two lectures on Trakl: "Language," from 1950, and "Language in the Poem," from 1952. Heidegger's correspondence (1952–1966) with Trakl's friend and patron Ludwig von Ficker deals primarily with the poet; however, as many of these references are cursory ("the beautiful picture of Trakl's bust," for example, MH/LF: 43), I cite or summarize only those that I have found most relevant to the themes of this book. Additionally, I have included, in parentheses, instances when people mentioned Trakl to Heidegger or provide a report that sheds light on Heidegger's engagement with Trakl's poetry. Regarding references from archival material that scholars are not permitted to cite, I paraphrase instead. I have organized these references chronologically when possible, although it should be noted that some refer back to earlier periods in Heidegger's life.

1950
In an unpublished letter to his brother from September 28, Heidegger discusses his upcoming lecture on language at Bühlerhöhe and explains that, given the time constraints of the presentation, he chose to condense his ideas on language into a close reading of a single poem by Trakl.

Ca. 1950 or after
Although the editor of GA 81 (p. 357) notes that part II of the volume, in which the following *Gedachtes* ("quasi-poetic thought") is contained, dates from the late 1930s to early 1940s, it seems more plausible to

situate the poem in the context of the 1950 lecture "Die Sprache," not only because of terminological overlap with the lecture but also because Heidegger would make updates to the manuscript of part II after its initial drafting. Later in the manuscript, for example (pp. 265, 270), one finds a reference to *Vier Hefte* (composed 1947–1950) as well as the date "March 11, 1950." Heidegger quotes Trakl's "Ein Winterabend" ("A Winter Evening") at the beginning of the *Gedachtes* (GA 81: 257):

Wir lesen

"Wenn der Schnee ans Fenster fällt . . ."
—
Er fiel und fiel
und lautlos klang ein zögernd Spiel,
das unsere Herzen suchen ließ
die Sammlung in ihr heiles Wesen,
daß' [sic] Vermögen uns verhieß,
rein den Unter-Schied zu lesen:
ungesagtes Zugetrautes,
kaum gewagtes Nie-Geschautes.

*

We read

"When the snow is falling on the window . . ."
—
It fell and fell
and soundless chimed a hesitant game
that let our hearts seek
the gathering into their hale essence,
that promised us power
to read purely the inter-scission:
the unsaid entrusted,
the barely ventured never-beheld.

1951
(In a letter to Ludwig von Ficker from April 23, in GS/LF, Gerhard Stroomann lays out some of his ideas for what would become the 1952

Trakl celebration at Bühlerhöhe. He relates that both he and Heidegger are interested in the poet.)

1952
GA 8: 153 (*Was heißt Denken?* [*What Is Called Thinking?*]): "Das lateinische Wort animus läßt sich auch durch unser deutsches Wort 'Seele' übersetzen. 'Seele' meint in diesem Falle nicht das Lebensprinzip, sondern das Wesende des Geistes, den Geist des Geistes, das Seelenfünklein des Meisters Eckhart. Die so gemeinte Seele ist im Gedicht Mörikes angesprochen: 'Denk es, o Seele.' Unter den heutigen Dichtern gebrauchte G. Trakl gern das Wort 'Seele' in einem hohen Sinne. Die dritte Strophe des Gedichtes 'Das Gewitter' beginnt: // 'O Schmerz, du flammendes Anschaun / Der großen Seele!'"

"The Latin word *animus* can also be translated with our German word *Seele* ["soul"]. In this case, 'soul' means, not the principle of life, but the essencing of spirit, the spirit of spirit, Meister Eckhart's little spark of the soul. The soul, in this sense, is addressed in Mörike's poem: 'Think, Oh Soul.' Among contemporary poets, G. Trakl likes to use the word 'soul' in an elevated sense. The third stanza of the poem 'The Thunderstorm' begins: // 'O pain, you flaming gaze / Of the great soul!'"

Ibid., 209 (citing Trakl's "Psalm"): "Und das *legein* als Sagen? Sagen ist die Sache der Sprache. Was sagt die Sprache? Ihr Gesagtes, das, was sie spricht und was sie schweigt, bleibt immer und überall das, was ist, sein kann, gewesen und im Ankommen ist; und all dies am unmittelbarsten und reichsten dort, wo die Wörter 'ist' und 'sein' gar nicht eigens in die Verlautbarung gelangen. Denn das, was im eigentlichen Sinne jeweils zur Sprache kommt, ist wesentlich reicher als das, was in die hörbaren und sichtbaren Gestalten der Verlautbarung eingeht und als solches dann im Geschriebenen der Schrift wieder verstummt. Gleichwohl bleibt alles Sagen verborgener Weise auf Jenes bezogen, das nennbar bleibt durch ein 'Es ist.' // 'Es ist ein Licht, das der Wind ausgelöscht hat. / Es ist ein Heidekrug, den am Nachmittag ein Betrunkener verläßt. / Es ist ein Weinberg, verbrannt und schwarz mit Löchern voll Spinnen. / Es ist ein Raum, den sie mit Milch getüncht haben. / Der Wahnsinnige ist gestorben . . .' // Das steht nicht in einem Lehrbuch der Logik, sondern anderswo. / Das Legen, als Vorliegenlassen in der weitesten Weise gedacht, bezieht sich auf das Vorliegende im weitesten Sinne, das lautlos spricht: es ist."

"And *legein* as saying? Saying is the affair of language. What does language say? What it says, that which it speaks and that which it keeps silent, always and everywhere remains what is, can be, has been, and is in the process of coming; and all this most immediately and richly where the words 'is' and 'to be' are not at all expressly uttered. For, that which in each case comes to language in the authentic sense is essentially richer than that which enters into the audible and visual shapes of the utterance and as such again falls silent in the written script. Nevertheless, all saying remains in a hidden way related to that which remains nameable through an '*Es ist*' ['There is,' or literally, 'It is'] // 'There is a light, which the wind has extinguished. / There is a heathland tavern, which a drunkard abandons in the afternoon. / There is a vineyard, burned and black with holes full of spiders. / There is a room, which they have whitewashed with milk. / The madman has died . . .' // This is not to be found in a logic textbook, but rather elsewhere. / Laying, thought of as letting-lie-before in the broadest manner, relates to what lies before in the broadest sense, which soundlessly speaks: there is."

(In letters to Ludwig von Ficker from August 25 and September 8, in GS/LF, Gerhard Stroomann relates that: "Heidegger bezeichnet Trakl in Briefen an mich als den Dichter unserer Generation." "Es ist wundervoll, wie Heidegger auf seiner 'Hütte,' wo er arbeitet, eindringt: 'Aber dieser Dichter wird mir täglich geheimnisvoller.'"

"In letters to me, Heidegger characterizes Trakl as the poet of our generation." "It is wondrous how Heidegger advances in his cabin where he works: 'But this poet is becoming more mysterious to me by the day.'")

In an unpublished letter dated September 26, Heidegger wrote from Todtnauberg to his lifelong friend Ernst Laslowski: "Ich bin hier oben im guten Arbeitsschwung trotz Schnee u. vielem Regen u. Sturm [. . .] Am 4./5. spreche ich auf Bühlerhöhe gemäß dem Wunsch von Prof. Stroomann über Georg Trakl [. . .]."

"I am up here, working with good momentum despite the snow and a lot of rain and storms [. . .] On the 4th/5th I will speak about Georg Trakl at Bühlerhöhe according to the request of Prof. Stroomann [. . .]." Heidegger conveyed similar information to his brother in an unpublished letter from October 1.

In a typescript version of "Language in the Poem" (as quoted in the preface to MH/LF: 8), Heidegger says the following, which is not contained in the published version in GA 12: "Zuerst ein persönliches Erlebnis: 1912 wurde ich durch die damalige Nummer des 'Brenner' mit den ersten Gedichten Trakls bekannt. 1913 kaufte ich mir die ersten Trakl-Gedichte und seither begleiten sie mich ständig."

"First a personal experience: in 1912, I became acquainted with the first poems of Trakl through the issue of *Der Brenner* at that time. In 1913, I purchased the first Trakl poems for myself, and they have accompanied me constantly ever since."

(Falk, "Heidegger und Trakl," 197, reports, without citing sources: "Und als [Heidegger] zum Doktor der Philosophie promoviert worden war, kaufte er sich zur Feier des Ereignisses die erste in Buchform erschienene Sammlung der Traklschen Gedichte."

"And when [Heidegger] had been promoted to doctor of philosophy [sc., in 1913], to celebrate the event he bought the first collection of Trakl's poems to appear in book form.")

In the Brenner archive, there are three transcripts of Heidegger's lecture "Language in the Poem." At the end of each is a brief account of the discussion period that took place the day after he delivered it. When Alfred Focke brought up the themes of Christianity and transcendence, Heidegger replied stating that it was important to ask about Trakl's relation to Christianity. Heidegger then mentioned that the poem "Herbstseele" ("Autumn Soul"), from which he had quoted only the penultimate stanza in his lecture, also had a final one, in which Trakl sings: "Rechten Lebens Brot und Wein, / Gott in deine milden Hände / Legt der Mensch das dunkle Ende, / alle Schuld und rote Pein" ("Bread and wine of proper living, / God into your mild hands / Layeth man the darksome ending, / All the guilt and scarlet torment"). Next, as reported by Alfred Focke's published summary of the discussion (*Georg Trakl: Liebe und Tod*, 179), which largely corresponds to that of the typescripts, Heidegger said: "das Gebet dieser letzten Strophe gilt für die Andern, von denen sich der Dichter der Herbstseele gerade getrennt hat, sie sprechen noch so, jedoch in der Abgeschiedenheit der blauen Seele wird nicht mehr so gesprochen" ("the prayer of the last stanza holds for the others, from whom the poet of the autumn soul has already separated himself; they still speak in this way, but there is no longer any such speaking in the detachment of the blue soul"). Regarding the second theme, Heidegger explained that "Transzendenz wäre hier nicht mehr nötig, da 'Gott ja gegenwärtig ist'" ("transcendence would no longer be necessary here, since 'God is indeed present'") (*Georg Trakl: Liebe und Tod*, 179), or in Ruth Horwitz's summary (in Ficker, *Briefwechsel 1940–1967*, 244), "'Gott ist da!' (In Trakl's Gedicht)" ("'God is there!' [In Trakl's poem]").

(Drawing presumably on personal recollections, the anonymous author of Schlosshotel Bühlerhöhe, ed., *Die Geschichte der Bühlerhöhe* writes, in both German (pp. 111–112) and English translation (p. 106, modified): "Aber es lag in der Natur der Sache, daß auch ein gewisses Selbstdarstellungsbedürfnis der Lokalprominenz die 'Mittwoch-Abende' zu einem gesellschaftlichen Ereignis werden ließen. Das war gewollt. Und die meisten der anwesenden Gäste scheinen sich dessen bewußt gewesen zu sein. Als einmal im Oktober 1952 Martin Heidegger zusammen mit einem Münchner Privatdozenten eine Ehrung des Dichters Georg Trakl vornahm, soll das nachdenkliche Bonmot die Runde gemacht haben: 'Was wäre wohl dem schüchternen, unansehnlichen Pharmaziegehilfen Trakl geschehen, wenn er, aus seinem Grabe auferstanden, beim Portier Zutritt zu jenem illustren Kreis erbeten hätte?'"

"But of course it was natural that a certain need for showmanship on the part of the local celebrities turned the 'Wednesday Evenings' into a social event. This was intentional. And most of the guests attending appeared to be aware of this. When, on an evening in October 1952, Martin Heidegger and a private university lecturer from Munich [Eduard Lachmann, who actually taught in Innsbruck at the time] undertook to honour the poet Georg Trakl, a thoughtful bonmot is said to have made the rounds: 'What would have happened to the shy, unsightly pharmacy assistant Trakl if he had risen from his grave and asked the porter to admit him to this illustrious gathering?'")

Letter to Kurt Bauch from October 14, in Heidegger and Bauch, *Briefwechsel 1932–1975*, 145: "In dem Trubel auf Bühlerhöhe ging alles so eilig, daß ich vergaß, Dir für Deinen Geburtstagsbrief zu danken. Nimm diese Zeilen dafür. Den Streit zwischen dem gesprochenen und geschriebenen Wort werde ich wohl nie zum Ausgleich bringen. Das eine und das andere gleichmäßig zu pflegen geht über die Kraft, wenn für diese noch einiges übrig bleiben soll, was der sog. 'Produktion' zugute kommt. Gern hätte ich mit Dir unmittelbar nach dem Vortrag gesprochen. Es war nur ein 'Ausschnitt' und das Eigentliche ist gar nicht zu sagen. Außerdem war es ein Wagnis, weil die ganze Dichtung Trakls vorausgesetzt war. Doch wenn jetzt einige der Hörer die Dichtungen deutlicher hören, mag es schon gut sein. Und Stroomann hat wohl auch eine Freude gehabt. Sonst aber ist das Milieu unmöglich."

"In the hubbub at Bühlerhöhe everything was so rushed that I forgot to thank you for your birthday letter. Take these lines as thanks. I will probably never settle the clash between the spoken and the written word. To cultivate the one and the other evenly goes beyond one's powers if anything is to be left over that is useful for so-called 'production.' I would have liked to speak with you immediately after the lecture. It was only an 'excerpt,' and the genuine thing is not at all to be said. Additionally, it was a gamble, because the entirety of Trakl's poetic work was presupposed. But it may be all right if some of the audience members hear the poems more clearly now. And I think Stroomann also enjoyed it. Otherwise, the milieu is impossible."

Letter to Hannah Arendt from December 15, in Arendt and Heidegger, *Briefe 1925 bis 1975*, 137: "Anfang Oktober hielt ich auf Bühlerhöhe zu Prof. Stroomanns 65. Geburtstag auf dessen besondern Wunsch einen Vortrag über Georg Trakl. Herr von Ficker, der Herausgeber des *Brenner* und Freund und Beschützer Trakls, war auch da. Es war eine schöne Begegnung. Ich wurde in das Jahr 1912 versetzt, wo ich als Student in der Freiburger Akademischen Lesehalle den *Brenner* las und dabei zum ersten Mal auf Gedichte Trakls stieß. Seitdem haben sie mich nicht mehr losgelassen. Der Vortrag (Eine Erörterung des Gedichtes) soll zum Frühjahr erscheinen."

"At the beginning of October, I gave a lecture on Georg Trakl in honor of Prof. Stroomann's sixty-fifth birthday at the latter's special request. Mr. von Ficker, the editor of *Der Brenner* and friend and protector of Trakl, was also there. It was a beautiful encounter. I was taken back to the year 1912, when as a student I read *Der Brenner* in the Freiburg Academic Reading Hall and thus came across Trakl's poems for the first time. They haven't let go of me ever since. The lecture (A Discussion of the Poem) should appear in the spring."

Undated (likely composed in conjunction with "Language in the Poem," 1952)

In the Deutsches Literaturarchiv Marbach, there are eight bundles of notes by Heidegger on Trakl, totaling 973 pages. The archive's online catalogue provides the following information about some of the content:

Bundle 1a–f

"Denken 'über' Gedichte" ("Thinking 'about' Poems")
"Das Gedicht Georg Trakls" ("The Poem of Georg Trakl")
"Die Dichtung" ("Poetry")
"Phi – Pi" ("Phi – Pi [Philosophy – Poetry]")
"Das Gespräch – die Dichtung" ("Dialogue – Poetry")
"Zu den Gesprächen" ("On the Dialogues")

Bundle 2

"Das Christliche bei G. T." ("The Christian Element in G[eorg]. T[rakl].")
"Nietzsche"
"Deutung des Dichters" ("Interpretation of the Poet")

Bundle 3

"Das Geschlecht – Der Schmerz" ("Gender/Lineage/Tribe/Etc. – Pain")
"Schwester" ("Sister")
"Frauen – Mütter" ("Women – Mothers")
"Das blaue Weite" ("The Blue Expanse")
"Das Böse" ("Evil")
"Offenbarung und Untergang" ("Revelation and Downfall")
"Vogelflug" ("Birdflight")
"Dichten" ("To Poetize")
"Das Anschauen" ("Gazing")
"Demut und Neige. Der Fromme. 'Geistliche'" ("Humility and Decline. The Pious One. 'Spiritual'")
"Der Gerechte" ("The Just One")
"Der Bruder" ("The Brother")

Bundle 4

"Stein" ("Stone")
"Dorn" ("Thorn")
"Jener" ("That One")
"Sageweisen" ("Ways of Saying")
"Scheinen" ("Seeming/Shining")
"transitiv. Verb" ("Transitive Verb")

"Die Bläue" ("Blueness")
"Gold"
"Die Farben" ("Colors")
"Weiher. Teich" ("Pond. Mere")
"Spiegel" ("Mirror")
"Sprache" ("Language")
"G.T.s Sprache" ("G[eorg]. T[rakl'].s Language")

Bundle 5

"Seele: Geist" ("Soul: Spirit")
"Das Ungeborene" ("What Is Unborn")
"Ein 'Fremdes'" ("Something 'Strange/Foreign'")
"Die Fremdlinge" ("The Strangers/Foreigners")
"Elis"
"Das 'O'" ("The 'Oh'")

Bundle 6

"Der Abgeschiedene" ("The Detached One")
"Dämmerung" ("Twilight")
"Die Toten. Der Tod" ("The Dead. Death")
"Der wohnende Mensch" ("The Dwelling Human")
"Antlitz" ("Countenance")
"Gott" ("God")
"Sprachliches" ("The Linguistic")
"Geist und Wahnsinn" ("Spirit and Madness")

Bundle 7

"Bilder" ("Images")
"Die Klage" ("The Lamentation")
"Geist und Schauen" ("Spirit and Gazing")
"Die Nacht" ("Night")

Bundle 8

"Geistliche Dämmerung" ("Spiritual Twilight")
"Seele" ("Soul")

"Geistlich" ("Spiritual")
"Abend – Land" ("Evening – Land")
"Auferstehen" ("Arising/Resurrecting")

1952/53–1957
GA 100: 33–34 (*Vigiliae und Notturno* [*Vigils and Nocturne*]): "Die erregenden und entscheidenden Jahre zwischen 1907 und 1914: / Die erste Begegnung mit der Frage *ti to on* anhand der Schrift von Franz Brentano 'Von der mannigfachen Bedeutung des Seienden bei Aristoteles'; die Begegnung mit Hölderlin; 1911 Erscheinen der vollständigen Ausgabe von Nietzsches 'Willen zur Macht'; das Erscheinen der Kierkegaardübersetzungen; Rilkes Neue Gedichte und der Malte; die ersten Gedichte Trakls im 'Jüngsten Tag' 1913 und die späteren im Brenner. Das Bekanntwerden *Hegels*, gegenüber der bisherigen Vernachlässigung. Husserls 'Logische Untersuchungen.' / Alles in nur einer einzigen suchenden Leidenschaft und zugleich noch innerhalb der von Schell und Braig bewegten Theologie; der Modernismus und Bergson. Vordem schon seit 1905: Stifter. // Nur das Nicht-Preisgegebene ist wahrhaft als Geschenk gewährt, je und je verwahrt im Aufbehaltenen des immer sanfter nahenden, seine eigene Verhüllung erhöhenden Geheimnisses."

"The exciting and decisive years between 1907 and 1914: / The first encounter with the question *ti to on* [what is being?] on the basis of Franz Brentano's text *On the Manifold Meaning of Being in Aristotle*; the encounter with Hölderlin; in 1911 the appearance of the complete edition of Nietzsche's *Will to Power*; the appearance of the Kierkegaard translations [in, among other places, *Der Brenner*]; Rilke's *New Poems* and *Malte*; the first poems by Trakl in [the book series] *Der Jüngste Tag* [*Judgement Day*] and the later ones in *Der Brenner*. Becoming acquainted with *Hegel*, compared to the previous neglect. Husserl's *Logical Investigations*. / All in only a single seeking passion and at the same time still within the theology animated by Schell and Braig; modernism and Bergson. Previously already since 1905: Stifter. // Only what is not abandoned is truly granted as a gift, again and again kept safe in what is retained of the ever more gently approaching mystery that elevates its own concealment."

Ibid., 63 (citing Trakl's "Jahr," "Year"): "*Ostergabe* aus dem 'Jahr' / '. . . unter grünenden Eschen / Weidet Sanftmut bläulichen Blickes; goldene Ruh. / Ein Dunkles entzückt der Duft der Veilchen; . . .'"

"*Easter gift* from 'Year' / '. . . under greening ash trees / grazes the gentle temperament of the bluish gaze; golden rest. / A dark thing is enraptured by the fragrance of violets; . . .'"

1953

On January 4, Ficker sent Heidegger a picture of Trakl as a child next to a candle. On January 9, Heidegger replied (quoting from Trakl's "Abendländisches Lied," "Song of the Occident," and alluding to Trakl's "Gesang des Abgeschiedenen," "Song of the Departed One") (MH/LF: 49): "Im Jugendbild blickt einen die Frühe an; ich muß immer an einen Hirtenbuben denken: 'Hirten gingen wir einst an dämmernden Wäldern hin'— / und das Kerzenlicht, das gute— / wie weit vorausblickend dieses Kinderbild ist."

"In the image of the youth, earliness gazes at one: I must always think of a shepherd boy: 'We shepherds once went to twilit forests'— / and the candlelight, the good— / how forward-looking this child's image is."

In the same letter to Ficker from January 9, Heidegger writes (quoting Trakl's "Verklärung," "Transfiguration") (MH/LF: 50): "Denn [Trakls] Werk wird erst ein Maßstab *werden* müssen für die heutige Maßlosigkeit und Willkür im Reden und Schreiben. Und die aufwachsende Generation muß erst lernen, das in diesem Werk Gesagte zu schauen und zu hören. [. . .] 'Blaue Blume, / die leise tönt in vergilbtem Gestein.'"

"[Trakl's] work will first have to become a measure for today's measurelessness and arbitrariness in speaking and writing. And the generation that is growing up must first learn to behold and hear what is said in this work. [. . .] 'Blue flower, / which resounds softly in the yellowed stone.'"

On Palm Sunday, March 29, Heidegger, along with Clemens and Sophie Dorothee von Podewils, traveled to Mühlau to see Ficker; Heidegger and Ficker discussed Trakl, and they visited the poet's gravesite (MH/LF: 146–147 et passim). In response, on May 4, Heidegger wrote to Ficker (MH/LF: 53): "Alles, [Trakls] Sagen und sein Schmerz, die verborgenste stille Zuversicht und die Schönheit seines Wesens rückte mir in eine neue Gegenwart. / Ganz Anderes als das nur historisch-biographisch Vorstellbare kam mir seit diesem Besuch näher und fließt in die immer besinnlicheren stillen Gespräche mit dem Dichter ein. / Gerade in diesen Wochen, die ich wieder [. . .] an Nietzsches 'Also sprach Zarathustra' mich abmühe, erfahre ich, *welchen* Schritt Georg Trakl in der Verwindung des Dionysischen bei allem Schmerz hat vollziehen dürfen."

"Everything, [Trakl's] saying and his pain, the most concealed, still confidence and the beauty of his essence, moved me into a new present. / Since this visit, something completely different from what can be merely represented historiographically and biographically came closer to me and flows into the ever more reflective, still dialogues with the poet. / Precisely in these weeks, in which I am again [. . .] toiling away on Nietzsche's *Thus Spoke Zarathustra*, I experience *what* a step Georg Trakl had to take in twisting free from the Dionysian, despite all the pain."

(In *Auf einen Stern zugehen*, Heinrich Wiegand Petzet recounts a conversation he had with Heidegger on April 24. He quotes Heidegger as follows (p. 89): "Es ist übrigens bezeichnend für die Heutigen, daß sie ihr Dichten auch immer noch meinen erklären zu müssen! Das stinkt von Arroganz den Dingen gegenüber. Nehmen Sie die '[Probleme der] Lyrik' [von Gottfried Benn]: wenn Sie ehrlich sind, werden Sie zugeben, daß das einfach schlecht geschrieben ist, völlig an der Peripherie. Was west vom Gedicht in dieser 'Lyrik'? Wie schon gesagt: viele, sehr viele von seinen eigenen Gedichten bestehen und werden bestehen. Aber Benn ist niemals vom Expressionismus los- und darüber hinausgekommen. [. . .] / Und nun wird man natürlich böse, wenn einer wie Heidegger plötzlich über Trakl schreibt und einem ins Handwerk pfuscht. Sie werden mir zugeben, daß das, was wir auf der Bühlerhöhe über Trakl erarbeiten konnten, weltenweit weg ist vom Bennschen 'Denken' über Gedichte. Die Folge: Benn, dem ich nie ein Haar gekrümmt habe, beginnt nun auch, sich unmanierlich und beißend über mich zu äußern. Schon meinen 'Hölderlin' hat er mir todübel genommen. In den Zynismus Benns, in die falsch verstandene 'Artistik'—wo er doch meint, Nietzsche zu begreifen!—paßt das natürlich niemals hinein."

"It is, by the way, characteristic of our contemporaries that they also think they always have to explain their poetizing! That stinks of arrogance with respect to the things at issue. Take [Gottfried Benn's] *Problems of Lyric Poetry*: if you are honest, you will admit that it is simply poorly written, completely peripheral. What of the poem essentially holds sway in this *Lyric Poetry*? As I said already: many, very many of his own poems endure and will endure. But Benn has never gotten free of and beyond expressionism. [. . .] / And now people of course get angry when someone such as Heidegger suddenly writes about Trakl and poaches on their territory. You will admit that what we were able to work out at Bühlerhöhe on Trakl is worlds away from Bennian 'thinking' about poems. The result: Benn, on whose head I have never harmed a hair, now also begins to speak rudely and acerbically about me. He already held my *Hölderlin* against me. That of course would never fit into Benn's cynicism, into the falsely understood '*Artistik*'—where he nevertheless thinks he grasps Nietzsche!" Regarding Nietzsche, see, for example, Benn, "Nietzsche—nach fünfzig Jahren," in *Gesammelte Werke*, 1: 482–493; see also GA 100: 69.)

(On May 8, Erhart Kästner, in Heidegger and Kästner, *Briefwechsel, 1953–1974*, 19–20, wrote to Heidegger: "ich muß fürchten, für undankbar gehalten zu werden, weil ich Ihnen noch nicht für die gütevolle und mich so ehrende Übersendung des Trakl-Aufsatzes gedankt habe. Dabei bin ich Ihnen sogar doppelten Dank schuldig. Die guten Freunde Podewils haben mir Ihr Typoskript von 'Dichterisch wohnet . . .' anvertraut und ich kann Ihnen kaum schildern, wie sehr ich wochenlang nun wiederum darin gewohnt habe. [. . .] [S]icher gehört dieser Zug des vereinsamten Schreibers und Lesers ins Bild unserer Zustände, die so oft in der Verzweiflung der Kontaktlosigkeit enden, was eigentlich ja das Leiden Kafkas, Rilkes und eben Trakls ausmacht. [. . .] man bewahrt, nach dem Lesen [von 'Dichterisch wohnet . . .'], nicht einzelne Sätze, Sentenzen und Resultate im Sinn (beim Trakl-Aufsatz ist das ganz anders), sondern ein allgemeines Befinden. [. . .] / Sehr muß ich Ihnen auch für den 'Trakl' danken, der so wunderbare Sätze enthält. Mein Exemplar ist von roten Anstrichen bedeckt. Die Einsicht, zum Beispiel, daß jeder Dichter nur aus einem einzigen Gedicht dichte: wie wunderbar und wie wahr. Beim Lesen Ihrer Schriften ist man so oft von einer Empfindung berührt, welcher in der Philosophie so selten Anwesenheit erlaubt wird, und in den Räumen der Theologie, wo man sie bei jeder Gelegenheit zu treffen vermutet, durchaus gar nie: der Rührung. Ihr Werben—ich hoffe, ich darf es so nennen—um eines Frühverstorbenen Gedichte, Ihr Werben um das Gedicht überhaupt, von einer solchen Höhe herab, denn es ist doch ein Unterschied, welcher Verstand es ist, der sich beugt vor dem Gedicht: das muß erschüttern, muß rühren, und diese Art Rührung wiederum kann, nach dem Maß ihrer Voraussetzungen nicht die übliche sein."

"I have to fear being taken for ungrateful, as I have not yet thanked you for kindly sending me the Trakl essay ["Language in the Poem"], which was such an honor. I thus owe you double thanks. Our good friends the Podewils entrusted me with your typescript of 'Poetically dwells . . . ,' and I can hardly depict to you how much I have, for weeks, again dwelled in it. [. . .] [T]his feature of the isolated writer and reader surely belongs in the picture of our circumstances, which so often end in the despair of contactlessness, which actually comprises the suffering of Kafka, Rilke, and precisely Trakl. [. . .] [A]fter reading it ['Poetically dwells . . .'], one retains, not individual sentences, maxims, or results (it is completely different with the Trakl essay), but a general feeling. [. . .] / I must also thank you for the 'Trakl,' which contains sentences that are so wonderful. My copy is covered with red marks. The insight, for example, that every poet poetizes only from one single poem: how wonderful and how true. In reading your writings, one is so often moved [berührt] by a sentiment that is so seldom allowed to be present in philosophy, and never at all in the realms of theology, where one expects to find it on every occasion: emotion [Rührung]. Your appeal—I hope I can call it that—on behalf of the poems of one who died early, your appeal on behalf of the poem in general, from such a height—for it makes a difference which mind bends before the poem—this must shake, must move, and this kind of emotion, according to the measure of its presuppositions, cannot in turn be the usual one.")

1953–1954
GA 12: 87–88 ("Aus einem Gespräch von der Sprache zwischen einem Japaner und einem Fragenden" ["From a Dialogue on Language Between a Japanese and a Questioner"]): "F Und ich habe das 1927 erschienene Buch 'Sein und Zeit' Husserl gewidmet, weil die Phänomenologie Möglichkeiten eines Weges schenkte. / J Mir scheint jedoch, die Thematik 'Sprache und Sein' blieb im Hintergrund. / F Sie blieb es schon in der von Ihnen genannten Vorlesung aus dem Jahre 1921 [sic; richtig: *Phänomenologie der Anschauung und des Ausdrucks*, 1920]. So stand es auch mit den Fragen nach der Dichtung und der Kunst. In jener Zeit des Expressionismus waren mir diese Bereiche stets gegenwärtig, mehr jedoch und schon aus meiner Studienzeit vor dem ersten Weltkrieg die Dichtung Hölderlins und Trakls."

"Q: I devoted the book *Being and Time* (1927) to Husserl, because phenomenology bestowed possibilities of a path. / J: The topic of 'language and being' nevertheless seems to me to have remained in the background. / Q: It remained there already in the lecture course from 1921 you mentioned [sic; should be *Phenomenology of Intuition and Expression*, 1920]. This was also the case with the questions concerning poetry and art. In that age of expressionism, these domains were constantly present for me, but even more, and already from my school days before the First World War, was the poetry of Hölderlin and Trakl."

Ibid., 115: "F insofern man in der Öffentlichkeit nicht ohne Titel auskommt. / J Dies kann Sie jedoch nicht hindern, auch die inzwischen aufgegebenen Namen 'Hermeneutik' und 'hermeneutisch' noch genauer zu erläutern. / F Ich versuche es gern, weil die Erläuterung in eine Erörterung übergehen kann. J In dem Sinne, wie Ihr Vortrag über Trakls Gedicht die Erörterung versteht. / F Genau so."

"Q: insofar as one does not get by in public without titles. / J: But that cannot prevent you from more precisely elucidating the terms 'hermeneutics' and 'hermeneutic,' which you have since abandoned. / Q: I am happy to attempt to do so, since elucidation can lead to an *Erörterung*. / J: In the sense that your lecture on Trakl's poetic work understands the term [as emplacement rather than discussion]. / Q: Precisely."

1954

(On March 22, one of the editors of *Merkur*, Hans Paeschke, wrote to Gottfried Benn [in Benn, Paeschke, and Moras, *Briefwechsel 1948–1956*, 107]: "erzählte ich Ihnen nicht davon, daß Heidegger mit seinen Jüngern nicht nur Hölderlin und Trakl, sondern auch Sie zu lesen und vorzulesen liebt und mir vor drei Jahren sagte, Sie seien unter den Lebenden der einzige, dem das 'dichtende Sagen' so wie Heidegger es auffasst, vergönnt sei. / Natürlich werden Preetorius und Podewils ihm nichts aus Ihrem Vortrag ["Altern als Problem für Künstler"] zitiert haben. Vielleicht haben Sie sich mit diesem Vortrag erspart, sich eines Tages von Heidegger auf dessen Weise so analysiert zu sehen, wie es dem armen Trakl passiert ist."

"Didn't I tell you that Heidegger loves to read and read aloud not only Hölderlin and Trakl but also you with his followers, and that three years ago he told me that you are the only one among the living to whom 'poetic saying,' as Heidegger conceives of it, has been granted? / Of course, Preetorius and Podewils won't have quoted to him anything from your lecture ["Aging as a Problem for Artists"]. Perhaps with this lecture you saved yourself from one day seeing yourself analyzed by Heidegger in the same way as it occurred with poor Trakl.")

(Tezuka Tomio's "An Hour with Heidegger" provides a report of a conversation Tezuka had with Heidegger in March. This conversation, among other things, served as a basis for "From a Dialogue on Language Between a Japanese and a Questioner," which I quote in the material under "1953–1954," above. On page 62, Tezuka writes: "When I mentioned 'the open' as a possible translation of *kū* (emptiness) I already had a premonition that this would sit well with [Heidegger] as an interpreter of Hölderlin and Rilke. He was pleased indeed! 'East and West,' he said, 'must engage in dialogue at this deep level. It is useless to do interviews that merely deal with one superficial phenomenon after another.' He then showed me several books containing his latest essays, and I was delighted to receive an offprint of his piece on Trakl.")

1957 (and 1972)

GA 1: 56 ("Vorwort zur ersten Ausgabe der 'Frühen Schriften' (1972)" ["Preface to the First Edition of the 'Early Writings' (1972)"]), reproducing material from a 1957 "Antrittsrede" ("Inaugural Speech"): "Was die erregenden Jahre zwischen 1910 und 1914 brachten, läßt sich gebührend nicht sagen, sondern nur durch eine Weniges auswählende Aufzählung andeuten: Die zweite um das Doppelte vermehrte Ausgabe von Nietzsches 'Willen zur Macht,' die Übersetzung der Werke Kierkegaards und Dostojewskis, das erwachende Interesse für Hegel und Schelling, Rilkes Dichtungen und Trakls Gedichte, Diltheys 'Gesammelte Schriften.'"

"I cannot properly say what the exciting years between 1910 and 1914 brought, but I can provide some indications through the following selective list: the second edition of Nietzsche's *Will to Power*, which was double the size of the first; the translation of the works of Kierkegaard and Dostoyevsky; the awakening interest in Hegel and Schelling, Rilke's poetic works and Trakl's poems [*Gedichte*, perhaps a reference to the 1913 collection], Dilthey's *Collected Writings*."

1958

(On May 11, Heidegger delivered the lecture "Dichten und Denken" ["Poetizing and Thinking"] in Vienna [cf. GA 12: 205–225]. During the trip back home, he stopped off in Mühlau to visit Ficker. Günther Neske, Heidegger's traveling companion, reports ["Nachwort des Herausgebers," 297–298]: "Wir reisten durch die Wachau zurück. Man freute sich während der Fahrt schon auf Salzburg und machte Pläne. Heidegger wollte den Park von Hellbrunn sehen, die Weiher, die durch Trakls

Gedichte gehen. Auf der Donaufähre, während uns die Kette mit der Strömung ans andere Ufer holte, kam die Sprache darauf. Heidegger begann zu zitieren, stockte und suchte den Fortgang. Ich griff in meine Tasche und reichte ihm Trakls Gedichte, einen der blauen Bände von Otto Müller, schon etwas verwittert vom vielen Gebrauch. 'Haben Sie das immer bei sich?' — 'Nicht immer, aber hierzuland schon.' / Manche Episode dieser Reise ist mir in Erinnerung geblieben, ganz besonders der Besuch bei Ludwig von Ficker in Mühlau bei Innsbruck, der uns an Trakls Grab führte, in einer hellen, sommerlichen Mittagsstunde. Damals fragte mich Heidegger, ob ich jenes Bild des zwölfjährigen Trakl mit der Kerze kennen würde. Ich verneinte. Ludwig von Ficker sandte mir bald darauf das Kalenderblatt: ein dem Leiden verschriebenes Kindergesicht von großem Ernst und ahnungsvoller Trauer, seltsam beschattet vom großen Hut und nicht erhellt von der kleinen Kerzenflamme im Windlicht, über die es hinwegsieht—*Grodek* vorweggenommen."

"We traveled back through the Wachau [Valley]. During the journey, we were already looking forward to Salzburg and made plans. Heidegger wanted to see the park of [the] Hellbrunn [palace], the ponds that recur throughout Trakl's poems. We spoke of this on the Danube ferry, while the chain was pulling us with the current to the other bank. Heidegger began to recite, faltered, and sought to go on. I reached into my pocket and handed him Trakl's poems, one of the blue volumes [published] by Otto Müller [Press], already somewhat weathered from much use. 'Do you always have this with you?' — 'Not always, but always when I'm in these parts.' / Many an episode from this trip has stayed with me, especially the visit to Ludwig von Ficker in Mühlau, near Innsbruck, who took us to Trakl's gravesite one bright summer afternoon. During that time, Heidegger asked me whether I was familiar with the picture of the twelve-year-old Trakl with the candle. I said no. Ludwig von Ficker soon sent me the calendar sheet [with the picture on it]: the face of a child dedicated to suffering, of great seriousness and foreboding sorrow, strangely shaded by the large hat and not illuminated by the small candle flame in the lantern, which [the face] looks away from—in anticipation of 'Gródek.'")

1959

On February 4, Heidegger wrote to Ingrid Strohschneider-Kohrs, relating that he had spent the morning with Trakl editor Walther Killy examining some of Trakl's manuscripts. He says that Killy provided him with some photocopies and intended to send more. Heidegger also mentions that he and Killy had discussed Strohschneider-Kohrs's habilitation lecture on Trakl, "Die Entwicklung der lyrischen Sprache in der Dichtung Georg Trakls" ("The Development of Lyrical Language in Georg Trakl's Poetry"). Later in the letter, Heidegger asks whether Strohschneider-Kohrs has a transcript of the second version of his first Trakl lecture, "Die Sprache." He tells her he has a copy ready for her along with other material.

On March 2, Heidegger wrote to Ingrid Strohschneider-Kohrs about a visit to Freiburg by Ludwig von Ficker. Heidegger says Ficker gave an impressive lecture (namely, "Der Abschied," "The Departure") and that Heidegger showed him a copy of Strohschneider-Kohrs's habilitation lecture on Trakl, "Die Entwicklung der lyrischen Sprache in der Dichtung Georg Trakls" ("The Development of Lyrical Language in Georg Trakl's Poetry"). Heidegger also tells Strohschneider-Kohrs that he would like to read to her the final version of a lecture on language (presumably, "Die Sprache," "Language," but "Der Weg zur Sprache," "The Way to Language," is also a possibility).

On October 12, Heidegger wrote to Ficker (MH/LF: 67): "Es gehört zu den schönsten Schickungen des vergangenen Jahrzehnts, daß ich Ihnen und Ihrer Umwelt begegnen durfte."

"It is among the most beautiful strokes of fate of the past decade that I was able to encounter you and your milieu."

GA 12: 242 ("Der Weg zur Sprache" ["The Way to Language"], citing Trakl's "Traum und Umnachtung" ["Dream and Lunacy"]): "Wir pflegen das Wort 'Sage,' wie manche anderen Worte unserer Sprache, jetzt meist in einem herabmindernden Sinne zu gebrauchen. Sage gilt als die bloße Sage, das Gerücht, was nicht verbürgt und daher unglaubwürdig ist. So wird 'die Sage' hier nicht gedacht, auch nicht in dem wesentlichen Sinne, den die Rede von der 'Götter- und Heldensage' meint. Aber vielleicht 'die ehrwürdige Sage des blauen Quells' (G. Trakl)? Nach dem ältesten Gebrauch des Wortes verstehen wir die Sage vom Sagen als dem Zeigen her und gebrauchen zur Benennung der Sage, insofern in ihr das Sprachwesen beruht, ein altes, gutbezeugtes, aber ausgestorbenes Wort: *die Zeige*. Das pronomen demonstrativum wird übersetzt durch 'Zeigewörtlin.' Jean Paul nennt die Erscheinungen der Natur 'den geistigen Zeigefinger.' / *Das Wesende der Sprache ist die Sage als die Zeige*."

"Today we tend to use the [German] word 'Sage,' like many other words of our language, mostly in a disparaging sense. Sage is considered to be mere say-so, rumor, which is unestablished and therefore untrustworthy. Here, we are not thinking of 'Sage' in this way, nor in the essential sense intended by the discourse of the 'saga [Sage] of gods and heroes.' But perhaps 'the venerable Sage of the blue source' (G. Trakl)? In accordance with the oldest use of the word, we understand Sage from saying [Sagen] as showing [Zeigen] and use an old, well-attested, but obsolete word to name this Sage: die Zeige ['the pointing']. The demonstrative pronoun is translated [into German] with 'Zeigewörtlin' [literally, 'little pointer word']. Jean Paul names the appearances of nature 'the spiritual pointer finger.' / The essencing of language is Sage as Zeige."

(In Auf einen Stern zugehen, 115, Petzet relates: "Zu Heideggers bevorstehendem 70. Geburtstag sollte ich einen Beitrag zu einer der Festschriften liefern. Die kleine Betrachtung, die damals entstand, blieb im Grunde ein Torso, weil sie nicht bis ins Letzte durchdacht war. 'Sie wissen anscheinend gar nicht, was Sie da angerührt haben!' sagte Heidegger, als er den Beitrag gelesen hatte. Ich wollte darin etwas vom Sich-Widerspiegeln eines Kunstwerks in einem anderen aufzeigen, von dem Goethe einmal gesprochen hat. Ein Bild in einem Gedicht. Als Beispiel hatte ich ein im Basler Kunstmuseum hängendes 'Stilleben' von Juan Gris und das 'Rondell' von Trakt gewählt."

"For Heidegger's upcoming seventieth birthday, I was supposed to make a contribution to one of the Festschrifts. The small consideration that emerged at the time remained basically a torso, since it was not thought through all the way to the end. 'You apparently don't realize at all what you have touched on there!,' said Heidegger when he had read the contribution. In it, I wanted to show something of the reflecting of one artwork in another that Goethe once spoke about. An image in a poem. As an example, I had chosen a 'still life' by Juan Gris that was hanging in the Basel Art Museum and Trakl's 'Rondel.'" See Petzet, "'. . . Reif ist die Traube / Und festlich die Luft . . . ,'" which takes its title from Trakl's "Stundenlied" ["Song of the Hours"]. It ambitiously sets itself the task of "leading one step further to that authentic site of Trakl's poetic work [einen Schritt weiter an jenen eigentlichen Ort des Gedichtes Trakls]" [243]. Incidentally, several other prominent authors with interests in Trakl and in Heidegger's reading of him contributed to the same Festschrift: Ilse Aichinger's poetic contribution, "Versuch"

["Attempt"], has been compared with other works she composed on "her favorite poet" Trakl, including a poem with the same title; Friedrich Georg Jünger read some of Trakl's poems aloud after Heidegger's delivery of "Language in the Poem" at Bühlerhöhe in 1952; Clemens Podewils attended the event as well and published an article about it in one of the most important newspapers of post-war Germany; Beda Allemann defended Heidegger's reading of Trakl against W. H. Rey's critique. For Aichinger, see Hina, "'Die heute undurchschaubare Strategie der Liebe." For F. G. Jünger and Heidegger's relation to him, see Morat, *Von der Tat zur Gelassenheit*, especially 352–353, 491. See also Podewils, "Erörterung eines Trakl-Gedichts" and "Eine Trakl-Feier"; Allemann, *Hölderlin und Heidegger*, 201; and F. G. Jünger's later text "Trakls Gedichte." Paul Celan, after much hesitation, refused to contribute to the Festschrift. See Bambach, "Celan and Heidegger," for details.)

1960
(On April 13, Heidegger gave a speech in Innsbruck in honor of Ficker's eightieth birthday. They visited numerous sites to which Trakl was connected, including, again, his gravesite, from which Heidegger took a cowslip and brought it home to his wife Elfride. Petzet, *Auf einen Stern zugehen*, 158; Heidegger, "*Mein liebes Seelchen!*," 341.)

1961
On December 22, Heidegger wrote to Ficker (MH/LF: 81): "Ich habe oft an Sie gedacht, und immer ist auch Georg Trakl mit im Andenken, dessen Dichtung mich in diesen Monaten wieder besonders anging. Die Gedichtanfänge 'Es ist ein . . .' beschäftigen mein Nachdenken (vgl. 'De Profundis' und 'Psalm')."

"I have often thought of you, and Georg Trakl is also always there in the remembrance, one whose poetizing was again especially relevant for me in these months. The 'There is a . . .' [or literally, 'It is a . . .'] at the beginning of poems occupies my thoughts (see 'De Profundis' and 'Psalm')."

Sometime between 1961 and 1965 (likely in conjunction with preparations for the 1962 lecture "Time and Being")
Heidegger wrote out Trakl's poem "De Profundis" and sent it to Ragnvi Maeter. In what appears to be the accompanying letter, Heidegger writes: "Dieser Gruß mitten aus der Arbeit in der Werkstatt möchte zu Dir."

"This greeting from the middle of labor in the workshop wishes to reach you."

1962
GA 14: 5 ("Zeit und Sein" ["Time and Being"]): "Könnte uns jetzt, und gar durch den Dichter Georg *Trakl* selbst, sein Gedicht 'Siebengesang des Todes' vorgesagt werden, dann möchten wir es oft hören und jeden Anspruch auf unmittelbare Verständlichkeit preisgeben."
  "If his poem 'Sevensong of Death' could be recited to us right now, and especially if the poet Georg *Trakl* could do so himself, we would wish to hear it often and would give up any claim to immediate intelligibility."

Ibid., 47–49 ("Protokoll zu einem Seminar über 'Zeit und Sein' " ["Protocol of a Seminar on 'Time and Being' "]): "Wegen des mitschwingenden Bezugs zum Menschen nennt das 'Es gibt' im unmittelbaren Sprachgebrauch das Sein deutlicher als das bloße 'sein,' das 'ist.' Daß aber auch das 'ist' nicht immer und nur den theoretisch abgeblaßten Sinn der Feststellung einer puren Vorhandenheit hat, zeigt sich in der dichterischen Sprache. Trakl sagt: // 'Es ist ein Licht, das der Wind ausgelöscht hat. / Es ist ein Heidekrug, den am Nachmittag ein Betrunkener verläßt. / Es ist ein Weinberg, verbrannt und schwarz mit Löchern voll Spinnen. / Es ist ein Raum, den sie mit Milch getüncht haben.' // Diese Verse stehen in der ersten Strophe des Gedichts 'Psalm.' In einem anderen 'De profundis' betitelten Gedicht, das zum selben Zyklus gehört wie das erstgenannte, sagt Trakl: // 'Es ist ein Stoppelfeld, in das ein schwarzer Regen fällt. / Es ist ein brauner Baum, der einsam dasteht. / Es ist ein Zischelwind, der leere Hütten umkreist— / Wie traurig dieser Abend. / . . . / . . . / Es ist ein Licht, das in meinem Mund erlöscht. // Und Rimbaud sagt in einem Stück aus 'Les Illuminations' // Au bois il y a un oiseau, son chant vous arrête et vous fait rougir. / Il y a une horloge qui ne sonne pas. [. . .]' // Das französische 'Il y a' (vgl. die süddeutsche mundartliche Wendung 'es hat') entspricht dem deutschen 'Es gibt,' hat aber eine größere Weite. Die sachgemäße Übersetzung des 'Il y a' bei Rimbaud wäre im Deutschen das 'Es ist,' wie es denn zu vermuten ist, daß Trakl das genannte Gedicht Rimbauds kannte. [. . .] Zunächst läßt sich sagen, daß es [das 'Es ist'] ebensowenig wie das 'Es gibt' das Vorhandensein von etwas feststellt. Im Unterschied zum gewöhnlichen 'Es gibt' nennt es aber nicht das Verfügbarsein dessen, was es gibt, sondern dieses gerade als ein Unverfügbares, das Angehende als ein Unheimliches, das Dämonische.

Somit ist mit dem 'Es ist' der Bezug zum Menschen, und zwar ungleich schärfer als im gewöhnlichen 'Es gibt,' mitgenannt."

"In the direct use of language, the phrase *Es gibt* [literally, 'It gives'], due to the relation to the human that resonates in it, names being more clearly than the mere 'to be,' the 'is.' That, however, the 'is' does not always and only have the theoretically discolored sense of ascertaining a pure presence-at-hand either, shows up in poetic language. Trakl says: // 'There is [or literally, 'It is'] a light, which the wind has extinguished. / There is a heathland tavern, which a drunkard abandons in the afternoon. / There is a vineyard, burned and black with holes full of spiders. / There is a room, which they have whitewashed with milk.' These verses appear in the first stanza of 'Psalm.' In another poem, titled 'De profundis,' which belongs to the same cycle as the first-named one, Trakl says: // 'There is a stubble field, on which a black rain falls. / There is a brown tree, which stands there all alone. / There is a hissing wind, which encircles empty shacks — / How sad this evening. / . . . / . . . / There is a light that is extinguished in my mouth.' // And Rimbaud says in a passage from *Illuminations* // 'In the forest there is a bird, its song arrests you and makes you blush. / There is a clock that does not sound. [. . .]' The French *Il y a* (cf. the South-German dialect phrase *es hat* ['it has']) corresponds to the German *Es gibt*, but has a broader scope. In German, the appropriate translation of *Il y a* in Rimbaud would be *Es ist*, which leads one to suppose that Trakl was familiar with the cited poem by Rimbaud. [. . .] Initially we can say that it [the *Es ist*] ascertains the being-present-at-hand of something as little as does the *Es gibt*. In contrast to the ordinary *Es gibt*, however, it names, not the availability of that which is given [*was es gibt*], but rather the latter as what is unavailable, that which concerns us as something uncanny, the demonic. Thus, the relation to the human is also named with the *Es ist*, indeed much more sharply than in the ordinary *Es gibt*."

1963 (or possibly later)
GA 102: 99 (*Vorläufiges I–IV* [*Preliminaries I–IV*]): "Weil die Sprache jeweils gelichtet-verborgen, bleibt die Sage mehrdeutig. / *Sage*: Zeigend, aber ihr Zeigen ein *Winken—Winken* zeigt in das Vermutbare—Unvermutete—deshalb ist die Sage mehrdeutig (vgl. Trakl-Aufsatz)."

"Because language is in each case cleared-concealed, the saying remains polysemous. / *Saying*: showing, but its showing a *hinting—hinting* points to the surmisable—unsurmised—for this reason, the saying is polysemous (cf. the Trakl essay)." See "Language in the Poem," GA 12: 70–71.

1964

On July 3, Heidegger wrote to Ficker (MH/LF: 91): "das früher auf Bühlerhöhe Versuchte und Gewagte war nur ein Tasten. Heute seh ich die Einzigkeit der Dichtung Trakls viel deutlicher, erkenne aber auch die gedankliche und sprachliche Rat- und Mittellosigkeit, ihr zu entsprechen."

"what was attempted and ventured earlier at Bühlerhöhe was only a groping. Today I see the uniqueness of Trakl's poetry much more clearly, but also recognize the conceptual and linguistic perplexity and lack of means when it comes to speaking in correspondence with it."

1966

On December 20, Heidegger wrote to Ficker (MH/LF: 98–99): "Immer wieder stoße ich auf die Spuren Ihres Wirkens und bedenke jedesmal, wie ganz anders Sie das Werk unseres Dichters hüteten im Vergleich mit dem heutigen literarischen Betrieb, der, statt das Hören auf den Dichter zu wecken und zu pflegen, alles auflöst und durch ein irregeleitetes Erklärenwollen das Wort zerstört."

"Again and again, I come across the traces of your work and consider every time how completely differently you tended the work of our poet in comparison with today's literary enterprise, which, instead of awakening and cultivating the act of listening to the poet, dissolves everything and destroys the word through a misguided will to explain."

1967

(On July 24, Paul Celan gave a legendary poetry reading at the University of Freiburg. Over one thousand people were in attendance, including Heidegger, who sat in the front row. Next to him was Ficker's daughter Birgit von Schowingen, whom Celan had already encountered many years prior during a visit to Innsbruck to meet with Ficker and lay flowers at Trakl's grave. After the poetry reading, Celan met with Heidegger, von Schowingen, the Germanist Gerhart Baumann, and the latter's student Gerhard Neumann at the Hotel Victoria, where they apparently discussed, among other things, Heidegger's reading of Trakl. Baumann told Celan that Heidegger had been acquainted with Ficker, who had passed away just a few months prior. As Hans-Peter Kunisch, drawing on a variety of sources, (imaginatively) reconstructs the encounter: "Jetzt hat Heidegger einen Anknüpfungspunkt. Vor Jahren habe er im Schlosshotel auf der Bühlerhöhe einen Vortrag über Trakl gehalten. Er habe natürlich gewusst, dass der Herr Papa der Gnädigen Frau im Publikum saß und habe ihm die Ehre erwiesen. Seither seien sie befreundet. [. . .] Heidegger strahlt. Er hat den Vortrag zu Georg Trakls 'Gedicht,' der, wie alle großen Dichter, nur eines geschrieben habe, noch genau im Kopf. Baumann bittet ihn. Alles dreht sich um das Fremde: 'Doch was heißt 'fremd'? Man versteht unter dem Fremdartigen gewöhnlich das Nichtvertraute, was nicht anspricht, solches, das eher lastet und beunruhigt. Allein, 'fremd,' althochdeutsch 'fram,' bedeutet eigentlich: anderswohin vorwärts, unterwegs nach . . . dem Voraufbehaltenen entgegen. Das Fremde wandert voraus. Doch es irrt nicht, bar jeder Bestimmung, rastlos umher. Das Fremde geht suchend auf den Ort zu, wo es als ein Wanderndes bleiben kann.' [. . .] 'Ich habe den Vortrag dem Herrn Vater gewidmet, und ich glaube, er hat ihn gefreut.'"

"Now Heidegger had a point of contact. Years ago, [Heidegger relates according to Kunisch,] he delivered a lecture on Trakl in the castle-hotel at Bühlerhöhe. He of course knew that the dear father of the madam sat in the audience, and he did him the honor. They've been friends ever since. [. . .] Heidegger is beaming. He still has in his head the lecture on the 'poem' of Georg Trakl, who, like all great poets, wrote only one. Baumann entreats him. Everything turns on the strange/foreign [*fremd*]: 'Yet what does '*fremd*' mean? Typically, by *fremd* and what pertains to it, one understands what is not familiar, what does not appeal to one, something that instead burdens and disquiets. Yet, '*fremd*,' '*fram*' in Old High German, authentically means: forward toward somewhere else, on the way to . . . , on toward what is already held in store for one. That which is *fremd* wanders out in advance. It does not restlessly roam about, however, devoid of any determination. That which is *fremd* goes, seeking, toward the place where it can remain as that which wanders.' [. . .] 'I dedicated the lecture to her father, and I believe he liked it.'" Kunisch, *Todtnauberg*, 107–108. See also Baumann, *Erinnerungen an Paul Celan*, 67–68, 70, and GA 12: 36–37.)

Letter to Arendt from October 30, in Arendt and Heidegger, *Briefe 1925 bis 1975*, 162: "Die Beispiele für den transitiven Gebrauch des Verbums ['schweigen'], die ich vergeblich suchte, lege ich Dir bei. [. . .] IM DUNKEL // Es schweigt die Seele den blauen Frühling. / Unter feuchtem Abendgezweig / Sank in Schauern die Stirne den Liebenden.

// ABENDLIED // Frühlingsgewölke steigen über die finstere Stadt, / Die der Mönche edlere Zeiten schweigt."
 "I have enclosed for you the examples of the transitive use of the verb [*schweigen*, 'to silence'] that I couldn't find before. [. . .] IN DARKNESS // The soul silences the blue Spring. / Under damp evening branches / the lovers' brow sank down shuddering. // EVENING SONG // Spring clouds rise over the gloomy city, / Which silences the nobler times of monks."

(Letter from Arendt to Heidegger from November 27, in Arendt and Heidegger, *Briefe 1925 bis 1975*, 163: "Dank für die 'Beispiele' des transitiven Gebrauchs des Schweigens (sehr schön, ich glaube ich verstand es gleich; bei Mallarmé geht es doch nicht, weil *tacite* nur Adjektiv ist, das Verb *taire* kann auch transitiv sein, taire la vérité)."
 "Thank you for the 'examples' of the transitive use of silencing (very beautiful, I believe I understood it right away; yet it doesn't work in Mallarmé, since *tacite* is only an adjective; the verb *taire* can also be transitive: *taire la vérité* [to silence the truth]).")

1969
(In an interview with Heidegger conducted by Frédéric de Towarnicki and Jean-Michel Palmier, and published in French in the October 20–26 issue of *L'express*, one reads, on page 84 [and here I place the interviewers' comments in italics]: "—*On s'est souvent étonné d'une cassure singulière survenue dans votre œuvre. On a parlé d'un Heidegger I et d'un Heidegger II. Brusquement, survient un changement de style. Vous semblez quitter le chemin aride de l'interrogation métaphysique et vous interrogez les poètes, Hölderlin, Mörike, Hebbel [sic], Rilke et surtout Trakl.* —Je l'ai écrit: la philosophie et la poésie se tiennent sur des monts opposés, mais elles disent la même chose. —*Pensez-vous qu'il soit possible de distinguer un Heidegger I d'un Heidegger II, comme le font des commentateurs américains?* —Absolument pas. Le Heidegger II n'est possible que par le Heidegger I, et le Heidegger I impliquait déjà le Heidegger II. —*Et votre nouveau style d'interrogation, disons poétique, après 'Etre et temps'?* —Ce n'est qu'un tournant."

"—*One is often surprised by a singular break in your work. One has spoken of a Heidegger I and a Heidegger II. Suddenly, a change of style occurs. You seem to leave the dry path of metaphysical interrogation, and you interrogate the poets, Hölderlin, Mörike, Hebbel* [sic; should be Johann Peter *Hebel*, not Christian Friedrich *Hebbel*], *Rilke, and above all Trakl.*

—I have written: philosophy and poetry stand on opposite mountains, but they say the same thing. —*Do you think it is possible to distinguish a Heidegger I from a Heidegger II, as American commentators do?* —Absolutely not. Heidegger II is only possible through Heidegger I, and Heidegger I already implies Heidegger II. —*And your new, let us say poetic, style of interrogation after* Being and Time? —This is just a turning.")

In or after 1969
GA 14: 80n12 (marginal note in "Das Ende der Philosophie und die Aufgabe des Denkens" ["The End of Philosophy and the Task of Thinking"], citing Trakl's "Im Weinland" ["In the Wine Country"]): " 'Ein Windstoß alte Linden lichtet' / G. Trakl, WW 1969, S. 274."

" 'A gust of wind clears old lindens' / G. Trakl, WW 1969 [see the 1st edition of volume 1 of HKA], p. 274." The note refers to the first instance of 'lichten' in the following passage: "Waldlichtung ist erfahren im Unterschied zum dichten Wald, in der älteren Sprache 'Dickung' genannt. Das Substantivum 'Lichtung' geht auf das Verbum 'lichten' zurück. Das Adjektivum 'licht' ist dasselbe Wort wie 'leicht.' Etwas lichten bedeutet: etwas leicht, etwas frei und offen machen, z. B. den Wald an einer Stelle frei machen von Bäumen."

"A clearing in the forest is experienced in contrast to the thick [*dichten*] forest, called in older [German] language a *Dickung* ['thicket']. The noun *Lichtung* ['clearing'] goes back to the verb *lichten* ['to clear']. The adjective *licht* is the same word as *leicht* ['light,' in the sense of 'not heavy']. *Etwas lichten* means: to make something light, something free and open, for example, to make the forest free of trees at a particular spot."

Undated (likely from 1969 or later)
On a single sheet sold to an undisclosed party by Kotte Autographs, Heidegger copied down four quotes by Trakl: "Ein Windstoß alte Linden lichtet" ("A gust of wind clears old lindens") (from "Im Weinland" ["In the Wine Country"]); "O das Wohnen in blauen Höhlen der Schwermut" ("Oh, dwelling in blue caves of melancholy") (from "Lange lauscht der Mönch" ["Long Listens the Monk"]); "Nur dem der das Glück verachtet, wird Erkenntnis" ("Knowledge comes only to one who has contempt for happiness") (Aphorism 1); and ". . . Die milde Stille | Erfüllt von leiser Antwort dunkler Fragen" (". . . The mild stillness / Filled by the faint answer of dark questions") (from "Der Herbst des Einsamen" ["Autumn of the Solitary One"]).

1970

(In the preface to the new edition of *Situation de Georg Trakl*, 18–19, 23, Jean-Michel Palmier relates that the idea for his book came from a meeting he had had with Heidegger: "Ce fut naturellement la lecture de l'essai de Heidegger qui l'orienta [l'auteur] vers le désir d'élucider cette [Trakl's] œuvre insolite. Par sa densité, sa profondeur, le commentaire de Heidegger était aussi fascinant que l'œuvre de Trakl elle-même. Comment pouvait-il affirmer sérieusement que ce poète mort en 1914 d'un excès de cocaïne dans un hôpital de Cracovie était 'le poète du destin de l'Occident non encore dévoilé'? Que signifiait cet étrange rapprochement qu'il effectuait ailleurs entre *L'Étranger* de Trakl et le Zarathoustra de Nietzsche? C'est après que j'eus consacré une maîtrise de philosophie à l'analyse du rectorat de Heidegger en 1933 [*Les écrits politiques de Heidegger*, L'Herne, 1968] que le philosophe allemand me convia à Fribourg-en-Brisgau. Et aujourd'hui encore je ne peux me souvenir de cette rencontre sans émotion. Je le questionnai entre autres sur son intérêt pour Trakl. Il me déclara l'avoir lu très tôt, pendant la guerre de 1914, et il me montra quelques photos—de Trakl lui-même et de sa sœur, je crois—qu'il gardait sur son bureau. Étrange attention de la part de quelqu'un qui, justement, affirmait bien haut son refus de prendre en considération tout élément biographique pour comprendre une œuvre. / Après avoir constaté avec regret qu'il n'existait aucune étude assez vaste consacrée au poète autrichien, je résolus de lui consacre une thèse de troisième cycle, sous la direction bienveillante mais un peu perplexe de Paul Ricœur, qui se demandait ce que ce poète toxicomane et alcoolique, amoureux de sa sœur, obsédé par un univers de couleurs et de ruines, pouvait avoir de philosophique. Mais la générosité de Paul Ricœur était si grande qu'il me laissa tenter l'aventure. [. . .] [Q]ue Heidegger ait pu s'intéresser à un travail réalisé par un étudiant et l'encourager à poursuivre témoigne aussi de la part de Heidegger d'une générosité qui invite à la plus extrême humilité."

"Reading Heidegger's essay ["Language in the Poem"] was naturally what oriented [me] toward the desire to elucidate [Trakl's] unusual work. In its density and depth, Heidegger's commentary was as fascinating as Trakl's work itself. How could he seriously claim that this poet who had died of an overdose of cocaine in 1914 in a hospital in Krakow was 'the poet of the destiny of the not-yet-revealed Occident'? What did this strange connection he made elsewhere between Trakl's Stranger and Nietzsche's Zarathustra mean? It was after I had devoted a master's degree in philosophy to the analysis of Heidegger's rectorate in 1933 [*Les écrits politiques de Heidegger* (*Heidegger's Political Writings*), L'Herne, 1968] that the German philosopher invited me to Freiburg im Breisgau. And even today, I cannot remember this meeting without emotion. I asked him about his interest in Trakl, among other things. He told me that he had read him very early on, during the war of 1914, and he showed me some pictures—of Trakl himself and of his sister, I believe—that he kept on his desk. Strange attention on the part of one who just had affirmed aloud his refusal to take into account any biographical element in order to understand a work. / After having noted with regret that there was no sufficiently substantial study on the Austrian poet, I resolved to devote a doctoral dissertation to him, under the benevolent but somewhat perplexed direction of Paul Ricœur, who wondered what could be philosophical about this drug-addicted and alcoholic poet, in love with his sister and obsessed by a universe of colors and ruins. But Paul Ricœur's generosity was so great that he let me undertake it [. . .] [T]hat Heidegger was able to take an interest in a work carried out by a student and encourage him to continue, testifies to a generosity, on Heidegger's part, that invites the most extreme humility." The date for Palmier's meeting can be found in Palmier, "Entretien avec Jean-Michel Palmier, réalisé par Peter Živadinović (en 1980)," 105; see also 77. In the dissertation version of his book, Palmier writes (p. 7): "Deux rencontres avec Martin Heidegger m'ont plus appris que deux ans de recherches." "Two meetings with Martin Heidegger taught me more than two years of research.")

1972
See the entry under 1957, above.

On May 9, Heidegger wrote to Jean-Michel Palmier about the latter's book on Trakl (letter available in Palmier's French translation in *L'Herne: Martin Heidegger*, 117–118, and excerpts of the original German in Sembera, *Unterwegs zum Abend-Lande*, 130n34, 168n127, and 177): "A l'exception de l'Avant-propos au volume II de l'édition historique et critique (p. 8) qui fait mention de mon essai sur Trakl, votre étude est à ma connaissance, la première qui ait compris le sens de ma réflexion. Celle-ci est certes, comme il est mentionné au début, délibérément partielle, mais dans un sens qui autorise l'interrogation: une œuvre de poésie (*Dichtung*) et par suite toute grande œuvre d'art peut-elle et doit-elle être expliquée par la biographie ou n'est-ce pas plutôt l'œuvre qui rend possible une interprétation de la biographie qui emprunterait le bon chemin? [Abgesehen vom Vorwort zu Bd. II der hist.-kritisch. Ausgabe S. 8, das meinen Trakl Aufsatz erwähnt, ist Ihre Untersuchung meines Wissens die erste, die den Sinn meiner Darlegung versteht. Diese ist freilich—wie schon eingangs vermerkt wird—bewußt einseitig, aber nach einer Seite, von der aus zu fragen bleibt: kann und muß das Werk der Dichtung und damit aller großen Kunst aus der Biographie erklärt werden, oder ermöglicht erst gerade das Werk eine recht geleitete Deutung der Biographie?] / Vous-même abordez en passant cette question et soulignez à juste titre la trilogie des poèmes en prose ["Verwandlung des Bösen," "Traum und Umnachtung," "Offenbarung und Untergang"] (p. 401 et sq.) / Vous avez dans votre langue un mot d'origine latine 'Transfiguration.' Pour autant que je comprenne jusqu'ici votre prudente interprétation de la trilogie, votre texte ne fait pas apparaître si vous assignez le rôle déterminant à l'œuvre ou à la biographie. / En tout état de cause, votre étude n'apporte pas seulement pour la France quelque chose de neuf, mais elle pose d'une manière générale la question qui conduit mes essais de réflexion: qu'est-ce qui dans l'ordre de préséance a pour la critique littéraire une place déterminante, la recherche ou le renvoi au poème et à l'écoute de la parole poétique? [In jedem Falle bleibt Ihre Untersuchung nicht nur für Frankreich neuartig, sondern stellt überhaupt vor die Frage, die meine Denkversuche leiten: was steht in der Rangordnung der Literaturbetrachtung an der maßgebenden Stelle: die Forschung oder die Weisung ins Gedicht und das Hören des dichterischen Wortes?] / Ma propre interprétation de Hölderlin, George, Rilke et Trakl, je ne la caractériserais pas comme 'métaphysique' mais au contraire comme ayant trait à l'histoire de l'Être. / Vos remarques critiques sur mon interprétation qui devait nécessairement, à de nombreux égards, demeurer incomplète, sont très justifiées surtout quant à la figure de l''Étranger' et des autres figures. [. . .] Moi-même, je fus touché pour la première fois par la poésie de Trakl au cours de l'été 1912, lorsque encore étudiant, je lus dans la salle de la bibliothèque universitaire de Fribourg, les numéros de la revue *Der Brenner*. / Pour l'interprétation de l'œuvre poétique de Georg Trakl, on devrait prendre en considération le fait que, au début de la première édition complète des œuvres de Trakl *Die Dichtungen* (1917) dont Trakl avait lui-même discuté le plan avec son éditeur et ami Karl Röck, se trouve le poème 'Verfall' (*Ruine*) qui figure déjà dans l'édition des poèmes de 1913, page 51. / Ce poème pense aux au 'destins plus clairs' et cette réflexion s'infléchit à partir de la troisième strophe: 'Alors me fait trembler un souffle de ruine.' Ce qui est nommé ici pour ainsi dire dans une succession temporelle, la poésie suivante pourra le dire dans une transfiguration unique en tant que situation. [Für die Deutung des dichterischen Werkes von G. T. wäre zu beachten, daß am Beginn der ersten Gesamtausgabe, 'Die Dichtungen' 1917, deren Plan Trakl selbst noch mit dem befreundeten Herausgeber Karl Röck besprach, das im Jahre 1909 entstandene Gedicht 'Verfall' steht, das schon in der Veröffentlichung von 'Gedichte' (1913) S. 51 gedruckt ist. / Dieses Gedicht denkt an die 'helleren Geschicke,' welches Denken von der 3. Strophe an sich wendet: 'Da macht ein Hauch mich von Verfall erzittern.' Was hier gleichsam noch in zeitlicher Abfolge genannt wird, vermag die folgende Dichtung in einer einzigen Transfiguration als die Situation zu sagen.] / A la différence de la fausse interprétation existentielle et anthropologique (chez Camus notamment), largement répandue en France, vous interprétez de manière ontologique, dans la direction exacte, le 'Verfallen' (*S.u.Z.* § 35 et sq.)"

"With the exception of the Preface to Volume II of the historical and critical edition (p. 8) [HKA 2: 8], which mentions my essay on Trakl ["Language in the Poem"], your investigation is, to my knowledge, the first that has understood the sense of my exposition. To be sure, the latter, as was already remarked at the beginning, is deliberately one-sided, but from a side from which it remains to be asked: can and must the work of poetry [*Werk der Dichtung*] and consequently every great work of art be explained on the basis of biography, or is it precisely the work that first makes possible an interpretation of the biography that would take the right path? / You yourself tackle this question in passing and rightly emphasize the trilogy of prose poems ["Transformation of Evil," "Dream and Lunacy," "Revelation and Downfall"] (p. 401 ff.). / You have in your language a word of Latin origin, 'Transfiguration.' As far as I understand your prudent interpretation of the trilogy up to this point, your text does not reveal whether you assign the decisive role to the work or to the biography. / In any case, your investigation not only brings something new to France, but it poses in a general manner the question that guides my attempts at thinking: what, for literary criticism, takes precedence, research or pointing to the poetic work [*Gedicht*] and to listening to the poetic word? / I would not characterize my own interpretation of Hölderlin, George, Rilke and Trakl as 'metaphysical,' but rather as having to do with the history of Being. / Your critical remarks on my interpretation, which necessarily had to remain incomplete in numerous regards, are quite justified, above all with respect to the figure of the 'Stranger' and other figures. [. . .] I myself was touched for the first time by Trakl's poetry in the summer of 1912, when, still a student, I read the issues of the journal *Der Brenner* in the hall of the Freiburg University library. / For the interpretation of the poetic work [*dichterischen Werkes*] of G. T., one would also have to take into consideration the fact that, at the beginning of the first complete edition, *Die Dichtungen* (1917), whose layout Trakl himself had discussed with his publisher and friend Karl Röck, there is the 1909 poem 'Verfall' ('Collapse') which is already printed in the publication of *Poems* from 1913, page 51. / This poem thinks of the 'clearer destinies,' a thinking that turns to itself with the third stanza: 'Then a breath of collapse makes me tremble.' What is named here, still in a temporal succession, so to speak, the subsequent poetry [*Dichtung*, possibly 'poem,' namely, 'Musik im Mirabell' ('Music in Mirabell')] will be able to say in a unique transfiguration as situation. / Unlike the false existentiell and anthropological interpretation (in Camus in particular), which is widespread in France, you interpret *Verfallen* [falling prey] ontologically, in the precise direction (*Being and Time*, § 35 and following)."

GA 13: 227 (and 226) ("Rimbaud vivant," alluding at least to Trakl's "Im Dunkel" ["In the Dark"] and "Abendlied" ["Song of Evening"]): "Ist der ursprünglich griechisch erfahrene *rhythmos* die Nähe des Unzugangbaren und als diese Gegend das den Menschen haltende Ver-Hältnis? Wird das Sagen des kommenden Dichters am Gefüge dieses Verhältnisses bauen und so dem Menschen den neuen Aufenthalt auf der Erde bereiten? Oder wird mit der drohenden Zerstörung der Sprache durch Linguistik und Informatik nicht nur ein Vorrang der Dichtung, sondern diese selbst in ihrer Möglichkeit untergraben? / Rimbaud bleibt lebendig, wenn wir uns diese Fragen stellen, wenn Dichtende und Denkende von der Notwendigkeit betroffen bleiben, 'sich sehend zu machen für das Unbekannte.' Dieses Unbekannte aber kann nur genannt werden (im Sinne des obigen Nennens [als 'ein Rufen, das in die Nähe des Unzugangbaren ruft und rufen kann, weil es 'zum voraus' in diese Nähe schon gehört und aus diesem Gehören das Ganze der Welt in den Rhythmus der dichtenden Sprache bringt']), indem es 'geschwiegen' (Trakl) wird. Indes vermag nur wahrhaft zu schweigen, wer Wegweisendes zu sagen hat und dies mit der ihm verliehenen Kraft des Wortes auch gesagt hat. Dieses Schweigen ist ein Anderes als das bloße Verstummen. Sein Nicht-mehr-sprechen ist ein Gesagt-haben."

"Is *ruthmos*, as it is originally experienced in Greek, the nearness of the inaccessible and, as this region, the holding relation that sustains the human? Will the saying of the coming poet build on the structure of this relation and thus prepare the new sojourn on earth for the human? Or will not only the precedence of poetry, but poetry itself in its possibility be undermined by the menacing destruction of language through linguistics and informatics? / Rimbaud remains vital when we pose these questions to ourselves, when those who poetize and think remain affected by the necessity 'to make themselves seers for the unknown.' / But this unknown can be named (in the above-mentioned sense of naming [as 'a calling that calls and can call into the nearness of the inaccessible because 'in advance' it belongs in this nearness and from this belonging brings the whole of the world into the rhythm of poetizing language']) only by being 'silenced' (Trakl). Yet only someone who has something pathbreaking to say and has also said this with the power of the word vested in him is capable of truly silencing. This silencing is something other than merely falling silent. Its no-longer-speaking is a having-said."

Appendix 3

References to Trakl's Works in "Language in the Poem"

In "Language in the Poem," Heidegger often cites or references Trakl without providing titles. If one does not have access to the edition Heidegger uses or to a concordance, it will be difficult or impossible to determine which poems he is referring to. The first part of the Italian edition of Heidegger's lecture, *La parola nella poesia*, helpfully includes dual-language versions of all the poems from which Heidegger quotes at least a phrase, but this is necessarily incomplete, since Heidegger sometimes cites just one word or provides only a page number. In this appendix, I have instead specified all of the poems that Heidegger cites or references on each page of his lecture. The reader will accordingly be able to determine, for example, that Heidegger's discussion of "bridal jewelry (150)" (GA 12: 51) refers to "Frühling der Seele" ("Springtime of the Soul"), the poem from which Heidegger takes his point of departure; that "64" (GA 12: 45) refers to the fraught figure of the "strange sister" in the third section of "Psalm"; and that Heidegger was much more familiar with Trakl's incest-laden "Passion" than one might otherwise expect. After the first instance, I will not mention additional citations of the sentence "Es ist die Seele ein Fremdes auf Erden" ("The soul is something strange on earth") from "Springtime of the Soul." By my count, Heidegger cites or references fifty-five poems in total, including the poems in prose.

GA 12: 35f.: quotation and 149f. = "Frühling der Seele"

GA 12: 36: 55 = "In ein altes Stammbuch"; 78 = "Ein Herbstabend"; 170 = "Jahr"; 177 = "Gesang des Abgeschiedenen"; 195 = second section of "Offenbarung und Untergang"; 78 = "Ein Herbstabend"; 101 = "Stundenlied"; 113 = "Am Mönchsberg"; 171 = first section of "Abendland"; 114 = "Hohenburg"; 138 = "Geburt"; 171 = first section of "Abendland"; 196 = third section of "Offenbarung und Untergang"

GA 12: 37: 107 = third section of "Sebastian im Traum"

GA 12: 38: 34 = "Verklärter Herbst"; "Geistlich dämmert [. . .]" is a quotation from "Frühling der Seele"

GA 12: 39: 169 = "Sommersneige"; 107 = third section of "Sebastian im Traum"; 34 = "Verklärter Herbst"; 99 = second section of "Elis"; 146 = "Passion"; "Bläue" and "geistlich dämmert" are quotations from "Frühling der Seele"

GA 12: 40: 139 = "Abendländisches Lied"; 97 = "An den Knaben Elis"; 104 = "Kindheit"; 110 = "Ruh und Schweigen"; 85 = "Nachtlied"

GA 12: 41: 85 = "Nachtlied"; "Unterwegs" alludes to Trakl's poem with this title

GA 12: 42: "blaues Wild" is a quotation from "Sommersneige"; 126 = "Ein Winterabend"; "Untergang" refers back to "Sebastian im Traum" or possibly to the poem "Untergang"; 146 = "Passion"; 142 = "Siebengesang des Todes"

GA 12: 43: 99 = second section of "Elis"; "läutenden Schrittes" is a paraphrase of a verse from "Sommersneige"; 169 = "Sommersneige"; 102 = "Unterwegs"; 137 = "Geistliche Dämmerung"

GA 12: 44: quotation of "Geistliche Dämmerung"

GA 12: 45: 134 = "Anif"; "schwarzer" is a reference to the black skiff in the first section of "Abendland" or, more likely, to the blackish ("schwärzlichem") one in "Siebengesang des Todes"; 64 = third section of "Psalm"; 87 = second section of "Helian"; 126 = "Ein Winterabend"; reference to "Sommersneige"; 124 = "Herbstseele"

Appendix 3 | 273

GA 12: 46: "verwesten Gestalt" is a quotation from "Siebengesang des Todes"; 186 = "Der Abend"; 162 = third paragraph of "Traum und Umnachtung"; "verfallene Geschlecht" is possibly an elliptical citation (without ellipsis) of "Unterwegs" ("sinkt ihr Lächeln in den verfallenen Brunnen, / [. . .] O, wie alt ist unser Geschlecht"); "blauen Seele" is a quotation from "Herbstseele"; "Jener" is a reference to "An einen Frühverstorbenen," among other poems

GA 12: 47: 87 = second section of "Helian"; 124 = "Herbstseele"

GA 12: 48: 177 and 178 = "Gesang des Abgeschiedenen"; 63 = first section of "Psalm"

GA 12: 49: quotations from first and second sections of "Psalm"; quotation from "Siebengesang des Todes"; 65 = fourth section of "Psalm"; 120 = "Die Verfluchten"; 161 = third paragraph of "Traum und Umnachtung"; 164 = fourth paragraph of "Traum und Umnachtung"; "sanfter" is presumably a reference to "sanftem Wahnsinn" from "Winkel am Wald" or "Passion"; quotation from "An einen Frühverstorbenen" (= 135, cited on the next page)

GA 12: 50: 105 = first section of "Sebastian im Traum"; 146 = "Passion"; 113 – "Am Mönchsberg"; 97 and quotation of "O, wie lange [. . .]" = "An den Knaben Elis"

GA 12: 51: 179 = "Das Herz"; 26 = third section of "Heiterer Frühling"; 150 = "Frühling der Seele"

GA 12: 52: 101 = "Stundenlied"; "des nächtigen Weihers [. . .]" and "schwarzer Wolke" are quotations from "Geistliche Dämmerung"; 33 = "Winkel im Wald"; "geistlichen Jahre" is a quotation from "Sommersneige"; 98 = first section of "Elis"; "O, wie lange [. . .]" is a quotation from "An den Knaben Elis"; 170 = "Jahr" (quoted on the next page)

GA 12: 53: "dunkle Geduld" is a quotation from "Jahr"; "Goldnen, Wahren" is a quotation from "Winkel im Wald"; 98 = first section of "Elis"; 200 = "Klage"

GA 12: 54: 200 = "Klage"; "geistlich" is a reference to "Frühling der Seele," "Geistliche Dämmerung" and "Sommersneige"; 191 = "In Hellbrunn" (with further quotations on this and the next page)

GA 12: 55: reference to "Frühling der Seele"; 20 = "Geistliches Lied"; "dunkle Wandern" and "blauen Seele" are quotations from "Herbstseele"

GA 12: 56: 201 = "Grodek"; 129 = first paragraph of "Verwandlung des Bösen"; 187 = "Die Nacht"

GA 12: 57: "nährt" is a quotation from "Grodek"; 55 = "In ein altes Stammbuch"; quotation from "An Luzifer" (in Trakl, *Nachlass und Biographie*, 14); 183 = "Das Gewitter" (with further quotations on this and the next page)

GA 12: 58: 26 = third section of "Heiterer Frühling" (with further quotations on the next page)

GA 12: 59: 135 = "An einen Frühverstorbenen" (quoted on the next page)

GA 12: 60: quotations from the third section of "Heiterer Frühling"

GA 12: 61: 144 = "Verklärung"; "sanfte Zyanenbündel" is a quotation from "Abendländisches Lied"; 201 = "Grodek" (with further quotations on the next page)

GA 12: 62: "geistlich" is a reference to "Frühling der Seele," "Geistliche Dämmerung" and "Sommersneige"; 136 = "An einen Frühverstorbenen"; 20 = "Geistliches Lied"; 81 = second section of "Im Dorf"

GA 12: 63: "Verwandlung" is a reference to "Verwandlung des Bösen"

GA 12: 64: 169 = "Sommersneige"; 135 = "An einen Frühverstorbenen"

GA 12: 65: 143 = "Der Wanderer"; "grüne Verwesung" is a quotation from "An einen Frühverstorbenen"; "schied" is a quotation from "Herbstseele"; 143 = "Der Wanderer"; "des weißen Magiers [. . .]" is a quotation from "Abendmuse"; 83 = "Abendlied"; "goldenen Kahn" is a quotation from the first section of "Elis"; 136 = "An einen Frühverstorbenen"

GA 12: 66: 177 = "Gesang des Abgeschiedenen"; 137 = "Geistliche Dämmerung"; 104 = "Kindheit"

GA 12: 67: 104 = "Kindheit"; 157 = first paragraph of "Traum und Umnachtung"; "geistliche Nacht" is a quotation from "Geistliche Dämmerung"; "goldenen Schauer" is a quotation from "Anif"

GA 12: 68: 134 = "Anif"; "unendliche Qual" and 187 = "Die Nacht"; "die steile Festung" is a quotation from "Das Herz"; 187 = "Die Nacht" (quoted on the next page)

GA 12: 69: 180 = "Das Herz"; Heidegger refers to the "triad" of poems "Das Herz," "Das Gewitter," "Die Nacht"; 55 = "In ein altes Stammbuch"; 54 = "In den Nachmittag geflüstert"

GA 12: 70: "Wahnsinnigen" is a quotation from the first section of "Psalm"; "Augenblicks" is a quotation from "Kindheit"; reference to "Gesang des Abgeschiedenen"; 194 = first section of "Offenbarung und Untergang"

GA 12: 71: 133 = "An die Verstummten"; "gerechten Anschauens" is a quotation from the first section of "Helian"

GA 12: 72: quotations of and references to "Klage" (= 200) and "Grodek"; "goldenen Antlitz des Menschen" is presumably a paraphrase of "Des Menschen goldnes Bildnis" from "Klage," although "weiße Antlitz des Menschen" appears in "Hohenburg"

GA 12: 73: 124 and "Bald entgleitet [. . .]" = "Herbstseele"; "beseelter Bläue wohnen" is a paraphrase of a verse from "Gesang des Abgeschiedenen"; "Abendland" refers to Trakl's poem of the same title, as well as to "Abendländisches Lied"; "Anbeginn" is a quotation from "Jahr"

GA 12: 74: 171ff. = "Abendland"; 139f. = "Abendländisches Lied"; reference to "Gesang des Abgeschiedenen"; "O der Seele [. . .]" and "*Ein*

Geschlecht" are quotations from "Abendländisches Lied"; "Sagen des Waldes," "Maß und Gesetz," and "mondenen Pfade der Abgeschiedenen" are quotations from "Gesang des Abgeschiedenen"

GA 12: 75: "*Einen* Geschlechts" is a quotation from "Abendländisches Lied"; 151 = "Im Dunkel"; 115 = "Kaspar Hauser Lied"; 97 = "An den Knaben Elis"; 113 = "Am Mönchsberg"; reference to "Abendländisches Lied"; 171ff. = "Abendland"

GA 12: 76: references to "Abendland, "Helian," and "Sebastian im Traum"; "leisen Geist" is possibly a paraphrase of a verse from "Jahr" ("Leise ist der Herbst, der Geist des Waldes"); "großen Städte" and "steinern aufgebaut [. . .]" are quotations from the third section of "Abendland"; "am grünenden Hügel" and "Frühlingswetter ertönt" are quotations from the first section of "Abendland"; 134 = "Anif"; 150 = "Frühling der Seele"; "Wahnsinnigen" is a quotation from the first section of "Psalm"

GA 12: 77: reference to "Gesang einer gefangenen Amsel"; "geistlich" and 149f. = "Frühling der Seele"

GA 12: 78: quotation of "Frühling der Seele"

Appendix 4

Selected Poems by Georg Trakl

ABENDLÄNDISCHES LIED

O der Seele nächtlicher Flügelschlag:
Hirten gingen wir einst an dämmernden Wäldern hin
Und es folgte das rote Wild, die grüne Blume und der lallende
    Quell
Demutsvoll. O, der uralte Ton des Heimchens,
Blut blühend am Opferstein
Und der Schrei des einsamen Vogels über der grünen Stille
    des Teichs.

O, ihr Kreuzzüge und glühenden Martern
Des Fleisches, Fallen purpurner Früchte
Im Abendgarten, wo vor Zeiten die frommen Jünger gegangen,
Kriegsleute nun, erwachend aus Wunden und Sternenträumen.
O, das sanfte Zyanenbündel der Nacht.

O, ihr Zeiten der Stille und goldener Herbste,
Da wir friedliche Mönche die purpurne Traube gekeltert;
Und rings erglänzten Hügel und Wald.
O, ihr Jagden und Schlösser; Ruh des Abends,
Da in seiner Kammer der Mensch Gerechtes sann,
In stummem Gebet um Gottes lebendiges Haupt rang.

O, die bittere Stunde des Untergangs,
Da wir ein steinernes Antlitz in schwarzen Wassern beschaun.
Aber strahlend heben die silbernen Lider die Liebenden:
E i n Geschlecht. Weihrauch strömt von rosigen Kissen
Und der süße Gesang der Auferstandenen.

AN DEN KNABEN ELIS

Elis, wenn die Amsel im schwarzen Wald ruft,
Dieses ist dein Untergang.
Deine Lippen trinken die Kühle des blauen Felsenquells.

Laß, wenn deine Stirne leise blutet
Uralte Legenden
Und dunkle Deutung des Vogelflugs.

SONG OF THE OCCIDENT

Oh nocturnal wingbeat of the soul:
Shepherds, we once walked along twilit forests
And there followed the wild red game, the green flower, and
 the babbling spring
Humbly. Oh, the ancient sound of the house cricket,
Blood blooming on the sacrificial stone,
And the cry of the solitary bird over the green stillness of
 the pond.

Oh, you crusades and blazing torments
Of the flesh, the falling of crimson fruits
In the evening garden, where ages ago pious disciples walked,
Warriors now, awaking from wounds and astral dreams.
Oh, the gentle cornflower-cluster of night.

Oh, you ages of stillness and golden harvests of autumn,
When we peaceful monks pressed the crimson grape;
And all around gleamed hill and forest.
Oh, you hunts and castles; repose of evening,
When in his chamber man pondered what was right,
In mute prayer strove for the living head of God.

Oh, the bitter hour of downfall,
When we behold a stony countenance in black waters.
But radiantly the lovers raise their silver eyelids:
One Being. Incense streams from rosy pillows,
And the sweet song of the resurrected ones.

TO THE BOY ELIS

Elis, when the blackbird calls in the black woods,
This is your downfall.
Your lips drink the coolness of the cliff's blue spring.

Let it be, when your brow quietly bleeds
Primeval legends
And dark augury.

Du aber gehst mit weichen Schritten in die Nacht,
Die voll purpurner Trauben hängt
Und du regst die Arme schöner im Blau.

Ein Dornenbusch tönt,
Wo deine mondenen Augen sind.
O, wie lange bist, Elis, du verstorben.

Dein Leib ist eine Hyazinthe,
In die ein Mönch die wächsernen Finger taucht.
Eine schwarze Höhle ist unser Schweigen,

Daraus bisweilen ein sanftes Tier tritt
Und langsam die schweren Lider senkt.
Auf deine Schläfen tropft schwarzer Tau,

Das letzte Gold verfallener Sterne.

AN NOVALIS

In dunkler Erde ruht der heilige Fremdling.
Es nahm von sanftem Munde ihm die Klage der Gott,
Da er in seiner Blüte hinsank.
Eine blaue Blume
Fortlebt sein Lied im nächtlichen Haus der Schmerzen.

DAS HERZ

Das wilde Herz ward weiß am Wald;
O dunkle Angst
Des Todes, so das Gold
In grauer Wolke starb.
Novemberabend.
Am kahlen Tor am Schlachthaus stand
Der armen Frauen Schar;
In jeden Korb
Fiel faules Fleisch und Eingeweid;
Verfluchte Kost!

But you go with soft steps into the night,
Which hangs full of crimson grapes
And more beautifully you move your arms in the blue.

A thornbush sounds,
Where your lunar eyes are.
Oh, how long, Elis, have you been dead.

Your body is a hyacinth,
Into which a monk dips his waxen fingers.
A black cave is our silence,

From which at times a gentle animal emerges
And slowly sinks the heavy lids.
On your temples drips black dew,

The last gold of fallen stars.

TO NOVALIS

In dark earth rests the holy stranger.
The god took lamentation from his gentle mouth,
As he sank down in his bloom.
A blue flower,
His song lives on in the nocturnal house of pains.

THE HEART

The wild heart turned white near the wood;
Oh, dark dread
Of death, thus died
The gold in a gray cloud.
November evening.
By the stark gate of the slaughterhouse stood
The throng of poverty-stricken women;
Into each basket
Foul flesh fell, and entrails;
Accursed fare!

Des Abends blaue Taube
Brachte nicht Versöhnung.
Dunkler Trompetenruf
Durchfuhr der Ulmen
Nasses Goldlaub,
eine zerfetzte Fahne
Vom Blut rauchend,
Daß in wilder Schwermut
Hinlauscht ein Mann.
O! ihr ehernen Zeiten
Begraben dort im Abendrot.

Aus dunklem Hausflur trat
Die goldne Gestalt
Der Jünglingin
Umgeben von bleichen Monden,
Herbstlicher Hofstaat,
Zerknickten schwarze Tannen
Im Nachtsturm,
Die steile Festung.
O Herz
Hinüberschimmernd in schneeige Kühle.

DE PROFUNDIS

Es ist ein Stoppelfeld, in das ein schwarzer Regen fällt.
Es ist ein brauner Baum, der einsam dasteht.
Es ist ein Zischelwind, der leere Hütten umkreist.
Wie traurig dieser Abend.

Am Weiler vorbei
Sammelt die sanfte Waise noch spärliche Ähren ein.
Ihre Augen weiden rund und goldig in der Dämmerung
Und ihr Schoß harrt des himmlischen Bräutigams.

Bei der Heimkehr
Fanden die Hirten den süßen Leib
Verwest im Dornenbusch.

The blue dove of evening
Brought no reconciliation.
Dark trumpet call
Drove through the elms'
Wet golden foliage,
A tattered flag
Smoking with blood,
That in wild melancholy
A man might harken.
Oh! you brazen ages
Buried there in the evening red.

From the dark hallway stepped
The golden figure
Of the youthess
Surrounded by pale moons,
Autumnal entourage,
Black firs snapped
In the night storm,
The steep fortress.
Oh heart
Shimmering across into snowy coolness.

OUT OF THE DEPTHS

There is a stubble field, on which a black rain falls.
There is a brown tree, which stands there all alone.
There is a hissing wind, which encircles empty shacks.
How sad this evening.

Past the hamlet
The gentle orphan gleans what is left of the corn.
Her eyes graze round and golden in the twilight
And her womb awaits the heavenly bridegroom.

Returning home
The shepherds found the sweet body
Decayed in the thornbush.

Ein Schatten bin ich ferne finsteren Dörfern.
Gottes Schweigen
Trank ich aus dem Brunnen des Hains.

DER TAU DES FRÜHLINGS

Der Tau des Frühlings der von dunklen Zweigen
Herniederfällt, es kommt die Nacht
Mit Sternenstrahlen, da des Lichtes du vergessen.

Unter dem Dornenbogen lagst <du> und es grub der Stachel
Sich tief in den kristallenen Leib
Daß feuriger sich die Seele der Nacht vermähle.

Es hat mit Sternen sich die Braut geziert,
Die reine Myrthe
Die sich über des Toten anbetendes Antlitz neigt.

Blühender Schauer voll
Umfängt dich endlich der blaue Mantel der Herrin.

FRÜHLING DER SEELE

Aufschrei im Schlaf; durch schwarze Gassen stürzt der
  Wind,
Das Blau des Frühlings winkt durch brechendes Geäst,
Purpurner Nachttau und es erlöschen rings die Sterne.
Grünlich dämmert der Fluß, silbern die alten Alleen
Und die Türme der Stadt. O sanfte Trunkenheit
Im gleitenden Kahn und die dunklen Rufe der Amsel
In kindlichen Gärten. Schon lichtet sich der rosige Flor.

Feierlich rauschen die Wasser. O die feuchten Schatten der
  Au,
Das schreitende Tier; Grünendes, Blütengezweig
Rührt die kristallene Stirne; schimmernder Schaukelkahn.
Leise tönt die Sonne im Rosengewölk am Hügel.
Groß ist die Stille des Tannenwalds, die ernsten Schatten
  am Fluß.

A shadow I am, far from gloomy villages.
God's silence
I drank from the font of the grove.

THE DEW OF SPRING

The dew of spring, which from darksome branches
Falls down here, the night comes
With star rays, since you forgot the light.

Under the arch of thorns you lay and the spike dug
Deeply into the crystalline body
That, more fiery, the soul would wed the night.

With stars the bride has adorned herself,
The pure myrtle
Who bends over the adoring countenance of the dead one.

Full of blossoming shudder
The blue mantel of the mistress embraces you at last.

SPRINGTIME OF THE SOUL

Outcry in sleep; the wind tumbles through black alleys,
The blue of spring beckons through breaking branches,
Crimson night-dew and all around the stars go out.
Greenish, the river dawns, silver, the old avenues
And the towers of the city. Oh, gentle drunkenness
In the gliding skiff and the dark calls of the blackbird
In the gardens of childhood. Already the rosy blossom becomes
    clearer.

Solemnly rush the waters. Oh, the damp shadows of the
    meadow,
The striding animal; greenery, flowering branches
Touch the crystalline brow; shimmering, swaying skiff.
Quietly the sun resounds in the rose-cloud by the hill.
Great is the stillness of the fir forest, the stern shadows at
    the river.

Reinheit! Reinheit! Wo sind die furchtbaren Pfade des Todes,
Des grauen steinernen Schweigens, die Felsen der Nacht
Und die friedlosen Schatten? Strahlender Sonnenabgrund.

Schwester, da ich dich fand an einsamer Lichtung
Des Waldes und Mittag war und groß das Schweigen des
    Tiers;
Weiße unter wilder Eiche, und es blühte silbern der Dorn.
Gewaltiges Sterben und die singende Flamme im Herzen.

Dunkler umfließen die Wasser die schönen Spiele der
    Fische.
Stunde der Trauer, schweigender Anblick der Sonne;
Es ist die Seele ein Fremdes auf Erden. Geistlich dämmert
Bläue über dem verhauenen Wald und es läutet
Lange eine dunkle Glocke im Dorf; friedlich Geleit.
Stille blüht die Myrthe über den weißen Lidern des
    Toten.

Leise tönen die Wasser im sinkenden Nachmittag
Und es grünet dunkler die Wildnis am Ufer, Freude im
    rosigen Wind;
Der sanfte Gesang des Bruders am Abendhügel.

GEISTLICHE DÄMMERUNG

Stille begegnet am Saum des Waldes
Ein dunkles Wild;
Am Hügel endet leise der Abendwind,

Verstummt die Klage der Amsel,
Und die sanften Flöten des Herbstes
Schweigen im Rohr.

Auf schwarzer Wolke
Befährst du trunken von Mohn
Den nächtigen Weiher,

Den Sternenhimmel.
Immer tönt der Schwester mondene Stimme
Durch die geistliche Nacht.

Purity! Purity! Where are the terrible paths of death,
Of gray, stony silence, the cliffs of night
And the peaceless shadows? Radiant sun-abyss.

Sister, when I found you in a lonesome clearing
Of the forest and it was noon and great was the silence of
    the animal;
White one, under a wild oak, and silver bloomed the thorn.
Violent dying and the singing flame in the heart.

More darkly did the waters flow about the lovely games of
    the fish.
Hour of grief, silent spectacle of the sun;
The soul is something strange on earth. Spiritually,
Blueness dawns over the thrashed forest and long
A dark bell tolls in the village; peaceful convoy.
In stillness the myrtle blooms over the white eyelids of the
    dead one.

Quietly the waters resound in the sinking afternoon
And the wilderness greens more darkly on the bank, joy in
    the rosy wind;
The gentle song of the brother on the evening hill.

SPIRITUAL TWILIGHT

In stillness at the forest's edge
A dark wild game is encountered;
By the hill the evening wind quietly dies away,

The lament of the blackbird goes mute,
And the gentle flutes of autumn
Keep silent in the reeds.

On a black cloud
You ride, drunken with poppy,
The nocturnal pond,

The spangled sky.
Ever the lunar voice of the sister sounds
Through the spiritual night.

GESANG DES ABGESCHIEDENEN

An Karl Borromaeus Heinrich

Voll Harmonien ist der Flug der Vögel. Es haben die grünen Wälder
Am Abend sich zu stilleren Hütten versammelt;
Die kristallenen Weiden des Rehs.
Dunkles besänftigt das Plätschern des Bachs, die feuchten Schatten

Und die Blumen des Sommers, die schön im Winde läuten.
Schon dämmert die Stirne dem sinnenden Menschen.

Und es leuchtet ein Lämpchen, das Gute, in seinem Herzen
Und der Frieden des Mahls; denn geheiligt ist Brot und Wein
Von Gottes Händen, und es schaut aus nächtigen Augen
Stille dich der Bruder an, daß er ruhe von dorniger Wanderschaft.
O das Wohnen in der beseelten Bläue der Nacht.

Liebend auch umfängt das Schweigen im Zimmer die Schatten der Alten,
Die purpurnen Martern, Klage eines großen Geschlechts,
Das fromm nun hingeht im einsamen Enkel.

Denn strahlender immer erwacht aus schwarzen Minuten des Wahnsinns
Der Duldende an versteinerter Schwelle
Und es umfängt ihn gewaltig die kühle Bläue und die leuchtende Neige des Herbstes,

Das stille Haus und die Sagen des Waldes,
Maß und Gesetz und die mondenen Pfade der Abgeschiedenen.

GRODEK

Am Abend tönen die herbstlichen Wälder
Von tödlichen Waffen, die goldnen Ebenen

SONG OF THE DEPARTED ONE

For Karl Borromaeus Heinrich

The flight of birds is full of harmonies. The green woods have
Gathered at evening to form lodges of greater stillness;
The crystalline pastures of the roe deer.
The dark makes gentle the splashing of the brook, the moist shadows

And the flowers of summer, which ring out beautifully in the wind.
Already the brow of meditative man enters into twilight.

And a little lamp, the good, shines in his heart
And the peace of the meal; for hallowed are bread and wine
By the hands of God, and from night-like eyes
In stillness the brother beholds you, that he may find rest from thorny wandering.
Oh, dwelling in the besouled blueness of night.

Silence in the room also lovingly embraces the shades of the elderly,
The crimson torments, lamentation of a great lineage,
Which now piously passes on in the solitary grandson.

For ever more radiantly does the tolerant one awaken
From black minutes of madness on a petrified threshold
And embracing him mightily is the cool blueness and the luminous decline of autumn,

The still house and the sayings of the forest,
Measure and law and the lunar paths of the departed ones.

GRÓDEK

At evening the autumn woods issue tones
Of deadly weapons, the golden plains

Und blauen Seen, darüber die Sonne
Düstrer hinrollt; umfängt die Nacht
Sterbende Krieger, die wilde Klage
Ihrer zerbrochenen Münder.
Doch stille sammelt im Weidengrund
Rotes Gewölk, darin ein zürnender Gott wohnt,
Das vergossne Blut sich, mondne Kühle;
Alle Straßen münden in schwarze Verwesung.
Unter goldnem Gezweig der Nacht und Sternen
Es schwankt der Schwester Schatten durch den schweigenden Hain,
Zu grüßen die Geister der Helden, die blutenden Häupter;
Und leise tönen im Rohr die dunkeln Flöten des Herbstes.
O stolzere Trauer! ihr ehernen Altäre,
Die heiße Flamme des Geistes nährt heute ein gewaltiger Schmerz,
Die ungebornen Enkel.

HERBSTSEELE

Jägerruf und Blutgebell;
Hinter Kreuz und braunem Hügel
Blindet sacht der Weiherspiegel,
Schreit der Habicht hart und hell.

Über Stoppelfeld und Pfad
Banget schon ein schwarzes Schweigen;
Reiner Himmel in den Zweigen;
Nur der Bach rinnt still und stad.

Bald entgleitet Fisch und Wild.
Blaue Seele, dunkles Wandern
Schied uns bald von Lieben, Andern.
Abend wechselt Sinn und Bild.

Rechten Lebens Brot und Wein,
Gott in deine milden Hände
Legt der Mensch das dunkle Ende,
Alle Schuld und rote Pein.

And blue lakes, over which the sun
Rolls on more gloomily; the night envelops
Dying warriors, the wild lamentations
Of their shattered mouths.
Yet quietly in the pasture red clouds,
In which a raging god dwells,
gather up the blood that was shed, lunar chill;
All streets enter the mouth of black decay.
Under golden boughs of night and stars
The shadow of the sister sways through the silent grove,
To greet the spirits of heroes, the bleeding heads;
And softly in the reeds the dark flutes of autumn resound.
Oh, prouder mourning! you brazen altars,
The hot flame of spirit is nourished today by a mighty pain,
The unborn grandchildren.

AUTUMN SOUL

Cry of hunters, bloodhounds' bay;
Mirror-pond, behind the cross
And brown hill, grows softly dim,
Harsh and bright the hawk is screaming.

Over stubble field and path
A black silence trembles now;
Purest heaven in the boughs;
Just the brook runs still and quiet.

Fish and game soon slip away.
Blue soul, darksome wand'ring, soon did
Sever us from loved ones, others.
Evening changes sense and image.

Bread and wine of proper living,
God into your mild hands
Layeth man the darksome ending,
All the guilt and scarlet torment.

HÖLDERLIN

Der Wald liegt herbstlich ausgebreitet
Die Winde ruhn, ihn nicht zu wecken
Das Wild schläft friedlich in Verstecken,
Indes der Bach ganz leise gleitet.

So ward ein edles Haupt verdüstert
In seiner Schönheit Glanz und Trauer
Von Wahnsinnn, den ein frommer Schauer
Am Abend durch die Kräuter flüstert.

IM WINTER

Wenn der Schnee ans Fenster fällt,
Lang die Abendglocke läutet,
Vielen ist der Tisch bereitet
Und das Haus ist wohlbestellt.

Mancher auf der Wanderschaft
Kommt ans Tor auf dunklen Pfaden.
Seine Wunde voller Gnaden
Pflegt der Liebe sanfte Kraft.

O! des Menschen bloße Pein.
Der mit Engeln stumm gerungen,
Langt von heiligem Schmerz bezwungen
Still nach Gottes Brot und Wein.

EIN WINTERABEND

Wenn der Schnee ans Fenster fällt,
Lang die Abendglocke läutet,
Vielen ist der Tisch bereitet
Und das Haus ist wohlbestellt.

Mancher auf der Wanderschaft
Kommt ans Tor auf dunklen Pfaden.
Golden blüht der Baum der Gnaden
Aus der Erde kühlem Saft.

HÖLDERLIN

The forest lies spread out in autumn
The winds repose, as not to wake it
The game sleeps hid away in peace,
The brook so softly glides along.

A noble head was thereby clouded
In shine and sadness of its beauty
By madnesss, which a pious shudder
At evening whispers through the herbs.

IN WINTER

When the snow falls on the window,
And the evening bell tolls long,
There's a table prepped for many
And the house arranged just so.

Several in their pilgrimage
Come on dark paths to the gate.
His wound so full of grace is
Tended by love's gentle might.

Oh! sheer agony of man.
He who strove with angels mutely,
Reaches, vanquished by holy pain,
So still, for God's bread and wine.

A WINTER EVENING

When the snow falls on the window,
And the evening bell tolls long,
There's a table prepped for many
And the house arranged just so.

Several in their pilgrimage
Come on dark paths to the gate.
Golden blooms the tree of grace
Rising from the earth's cool sap.

Wanderer tritt still herein;
Schmerz versteinerte die Schwelle.
Da erglänzt in reiner Helle
Auf dem Tische Brot und Wein.

IN EIN ALTES STAMMBUCH

Immer wieder kehrst du Melancholie,
O Sanftmut der einsamen Seele.
Zu Ende glüht ein goldener Tag.

Demutsvoll beugt sich dem Schmerz der Geduldige
Tönend von Wohllaut und weichem Wahnsinn.
Siehe! es dämmert schon.

Wieder kehrt die Nacht und klagt ein Sterbliches
Und es leidet ein anderes mit.

Schaudernd unter herbstlichen Sternen
Neigt sich jährlich tiefer das Haupt.

KARL KRAUS

Weißer Hohepriester der Wahrheit,
Kristallne Stimme, in der Gottes eisiger Odem wohnt,
Zürnender Magier,
Dem unter flammendem Mantel der blaue Panzer des Kriegers
    klirrt.

KLAGE

Schlaf und Tod, die düstern Adler
Umrauschen nachtlang dieses Haupt:
Des Menschen goldnes Bildnis
Verschlänge die eisige Woge
Der Ewigkeit. An schaurigen Riffen
Zerschellt der purpurne Leib
Und es klagt die dunkle Stimme
Über dem Meer.

Wanderer steps in, so still;
Pain has petrified the threshold.
There in purest brightness gleam
On the table bread and wine.

INTO AN OLD FAMILY ALBUM

Again and again you return, melancholy,
Oh, gentleness of the solitary soul.
A golden day gleams and comes to an end.

Humbly the patient one bends before pain
Ringing with sounds of harmony and soft madness.
Look! already it is twilight.

Again the night returns and something mortal laments
And another thing suffers in sympathy.

Shuddering under autumnal stars
Each year the head declines more deeply.

KARL KRAUS

White high priest of truth,
Crystalline voice, wherein God's icy breath dwells,
Raging magician,
Under whose flaming cloak the blue armor of the warrior
 clangs.

LAMENTATION

Sleep and death, the gloomy eagles
Whoosh about this head all night:
The golden image of man
Would be devoured by the icy wave
Of eternity. On dreadful reefs
Bursts the crimson body
And the dark voice laments
Over the sea.

Schwester stürmischer Schwermut
Sieh ein ängstlicher Kahn versinkt
Unter Sternen,
Dem schweigenden Antlitz der Nacht.

PASSION

Wenn Orpheus silbern die Laute rührt,
Beklagend ein Totes im Abendgarten,
Wer bist du Ruhendes unter hohen Bäumen?
Es rauscht die Klage das herbstliche Rohr,
Der blaue Teich,
Hinsterbend unter grünenden Bäumen
Und folgend dem Schatten der Schwester;
Dunkle Liebe
Eines wilden Geschlechts,
Dem auf goldenen Rädern der Tag davonrauscht.
Stille Nacht.

Unter finsteren Tannen
Mischten zwei Wölfe ihr Blut
In steinerner Umarmung; ein Goldnes
Verlor sich die Wolke über dem Steg,
Geduld und Schweigen der Kindheit.
Wieder begegnet der zarte Leichnam
Am Tritonsteich
Schlummernd in seinem hyazinthenen Haar.
Daß endlich zerbräche das kühle Haupt!

Denn immer folgt, ein blaues Wild,
Ein Äugendes unter dämmernden Bäumen,
Dieser dunkleren Pfaden
Wachend und bewegt von nächtigem Wohllaut,
Sanftem Wahnsinn;
Oder es tönte dunkler Verzückung
Voll das Seitenspiel
Zu den kühlen Füßen der Büßerin
In der steinernen Stadt.

Sister of stormy sadness
Look, an anxious skiff sinks
Under the stars,
The silent countenance of night.

THE PASSION

When, silverly, Orpheus plucks the lute,
Lamenting something dead in the evening garden,
Who are you, thing full of repose, under tall trees?
Autumnal reeds rustle the lamentation,
The blue pond,
Dying under greening trees
And following the shadow of the sister;
Dark love
Of a wild race,
From which the day rushes away on golden wheels.
Silent night.

Under gloomy firs
Two wolves mixed their blood
In stony embrace; something golden
Got lost, the cloud over the footbridge,
Patience and silence of childhood.
Again, the delicate corpse is met
At Triton Pond
Slumbering in its hyacinthine hair.
Would that the cool head shatter at last!

For always a wild blue game follows,
An eyeing one, under twilit trees,
Over these darker paths
Keeping vigil and moved by nocturnal consonance,
Gentle madness;
Or there sounded, replete with dark
Rapture, the string music
At the cool feet of the penitent woman
In the stony city.

NACHTERGEBUNG

Mönchin! schließ mich in dein Dunkel,
Ihr Gebirge kühl und blau!
Niederblutet dunkler Tau;
Kreuz ragt steil im Sterngefunkel.

Purpurn brachen Mund und Lüge
In verfallner Kammer kühl;
Scheint noch Lachen, golden Spiel,
Einer Glocke letzte Züge.

Mondeswolke! Schwärzlich fallen
Wilde Früchte nachts vom Baum
Und zum Grabe wird der Raum
Und zum Traum dies Erdenwallen.

SURRENDER TO THE NIGHT

Monkess! close me in your darkness,
Oh, you mountains cool and blue!
Downward bleeds the darksome dew
Cross doth rise in astral glitter.

Crimson, broke both mouth and lie
Coolly in the ruined room;
Laughter, golden play, yet shines,
Final tolling of a bell.

Mooncloud! Wild fruits fall blackly
From the tree while it is night.
All of space becomes a grave
And this earthly pilgrimage a dream.

Notes

Introduction

1. Several conferences have been held on Derrida's text (and therefore on Heidegger and Trakl) the past few years, including at Princeton, Texas A&M, and Goldsmiths, University of London. Partial proceedings from the first and second conferences are available in *Philosophy Today* 64, no. 2 (2020) and in *Política común* 14 (2021), respectively. There is also a special topic on this material in *Research in Phenomenology* 51, no. 1 (2021).

2. Krell, *Lunar Voices*, 61. For other comments on the idiosyncratic difficulty of Heidegger's reading of Trakl in "Language in the Poem," see Allemann, *Hölderlin und Heidegger*, 192 and note 66 ("so verliert sich jede Möglichkeit wissenschaftlicher Beurteilung in dem Maß, als sich Heidegger in seine denkerische Sprache findet [. . .] Das trifft vor allem auch auf die Trakl-Rede zu"); Bertorello, "La lentitud de las cosas," 93–94 ("contienen dificultades enormes de interpretación"); Caputo, "Thinking, Poetry and Pain," 163 ("an astonishingly dense text"); D'Angelo, "Einheit und Mannigfaltigkeit im dichterischen Wort," 64 ("extrem komplex"); GIII: 36n1, 87 ("déjà très difficile (secret) dans sa langue d'origine, on ne le dit pas assez. Il est à peine lisible dans les meilleures traductions," "Heidegger lit et écrit ici, sur la trace du lieu de Trakl, comme quelqu'un que les critiques littéraires, poéticiens ou philologues ou philosophes, hommes de savoir, jugeraient fou"); Hanly, "Dark Celebration," 254 ("*Die Sprache im Gedicht* travels much further [than does Heidegger's interpretation of Stefan George], travels even recklessly—impossibly, perhaps—toward a place, a site, *ein Ort*, within which language speaks as music"); Land, "Narcissism and Dispersion in Heidegger's 1953 Trakl Interpretation," 83 ("This mysterious text, at once intensely personal and strangely detached"); Moreiras, "'Another Topology for New Tasks'" ("extraordinary complexities"); Mullins, "Count Heidegger" ("one of the *maddest* texts of the Western philosophical tradition," "the essay's escalating or 'step' structure has so many supplementary complications, is so folded onto itself, that if it's a question of a staircase it's not even a spiral staircase, instead

rather more like the stairs of an M.C. Escher painting"); Palmier, "Préface à la nouvelle édition (1987)," 20 ("Pour Trakl, la lecture de Heidegger est d'autant plus difficile à utiliser qu'elle forme un système relativement clos qui exclut toute référence à l'histoire et à la biographie. Et il est infiniment plus difficile de réaliser un dialogue entre Trakl et Heidegger qu'entre Hölderlin et Heidegger"); Powell, ed., *Heidegger and Language*, 9 ("the strangeness of Heidegger's meditation on language meets with the strangeness that is Trakl's poetry, an encounter of strangeness that does not flinch in the face of strangeness [. . .] We would seem to be far from the philosophical tradition"); Rapaport, *Derrida on Exile and the Nation*, 5, 136 ("exceptionally enigmatic essay," "a highly compressed and secret literary sort of text, given Heidegger's poetic approaches to the German language, to say nothing of the essay's baffling transitions and surprising leaps of association"); Vietta, "Georg Trakl in Heideggers Sicht," 354 ("Sonderbar und ungewohnt, was hier vor sich geht"); Markus Wild, "Heidegger and Trakl," 45 ("one of Heidegger's arguably most difficult texts").

3. Hinze, "Heidegger und Trakl," 247.

4. The first quotation is reported in GS/LF: letter from August 25, 1952; the second is available in GA 12: 77.

5. *Pace* Rey, "Heidegger–Trakl: Einstimmiges Zwiegespräch."

6. Plato, *Republic*, 607b6. Aside from Derrida's seven seminar sessions on Heidegger's reading of Trakl (published in book-form in GIII), the only monograph on the Trakl/Heidegger connection that I am aware of is in Italian: Gagliardi, *L'azzurro dell'anima*. There is also a German-language PhD dissertation by Sembera, "Unterwegs zum Abend-Land." The latter two texts are largely expository and lacking in sufficient critical distance, even and especially at the level of language. In contrast to Derrida, with whom I am in constant dialogue throughout the book, I examine Trakl on his own terms, draw on other writings by Heidegger on Trakl, reconstruct the setting for Heidegger's engagement with Trakl, and devote significant attention to themes such as pain, madness, color, and detachment. Another frequent interlocutor, less vocal but always in my ear, is David Krell, in particular his reading of Derrida (and, by extension, of Heidegger and Trakl) in *Phantoms of the Other*. Krell first addressed Heidegger's Trakl interpretation in the 1977 essay "Schlag der Liebe, Schlag des Todes."

7. Ficker, *Der Briefwechel 1926–1939*, 246.

8. Celan, *Gesammelte Werke*, 3: 186.

Chapter 1

1. "The Trakl poem is for me an object of sublime existence. Only now does it really impress me how the figure—fleeting from the very beginning and spare in its description—was able to demonstrate the weight of its ongoing

decline in such precise images. It occurs to me that this entire work might have its likeness in the death of Li T'ai-po: both here and there, falling is a pretext for an inexorable ascension to heaven. [. . .] A new dimension of spiritual space appears [. . .] to be measured out and the emotional-material prejudice to be refuted, as if in the direction of the lament there were only lament—: there too, there is a world again." Rilke, *Briefe*, 2: 71. Partially translated, with discussion, in Yu, "The Poetics of Discontinuity," 273n1.

    2. "Today Ficker sent me poems by poor Trakl, which I find brilliant but do not understand. They did me good. God with me." Wittgenstein, *Geheime Tagebücher*, 45–46.

    3. Derrida, *De l'esprit*, 137. Badiou, *The Age of the Poets*, 41 (see also p. 6). Muschg, *Pamphlet und Bekenntnis*, 346. For Muschg's critique of Heidegger on Trakl specifically, see *Die Zerstörung der deutschen Literatur*, 214–230. Hinze, "Heidegger und Trakl," 251. See also Hamburger, *Reason and Energy*, 270 ("reads his own philosophy into Hölderlin and applies this reading to Trakl. The result is a fascinating, but ruthless, gesture, which sweeps away all evidence of Trakl's own thought in order to turn him into the prophet of an Occident regenerated by the philosophy of pure being"), and Kurrik, *Georg Trakl*, 22 ("The 'encyclopaedic' character of isolated words leads interpreters astray, but it has also produced such a wonderfully reflective essay as that of Heidegger on Trakl's words. Heidegger's thesis, however, is disputed by everyone, as well it might be, given the innumerable specification that the word reduced to zero degree allows").

    4. Celan owned over two dozen works by Heidegger, including a copy of *Unterwegs zur Sprache* that the philosopher had sent him in November 1959. France-Lanord, *Paul Celan und Martin Heidegger*, 222. Charles Bambach, in "Heidegger and Celan," points to many linguistic parallels in the work of both authors and holds that "Celan's enduring struggle with the poetic possibilities of the German language is virtually unthinkable without the constant presence of Heidegger." See also Schmidt, "Black Milk and Blue," and the first entry under "1967" in this book's appendix 2. I view Heidegger's turn to the self-speaking of language as complementary to his turn toward things, discussed in Mitchell, *The Fourfold*. See also Powell, ed., *Heidegger and Language*, 8. Prefiguration of the linguistic turn in Heidegger can be seen, for example, in GA 39: 23, 258.

    5. According to the translator, Peter D. Hertz, Heidegger agreed to the omission of "Language," which appeared instead in the same year in the mélange of Heidegger's works published under the title *Poetry, Language, Thought*. Hertz says nothing of his rearrangement of the remaining chapters, however. The English translation of "Language" was republished in two collections: Donkel, ed., *The Theory of Difference*, and Leitch, ed., *The Norton Anthology of Theory and Criticism*. Even the translation of Heidegger's second lecture reappeared under the title "Georg Trakl: Language in the Poem," in Bloom, ed., *Modern German Poetry*, although this reprint does not seem to have drawn much attention to it.

For numerous problems with Hertz's translation of "Language in the Poem," see Wills, "Which Way Back (way back)?," and especially Bennington, "*Geschlecht pollachos legetai*," who speaks, with Derrida, of a "suicide by translation": Hertz "seems to have taken a decision in principle simply to omit or change quite radically almost every occasion on which Heidegger's German explicitly remarks itself as German" (425).

6. Pöggeler, "Neue Wege mit Heidegger?," 44–45, 55 (cf. GIII: 153). Arendt, letter to Hugo Friedrich from July 15, 1953, in Arendt and Heidegger, *Briefe 1925 bis 1975*, 316–317. For Ficker, see MH/LF: passim; GS/LF: letters from October 10, 1952 and January 4, 1953. Roi, "Open letter to David Krell." Franz Fühmann's celebrated memoir about his transformative experience reading Trakl's poetry at the end of World War II and in the GDR is, doubtless, in dialogue with Heidegger, although Fühmann never mentions the philosopher by name. Even the singular *Gedicht* in the original German title (*Vor Feuerschlünden: Erfahrung mit Georg Trakls Gedicht*) reminds one of Heidegger's claim—echoed frequently by Fühmann—that all of Trakl's poetry is really just *one* poem. Fühmann, *At the Burning Abyss*, 28, 79, 142, 198, 260. See also Jorie Graham's Heidegger-inspired poem "What Is Called Thinking: After Trakl," as well as Steiner, *Martin Heidegger*, 143–144 ("many of [Heidegger's] readings are opportunistic fictions. / But not always. [. . .] If he augments the fitful, reiterative texture of the poems of Georg Trakl, Heidegger's reading of 'Ein Winterabend' ['A Winter Evening' in the lecture 'Language' of 1950] is, nevertheless, a marvel of sympathy. Heidegger's analysis of Trakl's oblique uses of tense and of epithets as predicate will stand").

7. First quotation reported in GS/LF: letter from August 25, 1952. Second available in GA 12: 77.

8. Cf. Heidegger and Bauch, *Briefwechsel 1932–1975*, 145.

9. On the uncertain status of some of Heidegger's literary remains, such as his hundreds of pages of notes on Trakl, see Held, *Marbach-Bericht über eine neue Sichtung des Heidegger-Nachlasses*, as well as my review of the latter under the title "On the History and Future of Heidegger's Literary Estate, with Newly Published Passages on Nazism and Judaism."

10. Arendt and Heidegger, *Briefe 1925 bis 1975*, 137.

11. Typescript version of "Die Sprache im Gedicht" ("Language in the Poem") (as quoted in MH/LF: 8). This recollection did not make its way into the published version of the lecture, nor is it in Heidegger's manuscript. See also GA 12: 87–88; GA 100: 33–34; GA 1: 56; Heidegger's 1972 letter to Palmier, 118; Palmier, "Préface à la nouvelle édition (1987)," 18; and Vezin, "Trakl au pays de Rimbaud," 135. Heidegger's personal copy of the 1913 *Gedichte* is still located in his family's library in Freiburg, along with his copies of the 1917 *Gesamtausgabe* (ed. Karl Röck), which is probably the copy he received as a gift for Christmas 1952 (MH/LF: 49); the sixth edition of the *Gesamtausgabe* (ed. Schneditz, Salzburg, 1938), which Heidegger referred to as his "workshop

volume" (MH/LF: 49); *Aus goldenem Kelch*, 2nd ed. (1939); *Nachlass und Biographie* (1949); and the second edition of Ficker's edited collection, *Erinnerung an Georg Trakl* (1959). Heidegger also owned the 1946 *Gesamtausgabe* (ed. Horwitz, Zurich, 1946), and perhaps HKA; he at least refers to the latter in his letter to Palmier, 118, and in the facsimile (located in the unprocessed collection of the Martin-Heidegger-Archiv der Stadt Meßkirch) of his description of how he acquired the manuscript of Trakl's "Afra."

12. Typescript version of "Die Sprache im Gedicht" (as quoted in MH/LF: 8).

13. For the sources of this report, as well as the lack of evidence in the records of *Der Brenner*, see Thonhauser, *Ein rätselhaftes Zeichen*, 141–145. Even if we must doubt the claim regarding subscription, which Heidegger himself never mentions, the year "1911" for Heidegger's acquaintance with Trakl's poetry, as opposed to "1912," is suggested by Heidegger's letter to Ficker from May 4, 1953 (MH/LF: 53). Additionally, another report suggests Heidegger may have kept up with the journal: in a conversation with Walter Methlagl, Ficker related that, at Bühlerhöhe in 1952, he (Ficker) had spoken with Heidegger about Paula Schlier's text "Geburt der Dichtung," which had appeared in vol. 17 of *Der Brenner*. Heidegger was familiar with it, or perhaps just her poetry in general, and praised her work. See Methlagl, *Brenner-Gespräche*, 61. Finally, it is also noteworthy that, after World War II but before Heidegger wrote on Trakl, Ficker republished three poems by Trakl in *Der Brenner* under the general title "Gedichte zur Erinnerung" ("Poems to Remember"), poems that would come to play a pivotal role in "Language in the Poem." They are "Abendländisches Lied" ("Song of the Occident"), "Frühling der Seele" ("Springtime of the Soul") and "Gesang des Abgeschiedenen" ("Song of the Departed One").

14. Hebel, less unruly than Trakl, is instead "the poet of the homeland [*Heimat*]" (GA 16: 494) or, in Julia Ireland's phrase, "the poet of *Gelassenheit*" ("Heidegger's *Hausfreund* and the Re-enchantment of the Familiar," 143).

15. Thomä puts it more strongly, saying that Heidegger "imitates" Trakl "quite obviously" in the poem. *Die Zeit des Selbst und die Zeit danach*, 34. I cite and translate "Abendgang auf der Reichenau" from the original 1917 publication, which accords with the facsimile of Heidegger's manuscript in Heidegger, *"Mein liebes Seelchen!,"* 46. The version in GA 13: 7 has "den" in the third line (thus "in or among [. . .] the gardens") and "sinnentrückte" ("sense-enraptured") in the antepenultimate. The latter variation is taken from Heidegger's personal copy (GA 13: 246). For other early poems by Heidegger see GA 13: 5–6; GA 16: 16–17, 36, 40.

16. For their possible influence on Trakl, see, respectively, Esselborn, "Novalis-Rezeption in der deutschen Moderne," and HKA 2: 756. For their influence on the early Heidegger, see, respectively, Moore, "Homesickness, Interdisciplinarity, and the Absolute," 283–291, and Moore, *Eckhart, Heidegger and the Imperative of Releasement*, 4–9. See also Hanly, *Between Heidegger and Novalis*.

Colombat, in "Heidegger, lecteur de Trakl," hears Hölderlin in Heidegger's lines, especially Hölderlin's late poem "Hälfte des Lebens" ("Half of Life").

17. On Hölderlin in and after the Third Reich, see Savage, *Hölderlin after the Catastrophe*, and Bambach, *Of an Alien Homecoming*. On Trakl, see Elliott, "'Und Gassen enden schwarz und sonderbar,'" and Sauermann, *Die Rezeption Georg Trakls in Zeiten der Diktatur*. For the quotation, see Hellingrath, *Zwei Vorträge*, 22. Heidegger goes further, calling the poet "the most German of the Germans" (GA 16: 333; see also GA 39: 214, 220; GA 54: 114).

18. In a 1939 newspaper article, Martin Kießig, "'Kristallene Tränen, geweint um die bittere Welt,'" 71, writes that, alongside Rilke and George, no other poet was more influential on the younger generation. Reference found in Elliott, "'Und Gassen enden schwarz und sonderbar,'" 83. The fifty-year-old Heidegger was perhaps too old to be included in this generation, but Kießig's quotation shows how important Trakl was, even during the period of National Socialism. In any case, it is noteworthy that Heidegger ranks Trakl above Rilke and George, as does, for example, Harold Bloom (ed., *Modern German Poetry*, vii).

19. Britting, *Briefe an Georg Jung*, 211.

20. Heidegger, *Briefwechsel mit seinen Eltern (1907–1927) und Briefe an seine Schwester (1921–1967)*, 148 (letter from April 6, 1950). Stroomann, *Aus meinem roten Notizbuch*, 207.

21. For more on Heidegger's audience and the postwar milieu, see Allen, "How Technology Caused the Holocaust," and Keiling, "Dwelling after 1945." On Heidegger's breakdown, treatment by the physician V. E. von Gebsattel, and subsequent recognition of the importance of health and healing for his thought, see Mitchell, "Heidegger's Breakdown."

22. Stroomann, *Aus meinem roten Notizbuch*, 181. For more on Stroomann, see Immo von Hattingberg, "Gerhard Stroomann: Ein Arzt in der Wandlung der Medizin," as well as Stroomann's own texts listed in the bibliography of the present book. Hattingberg, incidentally, was a student and friend of Heidegger, as well as senior physician at Bühlerhöhe from 1949 to 1956. Indeed, it was Hattingberg who first brought Heidegger to Bühlerhöhe in 1950. See Monika von Hattingberg, "Aus den Aufzeichnungen meines Vaters *Immo von Hattingberg*," 9, 11.

23. In GS/LF. "Unsere *Bemühungen* sind nicht Vorträge und Veranstaltungen. / Wir versuchen an '*Mittwochabenden*' dem *Geist* zu dienen in chaotischer, tief gefährdeter Zeit; nach Worten von Richard Benz einen '*Kosmos*' spürbar zu machen, 'in welchem der fühlende Mensch zu leben' vermag."

24. By May 1956, seventy-five events had taken place as a part of Stroomann's lecture series. Nineteen were devoted to poetry. Of these, there were events on Alfred Mombert, Georg Heym, Ernst Stadler, and Trakl. Information derived from invitations in GS/LF. In a letter to Ficker (GS/LF: October 16, 1952), Stroomann explains why poetry, and Trakl in particular, are so important for him: "I have indicated why I am summoning Georg Trakl's appearance: on a

harrowing mission, he signifies, for our generation and for the future, the poetic, with which, in my view (the view of a physician), humanity, sick humanity, must be permeated." "Ich habe angedeutet, warum ich die Erscheinung Georg Trakls beschwöre: In erschütternder Sendung bedeutet er für unsere Generation und für die Zukunft das Dichterische, von dem die Menschheit, die kranke Menschheit, nach meiner Meinung, der Meinung eines Arztes, durchdrungen werden muss." See also Podewils, "Erörterung eines Trakl-Gedichts": "[Stroomann], not least as a doctor, sees something curative about poetry in these destructive times." For more on Geiler, see Stroomann's obituary "Karl Geiler."

25. In GS/LW. "das Schaffen wertvoller Repräsentanten des europäischen Geisteslebens, die insbesondere die Sache der Freiheit des Einzelmenschen gegenüber allen kollektiven Parolen vertreten, zu unterstützen und ihre publizistische Betätigung zu fördern."

26. In GS/LF. "Mehr denn je gilt es, der Spaltung in eine gedankenlose Restauration auf der einen und einen bedenklichen Aktivismus auf der anderen Seite ein publizistisches Organ entgegenzustellen, das die Substanz bewahrt und sich gleichzeitig offenhält für das Neue. Denn nur, wo Altes und Neues, Tradition und Entwurf der Stunde sich ständig voreinander bewähren, entsteht echte Kontinuität. / Europäisches Denken heißt, in der Zeit wie im Raum den Zusammenhang sehen und bewahren: den Zusammenhang mit unserer Geschichte wie den zwischen den Völkern. In diesem Sinn ist es heute durch geschichtsfremde Utopien und die Spaltung zwischen West und Ost tödlich bedroht. Verbände und Organisationen für die Einheit Europas auf politischem Felde können die Bedrohung nicht bannen, wenn die Individuen fehlen, die eine Haltung des 'guten Europäers' von Gestern wie von Morgen verpflichtend vorleben."

27. Quoted in Kiessling, "Fruchtbare Zerrissenheit," 93. See Kiessling's entire article, as well as Schildt, *Medien-Intellektuelle in der Bundesrepublik*, especially 74–80, 188–201, for more on this little-studied, yet in many respects pivotal journal. See also Keiling, "Dwelling after 1945."

28. I compared the latter with an audio recording of the second half of Heidegger's lecture at Bühlerhöhe, and they are nearly identical. (A recording of the first half could not be located.)

29. Schildt, *Medien-Intellektuelle in der Bundesrepublik*, 384.

30. See Arendt and Heidegger, *Briefe 1925 bis 1975*, 134 (letter by Heidegger from February 17, 1952); Heidegger, "Mein liebes Seelchen!," 279 (letter from August 12, 1952); GA 83: 656; and Mendes-Flohr, "Martin Buber and Martin Heidegger in Dialogue."

31. In 1950: Trakl, "Gedichte"; Barth, "Zum Bilde Georg Trakls." In 1952: Heidegger's second Trakl lecture. In 1954: Lachmann, "Ende des Brenner." In 1958: Trakl, "Nachgelassene Gedichte"; Killy, "Gedichte im Gedicht," which Heidegger mentions in MH/LF: 65 (letter from December 29, 1958). See also the reviews of Walter Muschg's books *Die Zerstörung der deutschen Literatur*

(which includes a chapter that lampoons Heidegger's Trakl interpretation) and *Von Trakl bis Brecht*: Boehlich, "Schweizer Literaturforschung," and Demetz, "Grenzsituationen der Literaturwissenschaft." Heidegger would have had particular reason to read the former review, not just because of Muschg's attack on his thought, but also because Boehlich also reviewed, in the article, both Emil Staiger's *Kunst der Interpretation*, in which Heidegger's correspondence with Staiger about a poem by Mörike appears (more on this in chapters 2 and 5), and *Ironie und Dichtung*, by Heidegger's friend Beda Allemann. For other references to *Merkur*, see GA 76: 346, in which Heidegger cites Max Bense's "Kybernetik oder die Metaphysik einer Maschine," which appeared in *Merkur* in 1951; and Arendt and Heidegger, *Briefe 1925 bis 1975*, 141 (letter by Heidegger from April 21, 1954, about Karl Jaspers's critique of Rudolf Bultmann, which appeared in November and December 1953 in *Merkur* under the title "Wahrheit und Unheil der Bultmannschen Entmythologiesierung").

32. I derive this information from GA 7: 290; GA 12: 259; GA 13: 127–128; GA 16: 470; Gadamer, *Philosophische Lehrjahre*, 219; Heidegger, "Mein liebes Seelchen!," 269; Heidegger and Bauch, *Briefwechsel 1932–1975*, 138, 228; Heidegger, *Briefwechsel mit seinen Eltern (1907–1927) und Briefe an seine Schwester (1921–1967)*, 148; Heidegger, Podewils, and Stroomann, unpublished letter to Gottfried Benn; Morat, *Von der Tat zur Gelassenheit*, 485–486; Ortega y Gasset, "Anejo: En torno al 'Coloquio de Darmstadt, 1951,'" 625, 639; Petzet, *Auf einen Stern zugehen*, 69–74; Petzet, "Preetorius und Heidegger über abstrakte Kunst"; Speidel, *Aus unserer Zeit*, 303; Egon Vietta, "Die Vorträge Martin Heideggers 1949–1951," 1360; and the invitations in GS/LF. For other reports on and interpretations of Heidegger at Bühlerhöhe, see Allen, "How Technology Caused the Holocaust"; Anonymous, "Heidegger: Rückfall ins Gestell"; Britting, *Briefe an Georg Jung*, 211–212; F. [Frisé], "Bühler Höhen-Luft," 15; Ficker, *Briefwechsel 1940–1967*, 230, 243–244, 469–470, 534; Morat, *Von der Tat zur Gelassenheit*, 352–353, where Morat reproduces a previously unpublished letter by Friedrich Georg Jünger to his brother Ernst about the event; MH/LF: passim; Peters, "Durch Sprechen zur Sprache"; Petzet, *Auf einen Stern zugehen*, 55–60, 82, 88–89, 111, 114–115, 178, 221–222; Podewils, "Erörterung eines Trakl-Gedichts"; Safranski, *Ein Meister aus Deutschland*, 434–435; Stroomann, "Mittwoch-Abende auf Bühlerhöhe"; Egon Vietta, "Martin Heidegger über Georg Trakl"; Xolocotzi, *Facetas Heideggerianas*, 49–51. For descriptions of Bühlerhöhe, the surrounding area, and the political situation in 1952 (though without reference to Heidegger), see the recent historical spy-novel *Bühlerhöhe*, by Glaser.

33. Cf. Benn, Paeschke, and Moras, *Briefwechsel 1948–1956*, 106.

34. Cf. Allemann's 1957 book *Über das Dichterische*.

35. Haebler, "Metaphysik der Sprache"; F. [Frisé], "Bühler Höhen-Luft"; Peters, "Durch Sprechen zur Sprache"; Stroomann, "Mittwoch-Abende auf Bühlerhöhe"; Nora Kommerell, "Aufzeichnungen über die Max Kommerell-

Veranstaltung auf der Bühlerhöhe, Oktober 1950." Kommerell's work on Immermann would eventually be published as "Immermann und das neunzehnte Jahrhundert." Based on Haebler's description of Gadamer's presentation, some of the latter overlaps with Gadamer, "Zu Immermanns Epigonen-Roman." See also Gadamer's "Gedenkrede auf Max Kommerell." Buttlar would later invite Heidegger to speak at another memorial celebration for Kommerell. See Heidegger's contribution in GA 80: 1147–1172.

36. See also Arendt and Heidegger, *Briefwechsel*, 119, in which Heidegger mentions the event for Kommerell and that he has drafts for "Language" dating back to 1938–1939 (letter from November 2, 1950).

37. Transcribed letter given to me by Heinrich Heidegger. I am unsure why Heidegger mentions Kuwaki. Perhaps he had meaningful conversations about language with him, as he had and would continue to have with many other Japanese scholars. In any case, the East–West dialogue on language was important to Heidegger, as one can see in the third chapter of *Unterwegs zur Sprache* ("Aus einem Gespräch von der Sprache zwischen einem Japaner und einem Fragenden" ["From a Dialogue on Language between a Japanese and a Questioner"]). See also Heidegger's letter to Medard Boss from June 30, 1955: "My plans for Autumn are still undecided. Much depends on how I get the *discussion/emplacement of language* [Erörterung der Sprache] on the right track. Every day the issue [*Sache*] becomes more obscure and at the same time more exciting; today I am amazed that I ventured to give the language-lecture years ago. The biggest gap is that the possibility of a *sufficient* discussion of East-Asian languages *is lacking*" (Heidegger, *Zollikon*, 316). Cf. Powell, ed., *Heidegger and Language*, 8–9. For information on Kuwaki, who would go on to translate Heidegger and Finnish literature into Japanese, see Laitinen, "A War-time Guest Lecturer in Helsinki."

38. "Lieblingsgedanke" (GS/LF: April 23, 1951). "meine Lieblingsidee [. . .]. Für mich ist er [Trakl] seit Hofmannsthal die grosse österreichische Begabung und in der lyrischen Dichtung die letzte wahrhaft originale Kraft. [. . .] Ich bin sicher, dass *Martin Heidegger* sprechen wird, dessen grosse Zeit angebrochen ist und der seit Hegel und (anders) Nietzsche wieder ein philosophisches Zeitalter bedeutet" (GS/LF: January 5, 1952).

39. GS/LF: March 1, 1952. See Barth, "Zum Bilde Georg Trakls," and DD. The latter includes, on p. 227, an excerpt from Barth's *Georg Trakl: Zum Gedächtnis seines fünfzigsten Geburtstags* dealing with Trakl's "Grodek."

40. In GS/LF: June 22, 1952, and in published form in Ficker, *Briefwechsel 1940–1967*, 524.

41. James Lyon, in his 1970 study, "Georg Trakl's Poetry of Silence," provides a succinct analysis of the book's reception and a sensible reply to it: "The type of Trakl interpretation in Eduard Lachmann's *Kreuz und Abend* and similarly oriented studies [such as Focke's *Georg Trakl: Liebe und Tod*] has given

rise to such oversimplification and Procrustian stretching that it is now considered almost disreputable to view Trakl's poetry in light of the Christian religion. Yet if one considers questions of good and evil, sin and suffering, corruption and innocence, or guilt and redemption to be religious matters, Trakl's poetry has indisputable religious content, however devoid it might be of confessionally oriented matters" (349).

42. GS/LF: September 18, 1952. "gewaltige Aussage zu Ehren des Dichters." "Den Aufsatz in der Salzburger Traklausgabe lieben wir nicht." Lachmann's essay is titled "Trakl und Hölderlin: Eine Deutung" and can be found in the third volume, *Nachlass und Biographie*, of the Salzburg edition of Trakl's work. For Lachmann's other work on Hölderlin up to that point, which was also well known (or notorious) for its Christian emphasis, see, for example, his 1948 *Brenner* article "Hölderlin und das Christliche," as well as his 1938 and 1951 editions *Hymnen* and *Hölderlins Christus-Hymnen: Text und Auslegung*. A 1938 letter from Heidegger to Lachmann about the ending of "Wie wenn am Feiertage . . ." ("As When on a Holiday . . .") is available in Storck, "'Zwiesprache von Dichten und Denken,'" 354–355. Barth, incidentally, also offered a Christian reading of Trakl, although he criticized Lachmann's "Trakl und Hölderlin" in his *Merkur* essay, which Stroomann mentions in GS/LF: September 18, 1952.

43. GS/LF: September 18, 1952; HKA 2: 719.

44. Walter Manggold (who attended on behalf of the newspaper *Südkurier*), in Ficker, *Briefwechsel 1940–1967*, 251 (June 21, 1953). Others in attendance were the Jesuit priest Alfred Focke (whom the publisher of the Salzburg edition of Trakl's *Gesamtausgabe* had sent); Ruth Horwitz (daughter of the editor of the Zurich edition Kurt Horwitz); the publisher Vittorio Klostermann; physician and author Wilhelm Kütemeyer; Heidegger's friend the art historian Heinrich Wiegand Petzet; poet (and wife of Clemens Podewils) Sophie Dorothee von Podewils; the editor and journalist Benno Reifenberg; Swiss publisher Peter Schifferli (whose press Die Arche published the Zurich edition of Trakl's *Gesamtausgabe*); Ficker's daughter Birgit Schowingen-Ficker; Stroomann's wife; the jurist Roderich von Thun; Trott (the forest manager Heinrich von Trott zu Solz or perhaps his brother the philosophical author Heinrich; possibly both); and author and Heidegger enthusiast Egon Vietta. Ficker had also asked Stroomann to invite the family of Ficker's son's father-in-law Wilhelm von Krane; Franz Witt; Hans Hartung; Wilhelm Klunker (if this is the same person as Heidegger's student Will Klunker, then it is likely he did not attend); Erich Lissner (from the *Frankfurter Rundschau*); Albert Arnold Scholl; Paula Schlier (who did not attend); Willy Stadler; Ernst Ginsberg; Kurt Horwitz (who likely did not attend); Karlheinz Schmidthüs; and Max Picard (GS/LF: September 18, 1952). Stroomann wrote numerous letters trying to persuade Gottfried Benn to "come 'to Heidegger'" at the Trakl celebration, but Benn refused. See Benn, *Briefe an F. W. Oelze 1950–1956*, 142, and Benn, Paeschke, and Moras, *Briefwechsel 1948–1956*, 202.

Last, it is perhaps worth noting that Ernst Jünger had planned on attending, but was unable to at the last minute.

45. Key texts in the Marxist debate over expressionism are available in Schmitt, ed., *Die Expressionismusdebatte*. Those in the National-Socialist debate over the style/movement are available in the section "Aktualität und Abwehr des Expressionismus im 'Dritten Reich,'" in Fleckner and Steinkamp, eds., *Gauklerfest unterm Galgen*. For parallels between Heidegger's and *Der Brenner's* concerns, see Janik, "Carl Dallago und Martin Heidegger."

46. In Ficker, *Briefwechsel 1940–1967*, 243–245 (quotation on 244; see also 237, 533–534). Focke would go on to publish a Christian reading of Trakl titled *Georg Trakl: Liebe und Tod*. For more information, and for Ficker's *praise* both of Focke's comportment during the discussion at Bühlerhöhe and of his book, see Ficker, *Briefwechsel 1940–1967*, 230, 533. See also Ficker's earlier letters to Focke in ibid., 155, 198–200, as well as Stroomann's comment to Ficker from November 23, 1952, about a work that Focke had sent Stroomann. Perhaps Stroomann is referring to an earlier version of what would become Focke's book or to an article Focke wrote that served as its basis: "Von Dionysos zu Christus." Finally, see Podewils, "Erörterung eines Trakl-Gedichts," who says that Focke "supplemented [ergänzte] Heidegger's lecture in the discussion with references to the sacramental in Trakl's poems."

Another attack came almost immediately from the side of poetry and literary criticism, on whose territory Heidegger was accused of encroaching. See Heidegger's reaction in April 1953 to this attack as recorded in Petzet, *Auf einen Stern zugehen*, 89. Heidegger seems to be referring, at least, to the poet Gottfried Benn; see, for example, Benn, *Briefe an F. W. Oelze 1950–1956*, 97. For prominent literary and philological critiques from the 1950s, see Muschg, *Die Zerstörung der deutschen Literatur*, 214–230; Hamburger, *Reason and Energy*, 239–271; and Rey, "Heidegger–Trakl: Einstimmiges Zwiegespräch." One of the most famous Germanists of the time, Heidegger's friend Emil Staiger, critiqued the philosopher's Trakl-interpretation at the lectern, although, to my knowledge, never in print. See Pestalozzi, "Einzelinterpretation und literaturwissenschaftliche Synthese bei Emil Staiger," 29. Staiger's only essay on Trakl, "Zu einem Gedicht Georg Trakls," from 1961, does not even mention Heidegger, although his appeal to interpretive restraint and his repudiation of the import of the incommunicable on page 295 seem to be directed at the philosopher: "Sooner or later it will certainly be possible to press on into the dark. However, it would be false to believe that the important secret lies behind this limit and that one would miss what is essential if one were not to grasp it. The limit is where a completely incommunicable solitude begins. And a completely incommunicable solitude is madness [*Wahnsinn*]." Egon Vietta, finally, is an interesting case. He was a close friend and staunch defender of Heidegger (see especially *Die Seinsfrage bei Martin Heidegger*), but had already written a pamphlet on Trakl in 1947 (*Georg*

Trakl: Eine Interpretation seines Werkes) that could not be made compatible with Heidegger's reading of the poet. Rather than addressing their differences or explicitly retracting his earlier view, which centered on Trakl's Christian compassion, Vietta simply recapitulated Heidegger's interpretation when he turned back to Trakl in 1952–1953, declaring that, with this interpretation, "the scholasticism of our literary concepts has reached its end; the conception of what counts as language has changed" ("Georg Trakl in Heideggers Sicht," 353). See also Egon Vietta, "Martin Heidegger über Georg Trakl." For more on Vietta's and his family's relation to Heidegger, as well as his role as a middleman between Heidegger and Benn, see the reports by Vietta's son Silvio, who himself knew Heidegger and wrote on Trakl: "Dialog mit den Dingen"; "Egon Vietta und Gottfried Benn"; and "Briefwechsel mit Egon Vietta." For Silvio Vietta's early work on Trakl, see his 1975 book, co-authored with Kemper, titled *Expressionismus*, as well as his 1976 edited volume *Lyrik des Expressionismus*.

47. Quotation in *Briefwechsel 1940–1967*, 529. See also ibid., 230, 235, 533; GS/LF: October 10, 1952, November 16, 1952, January 4, 1953; MH/LF: passim. Ficker, for his part, was so moved that he sent Heidegger and Stroomann, respectively, the manuscripts of Trakl's "Afra" and the first version of "Verwandlung" ("Transformation") (MH/LF: 34; GS/LF: October 10, 1952).

48. Petzet, *Auf einen Stern zugehen*, 114. Petzet mistakenly writes that Ficker gave the "lecture" in the evening, but another comment allows us to discern some of its content: Petzet notes that Ficker repeated "it" later at the University of Freiburg. This Freiburg lecture, from 1959, is titled "Der Abschied" (MH/LF: 152). A first version of the text appeared already in 1926 in the first edition of Ficker, ed., *Erinnerung an Georg Trakl*. I discuss Ficker's text in greater detail in the final section of chapter 4.

49. Hinze, "Heidegger und Trakl," 247. See also Görner, *Georg Trakl: Dichter im Jahrzehnt der Extreme*, 28; Palmier, *Situation de Georg Trakl*, 525; and Sharp, "On Reading Trakl," 155. It is noteworthy that Heidegger's "Die Sprache im Gedicht" is appended to at least two collections of Trakl's poetry: a Spanish edition (*Poesías*), from 1956, and an Italian edition (*Il canto dell'esule / La parola nella poesia*), from 2003. Further, on the front of the dust jacket of the ninth, tenth, and eleventh editions of Trakl's *Die Dichtungen* (Salzburg edition), there is a long quotation from "Language in the Poem," and the back cover of the 1999 Reclam volume *Interpretationen: Gedichte von Georg Trakl*, ed. Kemper, contains the blurb: "Trakl's rank as one of the most significant German-language lyric poets of the twentieth century is undisputed; the one-of-a-kind 'Trakl tone' prompted Heidegger's adage that Trakl's slim poetic work is fundamentally just *one* poem."

50. Reports by Focke (*Georg Trakl: Liebe und Tod*, 179) and Horwitz (in Ficker, *Briefwechsel 1940–1967*, 244), respectively. These are nearly identical to the report of the discussion provided in the three typescripts of Heidegger's lecture located in the Forschungsinstitut Brenner-Archiv. I provide a fuller account under the heading "1952" in appendix 2.

51. Palmier, "Préface à la nouvelle édition (1987)," 18.
52. Heidegger sent Ficker a special, blue-bound printing of "Die Sprache im Gedicht," among many other texts. Ficker sent Heidegger a copy of the last issue of *Der Brenner* (in which Ficker, citing Podewils, summarizes Heidegger's Trakl-interpretation and discreetly offers a reading centered on Christian revelation as an alternative or supplement; see Ficker et al., "Nachträge und Notizen," 281–282); the second edition of his collection *Erinnerungen an Georg Trakl*; a copy of his Freiburg-lecture "Der Abschied"; and Drexel, ed., *Ludwig von Ficker zum Gedächtnis seines achtzigsten Geburtstags*, which includes an improvised speech, also in GA 16: 563–564, that Heidegger delivered at the ceremony for Ficker's eightieth birthday, during which Ficker was awarded an honorary doctorate from the Freie Universität Berlin (see the end of third chapter of this book for more details). Ficker's daughter also sent Heidegger her father's *Denkzetteln und Danksagungen*. Here is the secondary literature on Trakl that they sent one another or mention: Huder, "Der Dichter—Zeiger der Weltenuhr"; Killy, "Gedichte im Gedicht"; Strohschneider-Kohrs, "Die Entwicklung der lyrischen Sprache in der Dichtung Georg Trakls" (this was Strohschneider-Kohrs's "Probevorlesung," not identified by the editor of MH/LF; see 66 and 152); and a special issue of the *Cahiers du Sud* from 1957, titled "Georg Trakl." Finally, Ficker also recommended Leitgeb's "Die Trakl-Welt" to Stroomann and Heidegger (GS/LF: May 10, 1951), and Heidegger possibly forwarded Ficker "a long, wonderful letter," now lost, from "a young German" about "the Christian element in Trakl's *Gedicht*" (MH/LF: 75).
53. Diana Orendi Hinze sees here "a crass turn in [Heidegger's] relation to Trakl." "Heidegger," on her reading, "saw and had to admit that, within the framework of a new convergence of the world and poetizing [*Welt- und Dichtungsannäherung*], his old position on Trakl's poetizing was no longer tenable or able to answer to itself and the world" ("Heidegger und Trakl," 248). However, while noteworthy for my attempt to understand the Heidegger/Trakl connection, Heidegger's letter to Ficker is not especially remarkable in the broader context of Heidegger's trajectory, which, by his own admission, was always underway, always revising and rethinking what he had earlier elaborated. Heidegger was certainly not critiquing himself, as Hinze entertains, when he later wrote to Ficker: "Again and again I come across the traces of your work and consider every time how completely differently you tended the work of our poet in comparison with today's literary enterprise, which, instead of awakening and cultivating the act of listening to the poet, dissolves everything and destroys the word through a misguided will to explain" (MH/LF: 98–99; letter from December 20, 1966).
54. GA 12: 75; GA 13: 227; Arendt and Heidegger, *Briefe 1925 bis 1975*, 162. For a general account of Trakl's "transitivizations," see Sauermann, "Zu Valenzverstößen in poetischer Sprache," and Detsch, *Georg Trakl's Poetry*, 111–112.
55. Palmier, "Préface à la nouvelle édition (1987)," 18–19, 23. Paul Ricœur was the chair, and Emmanuel Levinas served as a member during the defense.

56. Quotations here and in the remainder of the paragraph come from Heidegger's letter to Palmier, 117–118. Heidegger's second lecture on Trakl, incidentally, is the only secondary source the editors, Walther Killy and Hans Szklenar, cite in their preface to the historical-critical edition, where they write, regarding Trakl's work: "It is not absolute poetry, but a poetry that [. . .] moves along the borders of the sayable and attempts to overtake the unsayable in sometimes compulsively repeated attempts. [. . .] It has been said [by Heidegger] that in the work of this poet we are ultimately—primordially—dealing with ONE poem [*EIN Gedicht*]. The reader will find this circumstance [. . .] confirmed in many respects" (HKA 2: 8). See also Heidegger's letter to Strohschneider-Kohrs from February 4, 1959, summarized in part in appendix 2.

57. For critiques of Palmier's study, see Stieg, "Une lettre de Heidegger à Jean-Michel Palmier (de 1972) justifie-t-elle la nouvelle édition de 'Situation de Georg Trakl' (en 1987)?," and Colombat, "Heidegger, lecteur de Trakl."

58. For these three critiques, see Palmier, *Situation de Georg Trakl*, 533n7, 533n8, 539; 537–539; and 540–541.

59. Compare Palmier, *Situation de Georg Trakl*, 531, and Heidegger's letter to Palmier, 117.

60. For information on the so-called Brenner Circle and Trakl's relation to it, see Detsch, *Georg Trakl and the Brenner Circle*; Morgan, "Georg Trakl (1887–1914) in Context"; and Methlagl, Sauermann, and Scheichl, eds., *Untersuchungen zum "Brenner."* A bibliography of all the texts appearing in the journal is available in Heinrich Wild, ed., "Der Brenner-Verlag."

61. Basil, *Georg Trakl*, 8.

62. Heidegger proceeds to quote Hölderlin's editor Norbert von Hellingrath: "above 'unpoetic,' variants are piled up in the likeness of a tower: 'unending,' 'unpeaceful,' 'uncontained,' 'unruly.' " Heidegger then explains what poetry is by way of an analysis of these words, absent their negative prefixes. For more on Hölderlin's poem and Heidegger's interpretation of these variants, see Mieszkowski, "The Next Word."

63. Compare Heidegger's preference for shorter, often fragmentary passages in interpreting ancient Greek authors. See Most, "Heidegger's Greeks," especially 88–89.

64. See also Horwitz's letter to Ficker from July 3, 1945, as he was planning the volume in the aftermath of World War II. After mentioning the devastation around him and the loss of loved ones, he writes: "I believe that today it comes down to showing the Georg Trakl who was moved by Christ, or better, to pointing to the, for now, last great poet who was absolutely a Christian." In Ficker, *Briefwechsel 1940–1967*, 117. For more on the planning of the volume, see ibid., 126–128.

65. The complete study can be found in *Erinnerung an Georg Trakl*, 2nd ed., 21–90. Quotation by McLary, "The Incestuous Sister or the Trouble with Grete," 30.

66. Here Mahrholdt is referring to Weininger, *Geschlecht und Charakter*, especially chapter 8 ("Ich-Problem und Genialität").

67. For more on these tendencies, see McLary, "The Incestuous Sister or the Trouble with Grete," and Zwerschina, "'Erinnerungen' an Georg Trakl und 'Erinnerungslücken.'"

68. Fichte, *Addresses to the German Nation*, 97. See also Derrida, "Onto-Theology of National-Humanism" and "Heidegger's Hand."

69. Although it would go beyond the scope of this study to discuss the status of Limbach's report in any detail, I should note that its authenticity is disputed: on one end of the spectrum, there is Walter Methlagl ("Hans Limbach: 'Begegnung mit Georg Trakl.' Zur Quellenkritik"), who argues that the conversation happened as Limbach recorded it; on the other end are Eberhard Sauermann ("Zur Authentizität in der Trakl-Rezeption") and Sieglinde Klettenhammer ("Hans Limbach als Schriftsteller und 'Brenner'-Leser"), who are quite skeptical. My present interest is, however, in Heidegger's reaction to this report, not its ultimate or literal veracity. For more on Dallago and his connection with topics I will discuss below—Whitman, Nietzsche, religion, and sexual difference—see Janik, "Carl Dallago and the Early Brenner," and Methlagl, "Hans Limbach."

70. Heidegger underlined the word *dumpf* (muffled, dull, apathetic) here and drew an exclamation mark next to it in the margin. I have rendered it in accordance with Limbach's report about Trakl's reticence and reserve, but Heidegger's surprise might come from hearing an element of perfunctoriness in it. Earlier in the report, Limbach writes: "[Trakl] once said, 'I'm only half-born!,' and claimed to have up until his twentieth year noticed nothing at all of his environment except *water*. His autobiographical sketch 'Traum und Umnachtung' ['Dream and Lunacy'] [. . .] wonderfully reproduces this *dumpfen*, agonizing state" (DD: 211). Cf. Heidegger's commentary on the word *dumpf* in Rilke, GA 5: 287.

71. For the development of Trakl's relation to Nietzsche, which began with discipleship and ended with Christian-Dostoevskyan repudiation, see Methlagl, "Nietzsche und Trakl."

72. Weininger, *Geschlecht und Charakter*, 265, 403, chapter 14, and 566. For more on Weininger, Trakl, and Dallago (who in 1912 published *Otto Weininger und sein Werk* in three parts in *Der Brenner* and also as a self-standing book), see McLary, "The Incestuous Sister or the Trouble with Grete"; Methlagl, "Hans Limbach"; and Heckmann, *Das verfluchte Geschlecht*.

Chapter 2

1. "And just as one lives in own's own truth, to live in the truth of a foreign being is love. To deviate from this truth is the danger of all language." Kommerell, "Die Sprache und das Unaussprechliche," 316.

2. "If we want to reach the Place of the texts, from which the so-called metaphysical or Christian texts come, we must stop believing in a certain univocity and read the latter as we read Trakl, giving them the same credit." GIII: 109.

3. Heidegger, *Zollikoner Seminare*, 322. GA 16: 364. On Kommerell as a poet, see Gadamer, "Gedenkrede auf Max Kommerell."

4. For Heidegger's relation to Kommerell, especially as regards Kommerell's famous critical letter to Heidegger about the latter's interpretation of Hölderlin, see Bernasconi, "Poets as Prophets and as Painters"; Busch, "Kommerell's Hölderlin"; Storck, "'Zwiesprache von Dichten und Denken'"; and Storck, "Hermeneutischer Disput." For the letter and Heidegger's response, see Kommerell, *Briefe und Aufzeichnungen*, 396–405; Heidegger, *Ausgewählte Briefe an Heinrich Wiegand Petzet*, 18–19; and GA 80: 1147–1172. The last text is a tribute to Kommerell and reveals Heidegger's extensive engagement with his work.

5. Agamben, "Kommerell, or On Gesture," 77. With a mixture of admiration and contempt, Benjamin, for his part, wrote that, "[i]f there were such a thing as a German conservatism worth its salt, it would have to regard this book [Kommerell's *Der Dichter als Führer in der deutschen Klassik*, written under the spell of Stefan George] as its Magna Carta." "Against a Masterpiece," 378. Kommerell's obscurity in the Anglophone world is due, in no small part, to the near absence of translations into English. See, however, Kommerell, "Hölderlin's Empedocles Poems."

6. Kommerell, *Jean Paul*, 47. My discussion of gesture draws largely on Fleming, "The Crisis of Art." See also Adler, "The Intermedial Gesture"; Agamben, "Kommerell, or On Gesture"; and Schmidt, *Between Word and Image*, especially chapter 3.

7. Kommerell, "Die Sprache und das Unaussprechliche," 243.

8. Kommerell, "Vom Wesen des lyrischen Gedichts," 41. This is the first chapter of Kommerell's last book, *Gedanken über Gedichte*, which Heidegger refers to three times in GA 80: 1165, 1168–1170, 1172.

9. Emerson, *The Complete Essays*, 329. Cf. GA 12: 28.

10. Kommerell, *Jean Paul*, 419.

11. The opening of the first version tries to justify the dearth of direct reference with the rhetorical question: "How could a commemoration [*Gedenken*] succeed better than by us thinking [*denken*]? We will endeavor to think by thoughtfully going *after* language [*denkend der Sprache nachgehen*]" (GA 80: 981). The second version, significantly emended, was delivered before the Württembergische Bibliotheksgesellschaft in Stuttgart on February 14, 1951. This version served as the basis for the chapter in *On the Way to Language* (1959). Both of the earlier versions were recently published in GA 80: 979–1032.

I might also note that, in unpublished letters to his brother from 1951, Heidegger says that the delivery of the second version was a success, but that the lecture is only a beginning and he does not want to make the material public property right away. Later in 1951, Heidegger had considered choosing "Language" for a lecture and discussion in Zurich but ultimately decided against it because, as he puts it in a letter to Medard Boss, "too much was packed into it" and because "it requires, as a counterpart, the logos-lecture [on Heraclitus, GA 7: 211–234]." In a letter to Beda Allemann, Heidegger provides a further explanation: "I dropped the theme 'Language,' not so much because it makes too high of demands on the audience, but because it is too difficult in itself and therefore also for me." Quotations in Heidegger and Staiger, "Der Briefwechsel," 71n94.

12. The sentences after the paragraph break are indented in the GA volume, as though separate from the main text. Reviews of the Bühlerhöhe celebration nevertheless prove that Heidegger mentioned Kommerell and the essay on Kleist during the event. F. [Frisé], "Bühler Höhen-Luft," 15, Peters, "Durch Sprechen zur Sprache"; see also Nora Kommerell, "Aufzeichnungen über die Max Kommerell-Veranstaltung auf der Bühlerhöhe, Oktober 1950." The first review, printed in the *Deutsche Zeitung und Wirtschaftszeitung*, is critical of Heidegger and of the general atmosphere of esotericism and deference at Bühlerhöhe. After acknowledging Gadamer's and Herbert von Buttlar's efforts to commemorate Kommerell, the reviewer provides the following commentary, which, due to its rarity and resonance with some of my own concerns, I will translate and cite here at length:

> Heidegger, who had also been close to Kommerell, held a *privatissimum* [a seminar or lecture for a select group of participants, used ironically here] on "Language," with reference to Kommerell's treatise "Language and the Inexpressible" (1937). [. . .] [O]ne instinctively thought of esotericism, of the airtight encapsulation of the circle [around Stefan George] from which Kommerell emerged. The shielding against the disquiet of everyday life, against contradiction from the "other side," mostly weakened his arguments rather than strengthening them. The aseptic and poison-free air up there, along with the deceptive security in social conventions that have become problematic, are now more than ever a questionable stimulus. Heidegger's diction underlined this danger: the danger of monologuing, of a thinking which spins about in its own head and seems, in its search for new ciphers, to lead to a frightening encryption of thoughts. Like hardly any other people [*Volk*], we [Germans] tend to absolutize an intellectual [*geistige*] figure without criticism and restraint; Stefan George was an example of this. Today, it looks like Heidegger is the next in line. [. . .] At this meeting with Heidegger, we had the impression that no one dared to admit openly what remained incomprehensible, indeed, what had to remain incomprehensible, and certainly not to ask why.

Contrast this with the report from the *Rhein-Neckar-Zeitung* (Haebler, "Metaphysik der Sprache," 2):

> Martin Heidegger's lecture presented a sort of metaphysics of language: in Heidegger's language. He does not want to talk about language: it is a matter of "thoughtfully grasping the speaking of language" ["*das Sprechen der Sprache denkend zu erfassen*"]. It was a masterful way of thinking through [this issue] with many abysses and backgrounds [*Abgründen und Hintergründen*], but again and again it was effectively and vividly taken out of the realm of thought [*Denkerischen*] and redeemed by exemplary recourse to a poem given to every audience member as a handout. Thus, in the midst of the dialectic of Heideggerian formulas, a philosophy came to [. . .] life.

Peters's review, published in *Die Zeit*, provides a neutral summary of Heidegger's lecture.

13. In his 1953 essay on "Language in the Poem," Egon Vietta was right to trace Heidegger's remarks back to Kommerell, although, perhaps because he did not hear or have access to the original version of "Language," Vietta missed the critical subtext ("Georg Trakl in Heideggers Sicht," 352):

> No sentence [in "Language in the Poem"] about the graveyards of the lyrical ego. In contrast, a decisive statement as a motto, to which Kommerell's interpretation of Kleist (Language and the Inexpressible) already pointed (although this emerged in a period of encounter between Heidegger and Kommerell): "The *Gedicht* of a poet remains unspoken."

14. Gadamer, "Europa und die Oikoumene," 273. See also Gadamer, "'Golden blooms the tree of grace,'" and, for an even earlier appearance of the peal of stillness, GA 85: 90.

15. This notion of *erörtern* as displacing *us*—or rather shifting the place of our concern to where we always already, albeit inconspicuously, are—does not appear in the first or second versions of "Language"; it therefore seems to be a development of, rather than a precursor to, Heidegger's emplacement of Trakl in "Language in the Poem." The word *Ortschaft*, which plays an important role in the third section of "Language in the Poem," does not appear in the earlier versions of "Language" either.

16. For more on what the self-speaking of language is *not* (such as an expression of inner states, a human function, or a presentation or representation of states of affairs), see GA 12: 9–13; GA 80: 1062. For further demarcations, and a helpful comparison of Heidegger's and Herder's "constitutive" theories of language, see Taylor, "Heidegger on Language." For Heidegger's lifelong engagement with

the problem of language, see Powell, ed., *Heidegger and Language*. It is not clear, in Heidegger's lecture, how dismissive of traditional views of language, whether expressive, pragmatic, or representationalist, he is being. Are they just derivative and superficial, in which case they would still have legitimacy within a restricted scope, or should Heidegger's reflections on language compel us to call them into question altogether? Heidegger says they are "correct" (*richtig*), but then, by sleight of etymology, he equates correctness with "conforming" (*sich richten*) to unquestioned presuppositions (GA 12: 13). Cf. Markus Wild, "Heidegger and Trakl."

17. For tautology as more than redundancy, see Roesner, "De la tautologie," and Ziarek, *Language after Heidegger*.

18. See also GA 12: 141–143, 231; GA 49: 156. The language of leaping (*springen*) appears in the first version of "Language," although not in the version Heidegger published in *On the Way to Language*. We can thoughtfully reach the speaking of language only through a "leap" (*Sprung*) into a *Gesprochenes*. Heidegger chooses "A Winter Evening" as his guiding example of the latter and does not, in contrast to the published version, hesitate to name Trakl as its author. "We will hear a *Gesprochenes*. It is a poem by Georg Trakl. Already in the choice of this poem the leap of our thinking shows itself" (GA 80: 985–986). In "Language in the Poem" Heidegger will speak of a *Blicksprung*, a "saccade" or, literally, "leap of the look" (GA 12: 35).

19. For an extensive treatment of this topic in Heidegger's Bremen Lectures (repeated at Bühlerhöhe), see Mitchell, *The Fourfold*. The terminology of these lectures is more present in the earlier versions of "Language," where one finds key terms such as *Spiegel-Spiel* ("mirror-play") (GA 80: 994, 1021).

20. Unlike the Latinate "gestate" and "gesture," *Gebären* and *Gebärde* do not appear to be related etymologically, even if there is historical precedent for connecting them, and even if language should speak this connection through the mouth of Heidegger. The first version of the lecture is more circumspect: "Our old language names *Austragen*: *bërn*—*bären*—whence the word *gebären*" (GA 80: 992). For a discussion of the etymologies, see Thomä, "Sprache," 301, who notes that "the transition from birth to gesture" allows Heidegger "to describe world as a space in which something *appears*—and precisely not: *emerges*." See also Boelderl, "Geburtsräume des Daseins."

21. The others are Hamann, Herder, Wilhelm von Humboldt, Kraus, and (in the first version) Kommerell (GA 12: 10–11, 15; GA 80: 1000). In the GA volume, there are also transcriptions of Heidegger's marginalia to his personal copy of *On the Way to Language*, where he refers critically to Mallarmé's idea of expression (GA 12: 28, note a). The first version also concludes not with another citation of "A Winter Evening" but with an allusion to Gottfried Benn's poem "Epilog 1949," which the editor of GA 80 does not identify. Heidegger writes: "The coming of the difference prepares us to go [or walk] when the heavens change their stars [*zu gehen, wenn die Himmel ihre Sterne wechseln*]" (GA 80: 1004). Cf. Benn, *Gesammelte Werke*, 3: 344: "Die Himmel wechseln

ihre Sterne—geh!" ("The heavens change their stars—go!") Benn is presumably also a hidden target of Heidegger's critique of expression (and of expressionism; cf. GA 98: 164). See Benn, "Probleme der Lyrik." "Language in the Poem" mentions, beside Trakl, only Aristotle, Ficker, Nietzsche, and Plato, and there is an uncredited citation of Sappho (GA 12: 35, 41, 44, 50, 53, 77).

22. *Pindari carmina cum fragmentis*, 1: 175, verses 1–3.

23. For echoes of Hölderlin in Trakl's poem and Heidegger's commentary, see Cooper, *Poetry and the Question of Modernity*, 62–77; see 115–118, 126–127 for their continued, albeit distorted, resonance in Paul Celan. See also Fynsk, "Noise at the Threshold."

24. See, however, GA 12: 20; GA 80: 1016; and the companion piece on Heraclitus, "Logos," in GA 7: 211–234.

25. Preface to Rickes, Ladenthin, and Baum, eds., *1955–2005: Emil Staiger und* Die Kunst der Interpretation *heute*, 7–8.

26. Quotation by Heidegger in Staiger, *Die Kunst der Interpretation*, 36, 46. This document contains, among other things, Staiger's lecture and an excerpted correspondence between Staiger and Heidegger about Mörike. For more on Heidegger, Staiger, and their exchange, see their complete correspondence (Heidegger and Staiger, "Der Briefwechsel"); Fóti, *Heidegger and the Poets*, chapter 1; Gelley, "Staiger, Heidegger, and the Task of Criticism"; Rickes, Ladenthin, and Baum, eds., *1955–2005: Emil Staiger und* Die Kunst der Interpretation *heute*; and Markus Wild, "Heidegger, Staiger, Muschg." Heidegger's relation to Mörike has been traced more broadly in Delobel, "Eduard Mörike et Martin Heidegger."

27. See GA 12: 16, and GA 80: 1019n10. Heidegger has been attacked pedantically for this reading. See Uhsadel, "[Review of] Martin Heidegger: Unterwegs zur Sprache," 219. I find the imperative plausible but only when considered alongside the indicative.

28. For the middle-voiced causality of letting and Heidegger's frequent deployment of *figurae etymologicae* or cognate nominative constructions, see Moore, *Eckhart, Heidegger, and the Imperative of Releasement*, 75–80, 97–102, and 133–137. For more on the peal of stillness, see Hanly, "Dark Celebration," 248–249; Gregory, *Speaking of Silence in Heidegger*, chapter 8; and von Herrmann, *Wege ins Ereignis*, 239–242.

29. Reports in Trakl, *Nachlass und Biographie*, 77–78, and Weichselbaum, *Georg Trakl: Eine Biographie*, 44–45.

30. In 1947, Heidegger's friend Egon Vietta referred to Trakl as a "patient sufferer [*Dulder*] who lives consubstantially [*wesenseins*] with the Bible." *Georg Trakl: Eine Interpretation seines Werkes*, 11.

31. Heidegger and Jaspers, *Briefwechsel 1920–1963*, 157. See 2 Corinthians 12:7.

32. Another target of Heidegger's attack seems to be Eduard Lachmann's "Trakl und Hölderlin," which Heidegger read and disliked (GS/LF: September 18,

1952). Lachmann's essay opens with a quotation of Trakl's poem "Lamentation," followed by the comment: "This, perhaps last message from Trakl, the lamentation from his Gethsemane-hour, has the tone of Christ's question: my God, why have you forsaken me? [. . .] In this possibility, albeit expressed in the subjunctive, Trakl's despair [*Verzweiflung*] and at the same time his poetry [*Dichtung*] are revealed to be truly Christian, to be a poetry of Christ's mortal dread [*Todesangst*], to be Good Friday poetry" (163).

33. See also the end of Derrida's *De l'esprit*.

34. Detsch, *Georg Trakl's Poetry*, 11–23. See also 35: "In the preceding quotation Heidegger spoke as a philosopher and drew from his own philosophical thought; however, now he appears to speak as a moralizing theologian and overlooks the fact that the sister herself had become for Trakl a kind of Christ figure."

35. *Expositio salutationis angelicae*, art. 2. On March 15, 2020, for example, as the COVID-19 pandemic was devastating Italy, Pope Francis went to the Basilica of Saint Mary Major to pray in front of the Marian icon "Salus Populi Romani." Cf., also, Novalis's idealization of his deceased beloved Sophie von Kühn as the Virgin Mary.

36. Noack, "Gespräch mit Martin Heidegger," 33.

37. Ibid., 33. Unlike in the previous quotation, this is not a direct citation of Heidegger but a paraphrase.

38. Lasker-Schüler, *Die gesammelten Gedichte*, 117.

39. Milton, *Paradise Lost*, 1.12–26.

40. From a diary entry by Trakl's friend and eventual editor Karl Röck. In Röck, *Tagebuch*, 3: 46.

41. Heidegger was acquainted with this aphorism, at least insofar as it appeared as the epigraph to Horwitz's afterword (DD: 228).

42. See the brief discussion and sources cited in Weichselbaum, *Georg Trakl: Eine Biographie*, 55, 65–66, 188n97, 191n157, 205–206n126.

43. Führmann, *At the Burning Abyss*, 229.

44. Heinrich, "Confiteor," 624. Quoted, with further discussion, in Methlagl, "'Der Brenner': Weltanschauliche Wandlungen vor dem ersten Weltkrieg," 243–244. See also Methlagl, "Theodor Haecker und 'Der Brenner'"; Wild, ed., "Der Brenner-Verlag: Eine Gesamtbibliographie," 40–41; Klessinger, "Schuld und Erlösung"; Neri, *Das abendländische Lied*, 131–144; and Levinas's favorite line from Dostoevsky's *The Brothers Karamazov*: "Each of us is guilty before everyone for everyone, and I more than the others" (quoted in *Otherwise than Being*, 146).

45. In person, Trakl seems to have been unable to hold onto even the slight shred of solace afforded by poetry. Ficker reports that, after Trakl handed him the aphorism under discussion, the poet said: "But of course no poem can atone for an iniquity [*kein Gedicht kann Sühne sein für eine Schuld*]." Ficker,

Denkzettel und Danksagungen, 226. For another reference to the concepts of *Schuld* and *Sühne*, see the early poem "Naturtheater," where Trakl speaks of "Lost days, without guilt and atonement" (HKA 1: 143).

46. For more biographical evidence, see Methlagl, *Brenner-Gespräche*, 86 (on Trakl's earnest and frequent use of the phrase "der liebe Gott," "our dear God"); Methlagl, "Hans Limbach," 9 (on Trakl's seemingly affirmative claim that "Christianity is the religion of criminals"); Röck, *Tagebuch*, 1: 189 (on Trakl's fondness for Dostoevsky; Trakl "more and more a confessor [*Bekenner*, sc., of faith]"), 1: 240 (on Trakl's distraught identification of a decapitated cow's head with "Our Lord Jesus"); and the reports by Röck and Trakl's sister Grete quoted in Weichselbaum, *Georg Trakl: Eine Biographie*, 116 (on decay and depravity as a means "for people to learn to recognize [*erkennen*] the Lord Jesus"). See, further, Ficker's correspondence with Dallago, Alfred Focke, and Werner Meyknecht about Trakl, in Ficker, *Briefwechsel*, passim, as well as Rusch and Schmidt, *Das Voraussetzungssystem Georg Trakls*, 131. "The most compelling reason for treating Trakl as a Christian writer," says Ben Morgan, "is that that is how he appeared to his contemporaries, even to those such as Carl Dallago, to whom being a Christian was not a recommendation." "Georg Trakl in Context," 331n9. In the acknowledgment section of his Christocentric reading of Trakl ("his poetry is an eminently and essentially *religious* poetry, in the concrete, Christian sense of the word," 5; see also 64–72) from 1935, *Das Bild des Menschen bei Georg Trakl*, Meyknecht, incidentally, thanks Heidegger for his "teaching activity," which, Meyknecht explains, "serves as the basis for what gives philosophical structure and direction to this work" (VII). Although Meyknecht had attended at least two of Heidegger's lecture courses (XII, 76), it is unclear whether they remained in touch. See also the excerpt of the book that appeared under the same title in *Der Brenner* in 1934, which Heidegger refers to in an unpublished note on Trakl.

47. Michel, "Vom Podvelež," 125.

48. HKA 2: 311, which is based on a faulty copy, has December 13, 1913. See Trakl, *Sämtliche Werke und Briefwechsel*, 3: 404.

49. Quotation by Kraus in Stieg, *Der Brenner und die Fackel*, 16. For details on Wittgenstein's interest in *Der Brenner* and in Trakl and some parallels in their work, see Janik, "'Ethik und Äesthetik sind Eins'"; Janik, "Wittgenstein: Ein österreichisches Rätsel"; and Janik and Toulmin, *Wittgenstein's Vienna*.

50. For more on the questionnaire and Trakl's relation to Kraus, see Stieg, *Der Brenner und die Fackel*, 37–53, 261–271, and Morgan, "Georg Trakl (1887–1914) in Context." For more on Kraus and his times, see, for example, Franzen, *The Kraus Project*; Janik and Toulmin, *Wittgenstein's Vienna*, 67–91; and Linden, *Karl Kraus and the Discourse of Modernity*. Eventually, *Der Brenner* would move in an explicitly Christian direction and distance itself from Kraus (despite the latter's secret conversion to Catholicism in 1911).

51. Mengaldo, "'Tönend von Wohllaut und weichem Wahnsinn,'" 74, reads the final line of "Psalm" as bleak, but fails to note the genuinely bleak first version of the poem—

In der zerstörten Stadt richtet die Nacht schwarze Zelte auf.

Wie eitel ist alles! (HKA 1: 202)

*

In the destroyed city the night raises black tents.

How vain is everything!

—in contrast to which the second stands out as a hopeful alternative. This is even more evident when we compare the second with a variant Trakl ended up rejecting:

Immer über der Schädelstätte tanzen grinsende / magnetene / Monde. (HKA 2: 107)

*

Over Golgotha dance grinning / magnetic / moons.

See Stieg, *Der Brenner und die Fackel*, 266.

52. The only reference I know of appears in a 1966 letter to Erhart Käster, in which Heidegger mockingly quotes Ulrich Sonnemann: "The Germans cannot truly be helped until Karl Kraus has become popular reading and Adorno required reading for a high-school diploma." *Briefwechsel 1953–1974*, 83.

53. For further references to bread and wine and an account of their broader role in Trakl's poems, see Millington, *Snow from Broken Eyes*, 276–289, and Lachmann, *Kreuz und Abend*, 22–28. Some of the biblical allusions I trace below were first identified by Reinhard Gerlach in his analysis of Anton Webern's atonal setting of Trakl's poem for soprano and orchestra. See Gerlach, "Anton Webern: Ein Winterabend op. 13, Nr. 4," 60–63.

54. Kaiser, "Brot und Wein," 146.

55. Casey, *Manshape that Shone*, 19.

56. Anonymous, "The 'Vita Adae,'" §§36, 40–42 (pp. 139, 140–142). For more on this text and its multilingual transmission, see Murdoch, *The Apocryphal Adam and Eve in Medieval Europe*.

57. The figure of Eve appears in Trakl's "Menschheit" ("Humanity") and "In Milch und Öde" ("In Milk and Wasteland"), for example. HKA 1: 24, 166.

58. Trakl, *Sämtliche Werke und Briefwechsel*, 3: 411.

59. This indeterminacy of petrification is reflected at the rhythmic level: "the 'te' verb ending of *versteinerte* lies on a stressed syllable, emphasizing this change in tense, but also undermining the taut regularity of the poem thus far, as the weak schwa vowel cannot sustain the development of the line's phrasing and meter. This line is characterized by the alliteration of three stressed / ʃ / phonemes, each part of a compound consonant: /Schmer/, /stei/, and /Schwe/, demanding a slower voicing and making the relative weakness of the /te/ even more glaring. The rending of pain is thus directed against the line itself, as *versteinerte* is rent prosodically, just as it would solidify and stabilize the threshold that permits such 'dif-ference' to articulate itself." Smith, *Sounding/Silence*, 168.

60. Bakhtin, *Problems of Dostoevsky's Poetics*, 61.

61. Dostojewski, *Literarische Schriften*, 1, 238.

62. Kaiser, "Brot und Wein," 151; Kudszus, *Poetic Process*, 32–33; Rey, "Heidegger–Trakl," 117.

63. Cf. GA 12: 13, in reference to John 1:1.

64. Ficker, *Der Briefwechsel 1926–1939*, 246.

Chapter 3

1. "The authentic image may be old, but the authentic idea is new. It is of today. Admittedly, this 'today' may be paltry. But whatever form it takes, our task is to seize it by the horns so that we can interrogate the past. It is the bull whose blood must fill the grave if the spirits of the departed are to appear at its edge." Benjamin, "Wider ein Meisterwerk," 259 / "Against a Masterpiece," 383.

2. Derrida, *Spectres de Marx*, 277–278.

3. One can see this in Derrida's personal copies of the original German and of a French translation, where he underlines and draws arrows next to Heidegger's most explicit association of detachment (*Abgeschiedenheit, Dis-cès*) with gathering (*Versammlung, rassemblement*): "Als Versammlung hat die Abgeschiedenheit das Wesen des Ortes" ("Comme rassemblant à soi, le Dis-cès a la nature du site"). Heidegger, *Unterwegs zur Sprache*, 67 / *Acheminement vers la parole*, 70.

4. Cf. Ezra Pound's most concise of definitions: "Dichten = condensare." *ABC of Reading*, 36.

5. Heidegger tacitly cites Sappho when, in reference to the "lunar voice of the sister [*mondene Stimme der Schwester*]" from Trakl's "Geistliche Dämmerung" ("Spiritual Twilight"), he speaks of "the shining of the mooness [*Möndin*]," after which he inserts the Greek word *selanna* in parentheses (GA 12: 44). The word *selanna* is an Aeolian form of *selēnē*, "moon" or "goddess of the moon."

Sappho uses it several times. (See also Pindar's 10th Olympian, verse 75, and GA 78: 78.) Heidegger cites its occurrence in fragment 34 of Sappho on two occasions (GA 40: 107, GA 16: 559), in the latter of which he calls her "the greatest poetess [*Dichterin*] of Greece." Elsewhere, in a preliminary remark to a poetry reading at Bühlerhöhe, he designates her "the greatest of all the lyric poets [*Lyriker*] of the West" (GA 16: 472). Despite this, Heidegger devotes little attention to her work (there are passing remarks in GA 8: 139, GA 75: 115, and GA 76: 392), and it is unclear how he understands the relation between *Lyriker* and *Dichter*: Heidegger, to my knowledge, never uses the word *Lyriker* for Pindar, for example, who is traditionally numbered among the "nine lyric poets."

6. On this circle and the Trakl lecture's relation to *Being and Time* generally, see Harries, "Language and Silence." For a different, deconstructive approach to Heidegger's method, centered on the need for counting, see Mullins, "Count Heidegger."

7. Phaedo 81c–e (drawing on Pythagoras), Phaedrus 246a–254e.

8. As Detsch, *Georg Trakl's Poetry*, 133n35, remarks.

9. There is also Paul Gerhardt's celebrated seventeenth-century Protestant hymn "Ich bin ein Gast auf Erden," which Trakl presumably would have sung in the Evangelische Christuskirche. Its first stanza conveys a sense of earthly alienation and an aspiration for heavenly restoration:

Ich bin ein Gast auf Erden Und hab hier keinen Stand;
Der Himmel soll mir werden, Da ist mein Vaterland.
Hier muß ich Unruh haben, Hier reis' ich ab und zu;
Dort will mein Gott mich laben Mit ewger Sabbatruh.

In Jane Borthwick's popular translation:

A pilgrim and a stranger, I journey here below;
Far distant is my country, The home to which I go.
Here I must toil and travail, Oft weary and opprest;
But there my God shall lead me To everlasting rest.

Trakl, moreover, was by no means deaf to the music of the Psalms: one need only read his own "Psalm" or the 1912 poem "De Profundis," whose title he takes from Psalm 130 (or 129 in the Vulgate) and which, as Gerald Stieg notes ("'Frühling der Seele,'" 164), one can read as a negative counterpart to "Springtime of the Soul." My interpretation of "Springtime of the Soul," which I will present below, is indebted to Stieg on several points.

10. For Heidegger's remarks on distinctively German thinking, see his lecture "Europa und die deutsche Philosophie" ("Europe and German Philosophy"), where he mentions Eckhart and Hegel (GA 80: 691–692), among others. See

also GA 31: 51; GA 39: 123, 133–134; and GA 41: 98. For Novalis, see, for example, GA 10: 19–20. Regarding Biblical verses, Levinas asks pointedly (against Heidegger): "Don't they have as much right as Hölderlin and Trakl to be cited? [. . .] Does philosophizing mean deciphering in a palimpsest a buried scripture?" Levinas goes on to offer an anti-Platonic interpretation of Psalm 119 that is nevertheless quite different from Heidegger's anti-Platonism:

> We read [. . .], "I am a stranger on the earth; do not hide your commandments from me." / Is this, as historical criticism claims, a later text from the Hellenistic period when oriental spirituality may have been seduced by the Platonic myth of the soul exiled in the body? But this psalm echoes texts recognized as dating from one century before Socrates and Plato, notably in Leviticus chapter 25, verse 23: "No land will be alienated irrevocably, because the land is mine, because you are but strangers, housed in my land." This has nothing to do with the strangeness of the eternal soul exiled amidst passing shadows, or the homesickness that can be surmounted by the edification of a house and possession of land, releasing by construction the hospitality of the site that the land envelops. Because, as in psalm 119, which calls for commandments, this difference between the ego and the world is extended by obligations toward others. Echo of the permanent *saying* of the Bible: the condition—or incondition—of strangers and slaves in the land of Egypt brings man closer to his fellow man. Men seek one another in their incondition of strangers. No one is at home. The memory of that servitude assembles humanity. The difference that gapes between ego and self, the non-coincidence of the identical, is a thorough non-indifference with regard to men. (*Humanism of the Other*, 66)

Trakl, I believe, had both: a Platonic sense of psychic exile and extreme solicitude for the stranger.

11. I here cite from the edition Trakl likely would have used, *Meister Eckeharts Schriften und Predigten*, which was extremely popular at the time (1: 74). The other widespread edition, *Meister Eckharts Mystische Schriften*, renders the passage similarly (40–41). Cf. Eckhart, *Die deutschen Werke*, 4: 490, lines 146–150. For parallels between Eckhart and Trakl, see Lyon, "Altered States of Consciousness," and, less so, Lyon, "Georg Trakl's Poetry of Silence."

12. Hegel, *Der Geist des Christentums und sein Schicksal*, 246–247; also 371.

13. For the quotations and further discussion, see Novalis, *Gedichte, Die Lehrlinge zu Sais*, 227–228, as well as Novalis's poem "Der Fremdling" ("The Stranger") on pages 54–55. For the motif of alienation on earth in Hölderlin, see the latter's *Sämtliche Werke und Briefe*, 1: 752.

14. Heidegger simply equates Elis with the figure of the stranger. For other possibilities, see Rainer, "Georg-Trakls 'Elis'-Gedichte," 405–406, and Ficker, *Briefwechsel 1926–1939*, 246.

15. The German philologist Gerald Stieg traces Trakl's phrase *verhauenen Wald* ("thrashed forest") back to an elegy by the Middle-High-German *Minnesänger* Walther von der Vogelweide, which laments the times and puts its hope in eternity. Stieg, "'Frühling der Seele,'" 168.

16. Eclogue VII, verse 62. There is also Clemens Brentano's "Das Märchen von dem Myrtenfräulein" ("Fairy Tale of the Myrtle-Girl"), in which a myrtle literally blooms over the buried corpse of a maiden before she is resurrected and weds the prince.

17. For these different translations, see McNulty, "Heidegger and the Poets," 88.

18. At the end of his lecture (GA 12: 77–78), Heidegger cites the final verse of the penultimate stanza of "Springtime of the Soul" ("Violent dying and the singing flame in the heart"), provides a one-sentence synopsis ("Then there follows the ascent of the song into the pure echo of the harmonious sound of the spiritual years, through which the stranger [*Fremdling*] wanders and which the brother, who begins to dwell in the land of evening, follows"), and concludes with a citation of the remaining verses. He thus omits the very scene that leads the narrator to speak of violent dying. Unfortunately, for all their care and attention to issues of citation and sexual difference, Derrida (GIII) and Krell (*Phantoms of the Other*) never consider this scene, either. Derrida even concludes his interpretation of "Language in the Poem" with a recitation of the same verses that Heidegger had cited; he adds a French translation—a noteworthy gesture in and of itself—but nothing else (GIII: 176–177). Fóti, *Heidegger and the Poets*, 26–29, cites and comments on "Springtime of the Soul" in its entirety, but she ignores or places little emphasis on the allusions to incest, murder, and Christian despair and accordingly does not recognize the redemptive significance of spirit. For her, the poet is missing

> the meaningful order of life [. . .]. The "spiritual blueness" which spreads over the mutilated forest cannot undo or heal the mutilation, but it encompasses and soothes it. [. . .] [It] is the gentle song, the very art of the poet, rather than any essential-historical vision [. . .], that promises reconciliation [. . .]. The subtle craft of the poem—the craft [. . .] of its *lexis* rather than of any encrypted or unconsummated meaning, its fragile and enigmatic self-sufficiency—is what the poet at last gives himself over to. Heidegger, however, remains reluctant thus to entrust himself. (29)

Fóti, however, for all her valuable insights, remains reluctant to entrust herself to any sort of transcendent truth. Trakl did not see his poems as self-sufficient. They were, rather, acts of partial expiation (HKA 1: 256). Nick Land, in his "Narcissism and Dispersion in Heidegger's 1953 Trakl Interpretation," misses this entirely.

The closest that Heidegger, for his part, comes to this scene of incest is in the second section of his lecture, when he refers to the "white eyelids" that, on his reading, "protect [the detached or dead one's] gazing into the blueness of the spiritual night." He says that these eyelids "gleam in the bridal jewelry that promises the softer twofold of (the) *Geschlecht*," and then quotes Trakl's "Springtime of the Soul": "In stillness the myrtle blooms over the white eyelids of the dead one" (GA 12: 51). Heidegger recognizes Trakl's botanical allusion to marriage and its promise of reconciliation, but, even here, Heidegger keeps a safe distance from what precipitates it and quickly moves on to other matters. It is remarkable, however, that the woman (the sister?) has an essential role to play in Heidegger's reading, even if this role seems merely decorative at first: without the shine of her jewelry, which Heidegger inserts for marital myrtle flowers, there is no promise of tender union. See chapter 6.

An earlier poem, which Heidegger would not have had access to when he wrote his lecture, but which resonates with the marital-redemptive theme of "Springtime of the Soul," is "Der Tau des Frühlings" ("The Dew of Spring"), where the soul (Christ?) weds the feminine night. I reproduce and translate the poem in appendix 4. Heidegger would have read its final three stanzas in the 1958 publication of Trakl's "Nachgelassene Gedichte" (page 1103), which appeared in the same issue of *Merkur* as Killy's "Gedichte im Gedicht." Heidegger refers to the latter in MH/LF: 65.

19. S.v. *fremd* in Kluge, *Etymologisches Wörterbuch der deutschen Sprache* (4th ed.); Schade, *Altdeutsches Wörterbuch*; Paul, *Deutsches Wörterbuch*.

20. Heidegger's use of the phrase "the old degenerate race [*alten entarteten Geschlecht*]" comes from Trakl's prose poem "Traum und Umnachtung" ("Dream and Lunacy") (HKA 1: 80), but it also calls to mind Isolde's wild rage at Tristan and his kind in the first scene of Wagner's opera *Tristan und Isolde*: "Entartet Geschlecht! Unwert der Ahnen!" "Degenerate race! Unworthy of its forebears!" (*Complete Vocal Score*, p. 23). Since Heidegger is writing in the wake of National Socialism, the loaded phrases *entartete Kunst* and *entartete Musik* resonate ominously as well. For Trakl's interest in Wagner, see Weichselbaum, *Georg Trakl: Eine Biographie*, 22, 38, 55, 72; HKA 1: 279, where Trakl plays on the alliteration of *w* words at the opening of *Das Rheingold*; and Methlagl, "Nietzsche und Trakl."

21. GA 12: 41, 45–46, 51, 56. Regarding the transformation of evil, see GA 12: 49, 56, 63.

22. Heidegger is presumably thinking of its derivation from the Gothic *sama* and the Greek *hama*, "the same," which is how he traces the meaning of *einsam* in a later essay of *Unterwegs zur Sprache*, where he reads *einsam*, not in accord with its typical sense as "solitary," but as "the same in the unifying of

what belongs together" (GA 12: 254; cf. 57). Why he does not go further back to the Proto-Indo-European *sem-, "same, one," seems to be tied to a linguistic-nationalist proclivity that we will return to later in this chapter.

23. Heidegger allows a connection between words related to *Geschlecht* (*verschlagen*, "to strike," *Schlag*, "blow, mark," *zerschlagen*, "to shatter") and the Greek *plēgē* ("stroke, curse"), as in a bad "stroke of fate" (GA 12: 46; cf. the English word "plague"). And yet Heidegger never, in his reading of Trakl, makes use of similar connections with Latinate terms, such as the derivation of *Konflikt* from *fligere*, "to strike."

24. Oddly, the inverse does not hold. Heidegger translates—from within German—Trakl's "Vesper" as "Abendland" without further ado (GA 12: 47). Perhaps he would say that this is legitimate because the Latin *vesper* is related to the Greek *hesperos*, and both mean "western," "evening," "the evening star Venus."

25. In February and March 1913, *Der Brenner* published Heinrich's "Briefe aus der Abgeschiedenheit I (Tempo, Zeit und Stellungslosigkeit: Furcht vor dem Tode und Wert des Lebens)" and his ecstatic tribute to his "prophetic" friend Trakl: "Briefe aus der Abgeschiedenheit II: Die Erscheinung Georg Trakl's." In the same issues, respectively, Trakl published "Zwei Gedichte" (namely, "Nähe des Todes" ["Nearness of Death"] and "Abendlied" ["Evening Song"]) and "Untergang" ("Downfall"), the last of which he dedicated to Heinrich. Heinrich and Trakl had asked Ficker to publish their texts in the March issue together (HKA 1: 289, HKA 2: 768). Among other things, the publication of these texts, together with Heinrich's attempted suicide shortly thereafter, led to the composition of Trakl's poem "Song of the Departed One [*Abgeschiedenen*]" in 1914 and its dedication to Heinrich. The two friends were so close they called one another brother, which, judging by the valediction of one of Heinrich's letters ("frater minor," HKA 2: 768), had a Franciscan connotation to it. Heinrich viewed Trakl's poetic endeavors as a mission from God (HKA 2: 769–770). Heidegger, who claimed he had been an avid reader of *Der Brenner* since 1911 or 1912, may have taken *Abgeschiedenheit* as the place of Trakl's *Gedicht*, not just from "Song of the Departed One," which I will discuss below, but from Trakl's relation to Heinrich and from the latter's texts on *Abgeschiedenheit* in particular—Heidegger's protestations against biography notwithstanding. Heinrich's second *Abgeschiedenheit* text was, after all, reprinted several times, including in Ficker, ed., *Erinnerung an Georg Trakl*, 93–104, and, in the form of excerpts, in Karl Kraus's journal *Die Fackel* 15, nos. 389–390: 27. It is any case noteworthy that Trakl never actually uses the noun *Abgeschiedenheit* in any of his poems, and that *abgeschieden* does not seem to have a positive sense in "Elis" or in the prose poem "Offenbarung und Untergang" ("Revelation and Downfall") (HKA 1: 49, 96). For the latter point, see Rey, "Heidegger–Trakl," 125. On Trakl's relation to Heinrich, see Detsch, "Die Beziehungen zwischen Karl Borromäus Heinrich und Georg Trakl."

As for Heidegger, I know of no references to Heinrich in his corpus. However, in his personal copy of DD: 207, Heidegger did annotate Heinrich's tribute to Trakl (titled "Die Erscheinung Georg Trakls").

26. According to Thrax's *Technē grammatikē*, the first Greek grammar, etymology is an essential component of literary criticism.

27. Again, we might ask, what does resurrection mean in a non-Christian or this-worldly context, and how can we be so sure Trakl is not thinking in terms of Christianity here, whether or not he intends it in orthodox fashion?

28. Martin and Fritz Heidegger, "Ausgewählte Briefe," 129–130; GA 16: 396, 679; GA 73: 857; GA 97: 51.

29. "Nationalité et nationalisme philosophiques" was the general title given to four seminars Derrida held at the EHESS in Paris, of which "Le fantôme de l'autre" (1984–1985), with its seven sessions on Heidegger's reading of Trakl, is the first. For more details, and for the context of the first seminar as a whole, see Rapaport, *Derrida on Exile and the Nation*, and Therezo, "Heidegger's National-Humanism." The first session of the first seminar is available, only in English, under the title "Onto-Theology of National-Humanism." On the general problem of nationalism in Heidegger, see Bambach, *Heidegger's Roots*. See also the proceedings from the conference "*Geschlecht III* and the Problem of 'National Humanism,'" ed. Rosenthal and Therezo.

30. Derrida, *Le monolinguisme de l'autre*. See also Haddad, "More than a Language to Come."

31. Eckhart, *Die deutschen Werke*, 5: 283, line 8.

32. For Heidegger's relation to Eckhart, see Moore, *Eckhart, Heidegger, and the Imperative of Releasement*. For Heidegger's marginalia, see ibid., 168–176. For Eckhart's coinage of *abegescheidenheit* and *gelâzenheit*, see, respectively, Eckhart, *Die deutschen Werke*, 5: 438n1, and Panzig, "gelâzenheit und abegescheidenheit," 338n11. Finally, for a passage in which Heidegger himself cites Trakl alongside Eckhart, see GA 8: 153.

33. Eckhart, *Die deutschen Werke*, 2: 528, lines 5–6.

34. For example, as Derrida points out, the Latinate German word *nationalistisch* is itself, on Heidegger's account, a superficial way of understanding *Heimat*, homeland (GIII: 121–122); yet, we might add, is there not something *nationalistisch* about this very restriction?

35. Eckhart, *Die deutschen Werke*, 5: 11, lines 7–10.

36. Eckhart, *Die deutschen Werke*, 3: 336, lines 1–4.

37. Silesius, *Cherubinischer Wandersmann*, Erstes Buch, #289, p. 69.

38. Although Heidegger claimed to have destroyed his manuscript for this course, a substantial portion of it actually survives on the versos of pages that he had used for later lecture courses and notes. For details, see Moore, *Eckhart, Heidegger, and the Imperative of Releasement*, 6 and 222n10.

39. This note is published in German and in English translation in Kisiel, "Notes for a Work on the 'Phenomenology of Religious Life' (1916–19)," 319, 327n35. It is not available in GA 60. See *Meister Eckhart*, ed. Pfeiffer, 479, lines 25–28, for the original.

40. For Derrida's reading of *Geist* in Heidegger, and for his puzzlement over the absence of a discussion of *ruach*, see *De l'esprit*, especially 165, as well as my discussion in chapter 7. Interestingly, the question of *Geist* (as mind, soul, spirit) is a frequent theme in the notes that have survived from Heidegger's 1915–1916 course.

41. See the report by Welte, "Erinnerung an ein spätes Gespräch." Other important references to *Abgeschiedenheit* in Heidegger's corpus can be found in GA 60: 308–309, 314, 317–318; GA 65: 504; GA 71: 68, 218–19, 279; GA 80: 571; GA 95: 142; GA 100: 119; and SZ 310, where Heidegger uses *Abgeschiedenheit* in a vein similar to Trakl's friend Karl Borromäus Heinrich when he (Heidegger) is trying to demarcate the sense of being-toward-death. Reiner Schürmann was one of the few people to recognize the Eckhartian background of detachment in Heidegger's reading of Trakl: "In earlier texts, Heidegger suggested the undertow toward absencing, for instance through the term *Abgeschiedenheit*, taken only secondarily from Trakl, but primarily from Meister Eckhart." "'Only Proteus Can Save Us Now,'" 62.

42. It would be worth comparing here Paul Celan's critical engagement with Eckhart in the final three poems of *Lichtzwang* (*Light Compulsion*). Celan, like Heidegger, is apprehensive about the universalist thrust of Eckhart's preaching of detachment, although, unlike Heidegger, the singular for which Celan advocates lacks specificity; it is wholly other. I take up this comparison, with occasional reference to Heidegger, in "Memory and Mystical Detachment in Paul Celan's Eckhart-Poems" and in "'statt aller / Ruhe.'"

43. This is most conspicuous in a text unavailable to Derrida, namely, Heidegger's 1945 lecture "Armut" ("Poverty"), which comments on a line from Hölderlin ("With us, everything is concentrated on the spiritual [*Geistige*], we have become poor in order to become rich") and contains *in nuce* several of the ideas and phrases that will be developed in the Trakl material.

44. Derrida, *De l'esprit*, 56, 113–114, 152–156.

45. Derrida, *De la grammatologie*, 71–72.

46. For more details on the event, see MH/LF: 156–159. Attendees included Trakl scholar Walther Killy, Heidegger's friend Heinrich Wiegand Petzet, and, at least during the final meal, theologian Karl Rahner.

47. It is often claimed that Heidegger considered *The Little Prince* the first work of existentialism and that it was his favorite book. I have been unable to locate a reliable source for the former claim, which seems dubious, as Heidegger says nothing of the sort in his genealogy of the concept of existence in GA 49,

for example, and "existentialism" was not a positive label in his eyes; however, the latter claim finds support in a newspaper article from April 1950: " 'Here is the beginning of a philosophy of technology [*Technik*],' Heidegger once said to a French inquirer, grabbing his favorite book from the shelf: Saint-Exupéry's *The Little Prince*, a copy marked with the traces of an intense labor of thinking." Anonymous, "Heidegger: Rückfall ins Gestell," 36. Ingrid Strohschneider-Kohrs, in *Seltsame Situationen*, 93, also mentions discussing Saint-Exupéry's *The Little Prince* with Heidegger in August 1947.

48. Heidegger often cites this phrase, although it does not appear in Augustine as such. Presumably, he is taking the idea from Book XI of Augustine's *De civitate dei* (see GA 86: 547).

49. Heidegger later acknowledges Trakl's debt to Rimbaud (GA 14: 47–49). He also brings the two poets together in GA 13: 227. For more on the two poets, see Böschenstein, *Von Morgen nach Abend*, and Lindenberger, "Georg Trakl and Rimbaud."

50. Derrida, "Of Writing, Heritage and the Other," 14. See also Kamuf, *Book of Addresses*, chapter 1.

Chapter 4

1. From the poem that begins "This World is not Conclusion," in Dickinson, *The Complete Poems*, #501, p. 243.

2. "[Trakl] compels our fraternity with the compulsion inherent to poetry: that of an open wound, an unsoothable pain." Fühmann, *Vor Feuerschlünden*, 137 / *At the Burning Abyss*, 150.

3. See Capobianco, *Engaging Heidegger*, 8, 142.

4. Bernasconi, "Being is Evil," 164. Derrida, for instance, only mentions pain in GIII on page 93, and he treats it, all too briefly, in *De l'esprit*, 173–175. David Krell, who on many occasions had encouraged Derrida to devote more time and attention to the topic, only recently addressed it in detail in a few pages (283–289) of "Derrida, Heidegger, and the Magnetism of the Trakl House," pages to which this chapter is indebted. See also Krell, *Phantoms of the Other*, 93, 141–142, 152, 160–161. For explications of Heidegger's account of pain, see Clark, "Heidegger and the Mystery of Pain"; Clark, "Pain and Being"; and Emad, "Heidegger on Pain." Mitchell, "Entering the World of Pain," advances Heidegger's comments in the direction of mortal exposedness and constitutive relationality, and Nielsen, "Der Schmerz," advances them in the direction of a non-ecstatic, infra-phenomenological vitality. Caputo, "Thinking, Poetry, and Pain," lambastes Heidegger's insensitivity to the flesh and to the Judeo-Christian elements of Trakl's poetry. While my objections overlap in part with those of Caputo and of Krell, I place greater emphasis on etymology and, because of the publication of *On Pain*,

pain at the level of being itself. Muschg, *Die Zerstörung der deutschen Literatur*, 223, calls two of Heidegger's remarks on pain (GA 12: 59, 60) "abracadabra" and an "assassination attempt on the German language." For parallels between Heidegger and Paul Celan on pain and language, see Schmidt, "Black Milk and Blue." Last, see Ferber, *Language Pangs*, chapter 4, for a discussion primarily of Heidegger's earlier remarks on pain in his 1939 seminar on Herder.

    5. Held, *Marbach-Bericht über eine neue Sichtung des Heidegger-Nachlasses*, 24.

    6. Also Titled "Über den Schmerz," call number 75.7300,3.

    7. In the archives are numerous other manuscripts by Heidegger that contain material on pain, including one on Trakl titled "Das Geschlecht Der Schmerz," call number 75.7372,3.

    8. Ernst Jünger, *Blätter und Steine*, 12–13.

    9. Ernst Jünger, *Der Arbeiter*, 89 et passim.

    10. His marginalia are reproduced in GA 90: 436–459. For his references, see, in addition to the above-mentioned, GA 9: 391; GA 71: 116; GA 73: 800; GA 87: 284; GA 90: 125, 201, 242, 244–245, 257, 335, 346, 387, 391; and his letter to Kurt Bauch, dated February 18, 1945, in Heidegger and Bauch, *Briefwechsel 1932–1975*, 96–97. Incidentally, on page 10 of *Blätter und Steine*, Jünger mentions Trakl: "Old Austria's connection with decay, in terms of both its promotion and its reflection, is remarkable. Alongside Kubin, who grasps decay's grotesque-demonic side, we should mention, above all, Trakl, who has plumbed the deepest depths of its silent pain [*lautlosen Schmerzes*]." See also page 105: "What is reflected in particular here is the downfall of Old Austria, as can be painfully felt in *Trakl's* lyric poetry."

    11. In the 1945 letter to Bauch that I mentioned in the previous note, Heidegger claims that he had just read Ernst Jünger's "Über den Schmerz" for the first time, though this can hardly be taken literally given Heidegger's numerous, substantive references to Jünger's text prior to 1945.

    12. For instance, Blok's study on Jünger and Heidegger, *Ernst Jünger's Philosophy of Technology*, makes only one reference to Jünger's "On Pain" (37n29). For a study that does consider Jünger's text and Heidegger in some detail, however, see Giubilato, "Dolor e historia del Ser."

    13. Ernst Jünger, *Blätter und Steine*, 155.

    14. Kierkegaard, *Der Pfahl im Fleisch*, 44–45 / *Eighteen Upbuilding Discourses*, 344. Trakl is reported to have said, "If you were carefree, you wouldn't understand my poems." In Rusch and Schmidt, *Das Voraussetzungssystem Georg Trakls*, 130.

    15. DW 5: 300, lines 1–2 (cf. GA 73: 878); *The Complete Works of Zhuangzi*, 6, 231 (cf. GA 77: 239 and GA 80: 1177–1178).

    16. Cf. Blanchot, *L'écriture du désastre*, 219: "Apprends à penser avec douleur," "Learn to think with pain."

    17. HKA 1: 256. See also Trakl's poem "Im Schnee" ("In the Snow") ("Pondering the truth— / Much pain!," HKA 1: 229), Job 6:10, and 2

Corinthians 7:9 ("Now I rejoice, not that ye were made sorry [elupēthēte], but that you were sorrowed to repentance; for you were made sorry after a godly manner"). Classical analogues can be found in Aeschylus's *Agamemnon*, verse 177: *pathei mathos*, "learning through suffering"; and in Democritus B 182 (in Diels, ed., *Die Fragmente der Vorsokratiker*): "learning accomplishes fine things by means of toils [*ponois*], but one reaps the fruits of shameful things automatically, without any toils."

18. In *On Pain*, Heidegger associates the will with Aristotelian terminology: "([. . .] How did the will enter into the self of the human being? The will appears initially in the shape of *actio*, that is, in the shape of the *energeia* of *noein*. Within this essential delimitation of the human being, which is also that which is carried out by Christianity, the only thing remaining is to renounce one's own will before the will of God.) But it is not just one's own will that must be sacrificed; rather the will-essence in general must come to appear as the computational transformation into the monstrous non-essence of being [*die Verrechnung in das Unwesen des Seins*]" (47). For further discussion of the connection between metaphysics and the will, see Davis, *Heidegger and the Will*, and especially pages 161–164 for the role of Plato and Aristotle.

19. Definition proposed in Raja et al., "The Revised International Association for the Study of Pain Definition of Pain."

20. Heidegger jots down passages from Aquinas's *Summa theologiae* (3.15.6) and *Quaestiones disputatae de veritate* (22.5 and 26.3 ad 9); he refers to Aristotle's *Metaphysics*, 9.10; and he quotes from part 2, book 4, chapter 46 of Schopenhauer's *Die Welt als Wille und Vorstellung*. Incidentally, when asked for an evaluation of Hans Wenke in 1945, Heidegger mentioned the latter's co-authored book on pain, which contains discussions of several works by authors relevant to Heidegger's analysis (including the same question from Aquinas's *Summa theologiae*, the same work by Schopenhauer, and Ernst Jünger's "On Pain"). See Sauerbruch and Wenke, *Wesen und Bedeutung des Schmerzes*. Heidegger called the book "diligent but paltry" (GA 16: 407).

21. Hegel, *Phänomenologie des Geistes*, 61, 14–15; "Glauben und Wissen," 432–433; *Vorlesungen über die Philosophie der Religion II*, 273–274.

22. Heidegger brings these two sets of terms together in the final chapter of GA 12, although not in the context of a discussion of pain. For details, see Powell, "The Way to Heidegger's 'Way to Language,'" 194–197.

23. Hegel, *Wissenschaft der Logik: Die Lehre vom Sein (1832)*, 101–102.

24. For reasons of space, I must pass over the "reißende Zeit" ("rending time") from the conclusion of Hölderlin's "Der Archipelagus" (*Sämtliche Werke und Briefe*, 1: 304, verse 293) and its influence on Heidegger's understanding of the origin of ecstatic temporality. For details, see McNeill, "Remains." See also Polt, *Time and Trauma*, chapter 1.

25. Gadamer, "Pain," 64. For more on the community-founding and linguistic dimensions of pain, see Ferber, Language Pangs.

26. Cicero, Tusculanae disputationes, 2.31.

27. Hölderlin, Sämtliche Werke und Briefe, 1: 436, verses 1–3; see also 3: 257, and GA 7: 135.

28. GA 7: 137; GA 39: 135; GA 53: 190; GA 73: 755–757; GA 75: 55–56; GA 79: 57.

29. Hölderlin, Sämtliche Werke und Briefe, 1: 476, verses 50–51.

30. For more on this manuscript and a brief discussion of the role of pain in it, see Vallega-Neu, Heidegger's Poietic Writings, chapters 8 and 9 (especially 157–158).

31. For more on this essential, indeed eschatological containment, see Krell, "Derrida, Heidegger, and the Magnetism of the Trakl House," and my chapter 7.

32. Anonymous, ΕΤΥΜΟΛΟΓΙΚΟΝ ΤΟ ΜΕΓΑ, s.v. Ἀληθὲς. For a discussion of one of the most prominent attacks on Heidegger's etymology and the ultimate retraction of that attack, see Bernasconi, The Question of Language in Heidegger's History of Being, 17–27 (who nevertheless does not mention this lexicon).

33. Anonymous, ΕΤΥΜΟΛΟΓΙΚΟΝ ΤΟ ΜΕΓΑ, s.v. Ἄλγος.

34. Chantraine, Dictionnaire étymologique de la langue grecque, Vol. 1, s.v. ἄλγος and ἀλέγω. For Hegel's place in the passage and what Heidegger calls a "transcendental pain" (GA 68: 103), see Malabou, "Négativité dialectique et douleur transcendantale." In the Greater Logic, pain appears as the concept qua living nature. Hegel, Wissenschaft der Logik: Die Lehre vom Sein (1832), 132; Wissenschaft der Logik: Die Lehre vom Begriff (1816), 222–223.

35. Seebold, Chronologisches Wörterbuch des deutschen Wortschatzes, s.v. smerzan.

36. Homer, The Iliad, book 11, lines 574–575 (Pope's translation).

37. For luein, see Anonymous, ΕΤΥΜΟΛΟΓΙΚΟΝ ΤΟ ΜΕΓΑ, s.v. Λύπη; for loptum, see Frisk, Griechisches Etymologisches Wörterbuch, s.v. λύπη. Neither of these connections survives scientific scrutiny: Frisk calls the latter (loptum) into question, and does not even mention the former (luein) as a possibility; likewise with Chantraine's discussion of the same term in Dictionnaire étymologique de la langue grecque, Vol. 3. Such would not, in other cases, stop Heidegger's speculations, however.

In his early work on Aristotle, Heidegger always follows the Stagarite in viewing lupē in a pejorative light. Aristotle contends that pleasure and pain, hēdonē and lupē, threaten to make us lose sight of the true end of our actions (Nic. Eth.: 6.5, 1140b11–20). To lupēron, which Heidegger renders not as "what is painful or distressing" but as what "oppresses or depresses [niederdrückt]," cannot, for all that, be eliminated; it is, in Heidegger's words, "a fundamental determination of the human being," who is thus "constantly in danger of becoming concealed [*verdeckt*] to himself by himself" (GA 19: 52). Rather than bringing us to ourselves, pain propels flight from ourselves (GA 18: 247). It is thus a source of inauthenticity. To *lupēron* can, however, be resisted; indeed, in our circumspective comportment (*phronēsis*) we are "*in a constant battle against the tendency to concealment* [Verdeckungstendenz] *that lies in Dasein itself*" (GA 19: 52). Here, pain is precisely the enemy of truth (*alētheia*), even as it allows for the possibility of un-concealment (*a-lētheia*). As one might expect, it is also centered on Dasein, not *Sein* itself.

38. Focke, "Von Dionysos zu Christus," 81–83. See also Focke's 1955 monograph *Georg Trakl: Liebe und Tod*, 27, 44–45, 56–57, 236, and Methlagl, "Nietzsche und Trakl."

39. Krell, *Lunar Voices*, 94. I agree with Krell's critique, although, as should be clear by this point, I do not read Trakl solely in terms of "horizontality," where *Geschlecht* would "always" be "a race of lovers" or, as Krell puts it in *Phantoms of the Other* (231), "that unhappy house, which is the only house there ever was." See also Krell, "Derrida, Heidegger, and the Magnetism of the Trakl House," 287–288; Krell, "We, the Unborn"; Palmier, *Situation de Georg Trakl*, 540–541; and especially Mullins, "Count Heidegger," who, without apologetics, demonstrates the extreme complexity of this passage and its counterfactual conditional. For the complicated and contradictory reception of "Grodek" in the context of both world wars, see Holzner, "Lyrik im Umfeld von Trakls 'Grodek,' " and Sauermann, *Die Rezeption Georg Trakls in Zeiten der Diktatur*, 101.

40. Petzet, *Auf einen Stern zugehen*, 114. Ficker, *Briefwechsel 1940–1967*, 230. It is possible Heidegger had already read Ficker's account in DD: 213–222, although there are no markings in his personal copy. In any case, he had surely read the brief biographical report in his personal copy of the Salzburg edition (6th ed.), where one reads: "After the battle of Grodek, [Trakl] had to care for ninety severely wounded men by himself in a barn, without being able to help them. In extreme despair [*Verzweiflung*] he wanted to shoot himself" (6). Heidegger also heard Ficker deliver a version of the speech again on March 1, 1959, before publishing *Unterwegs zur Sprache* (MH/LF: 65, 152; letter to Strohschneider-Kohrs, March 2, 1959; Heidegger and Pöggeler, *Briefwechsel 1957–1976*, 37–41).

41. Ficker, "Der Abschied," 83–84. In a footnote to a later version of the lecture, which Heidegger could have read in his copies of Ficker, ed., *Erinnerung an Georg Trakl* (2nd ed., 1959), 187n, and Ficker, *Denkzettel und Danksagungen*, 332n2, Ficker cites an eyewitness report: "I saw Trakl leaning against the wall of the barn, his eyes wide open with horror. The cap had slipped from his hands. He didn't notice, and, deaf to encouragement [*ohne auf Zuspruch zu hören*], he gasped: 'What can I do? How am I supposed to help? It's unbearable.' " For specifics regarding the battle of Gródek and the retreat, see Weichselbaum, *Georg Trakl: Eine Biographie*, 166–168.

42. Ficker, "Der Abschied," 87.
43. Ibid., 88–90. Günther, *Gedichte*, 7, 184. For details about Trakl's personal copy of this volume, which he appears to have given to Ficker before the latter's departure, see Sauermann, "Trakl-Lektüre aufgefunden."
44. Ficker, "Der Abschied," 92. HKA 1: 324.
45. Trakl, *Sämtliche Werke und Briefwechsel*, 4.2: 333–334. Cf. Aichinger, "Der geheime Leonce."

Chapter 5

1. From the poem "Blue Moles," in Plath, *Collected Poems*, 126.
2. Bonaventure, *Itinerarium mentis in deum*, §5.4. Braig, *Vom Sein*, v. For Heidegger's relation to Braig, see Schaber, "Der Theologiestudent Martin Heidegger und sein Dogmatikprofessor Carl Braig."
3. Otto, *Das Heilige*, chapters 2–3. Troeltsch, "Zur Religionsphilosophie: Aus Anlaß des Buches von Rudolf Otto über 'Das Heilige' "; Windelband, *Präludien*, 2: 295–332 ("Das Heilige [Skizze zur Religionsphilosophie]"). Heidegger refers to the latter two texts in GA 60: 26, 314–315, 334. For Heidegger's relation to Otto and some parallels between their work, see Camilleri, *Phénoménologie de la religion et herméneutique théologique dans la pensée du jeune Heidegger*, chapter 19.
4. In Kisiel and Sheehan, eds., *Becoming Heidegger*, 362, 367.
5. See Heidegger's elucidation of the verse "Von goldenen Träumen schwer," from Hölderlin's "Andenken" ("Remembrance"), in GA 52: §§35–43 (especially p. 130), where Heidegger draws on Pindar's 8th Pythian. On page 121 of this Winter Semester 1941–1942 lecture course, Heidegger characterizes the golden dreams of Hölderlin's poem as "heavy from the solidity of the essential," "gleaming from the preciousness of the approaching gift," and "noble from the purity of what is decided here." In the parallel passage of Heidegger's 1943 essay on "Remembrance," he inserts the language of the holy, which had been peripheral in the discussion of gold in the lecture course: "The golden dreams are, like gold, heavy from the solidity of the essential character of their poem. They are, like gold, gleaming from the luminous glow of the holy. They are, like gold, noble from the purity of what is decided and sent from the holy" (Heidegger, "Andenken," 294–295 = GA 4: 114). Heidegger's intervening commentary, from 1942, on the gold of Pindar's "holy songs" (GA 78: 97) is, I believe, responsible for the shift in emphasis. Heidegger's later analysis (composed sometime after July 1970) of the words "goldne Pracht" ("golden splendor") from one of Hölderlin's last poems, "Der Herbst" ("Autumn"), is also clearly indebted to Pindar (GA 75: 205–209).

For Hölderlin's engagement with Pindar, see Hellingrath, *Pindarübertragungen von Hölderlin*. It is not an exaggeration to say that Hellingrath's efforts on behalf of Hölderlin, and of the latter's Pindar translations in particular, were life changing for Heidegger. See especially Heidegger's correspondence with Hellingrath's erstwhile fiancée Imma von Bodmershof: *Briefwechsel 1959–1976*, passim. For a concise overview of Heidegger's relation to Hölderlin (and the holy), see McNeill, "Heidegger's Hölderlin Lectures." For a more extended treatment, which also addresses the Hellingrath/Heidegger connection, see Bambach, *Of an Alien Homecoming*.

6. Reported in Noack, "Gespräch mit Martin Heidegger," 33.

7. Brief discussions of the Pindar material are available in Blanchet, "De bleu et d'or," 74, 82–83, 86–87; Capobianco, "Heidegger on Heraclitus," 466–467; and Capobianco, *Heidegger's Way of Being*, chapter 2 (especially pp. 35, 108n7). Little has been written on Heidegger's relation to Pindar more broadly. See, however, Froidecourt, "La poésie de Pindar à l'aube de la métaphysique," who focuses mainly on GA 40. Michael Theunissen, in his massive study *Pindar: Menschenlos und Wende der Zeit*, analyzes Heidegger's treatment of time (925–951) but says nothing about his direct engagement with the Greek lyricist.

8. *Pindari carmina cum fragmentis*, 1: 175.

9. *Pindar*, trans. Dornseiff, 56. See also Pindar, *Die Dichtungen und Fragmente*, trans. Wolde, 182: "den Menschen dünkt das Gold herrlich und mächt'ger als Anderes." GA 78: 291–292.

10. The first version of Heidegger's translation (GA 78: 285) is the same as the second, although in the first version of his commentary Heidegger also offers a more conventional way to render verses 2–3: "Dich in der Acht denn auch großmächtig erachten / das Gold die Menschen hervorragender denn Anderes" (GA 78: 294). "You, in consideration, because humans also consider gold / mighty, more outstanding than other things."

11. For background to the poem and various interpretations of it, see Burnett, *Pindar's Songs for Young Athletes of Aigina*, chapter 6 ("Isthmian 5: Achilles and Telephos"); Bury, ed., *The Isthmian Odes of Pindar*, 85–103; and Willcock, "On First Reading Pindar." The last-named commentator recommends that one start one's study of Pindar with the 5th Isthmian. Heidegger, it seems, would agree, but for radically different reasons. According to the philosopher, the 5th Isthmian is the "most magnificent [*herrlichste*] of Pindar's odes": "The first three verses [. . .] gleam over and beyond [*überglänzen*] the entire opening of the song, gleam over and beyond the entire ode, gleam over and beyond the entire poetic work [*Dichtung*] of Pindar, clear [*lichten*] the relation of being to the word and language"; verses 2–17 are "the pure poem of the godhead of the gods, and nothing else besides" (GA 78: 76, 78, 97). Heidegger's interpretation, unsurprisingly, differs from that of traditional scholarship. Although Heidegger is correct to link Theia with gold—Bury, for example, relates that Theia was also referred to as *Chryse*, "golden goddess" (85)—other commentators have argued for a contrast between the invocation of Theia and the courage (*alka*)

displayed in contest or battle. Burnett (94–95), for example, interprets *alka* and the *daimones* of verse 11 as marking a shift to the unseen and thus to what is independent from Theia and from the gold that the goddess makes visible. Or, in Bury's pithy summary (85n3): "Gold is chased for the sake of Theia σέο Ϝέκατι l. 2; glory for the sake of Zeus, Διὸς ἕκατι, l. 29, in the same position in the same verse of the strophe. This is as much as to say that Theia is merely introduced in order to be shown her place."

12. *Pindari carmina cum fragmentis*, 2: 131, verse 1: κεκρότηται χρυσέα κρηπὶς ἱεραῖσιν ἀοιδαῖς. Heidegger translates (GA 78: 97): "Geschmiedet ist der goldene Grund / den heiligen Gesängen," "Forged is the golden ground / unto the holy songs."

13. Although the language of *Ereignis*, intimated here, is largely absent from the Pindar interpretation (see, however, GA 78: 68), Heidegger could have brought it into connection with *periōsion* by considering the Greek word's Biblical trajectory, which presents an alternative to his narrative about the word's lapse into substance metaphysics. In Titus 2:14, it refers to a people who, through the sacrifice of Jesus, will come to belong to, and be cherished by, God, thereby, we might add, coming into their own: "[Christ Jesus] gave himself for us in order that he might redeem us from all lawlessness and purify for himself [for his own possession] a select people [*heautōi laon periousion*] who are zealous to do fine works." A hapax legomenon in the New Testament, the word is also found in the Septuagint, Exodus 19:5 et passim. For details, see Cremer, *Biblico-Theological Lexicon of New Testament Greek*, s.v. Περιούσιος.

14. Silesius, *Cherubinischer Wandersmann*, #289, page 69. Compare GA 40: 16 (on the opening up of a rose as an example of originary *phusis*) and Pindar's 7th Olympian, which plays on the anthetic birth of the island of Rhodes, the Greek *rhodon* ("rose"), and the nymph Rhode, wife of Helios. In this victory song, Pindar sings of the time when Zeus "inundated" one of the cities of Rhodes "with snowy gold" (βρέχε θεῶν βασιλεὺς ὁ μέγας χρυσέαις νιφάδεσσι πόλιν) after the birth of Athena. *Pindari carmina cum fragmentis*, 1: 28, verse 34. Pindar's ode ended up dedicated in letters of gold in the Temple of Athena Lindia on the island. See also, regarding Silesius's rose and Mörike's *Scheinen*, GA 10: 101–102.

15. For *legein* qua gathering, see GA 78: 93, 96. In the Pindar commentary, Heidegger does not specifically use the word *sanft*, "gentle," which will play a crucial role in his reading of the spirit of Trakl's poetry; however, it is implied by the "exotic superlative" (Burnett, *Pindar's Songs for Young Athletes of Aigina*, 94–95) of verse 12, *alpniston*, "gentlest" or "smoothest," which Heidegger renders as *lieblich*, "lovely," "charming" (GA 78: 66). Note, moreover, Pindar's floral metaphor: δύο δέ τοι ζωᾶς ἄωτον μοῦνα ποιμαίνονται τὸν ἄλπνιστον, εὐανθεῖ σὺν ὄλβῳ / εἴ τις εὖ πάσχων λόγον ἐσλὸν ἀκούῃ (verses 12–13). "Eins und ein Anderes aber des Lebens Herrliches einzig hütet das liebliche, blühend im Glück: / Wenn einer, geschicklich seinem Geschick, gesammelt dem Ruhm des

Edlen gehöret" (GA 78: 66). "Yet one and the other, the glorious of life, solely guards the lovely, blooming in happiness: / When one, collected and skillfully compliant with his fate, listens and belongs to the glory of the noble."

16. One might wonder: if Theia is simply the godhead, why, beyond the fact that the Greek suffix makes any noun to which it is attached feminine, retain the gender? Heidegger might reply that he is simply thinking through Pindar's poetry, which, after all, refers to Theia as a mother. And yet, Heidegger continues to use feminine and maternal tropes for being and language in his commentary, tropes that will reappear in his later interpretation of Trakl. Despite Heidegger's early claims about the nongendered status of Dasein, perhaps what he is seeking is something along the lines of a maternity more motherly than all mothers, a femininity more womanly than all women. Compare Heidegger's claim that "*Theia*, spoken from the perspective of later representations, is more spiritual [*geistiger*] than the 'spirits' that are otherwise known, and yet at the same time more sensuous [*sinnlicher*, "sensual"] than any 'sensuousness' has ever been capable of" (GA 78: 88). See my chapter 6.

17. I have been unable to determine, at the philological level, why Heidegger has *pantōn* rather than *allōn* here, especially since the earlier versions of his lecture both have *allōn* (GA 80: 994, 1017), as do his citations of the verse in GA 78: passim; GA 74: 177; and GA 81: 249. As a matter of interpretation, however, *pantōn* makes sense.

18. Pindari carmina cum fragmentis, 1: 105, verse 95: *epameroi*, *Tagwesen*, "creatures of the day." GA 78: 79, 86–87, 326; GA 52: 111–112.

19. Heidegger and Staiger, "Der Briefwechsel," 53–67.

20. Blanchet, "De bleu et d'or," 78. See also 75.

21. Martin Heidegger, *Auszüge zur Phänomenologie aus dem Manuskript "Vermächtnis der Seinsfrage,"* 94. Cf. John 1:1. For more on this "last word of phenomenology" and its connection to the "saying of Being," see McNeill, *The Fate of Phenomenology*, chapter 7.

22. HKA 1: 66. GA 12: 74. Novalis, *Heinrich von Ofterdingen*, 252. For Boehme as Novalis's source, see Ederheimer, *Jakob Boehme und die Romantiker*, 113, 123.

23. HKA 1: 46 ("Unterwegs," "Underway"), 79 ("Gesang des Abgeschiedenen," "Song of the Departed One"), 37 ("Im Dorf," "In the Villiage"), 59 ("Entlang," "Along"), 46 ("Stundenlied," "Song of the Hours"), 78 ("Frühling der Seele," "Springtime of the Soul"). For more examples and a helpful overview of Trakl's use of colors, see Grube, *"so oder so, es bleibt blau oder braun, das Gedicht,"* especially chapter 5.

24. Cf. Harrison, *1911*, 40: "Georg Trakl, the most ambivalent poet of the twentieth century."

25. Perhaps most conspicuously, for our purposes, is Trakl's poem "Vorhölle" ("Limbo"): "Bläue, die Todesklagen der Mütter. [. . .] Mit knöchernen Händen

/ Tastet im Blau nach Märchen / Unheilige Kindheit" ("Blueness, the dirges of the mothers. [. . .] With bony hands / Unholy childhood / Gropes for fairy tales in the blue"). HKA 1: 73. For a critique of Heidegger's and other commentators' overemphasis on blue and its holiness, which dates back at least to Erwin Mahrholdt's 1925 study on Trakl (excerpted in the Zurich edition of Trakl's poems), see Rovini, *La fonction poétique de l'image dans l'œuvre de Georg Trakl*, 101–102, 104–105.

26. The preposition "in" in this and the previous sentence translates the German *in*, which Heidegger, oddly, uses with accusative nouns, thereby suggesting directionality and movement. Hence, "into" would perhaps be better. See my chapter 7.

27. Cf. *Pindari carmina cum fragmentis*, 1: 69, verse 72 (2nd Pythian): γένοι', οἷος ἐσσὶ μαθών.

28. Cf. GA 5: 319; GA 9: 352, 359–360; GA 78: 305–307.

29. Celan, *Gesammelte Werke*, 3: 167.

30. Hölderlin, *Sämtliche Werke*, 2: 340–341, 353, 361, 371.

31. Hölderlin, *Dramen und Übersetzungen*. Trakl would have been able to read the passages mentioned in the previous note on pages 242–244, 259, 268, and 291 of his personal copy. For details on the discovery, see Weichselbaum, "Ein überraschender Fund," and Weichselbaum, "Unbekannte Gedichte und Prosa Georg Trakls entdeckt," 421–423.

32. Mann, *Der Wendepunkt*, 104. See also Böschenstein, "Hellingrath–Hölderlin–George," 21.

33. Ficker's report is reproduced in Riese, *Das Sinnesleben eines Dichters*, 52. The source for the quote can be found in the introduction to the first volume of Böhm's edition: Hölderlin, *Hyperion: Mit Einleitung und Auswahl seiner Briefe*, xliv. For discussion, see Methlagl, "'Versunken in das sanfte Saitenspiel seines Wahnsinns . . . ,'" 37, 57.

34. Hölderlin, *Gedichte*, 319.

35. Weichselbaum, "Ein überraschender Fund," 170. Hölderlin, *Gedichte*, 311. For Trakl's relation to Hölderlin more broadly, see Böschenstein, *Von Morgen nach Abend*.

36. As Hölderlin-translator Michael Hamburger called them. See *Reason and Energy*, 11. For an influential contrasting view, see Helligrath, *Zwei Vorträge*, 49–85 ("Hölderlins Wahnsinn"), and Heidegger's references and allusion to Hellingrath's study in GA 4: 180–181; GA 52: §18; and GA 75: 205.

37. Strohschneider-Kohrs, "Ein Gedicht Georg Trakls," 71. For Heidegger's relation to Strohschneider-Kohrs, see MH/LF: 66; Strohschneider-Kohrs, *Seltsame Situationen*; and the report by her student Werner Herzog, in the latter's *A Guide for the Perplexed*, 6. Heidegger's extensive correspondence with her (1947–1974) is available in the Deutsches Literaturarchiv Marbach. For summaries of excerpts, see the first two entries under "1959" in my appendix 2. Interestingly, Strohschneider-

Kohrs's first published article, "Ein Gedicht Georg Trakls," from 1952, ends on an unmistakably Heideggerian note: "Here an unspoken has been properly delivered over to language. [. . .] The interpretation itself can only attempt to let the signatures and ciphers endure [*gewähren zu lassen*] in the complete unsayability of the unspoken" (74). Much later, she would publish a monograph on Trakl's "Klage" ("Lamentation") under the title *Fast schon jenseits der Welt*, which would influence Toshio Hosokawa's 2013 composition for soprano and orchestra *Klage*. See Meyer-Kalkus, "Zerwürfnis mit Nachspiel," 48–49.

38. Additionally, in marginalia to "In ein altes Stammbuch" ("Into an Old Family Album") in his personal copy of the Salzburg edition, Heidegger cross-referenced "soft madness" with the third version of Trakl's "Passion" ("moved by nocturnal harmony, / By gentle madness") and the second section of "Helian" ("sunk in the gentle string music of his madness"). See my appendix 1, §3.

39. Heidegger fails to mention that there is no Middle or Old High German version of *Wahnsinn*. The word, a back-formation of *wahnsinnig*, was coined in analogy to *Wahnwitz* (MHG: *wanwiz*; AHG: *wanawizzi*), "out of one's wits." See Muschg, *Die Zerstörung der deutschen Literatur*, 222. So far, I have refrained from citing the published English translation of Heidegger's lecture. The following is an example of why. In this passage, the translator effaces Heidegger's etymologies and restricts the universal scope of Heidegger's characterization of *Wahnsinn*. There is no "here" in the German:

> Does [the madman] mean someone who is mentally ill? Madness here does not mean a mind filled with senseless delusions. The madman's mind senses—senses in fact as no one else does. Even so, he does not have the sense of the others. He is of another mind. The departed one is a man apart, a madman, because he has taken his way in another direction. From that other direction, his madness may be called "gentle," for his mind pursues a greater stillness. (Heidegger, *On the Way to Language*, 173).

40. Trakl, *Dichtungen und Briefe*, 55 ("Verwandlung des Bösen," "Transformation of Evil"), 68 ("An die Verstummten," "To the Silenced"), 83. Heidegger uses etymology once again to salvage a positive sense of *Umnachtung*, literally "benightedness" or "a state of being surrounded by night":

> The *Umnachtung* named here [in Trakl's prose poem "Dream and Lunacy"] is not a mere darkening of the spirit or mind [*Verfinsterung des Geistes*], as little as *Wahnsinn* is insanity [*Irrsinn*, literally, "errant or erroneous sense"]. The night [*Nacht*] that surrounds [*umnachtet*] the singing brother of the stranger remains the "spiritual night" of that death which the detached one has died into [*sic*] the "golden

shudder" of earliness. (GA 12: 67, citing "Geistliche Dämmerung," "Spiritual Twilight," and "Anif").

Cf., regarding Hölderlin, GA 16: 715; GA 75: 205.

41. This, I believe, is how Heidegger would respond to Rodrigo Therezo's noteworthy attempt to deconstruct Heidegger's phonocentric, as opposed to typographical, fixation on the "O n e." Therezo might reply, however, with Mallarmé and Derrida, by drawing our attention to the blank spaces on the far sides of the word. See Therezo, "When Silence Strikes." It should, in any case, be noted that, in the original publication of the second Trakl lecture in *Merkur* ("Georg Trakl: Eine Erörterung seines Gedichtes," 255–257), Heidegger did retain the spacing; only later, for the publication of *Unterwegs zur Sprache*, was it changed to italics, presumably as a typographical policy of the publisher.

42. Hölderlin, *Sämtliche Werke und Briefe*, 1: 909 ("In lieblicher Bläue . . ."). Cf. GA 4: 47.

43. For strategies of fragmentation and fractured citation in Trakl's work, especially in the poem "Helian," see Degner, "'Infirme' Autorschaft" (who also discusses Trakl's "Hölderlin" on pp. 110–111). Drawing on manuscript variants, Killy develops his position in two works that were influential on Celan: "Gedichte im Gedicht" (which Heidegger also read and admired [MH/LF: 65]) and *Wandlungen des lyrischen Bildes*, 116–135. For Celan's appreciation and meticulous annotation of Trakl's use of colors, see Grube, *"so oder so, es bleibt blau oder braun, das Gedicht."*

44. Michel, *Das Leben Friedrich Hölderlins*, 464.

45. Celan, *Gesammelte Werke*, 3: 186.

46. Celan, *Gesammelte Werke*, 1: 226. For a powerful reading of this poem, along the lines I have intimated, see Bambach, *Thinking the Poetic Measure of Justice*, 204–213. See also Celan's poem "Ich trink Wein" ("I Drink Wine"), which is a later response to Hölderlin and to the 1805 report that the latter, "always half-deranged [*halbverrückt*], harrows away at Pindar." For discussion, see ibid., 253–265.

Chapter 6

1. "Neither man nor woman shall possess the kingdom of God, but the virgin born from the death of man and woman shall be queen of heaven. One sex [*Ein Geschlecht*], not two; one tree, not many! Christ was the trunk because he was the root of the new body that emerged from death, that led the deceased virgin again as a beautiful branch out from death. And all of us are the boughs and all of us stand on one trunk, which is Christ." Böhme, "De incarnatione verbi," 227.

2. "Humans, animals, plants, stones and stars, elements, tones, colors, come together like One Family, act and speak like One *Geschlecht*." Novalis, *Heinrich von Ofterdingen*, 252.

3. "One day all will be body, / O n e body, / In heavenly blood / the blessed pair will swim." From "Geistliche Lieder," no. 7, in Novalis, *Gedichte, Die Lehrlinge zu Sais*, 111.

4. Pinthus, *Menschheitsdämmerung*, 35, 382. GA 12: 38. George Steiner claims that Pinthus's collection, which features ten poems by Trakl, "marked Heidegger's whole view of poetry, and it may well have prepared his later uses of Rilke and Trakl." *Martin Heidegger*, 75. For the anti-Nietzschean background to "Into an Old Family Register," see Methlagl, "Nietzsche und Trakl," 98–101.

5. Throughout his career, Heidegger's uses the word *Geschlecht* in manifold ways, as: generation (GA 27: 216; GA 86: 205; GA 97: 479); grammatical gender (GA 99: 114); stock, e.g., the *Geschlecht* of farmers, gods, or thinkers (GA 16: 247; GA 83: 349; GA 97: 450); ancestral family name (GA 97: 7); sexual intercourse (GA 29/30: 292, 363–364); sex/gender (GA 26: 172–175; GA 27: 146–147); genitals (GA 66: 34); species (GA 16: 499, citing Hebel on the caterpillar *Geschlecht*); animals and plants writ large (GA 74: 50); genus, in the sense of the *Geschlecht* "house" vis-à-vis individual houses (GA 45: 63); the *Geschlecht* of those who are without pain, without gods, or without gratitude (GA 73: 685, 756–757; GA 75: 55, 261); and, last but not least, race, even if he does not intend to base it on blood or biology. Regarding the last, in transcripts of speeches delivered in support of the Nazi party, for example, Heidegger speaks of the need for *ein hartes Geschlecht*: "a hard generation," yes, but one with exclusive ties to the German *Volk* and all it entails (GA 16: 763, 772; see also GA 16: 282, 284; GA 66: 61). Merely speaking German does not seem sufficient for membership in what Heidegger, following Hölderlin, calls "the German *Geschlecht*" (GA 39: 205; GA 75: 171; GA 94: 374), which is connected to the *Geschlecht* to come (GA 94: 299, 320; GA 97: 128). The phrase "ein hartes Geschlecht," which is the title of a 1931 novel by Will Vesper, was, incidentally, also used by Hitler in a sentence from 1935 that would serve as a motto for childhood education: "We want to raise a hard *Geschlecht* that is strong, reliable, loyal, obedient, and respectable, so that we need not be ashamed of our people [*Volk*] before history." See Wasmuth, *Kindertageseinrichtungen als Bildungseinrichtungen*, 434, and Sommer, "'Das harte Geschlecht.'"

6. Kluge, *Etymologisches Wörterbuch der deutschen Sprache* (4th ed.), 112 / *An Etymological Dictionary of the German Language*, 115–116 (translation modified). Heidegger, notes on Trakl, bundle 3. Derrida, "Geschlecht I," 7. Derrida's other three texts on *Geschlecht* are "Heidegger's Hand," GIII, and "Heidegger's Ear." For commentary on the status of the word/mark *Geschlecht* (and on Derrida's *Geschlecht* series more broadly), see Bennington, "*Geschlecht pollachos legetai*"; Dastur, "*Geschlecht et Geist*"; Hoffman-Schwartz, "'Étranger,' ou plutôt 'fremd'";

Krell, *Phantoms of the Other*; Rapaport, *Derrida on Exile and the Nation*, especially 149–150; and Therezo, "When Silence Strikes."

7. Agamben, *The Open*, 39. See also Franck, "Being and the Living," 146.

8. Paul, *Deutsches Wörterbuch*, s.v. *Geschlecht*.

9. Mitchell, "Heidegger's Later Thinking of Animality," 74. For more on Heidegger's enigmatic earlier work on the human/animal problem, see, for example, Buchanan, *Onto-Ethologies*; Derrida, *The Beast and the Sovereign*; and McNeill, "Life Beyond the Organism."

10. As David Krell notes, it is peculiar that, of all the poems by Trakl that deal with the figure of the *Enkel*, Heidegger here refers only to "Song of the Departed One," with its aura of piety. A more extensive survey paints a darker picture. See Krell, "Derrida, Heidegger, and the Magnetism of the Trakl House," 301–302n23, 303n29, and 303n31 for this and other comments on Heidegger's marginalia.

11. In *Georg Trakl: Liebe und Tod*, 74, Alfred Focke mis-cites the phrase as "mondenen Pfade des Abgeschiedenen." Lachmann, *Kreuz und Abend*, remarks that the genitive definite article is surprising (187) but does not appear to be a typo (112).

12. Paul, *Deutsches Wörterbuch*, s.v. *fremd*.

13. Epigraph of *Meister Eckehart Schriften*, Vol. 2.

14. See also GA 7: 36, and Derrida's long footnote, dedicated to Françoise Dastur, in *De l'esprit*, 147–154.

15. If true, this latter possibility would support a *terminus post quem* of 1969 for this marginalium, the year in which HKA appeared. Since this marginalium is in blue pen, whereas the others to "Song of the Departed One" are in lead pencil, perhaps Heidegger made them at different time periods. In any case, if he did consult HKA 2, Heidegger would have also been able to see another connection with "Grodek," namely, that an earlier version of "Song of the Departed One" has the lunar paths of the *Ungeborenen* ("unborn") instead of *Abgeschiedenen* (263).

16. Krell, *Phantoms of the Other*, 236. In what follows, I have benefited greatly from ibid., especially chapter 6, and Krell, *Lunar Voices*, chapter 4.

17. Despite his extensive discussion of Trakl's poem "Abendland" ("Occident") in "Language in the Poem," Heidegger also neglects to mention that the poem's dedicatee is the great expressionist poetess Else Lasker-Schüler, whom Trakl befriended in Berlin, and who would go on to compose two poetic tributes to Trakl after his death. This neglect becomes more poignant when we recall that Heidegger mentions Ficker as the dedicatee of "Gesang einer gefangenen Amsel" ("Song of a Captured Blackbird") (GA 12: 77).

18. It is noteworthy that "87" refers to the second section of "Helian" (which Heidegger goes on to cite in GA 12: 47), since it is the brother who precedes the stranger and not the other way around. Perhaps Heidegger would

reply that this brother, "the holy brother" (read: Hölderlin), is different from the other brothers he had been discussing. Or might he try to claim that "Where the holy brother had previously gone [Wo vordem der heilige Bruder gegangen]" (HKA 1: 40) means the opposite of what the words say? After all, a few pages later, Heidegger contends that the verse from "Am Mönchsberg" ("At the Mönchsberg")—

> Immer folgt dem Wandrer die dunkle Gestalt der Kühle (HKA 1: 53)
>
> *
>
> Always the dark shape of coolness follows the wanderer

—actually means that the dark shape of coolness "goes out ahead" of the wanderer, "insofar as the blue voice of the boy [Elis] retrieves what has been forgotten and *says it in advance* [vorsagt]" (GA 12: 50).

19. Heidegger also used the word to characterize Hannah Arendt in a poem he wrote for her in February 1950 titled "Das Mädchen aus der Fremde" ("The Girl from Abroad"). See Arendt and Heidegger, *Briefe 1925 bis 1975*, 79–80. For discussion, see Travers, "'Die Blume des Mundes,'" 95–98.

20. See Grimm, *Deutsches Wörterbuch*, s.v. *Jünglingin* and *Mönchin*.

21. Derrida, "*Geschlecht* I"; Derrida and McDonald, "Choreographies"; Brennan, Cornell, and Derrida, "Opening Plenary." See also GA 27: 146, and Grosz, "Ontology and Equivocation"; Krell, *Phantoms of the Other*, chapter 1; Raffoul, "Sexual Difference and Gathering in *Geschlecht III*"; and Therezo, "From Neutral Dasein to a Gentle Twofold." On Heidegger and counting, see Elden, *Speaking against Number*, and Mullins, "Count Heidegger."

22. If we restrict the scope of Heidegger's claim to his workshop volume, namely, the 6th Salzburg edition, then he is correct. However, the volume *Nachlass und Biographie*, which Heidegger also cites in "Language in the Poem" (GA 12: 57), uses spacing to emphasize the first word of Trakl's "Herbstliche Heimkehr" ("Autumnal Homecoming"): "E r i n n e r u n g , begrabene Hoffnung," "R e c o l l e c t i o n , buried hope" (p. 12). Heidegger cites this poem in his marginalia to "Into an Old Family Register." See also DD: 212 for the spaced "O n e   F l e s h" in Limbach's report about his encounter with Trakl.

23. Several scholars have made strides in this direction. See, for instance, Armour, "'Through Flame or Ashes,'" who draws on the work of Luce Irigaray; Ewegen, "Gestures of the Feminine in Heidegger's 'Die Sprache'"; Gosetti, "Feminine Figures in Heidegger's Theory of Poetic Language," and Graybeal, *Language and "the Feminine" in Nietzsche and Heidegger*, especially chapter 7, who draw on Julia Kristeva; Krell, *Lunar Voices*, especially chapter 4; and Marder, "Still (Un)Born."

24. See the image on the cover of this book and image 8, as well as Weichselbaum, "'Eine bleiche Maske mit drei Löchern.'" Trakl considered the title "Münch" for the above-cited poem "The Heart," as he did also for "Herbstseele" ("Autumn Soul"). "Traum und Umnachtung" ("Dream and Lunacy") was originally titled "Der Untergang des Kaspar Münch" ("The Downfall of Kaspar Münch")—an allusion to Kaspar Hauser. Might we be justified in hearing an allusion to Edvard Munch, too?

25. Although I cannot do so here, it would be interesting to study the role that Trakl's sister Grete played in this mythos, as evinced by the poem "Helians Schicksalslied" ("Helian's Song of Fate"), which she either penned herself or copied from Georg's papers and preserved for posterity.

> Einst wird ein Tag voll Freude sein
> Da schreiten wir durch den trunkenen Hain
> —Einst wird ein Tag voll Freude sein
> An solchem Tage will ich Dich frein'
> Und ward uns Freude aus tiefstem Leid
> Dann feiern wir unsere hohe Zeit
> Und ward uns Freude aus tiefstem Leid
> Wir sind die Kinder der Ewigkeit
> Und bleibt uns aus Freude tiefste Not
> Wir grüßen jauchzend den heiligen Tod
> Und bleibt uns aus Freude tiefste Not
> Wir glühen von Morgen zu Morgenrot.

*

> A day will come that is full of joy
> When we stride through the drunken grove
> —A day will come that is full of joy
> On such a day will I free you
> And joy from deepest sorrow became ours
> Then we will celebrate our wedding
> And joy from deepest sorrow became ours
> We are the children of eternity
> And from joy we are left with deepest need
> Cheerfully we greet holy death
> And from joy we are left with deepest need
> We glow from morning to dawn.

Whoever the legal author may be, neither Georg nor Grete could have written it without the other, and it is fitting that the androgynous indeterminacy that Georg dreams of matches the indeterminacy of this poem's authorial beginning. The poem is published in German in Rusch and Schmidt, *Das Voraussetzungssystem Georg Trakls*, 161, although I have amended it slightly based on the original manuscript in the Brenner-Archiv. On account of similarities with other transcripts, Weichselbaum, "Unbekannte Gedichte und Prosa Georg Trakls entdeckt," 408–409 and 423n8, speculates that it may have been written by Georg and not, as previously thought, by Grete. The manuscript, at any rate, does not contain an attribution to "Margarete Langen," as Rusch and Schmidt lead one to believe. For more on Grete Trakl (although not on the poem itself), see Bax, *Immer zu wenig Liebe*, and McLary, "The Incestuous Sister or the Trouble with Grete."

26. For a systematic study of the term in Trakl and parallels with Hölderlin, see Böschenstein, "Motivwanderung in Trakls Gedichten: Am Beispiel des 'Wilds,'" in *Von Morgen nach Abend*, 258–266. See also GA 75: 98, 146–147.

27. Kluge, *Etymologisches Wörterbuch der deutschen Sprache* (4th ed.), 386 / *An Etymological Dictionary of the German Language*, 395.

28. *Karfreitagskind* stands out as the only unrhymed final word in the poem, as Lachmann, *Kreuz und Abend*, 114, remarks.

29. It is possible, although unlikely, that Heidegger would have been familiar with this earlier version the poem, published in *Der Brenner* (February 15, 1914). Heidegger provides page numbers for, or quotes from, the third version of "Passion" in "Language in the Poem" (GA 12: 39, 42, 49, 50), although, perhaps wishing to avoid the incest-motif, he never mentions it by name in the lecture. He does refer to it overtly in his notes on *Geschlecht*, though.

30. Which, admittedly, is not without its own complications. See the interview with Levinas and the essays in Atterton and Wright, eds., *Face to Face with Animals*.

31. Freud, *Introductory Lectures on Psychoanalysis (Part III)*, 284.

32. Cf. Grimm, *Deutsches Wörterbuch*, s.v. *sanft*: "sanft würde also auf dieselbe wurzel zurückgehen, die in griech. *homos*, deutsch *sam*, gleich *sammeln*, *zusammen*, vorliegt."

33. Cf. Krell, *Phantoms of the Other*, 159.

34. Mitchell, "Heidegger's Later Thinking of Animality." See also Mitchell, "Contamination, Essence, and Decomposition," 143, 149n21; and Mitchell, "Heidegger's Poetics of Relationality," 223. Phillips makes a similar argument in *Heidegger's Volk*, chapter 5. On the other end of the spectrum is Pimentel, *Heidegger with Derrida*, 271, who sees Heidegger as identifying degeneration and animality as such.

35. Novalis, *Heinrich von Ofterdingen*, 252. Novalis, the poet of the blue flower, also includes plants and stones in his vision of unification. There is, indeed, ample material in "Language in the Poem" that would allow us to push the boundaries further, not just those between human and animal but

also between animal and plant (which Heidegger typically ignores) and even between animal and stone (the latter of which, on several occasions, he calls worldless). Briefly, regarding the animal/plant distinction, in order to understand the wild blue game, Heidegger looks to the "the gentle cornflower cluster of night" from "Song of the Occident," which he associates with the holy. He then associates plant and animal more explicitly by way of "the holy character of blue flowers" and "the black flight of birds" in Trakl's "Ruh und Schweigen" ("Tranquility and Silence") (HKA 1: 62, 65). Regarding the animal/stone distinction, Heidegger links them via pain: the stone is the *gathering* of *pain*; like the animal face, *pain* is lit by the *blue*; in view of *blueness*, the wild game goes back into gentleness, which means *gathering* (GA 12: 39–41). See also the speaking stone (GA 12: 59), the bird-call of the friend (GA 12: 65, 77), the wingbeat (*Flügelschlag*) of the soul (GA 12: 74), and the possibility of playing with pacified snakes (GA 12: 49).

36. Nietzsche, *Jenseits von Gut und Böse*, no. 62, in *Kritische Studienausgabe*, 5: 81.

Chapter 7

1. Eckhart, *Die deutschen Werke*, 4: 430. "The wind bloweth where it listeth, and thou hearest the sound thereof, but canst not tell whence it cometh, and whither it goeth."

2. Martin and Fritz Heidegger, "Ausgewählte Briefe," 129–130; GA 12: 56; GA 16: 396.

3. Is this really so incompatible with Christianity, though? Is not spirit, as *Pneuma Hagion*, associated precisely with fire (*pur*) in Baptism and Pentecost (Matthew 3:11, Luke 3:16, Acts 2:3–4; cf. Trakl's variant for "Ein Winterabend," "A Winter Eveing," in HKA 2: 176: "Spricht mit feurigen Zungen," "Speaks with fiery tongues")? Is the author of Acts really thinking of language as a tool (GA 12: 11, 192) here? Do not evil spirits (*ta pneumata ta ponēra*) populate the Bible (Acts 19:13 et passim)? Is not God, too, a consuming fire (Deuteronomy 4:24, Hebrews 12:29, et passim)? For more along these lines of interrogation, see Roesner, "De la tautologie." For a consideration of Hebrew *ruah* and the idea of spirit in languages other than Greek, Latin, and German, see Derrida, *De l'esprit*, 165–167, and Dastur, "Geschlecht et Geist," 224–229.

4. According to the recent, twenty-fifth edition of Kluge's *Etymologisches Wörterbuch der deutschen Sprache*, the word *Geist* does indeed stem from the Indo-Germanic **gheis-d*, "to be outside of oneself" (*außer sich sein*). Heidegger, I suspect, consulted an earlier edition of this dictionary, as he definitely did for *Geschlecht*, although the version on which I have frequently relied, from 1889, does not mention *gheis* specifically. The entry on *Geist* is nonetheless instructive:

GEIST, m. "spirit, genius, spectre," from MidHG. and OHG *geist*, m., "spirit (in contrast to body), supernatural being"; corresponding to OSax. *gêst*, Du. *geist*, AS *gâst* (*gǽst*), E. *ghost*; common to Teut. in the same sense [. . .]. The prim. meaning [*Grundbedeutung*] of the word ("agitation" ["*Aufgeregtheit*"]?) is not quite certain; yet OIc. *geisa*, "to rage" ["*wüten*"] (of fire, passion), and Goth. *us-gaisjan*, "to enrage" ["*außer sich bringen*," literally "to bring outside oneself"] seem to be allied. Respecting the dental suffix of the Teut. GEIST (pre-Teut. *ghaisdos*), note the Sans. root *hîḍ* (from *hizd*), "to get angry" ["*zürnen*"], *hêḍas*, n., "anger," to which E. *aghast* [the German edition adds: "aufgeregt, zornig," "agitated, angry"] also corresponds.

Kluge, *Etymologisches Wörterbuch der deutschen Sprache* (4th ed.), 108 / *An Etymological Dictionary of the German Language*, 111.

5. For Heidegger's earlier treatment of evil, see GA 42: 167 to end; GA 49: 95–104, 136–138 et passim; the "Abendgespräch" ("Evening Conversation") in GA 77; and Heidegger and Blochmann, *Briefwechsel 1918–1969*, 31–33. For commentary (although not on the Trakl material), see Bernasconi, "Being Is Evil"; Moore, "Science, Thinking, and the Nothing as Such," 553–555; and Novák, *Heideggers Bestimmung des Bösen*.

6. Regarding the Bible verse, see Röck, *Tagebuch*, 3: 46. Regarding evil, see Trakl's accusation, during his exchange with Dallago, that the latter "knows nothing of evil" (not in DD) and the discussion in Methlagl, "'Der Brenner': Weltanschauliche Wandlungen vor dem ersten Weltkrieg," 242–245. When, in a 1945 lecture titled "Armut" ("Poverty"), Heidegger does reflect on spiritual poverty, it is a matter of lacking what is not necessary, that is to say, of belonging to being (GA 73: 871–883). Material poverty, helping the poor, welcoming the stranger, the Bible, are all irrelevant. Curiously, in 1945, it is the adjective *geistig* that characterizes genuine, i.e., ontological poverty, whereas, in the 1952 Trakl lecture, everything instead comes down to being *geistlich* rather than *geistig*, the latter, in Heidegger's interpretation, signifying metaphysical opposition to materiality (GA 12: 55). Heidegger conveniently disregards Trakl's own use of *geistig* in early poems, such as in the second version of "An Angela" ("To Angela"): "Thus bread and wine, nourished by the flesh of the earth, / show their *Geistiges* to Sebastian in dream" (HKA 1: 165; see also 194).

7. Thomas Aquinas, *Summa theologiae* I.2.3.

8. In *De l'esprit*, Derrida frequently points to the fact that Heidegger's reading is "literally Schellingian" (102, 168, 169, 175–176). Indeed, one of the few non-translational words in Derrida's marginalia to Heidegger's essay (*Acheminement vers la parole*, 63) is "Schelling" (cf. GA 12: 56). Typically, Derrida just provides translations or non-lexical marks. For Heidegger's relation to Boehme and passages in which he cites the baroque theosophist, see Bernasconi, "Being Is Evil," and

Moore, *Eckhart, Heidegger, and the Imperative of Releasement*, 236–237n59. For Baader, see Wolfson, *Heidegger and Kabbalah*, passim. The theosophic tradition also seems to be in the background of Heidegger's comments on the circular or reciprocal causality of masculine spirit (<u>der</u> Geist) and feminine soul (<u>die</u> Seele) in "Language in the Poem" (GA 12: 56–57). See Schelling, *Philosophische Untersuchungen über das Wesen der menschlichen Freiheit*, 30–31, and the sources supplied by the editor on pages 119–123.

     9. Schelling, *Philosophische Untersuchungen über das Wesen der menschlichen Freiheit*, 75–77 / *Philosophical Investigations into the Essence of Human Freedom*, 66–67.

     10. It is worth noting that Schelling encounters similar problems with his notion of the *Ungrund* or "non-ground," or what he also calls the love that stands higher than spirit, that "is" before ground and existence, and that "is" their "absolute *indifference*" (ibid., 78 / 68). As the translators of Schelling's treatise explain, "Schelling's notion of indifference does little to explain how difference can come to be, that is, how anything can come to be—the origin remains necessarily mysterious, ever a challenge to thought, and a stern reminder of the possible limits to thought" (169n95).

     11. Killy, "Gedichte im Gedicht," 1115. Also in HKA 2: 308.

Postscript

     1. "The concern for the *single* Germany will have never left him." Lacoue-Labarthe, "Présentation," 21.

     2. Hellingrath, *Zwei Vorträge*, 16–17, as translated by Charles Bambach in his monograph on, among other things, the leitmotif of a secret Germany in Heidegger's engagement with Hölderlin. See Bambach, *Of an Alien Homecoming*, 47. See also Kisiel, "The Siting of Hölderlin's 'Geheimes Deutschland' in Heidegger's Poetizing of the Political"; Mitchell, "Die Politik des geheimen Deutschland"; and Trawny, "Politik und Dichtung bei Heidegger."

     3. I would therefore amend Bambach's claim that, "[a]s the poet of/for this time of destitution, Hölderlin comes to stand for Heidegger as the one undefiled figure whose voice cries out in the wilderness of modern nihilism to prepare for what is coming" (*Of an Alien Homecoming*, xxiii; see also 322). Hölderlin is one of *two* undefiled figures. He is not, as Paul de Man claims, "the only one whom Heidegger cites as a believer cites Holy Writ." "Heidegger's Exegeses of Hölderlin," 250. For recognition of the two poets' similar if not identical status in Heidegger's estimation, see Dastur, "Heidegger et Trakl" ("[Trakl] est sans doute après Hölderlin le poète dont Heidegger se sent le plus proche et auquel il voue la plus grande admiration"), and Markus Wild, "Heidegger and Trakl," 45 ("Although Hölderlin is quoted in virtually all of Heidegger's poetry analyses,

in the essays on Trakl, Hölderlin is neither mentioned nor quoted. I take it that Trakl is not measured against Hölderlin because he stands right next to him").

4. DD: 201. Röck, *Tagebuch*, 3: 99. Heidegger would have read the former quotation in his personal copy of the Zurich edition. He annotated a different passage on the same page. See also the reports in DD: 212, and Röck, *Tagebuch*, 1: 249.

5. Hölderlin, *Sämtliche Werke und Briefe*, 1: 453. HKA 1: 61. See also HKA 1: 41 ("Helian") and 56 ("Verwandlung des Bösen," "Transformation of Evil"), as well as Böschenstein, *Von Morgen nach Abend*, 86–87, 232–234, 244.

6. For further discussion of the expressionist "emancipation of dissonance," see Harrison, *1910*, who quotes Benn on page 1, as well as Sokel, *The Writer in Extremis*. For Wolff's series, see Göbel, "Der Kurt Wolff Verlag," 573, and Herweg, *Helen und Kurt Wolff in Marbach*, 4.

7. Adorno, "Parataxis," 463.

8. Schürmann, *Broken Hegemonies*, 515, 9, 348 / *Des hégémonies brisées*, 593, 17, 409.

9. Ibid., 526/607 (translation modified). For more on Schürmann's reading of the *Beiträge* and the relevance of this reading today, see Guercio and Moore, "Heidegger, Our Monstrous Site."

10. Cf. Schürmann, *Broken Hegemonies*, 527 / *Des hégémonies brisées*, 608.

Works Cited

Unpublished Sources

Derrida, Jacques. Marginalia to Martin Heidegger, *Acheminement vers la parole*, translated by Jean Beaufret, Wolfgang Brokmeier, and François Fédier. Paris: Gallimard, 1976. The Library of Jacques Derrida, Studio Series, Box B-000204 Folder 5; Rare Book Division, Department of Rare Books and Special Collections, Princeton University Library.

———. Marginalia to Martin Heidegger, *Unterwegs zur Sprache*, 6th ed. Pfullingen: Neske, 1979. The Library of Jacques Derrida, Studio Series, Box B-000210 Folder 2; Rare Book Division, Department of Rare Books and Special Collections, Princeton University Library.

Heidegger, Martin. An undated note on detachment, presumably from the conclusion of Heidegger's Winter Semester 1915–1916 lecture course, found on the back page of one of the sheets of the manuscript of the Winter Semester 1925–1926 lecture course *Logik: Die Frage nach der Wahrheit*. Deutsches Literaturarchiv Marbach, call number 75.7051.

———. Facsimile of the manuscript of Trakl's "Afra" and of Heidegger's description of receiving and donating it. Unprocessed collection of the Martin-Heidegger-Archiv der Stadt Meßkirch.

———. Letter to Ernst Laslowski from September 27, 1952. Partial transcription available through Kotte Autographs: www.kotte-autographs.com/de/autograph/heidegger-martin

———. Letters (unpublished) to Fritz Heidegger. Typewritten transcriptions made available to me by Martin Heidegger's nephew Heinrich Heidegger.

———. Letters to Ingrid (Strohschneider-)Kohrs. Deutsches Literaturarchiv Marbach, call numbers HS000355364, HS.1998.0013.00006.

———. Manuscript of "Die Sprache im Gedicht." Deutsches Literaturarchiv Marbach, call number 75.7343,8.

———. Marginalia to *Die Dichtungen: Gesamtausgabe, mit einem Anhang Zeugnisse und Erinnerungen*, edited by Kurt Horwitz. Zurich: Die Arche, 1946. Unprocessed collection of the Martin-Heidegger-Archiv der Stadt Meßkirch.

———. Marginalia to Georg Trakl, *Die Dichtungen*, 6th ed. [Edited by Wolfgang Schneditz.] Salzburg: Otto Müller, 1938. Located in the Literaturmuseum der Moderne, Marbach, Germany.

———. Notes on Trakl. Deutsches Literaturarchiv Marbach, call numbers 75.7372,1a–f and 75.7372,2–8.

———. Note to Ragnvi Maeter. Partial transcription available through Kotte Autographs: www.kotte-autographs.com/TOOLS/content/wp-content/uploads/download/40.pdf (p. 141)

———. Note with four quotes by Trakl in Heidegger's hand. Formerly available through Kotte Autographs: www.kotte-autographs.com/de/autograph/heidegger-martin

———. Recording of the second half of Heidegger's "Die Sprache im Gedicht." Unprocessed collection of the Martin-Heidegger-Archiv der Stadt Meßkirch.

———. Three typescript versions of "Die Sprache im Gedicht," all titled "Martin Heidegger deutet Georg Trakl. Bühlerhöhe am 4. Oktober 1952." Research Institute Brenner-Archiv at the University of Innsbruck, call number 65/33–1.

———. "Über den Schmerz." Deutsches Literaturarchiv Marbach, call number 75.7300,3.

Heidegger, Martin, Clemens Podewils, and Gerhard Stroomann. Letter from March 13, 1954 to Gottfried Benn. Deutsches Literaturarchiv Marbach, call number 91.114.515,1.

Kommerell, Nora. "Aufzeichnungen über die Max Kommerell-Veranstaltung auf der Bühlerhöhe, Oktober 1950." Deutsches Literaturarchiv Marbach, call number 93.15.56.

Langen, Margarete (or possibly by Georg Trakl). "Helians Schicksalslied." Forschungsinstitut Brenner-Archiv, Nachlass Ludwig von Ficker, call number 041-068-032.

Strohschneider-Kohrs, Ingrid. *Seltsame Situationen: Menschen und Begebenheiten in Kriegs- und Nachkriegsjahren*. Private printing, Gauting 2013, made available to me by Helmut Berthold.

Published Sources

Adler, Anthony Curtis. "The Intermedial Gesture: Agamben and Kommerell." *Angelaki* 12, no. 3 (2007): 57–64.

Adorno, Theodor W. "Parataxis." In *Noten zur Literatur*, edited by Rolf Tiedemann, 447–491. Frankfurt: Suhrkamp, 1981.

Aeschylus. *Agamemnon*. Vol. 1. Edited by Eduard Fraenkel. Oxford: Clarendon, 1950.

Aichinger, Ilse. "Der geheime Leonce: Zu Georg Trakl." In *Kleist, Moos, Fasane*. Frankfurt: Fischer E-Books, 2015.

———. "Versuch (für Georg Trakl)." "*SALZ*" 2, no. 7 (March 1977): 7.
———. "Versuch." In *Martin Heidegger zum siebzigsten Geburtstag: Festschrift*, edited by Günther Neske, 298. Pfullingen: Neske, 1959.
Agamben, Giorgio. "Kommerell, or On Gesture." In *Potentialities*, edited and translated by Daniel Heller-Roazen, 77–85. Stanford, CA: Stanford University Press, 1999.
———. *The Open: Man and Animal*. Translated by Kevin Attell. Stanford, CA: Stanford University Press, 2004.
Allemann, Beda *Hölderlin und Heidegger*. 2nd ed. Zurich: Atlantis, [1956].
———. *Ironie und Dichtung*. Pfullingen: Neske, 1956.
———. *Über das Dichterische*. Pfullingen: Neske, 1957.
Allen, Michael Thad. "How Technology Caused the Holocaust: Martin Heidegger, West German Industrialists, and the Death of Being." In *Lessons and Legacies, Vol. 7: The Holocaust in International Perspective*, edited by Dagmar Herzog, 285–302. Evanston, IL: Northwestern University Press, 2006.
Anonymous. *ΕΤΥΜΟΛΟΓΙΚΟΝ ΤΟ ΜΕΓΑ*. Ed. Friderici Sylburgii, editio nova correctior. Lipsiae apud Io. Aug. Gottl. Weigel, 1816.
Anonymous. "Heidegger: Rückfall ins Gestell." *Der Spiegel*, April 6, 1950.
Anonymous. "The 'Vita Adae.'" Edited by J. H. Mozley. *The Journal of Theological Studies* 30, no. 118 (January 1929): 121–149.
Arendt, Hannah, and Martin Heidegger. *Briefe 1925 bis 1975 und andere Zeugnisse*. Edited by Ursula Ludz. Frankfurt: Klostermann, 1998.
Aristotle. *Ethica Nicomachea*. Edited by I. Bywater. Oxford: Clarendon, 1894.
Armour, Ellen T. "'Through Flame or Ashes': Traces of Difference in *Geist*'s Return." In *Feminist Interpretations of Martin Heidegger*, edited by Nancy J. Holland and Patricia Huntington, 316–333. University Park: Pennsylvania State University Press, 2001.
Atterton, Peter, and Tamra Wright, eds. *Face to Face with Animals: Levinas and the Animal Question*. Albany, NY: SUNY Press, 2019.
Badiou, Alain. *The Age of the Poets and Other Writings on Twentieth-Century Poetry and Prose*. Edited and translated by Bruno Bosteels. London: Verso, 2014.
Bakhtin, Mikhail. *Problems of Dostoevsky's Poetics*. Edited and translated by Caryl Emerson. Minneapolis: University of Minnesota Press, 1984.
Bambach, Charles. "Heidegger and Celan." In *Heidegger and Literature*, edited by Andrew Benjamin. Cambridge: Cambridge University Press, forthcoming 2023.
———. *Heidegger's Roots: Nietzsche, National Socialism, and the Greeks*. Ithaca, NY: Cornell University Press, 2003.
———. *Thinking the Poetic Measure of Justice: Hölderlin–Heidegger–Celan*. Albany, NY: SUNY Press, 2013.
———. *Of an Alien Homecoming: Heidegger and Hölderlin*. Albany, NY: SUNY Press, 2022.

Barth, Emil. *Georg Trakl: Zum Gedächtnis seines fünfzigsten Geburtstags am 3. Februar 1937*. Mainz: Eggebrecht, 1937.
———. "Zum Bilde Georg Trakls." *Merkur* 4, no. 7 (29) (July 1950): 793–800.
Basil, Otto. *Georg Trakl: In Selbstzeugnissen und Bilddokumenten*. Reinbek: Rowohlt, 1965.
Baumann, Gerhart. *Erinnerungen an Paul Celan*. Frankfurt: Suhrkamp, 1992.
Bax, Marty. *Immer zu wenig Liebe: Grete Trakl*. Amsterdam: Bax, 2014.
Benjamin, Walter. "Wider ein Meisterwerk." In *Gesammelte Schriften*, edited by Hella Tiedemann-Bartels, Vol. 3, 252–259. Frankfurt: Suhrkamp, 1991. "Against a Masterpiece." In *Selected Writings, Vol. 2, Part 1: 1927–1934*. Translated by Rodney Livingstone et al. Edited by Michael W. Jennings, Howard Eiland, and Gary Smith, 378–385. Cambridge, MA: Belknap, 1999.
Benn, Gottfried. "Altern als Problem für Künstler." In *Gesammelte Werke*, 1: 552–582. A different version is published in *Merkur* 8, no. 4 (74) (April 1954): 301–319.
———. *Briefe an F. W. Oelze 1950–1956*. Edited by Harald Steinhagen and Jürgen Schröder. Stuttgart: Klett-Cotta, 2016.
———. "Probleme der Lyrik." In *Gesammelte Werke*, 1: 494–532.
———. *Gesammelte Werke*. 4 vols. Wiesbaden: Limes, 1962.
Benn, Gottfried, Hans Paeschke, and Joachim Moras, *Briefwechsel 1948–1956*. Edited by Holger Hof. Stuttgart: Klett-Cotta, 2004.
Bennington, Geoffrey. "*Geschlecht pollachos legetai*: Translation, Polysemia, Dissemination." *Philosophy Today* 64, no. 2 (Spring 2020): 423–439.
Bense, Max. "Heideggers Brief über den Humanismus." *Merkur* 3, no. 10 (20): 1021–1026.
———. "Kybernetik oder Die Metaphysik einer Maschine," *Merkur* 5, no. 3 (37) (1951): 205–218.
Bernasconi, Robert. "Being Is Evil: Boehme's Strife and Schelling's Rage in Heidegger's 'Letter on 'Humanism.'" *Gatherings* 7 (2017): 164–181.
———. "Poets as Prophets and as Painters: Heidegger's Turn to Language and the Hölderlinian Turn in Context." In *Heidegger and Language*, edited by Jeffrey Powell, 146–162. Bloomington: Indiana University Press, 2013.
———. *The Question of Language in Heidegger's History of Being*. Amherst, NY: Humanity, 1989.
Bertorello, Adrián. "La lentitud de las cosas: El lugar de lo alsosemiótico en la lectura heideggeriana de Georg Trakl." *Tópicos del Seminario* 26 (July–December 2011): 93–110.
Blanchet, Vincent. "De bleu et d'or: *Das Heilige* et Heidegger." *Les Études philosophiques* 161, no. 1 (2016): 73–88.
Blanchot, Maurice. *L'écriture du désastre*. Paris: Gallimard, 1980.
Blok, Vincent. *Ernst Jünger's Philosophy of Technology: Heidegger and the Poetics of the Anthropocene*. New York: Routledge, 2017.

Bloom, Harold, ed. *Modern German Poetry*. New York: Chelsea, 1989.
Boehlich, Walter. "Schweizer Literaturforschung." *Merkur* 11, no. 5 (111) (1957): 494–498.
Boelderl, Artur R. "Geburtsräume des Daseins: Über Heideggers Sprachgebär(d)en." In *Zugänge. Ausgänge. Übergänge: Konstitutionsformen des sozialen Raums*, edited by Thomas Bedorf and Gerhard Unterthurner, 27–39. Würzburg: Königshausen & Neumann, 2009.
Böhme, Jakob. "De incarnatione verbi, oder: Von der Menschwerdung Christi." In *Sämmtliche Werke*, edited by K. W. Schiebler, Vol. 6. Leipzig: Barth, 1846.
Bonaventure. *Itinerarium mentis in deum*. Translated by Philotheus Boehner. Saint Bonaventure, NY: The Franciscan Institute, Saint Bonaventure University, 1956.
Böschenstein, Bernhard. "Hellingrath–Hölderlin–George: Bernhard Böschenstein im Gespräch mit Ulrich Raulff und Jürgen Brokoff." In *Norbert von Hellingrath und die Ästhetik der europäischen Moderne*, 15–29. Edited by Jürgen Brokoff, Joachim Jacob, and Marcel Lepper. Göttingen: Wallstein, 2014.
———. *Von Morgen nach Abend: Filiationen der Dichtung von Hölderlin zu Celan*. Munich: Fink, 2006.
Braig, Carl. *Vom Sein: Abriß der Ontologie*. Freiburg: Herder, 1896.
Brennan, Teresa, Drucilla Cornell, and Jacques Derrida. "Opening Plenary: Is Feminist Philosophy Philosophy?" In *Is Feminist Philosophy Philosophy?*, edited by Emanuela Bianchi, 3–31. Evanston, IL: Northwestern University Press, 1999.
Brentano, Clemens. "Das Märchen von dem Myrtenfräulein." In *Die Märchen des Clemens Brentano*. Vol. 2. Edited by Guido Görres. Stuttgart: 1847.
Britting, Georg. *Briefe an Georg Jung 1943 bis 1963*. Georg Britting-Stiftung www.britting.de/wordpress/wp-content/uploads/Band20_d.pdf
Buchanan, Brett. *Onto-Ethologies: The Animal Environments of Uexküll, Heidegger, Merleau-Ponty, and Deleuze*. Albany, NY: SUNY Press, 2008.
Buber, Martin. "Hoffnung für diese Stunde." *Merkur* 6, no. 8 (54) (1952): 711–718.
———. "Religion und modernes Denken." *Merkur* 6, no. 2 (48) (1952): 101–120.
Burnett, Anne Pippin. *Pindar's Songs for Young Athletes of Aigina*. Oxford: Oxford University Press, 2005.
Busch, Walter. "Kommerells Hölderlin: Von der Erbschaft Georges zur Kritik an Heidegger." In *Kommerell: Leben–Werk–Aktualität*, edited by Walter Busch and Gerhart Pickerodt, 278–299. Göttingen: Wallstein, 2003.
Bury, J. B., ed. *The Isthmian Odes of Pindar*. Amsterdam: Hakkert, 1965.
Camilleri, Sylvain. *Phénoménologie de la religion et herméneutique théologique dans la pensée du jeune Heidegger: Commentaire analytique des Fondements philosophiques de la mystique médiévale (1916–1919)*. Dordrecht: Springer, 2008.
Capobianco, Richard. *Engaging Heidegger*. Toronto: University of Toronto Press, 2010.

---. "Heidegger on Heraclitus: *Kosmos*/World as Being Itself." *Epoché* 20, no. 2 (Spring 2016): 465–476.
---. *Heidegger's Way of Being*. Toronto: University of Toronto Press, 2014.
Caputo, John D. "Thinking, Poetry and Pain." *The Southern Journal of Philosophy* 288 (1989): 155–181.
Casey, T. J. *Manshape that Shone: An Interpretation of Trakl*. Oxford: Basil Blackwell, 1964.
Celan, Paul. *Gesammelte Werke*. 5 vols. Edited by Beda Allemann and Stefan Reichert. Frankfurt: Suhrkamp, 1986.
Chantraine, Pierre. *Dictionnaire étymologique de la langue grecque: Histoires des mots*. Vols. 1 and 3. Paris: Éditions Klincksieck, 1968, 1974.
Cicero. *Tusculanae disputationes*. Edited by M. Pohlenz. Stuttgart: Teubner, 1965.
Clark, Orville. "Heidegger and the Mystery of Pain." *Man and World* 10, no. 3 (1977): 334–350.
---. "Pain and Being: An Essay in Heideggerian Ontology." *The Southwestern Journal of Philosophy* 4, no. 3 (1973): 179–190.
Colombat, Rémy. "Heidegger, lecteur de Trakl." *Études Germaniques* 271 (2013): 395–420. www.cairn.info/revue-etudes-germaniques-2013-3-page-395.htm#
Cooper, Ian. *Poetry and the Question of Modernity: From Heidegger to the Present*. New York: Routledge, 2020.
Cremer, Hermann. *Biblico-Theological Lexicon of New Testament Greek*. 4th ed. Translated by William Urwick. New York: Scribner, 1895.
D'Angelo, Diego. "Einheit und Mannigfaltigkeit im dichterischen Wort: Perspektiven auf Heideggers Trakl-Interpretation." In *Perspektiven mit Heidegger: Zugänge–Pfade–Anknüpfungen*, edited by Gerhard Thonhauser, 55–70. Freiburg: Alber, 2017.
Dallago, Carl. *Otto Weininger und sein Werk*. Innsbruck: Brenner, 1912. First published in installments in the journal *Der Brenner*, 3, nos. 1–3 (1912).
Dante. *Paradiso*. In Italian and an English translation by Robert Hollander and Jean Hollander. New York: Random, 2007.
Dastur, Françoise. "*Geschlecht* et *Geist*: Derrida, Heidegger, Trakl." In *Déconstruction et phénoménologie: Derrida en débat avec Husserl et Heidegger*, 191–229. Paris: Hermann, 2016.
---. "Heidegger et Trakl: Le site occidental et le voyage poétique." *Noesis* 7 (2004). https://journals.openedition.org/noesis/22
Davis, Bret W. *Heidegger on the Will: On the Way to Gelassenheit*. Evanston, IL: Northwestern University Press, 2007.
De Beauvoir, Simone. *Das andere Geschlecht: Sitte und Sexus der Frau*. Translated by Uli Aumüller and Grete Osterwald. Reinbek: Rowohlt, 1992.
Degner, Uta. "'Infirme' Autorschaft: Trakls *Helian* als poetologischer Selbstentwurf." In *Autorschaft und Poetik in Texten und Kontexten Georg Trakls*, edited by Uta Degner, Hans Weichselbaum, and Norbert Christian Wolf, 95–115. Salzburg: Otto Müller, 2016.

Delobel, Cécile. "Eduard Mörike et Martin Heidegger: Faire du chemin avec. . . ." *Heidegger Studies* 36 (2020): 139–175.
De Man, Paul. "Heidegger's Exegeses of Hölderlin." In *Blindness and Insight: Essays in the Rhetoric of Contemporary Criticism*, 2nd ed., 246–266. Minneapolis: University of Minnesota Press, 1983.
Demetz, Peter. "Grenzsituationen der Literaturwissenschaft." *Merkur* 16, no. 8 (174) (1962): 784–787.
Derrida, Jacques. *De l'esprit: Heidegger et la question.* Paris: Galilée, 1987.
———. *De la grammatologie.* Paris: Minuit, 1967.
———. *Le monolinguisme de l'autre ou la prothèse d'origine.* Paris: Galilée, 1996.
———. "Geschlecht I: Sexual Difference, Ontological Difference." In *Psyche: Inventions of the Other*, Vol. 2, edited by Peggy Kamuf and Elizabeth Rottenberg, 7–26. Stanford, CA: Stanford University Press, 2008.
———. "Heidegger's Ear: Philopolemology (*Geschlecht* IV)." Translated by John P. Leavey. In *Reading Heidegger: Commemorations*, edited by John Sallis, 163–218. Bloomington: Indiana University Press, 1993.
———. "Heidegger's Hand (*Geschlecht* II)." In *Psyche: Inventions of the Other*, Vol. 2, edited by Peggy Kamuf and Elizabeth Rottenberg, 27–62. Stanford, CA: Stanford University Press, 2008.
———. *L'animal que donc je suis.* Paris: Galilée, 2006.
———. "Of Writing, Heritage and the Other: An Interview with Jacques Derrida." By Nikhil Padgaonkar. *Biblio: A Review of Books* 3, no. 1 (January–February 1997): 14–15.
———. "Onto-Theology of National Humanism (Prolegomena to a Hypothesis)." *Oxford Literary Review* 14, no. 1 (1992): 3–23.
———. *Spectres de Marx: L'état de la dette, le travail du deuil et la nouvelle Internationale.* Paris: Galilée, 2006.
———. *The Beast and the Sovereign.* 2 vols. Translated by Geoffrey Bennington. Chicago: University of Chicago Press, 2011.
Derrida, Jacques, and Christie V. McDonald. "Choreographies." *Diacritics* 12, no. 2 (Summer 1982): 66–76.
Detsch. Richard. "Die Beziehungen zwischen Karl Borromäus Heinrich und Georg Trakl." *Modern Austrian Literature* 16, no. 2 (1983): 82–104.
———. *Georg Trakl and the Brenner Circle.* New York: Lang, 1991.
———. *Georg Trakl's Poetry: Toward a Union of Opposites.* University Park: Pennsylvania State University Press, 1983.
Dickinson, Emily. *The Complete Poems.* Edited by Thomas H. Johnson. Boston: Little, Brown, 1960.
Diels, Hermann, ed. *Die Fragmente der Vorsokratiker.* 3 vols. Zurich: Weidmann, 1964.
Dostojewski, F. M. *Literarische Schriften.* Munich: Piper, 1921.
Drexel, Joseph E., ed. *Ludwig von Ficker zum Gedächtnis seines achtzigsten Geburtstags.* Nuremberg: Druckhaus Nürnberg, 1960.

Eckhart. *Die Deutschen Werke*. 5 vols. Herausgegeben im Auftrag der Deutschen Forschungsgemeinschaft. Stuttgart: Kohlhammer, 1936–2016.

———. *Meister Eckhart*. Edited by Franz Pfeiffer. Leipzig: Göschen, 1857.

———. *Meister Eckeharts Schriften und Predigten*. Edited and translated by Herman Büttner. 2 vols. Leipzig: Diederichs, 1903, 1909.

———. *Meister Eckharts Mystische Schriften*. Translated by Gustav Landauer. Berlin: Schnabel, 1903.

Ederheimer, Edgar. *Jakob Boehme und die Romantiker. I. und II. Teil: Jakob Boehmes Einfluß auf Tieck und Novalis*. Heidelberg: Winter, 1904.

Elden, Stuart. *Speaking against Number: Heidegger, Language and the Politics of Calculation*. Edinburgh: Edinburgh University Press, 2006.

Elliott, Mark. "'Und Gassen enden schwarz und sonderbar': Poetic Dialogues with Georg Trakl in the 1930s and 40s." *Austrian Studies* 12 (2004): 80–97.

Emad, Parvis. "Heidegger on Pain: Focusing on a Recurring Theme of His Thought." *Zeitschrift für philosophische Forschung* 36 (1982): 345–360.

Emerson, Ralph Waldo. *The Complete Essays and Other Writings*. Edited by Brooks Atkinson. New York: Modern Library, 1950.

Esselborn, Hans. "Novalis-Rezeption in der deutschen Moderne." In *"Blüthenstaub": Rezeption und Wirkung des Werkes von Novalis*, edited by Herbert Uerlings, 289–310. Tübingen: Niemeyer, 2000.

Ewegen, S. Montgomery. "Gestures of the Feminine in Heidegger's 'Die Sprache.'" *The Journal of Speculative Philosophy* 30, no. 4 (2016): 486–498.

F., A. [Frisé, Adolf]. "Bühler Höhen-Luft." *Deutsche Zeitung und Wirtschaftszeitung* 5, no. 82 (October 14, 1950): 15.

Falk, Walter. "Heidegger und Trakl." *Literaturwissenschaftliches Jahrbuch der Görresgesellschaft* 4 (1963): 191–204.

Ferber, Ilit. *Language Pangs: On Pain and the Origin of Language*. Oxford: Oxford University Press, 2019.

Fichte, Johann Gottlieb. *Addresses to the German Nation*. Edited by Gregory Moore. Cambridge: Cambridge University Press, 2008.

Ficker, Ludwig von. *Briefwechsel 1909–1914*. Edited by Ignaz Zangerle et al. Innsbruck: Müller, 1986.

———. *Briefwechsel 1914–1925*. Edited by Ignaz Zangerle et al. Innsbruck: Haymon, 1991.

———. *Briefwechsel 1926–1939*. Edited by Ignaz Zangerle et al. Innsbruck: Haymon, 1991.

———. *Briefwechsel 1940–1967*. Edited by Martin Alber et al. Innsbruck: Haymon, 1996.

———. *Denkzettel und Danksagungen: Aufsätze–Reden*. Edited by Franz Seyr. Munich: Kösel, 1967.

———. "Der Abschied." In *Denkzettel und Danksagungen: Aufsätze–Reden*, edited by Franz Seyr, 80–101. Munich: Kösel, 1967. First published in 1926.

Ficker, Ludwig von, et al. "Nachträge und Notizen." *Der Brenner* 18 (1954): 280–285.
Ficker, Ludwig von, ed. *Erinnerung an Georg Trakl: Zeugnisse und Briefe*. 2nd ed. Salzburg: Müller, 1959. First published in 1926.
Fleming, Paul. "The Crisis of Art: Max Kommerell and Jean Paul's Gestures." *MLN* 15 (2000): 519–543.
Focke, Alfred. *Georg Trakl: Liebe und Tod*. Vienna: Herold, 1955.
———. "Von Dionysos zu Christus: Rainer Maria Rilke, Georg Trakl, Gertrud von Le Fort." *Wissenschaft und Weltbild* 4 (1951): 79–84.
Fleckner, Uwe, and Maike Steinkamp, eds. *Gauklerfest unterm Galgen: Expressionismus zwischen "nordischer" Moderne und "entarteter" Kunst*. Berlin: De Gruyter, 2015.
Fóti, Véronique M. *Heidegger and the Poets: Poiēsis/Sophia/Technē*. Atlantic Highlands, NJ: Humanities, 1992.
Franck, Didier. "Heidegger and the Living." Translated by Peter T. Connor. In *Who Comes after the Subject?*, edited by Eduardo Cadava, Peter Connor, and Jean-Luc Nancy, 135–147. New York: Routledge, 1991.
Franzen, Jonathan. *The Kraus Project*. New York: Farrar, Straus and Giroux, 2013.
Freud, Sigmund. *Introductory Lectures on Psychoanalysis (Part III)*. Standard edition vol. XVI. Edited and translated by James Strachey. London: Hogarth, 1963.
Frisk, Hjalmar. *Griechisches Etymologisches Wörterbuch*. Vol. 2. Heidelberg: Winter, 1970.
Froidecourt, Adéline. "La poésie de Pindare à l'aube de la métaphysique." *Heidegger Studies* 28 (2012): 67–100.
Fühmann, Franz. *Vor Feuerschlunden: Erfahrung mit Georg Trakls Gedicht*. Rostock: Hinstorff, 2000. *At the Burning Abyss: Experiencing the Georg Trakl Poem*. Translated by Isabel Fargo Cole. London: Seagull, 2017.
Fynsk, Christopher. "Noise at the Threshold." *Research in Phenomenology* 19, no. 1 (1989): 101–120.
Gadamer, Hans-Georg. "Europa und die Oikoumene." In *Gesammelte Werke*, Vol. 10, 267–284. Tübingen: Mohr, 1995.
———. "Gedenkrede auf Max Kommerell." In Max Kommerell, *Dichterische Welterfahrung: Essays*, edited by Hans-Georg Gadamer, 205–229. Frankfurt: Klostermann, 1952.
———. "'Golden blooms the tree of grace': On Georg Trakl's *Ein Winterabend*." Edited and translated by Ian Alexander Moore. *Journal of Continental Philosophy* 3, no. 1 (forthcoming 2022).
———. "Pain: Reflections of a Philosopher." Translated by Alexander Crist. *The Journal of Continental Philosophy* 1, no. 1 (2020): 63–75.
———. "Zu Immermanns Epigonen-Roman." In *Gesammelte Werke*, Vol. 9, 193–206. Tübingen: Mohr, 1993.

Gagliardi, Francesco. *L'azzurro dell'anima: Heidegger e la poesia di Trakl.* Perugia: Morlacchi, 2007.
Gelley, Alexander. "Staiger, Heidegger, and the Task of Criticism." *Modern Language Quarterly* 23, no. 3 (1962): 195–216.
"Georg Trakl." Special issue of the *Cahiers du Sud*, no. 341 (1957).
Gerlach, Reinhard. "Anton Webern: Ein Winterabend op. 13, Nr. 4: Zum Verhältnis von Musik und Dichtung oder Wahrheit als Struktur." *Archiv für Musikwissenschaft* 30, no. 1 (1973): 44–68.
Giubilato, Giovanni Jan. "Dolor e historia del Ser: El debate entre Heidegger y Jünger sobre el dolor en la épocha de la técnica." *Naturaleza humana* 18, no. 1 (2016): 55–68.
Glaser, Brigitte. *Bühlerhöhe: Roman.* Berlin: Ullstein, 2016.
Göbel, Wolfram. "Der Kurt Wolff Verlag: Expressionismus als verlegerische Aufgabe." *Archiv für Geschichte des Buchwesens* 15 (1975): 521–962.
Görner, Rüdiger. *Georg Trakl: Dichter im Jahrzehnt der Extreme.* Vienna: Zsolnay, 2014.
Gosetti, Jennifer Anna. "Feminine Figures in Heidegger's Theory of Poetic Language." In *Feminist Interpretations of Martin Heidegger*, edited by Nancy J. Holland and Patricia Huntington, 196–218. University Park: Pennsylvania State University Press, 2001.
Graham, Jorie. "What Is Called Thinking: After Trakl." *The Antioch Review* 48, no. 3 (Summer 1990): 342–344.
Graybeal, Jean. *Language and "the Feminine" in Nietzsche and Heidegger.* Bloomington: Indiana University Press, 1990.
Gregory, Wanda Torres. *Speaking of Silence in Heidegger.* Lanham, MD: Lexington, 2021.
Grimm, Jacob and Wilhelm. *Deutsches Wörterbuch.* Leipzig: 1854–1961.
Grosz, Elizabeth. "Ontology and Equivocation: Derrida's Politics of Sexual Difference." *Diacritics* 25, no. 2 (Summer 1995): 114–124.
Grube, Christoph. *"so oder so, es bleibt blau oder braun, das Gedicht": Aspekte der Trakl-Rezeption Paul Celans.* Würzburg: Königshausen & Neumann, 2014.
Gründgens, Gustav. "Das Theater und die moderne Kunst." In *Gustav Gründgens: Briefe, Aufsätze, Reden*, edited by Rolf Badenhausen and Peter Gründgens-Gorski, 350–366. Munich: Deutscher Taschenbuch, 1970.
Günther, Johann Christian. *Gedichte.* Edited by Berthold Litzmann. Leipzig: Reclam, n.d.
Guercio, Francesco, and Ian Alexander Moore. "Heidegger, Our Monstrous Site: On Reiner Schürmann's Reading of the *Beiträge*," *Graduate Faculty Philosophy Journal* 42, no. 1 (2021): 93–114.
Haddad, Samir. "More than a Language to Come." *Philosophy Today* 64, no. 2 (Spring 2020): 379–394.
Haebler, R. G. "Metaphysik der Sprache: Max-Kommerell-Tagung auf Bühlerhöhe." *Rhein-Neckar-Zeitung* 235 (October 10, 1950): 2.

Hamacher, Werner. "Other Pains." Translated by Ian Alexander Moore. *Philosophy Today* 61, no. 4: (Fall 2017): 963–989.
Hamburger, Michael. *Reason and Energy: Studies in German Literature*. London: Routledge & Kegan Paul, 1957.
Hanly, Peter. *Between Heidegger and Novalis*. Evanston, IL: Northwestern University Press, 2021.
———. "Dark Celebration: Heidegger's Silent Music." In *Heidegger and Language*, edited by Jeffrey Powell, 240–264. Bloomington: Indiana University Press, 2013.
Harries, Karsten. "Language and Silence: Heidegger's Dialogue with Georg Trakl." *boundary 2* 4, no. 2 (1976): 495–511.
Harrison, Thomas. *1910: The Emancipation of Dissonance*. Berkeley: University of California Press, 1996.
Hattingberg, Immo von. "Gerhard Stroomann: Ein Arzt in der Wandlung der Medizin." *Merkur* 11, no. 7 (113) (July 1957): 653–659.
Hattingberg, Monika von. "Aus den Aufzeichnungen meines Vaters Immo von Hattingberg: Über seine Begegnung mit Martin Heidegger und seiner Philosophie und deren Bedeutung für sein Leben." *Heidegger Studies* 34 (2018): 9–13.
Heckmann, Ursula. *Das verfluchte Geschlecht: Motive der Philosophie Otto Weiningers im Werk Georg Trakls*. Frankfurt: Lang, 1992.
Hegel, Georg Wilhelm Friedrich. "Glauben und Wissen." In *Werke*, Vol. 2: *Jenaer Schriften 1801–1807*, 287–433. Frankfurt: Suhrkamp, 1986.
———. *Phänomenologie des Geistes*. Hamburg: Meiner, 1952.
———. "Der Geist des Christentums und sein Schicksal." In *Theologische Jugendschriften*, edited by Herman Nohl, 241–342. Tübingen: Mohr, 1907.
———. *Vorlesungen über die Philosophie der Religion II: Vorlesungen über die Beweise vom Dasein Gottes*. Werke, Vol. 17. Frankfurt: Suhrkamp, 1986.
———. *Wissenschaft der Logik: Die Lehre vom Begriff (1816)*. Edited by Hans-Jürgen Gawoll. 2nd ed. Hamburg: Meiner, 2003.
———. *Wissenschaft der Logik: Die Lehre vom Sein (1832)*. Edited by Hans-Jürgen Gawoll. 2nd ed. Hamburg: Meiner, 2008.
Heidegger, Martin. "Abendgang auf der Reichenau." In *Das Bodenseebuch 1917: Ein Buch für Land und Leute* 4, p. 152. Konstanz: Reuß & Itta.
———. "Andenken." In *Hölderlin: Tübinger Gedenkschrift zu seinem 100. Todestag*, edited by Paul Kluckhohn, 267–325. Tübingen: Mohr, 1943.
———. *Ausgewählte Briefe an Heinrich Wiegand Petzet*. Jahresgabe der Martin-Heidegger-Gesellschaft, 2003.
———. *Auszüge zur Phänomenologie aus dem Manuskript "Vermächtnis der Seinsfrage."* Jahresgabe der Martin-Heidegger-Gesellschaft, 2011–2012.
———. *Briefwechsel mit seinen Eltern (1907–1927) und Briefe an seine Schwester (1921–1967)*. Edited by Jörg Heidegger and Alfred Denker. Freiburg: Karl Alber, 2013.

———. "Georg Trakl: Eine Erörterung seines Gedichtes." *Merkur* 7, no. 3 (61) (March 1953): 226–258.

———. "Georg Trakl: Language in the Poem." In *Modern German Poetry*, edited by Harold Bloom, 93–121. New York: Chelsea, 1989.

———. Interview with Frédéric de Towarnicki and Jean-Michel Palmier. *L'Express* 945 (20–26 October 1969): 78–85.

———. "Language." In *Poetry, Language, Thought*, translated by Albert Hofstadter, 187–208. New York: Harper & Row, 1971. Republished in *The Theory of Difference: Readings in Contemporary Continental Thought*, edited by Douglas L. Donkel, 41–56. Albany, NY: SUNY Press, 2001. Republished in *The Norton Anthology of Theory and Criticism*, edited by Vincent B. Leitch, 982–998. New York: Norton, 2001.

———. Letter to Jean-Michel Palmier, May 9, 1972. Translated into French by Jean-Michel Palmier. In *L'Herne: Martin Heidegger*, edited by Michel Haar, 117–18. Paris: Éditions de l'Herne, 1983.

———. "Mein liebes Seelchen!": *Briefe Martin Heideggers an seine Frau Elfride 1915–1970*. Edited by Gertrud Heidegger. Munich: Deutsche Verlags-Anstalt, 2005.

———. *On the Way to Language*. Translated by Peter D. Hertz. New York: Harper & Row, 1971.

———. *Poetry, Language, Thought*. Translated by Albert Hofstadter. New York: Harper & Row, 1971.

———. *Unterwegs zur Sprache*. Pfullingen: Neske, 1959.

———. "Was heisst Denken?" *Merkur* 6, no. 7 (53) (July 1952): 601–611.

———. *Zollikoner Seminare: Protokolle–Zwiegespräche–Briefe*. 2nd ed. Edited by Medard Boss. Frankfurt: Klostermann, 1994.

Heidegger, Martin, and Elisabeth Blochmann. *Briefwechsel 1918–1969*. 2nd ed. Edited by Joachim W. Storck. Marbach: Deutsche Schillergesellschaft, 1990.

Heidegger, Martin, and Emil Staiger. "Der Briefwechsel." Edited by Werner Wögerbauer. *Geschichte der Germanistik* 25/26 (2004): 34–79.

Heidegger, Martin, and Erhart Kästner. *Briefwechsel, 1953–1974*. Edited by Heinrich W. Petzet. Frankfurt: Insel, 1986.

Heidegger, Martin, and Fritz Heidegger. "Ausgewählte Briefe." In *Heidegger und der Antisemitismus: Positionen im Widerstreit*, edited by Walter Homolka and Arnulf Heidegger. Freiburg: Herder, 2016.

Heidegger, Martin, and Imma von Bodmershof. *Briefwechsel 1959–1976*. Edited by Bruno Pieger. Stuttgart: Klett-Cotta, 2000.

Heidegger, Martin, and Karl Jaspers, *Briefwechsel 1920–1963*. Edited by Walter Biemel and Hans Saner. Frankfurt: Klostermann, 1990.

Heidegger, Martin, and Kurt Bauch. *Briefwechsel 1932–1975*. Edited by Almuth Heidegger. Freiburg: Karl Alber, 2010.

Heidegger, Martin, and Otto Pöggeler, *Briefwechsel 1957–1976*. Edited by Kathrin Busch and Christoph Jamme. Freiburg: Karl Alber, 2021.

Heinrich, Karl Borromäus. "Briefe aus der Abgeschiedenheit I (Tempo, Zeit und Stellungslosigkeit. Furcht vor dem Tode und Wert des Lebens)." *Der Brenner* 3, no. 10 (February 15, 1913): 460–468.

———. "Briefe aus der Abgeschiedenheit II: Die Erscheinung Georg Trakl's." *Der Brenner* 3, no. 11 (March 1, 1913): 508–516.

———. "Confiteor." *Der Brenner* 3, no. 14 (April 15, 1913): 624–644.

Held, Klaus. *Marbach-Bericht über eine neue Sichtung des Heidegger-Nachlasses*. Frankfurt: Klostermann, 2019.

Hellingrath, Norbert, von. *Zwei Vorträge: Hölderlin und die Deutschen, Hölderlins Wahnsinn*. 2nd ed. Munich: Bruckmann, 1922.

———. *Pindarübertragungen von Hölderlin: Prolegomena zu einer Erstausgabe*. Leipzig: Breitkopf & Härtel, 1910.

Herweg, Nikola. *Helen und Kurt Wolff in Marbach*. Marbach: Deutsche Schillergesellschaft, 2015.

Herzog, Werner. *A Guide for the Perplexed: Conversations with Paul Cronin*. London: Faber & Faber, 2014.

Hina, Atsuhiro. "'Die heute undurchschaubare Strategie der Liebe': Zur Trakl-Rezeption bei Ilse Aichinger." *Neue Beiträge zur Germanistik* 13, no. 1 (2014): 147–164.

Hinze, Diana Orendi. "Heidegger und Trakl: Aus dem unveröffentlichten Briefwechsel Martin Heidegger–Ludwig von Ficker." *Orbis litterarum* 32 (1977): 247–253.

Hoffman-Schwartz, Daniel. "'Étranger,' ou plutôt 'fremd': Philosophical-Poetic Nationalism in Derrida's *Geschlecht III* and Beyond." *Philosophy Today* 64, no. 2 (Spring 2020): 361–378.

Hölderlin, Friedrich. *Dramen und Übersetzungen*. Edited by Wilhelm Böhm. Jena: Diederichs, 1905.

———. *Gedichte*. Edited by Paul Ernst. Jena: Diederichs, 1905.

———. *Hölderlins Christus-Hymnen: Text und Auslegung*. Edited by Eduard Lachmann. Vienna: Herold, 1951.

———. *Hymnen*. Edited by Eduard Lachmann. Frankfurt: Klostermann, 1938.

———. *Hyperion: Mit Einleitung und Auswahl seiner Briefe*. Edited by Wilhelm Böhm. Jena: Diederichs, 1905.

———. *Sämtliche Werke und Briefe in drei Bänden*. Edited by Michael Knaupp. 3 vols. Munich: Hanser, 2019.

Holzner, Johann. "Lyrik im Umfeld von Trakls 'Grodek.'" In *Georg Trakl und die literarische Moderne*, edited by Károly Csúri, 235–248. Tübingen: Niemeyer, 2009.

Homer. *The Iliad*. Translated by Alexander Pope. Chicago: Belford, 1884.

Huder, Walther. "Der Dichter—Zeiger der Weltenuhr: Über Georg Trakl. Zur 50. Wiederkehr seines Todestages." *Welt und Wort* 19 (1964): 331–335.

Ireland, Julia A. "Heidegger's *Hausfreund* and the Re-enchantment of the Familiar." *Gatherings* 7 (2017): 142–163.

Janik, Allan. "Carl Dallago and the Early Brenner." *Modern Austrian Literature* 11, no. 2 (1978): 1–17.

———. "Carl Dallago und Martin Heidegger: Über Anfang und Ende des 'Brenner.'" In *Untersuchungen zum "Brenner,"* edited by Walter Methlagl, Eberhard Sauermann, and Sigurd Paul Scheichl, 21–34. Salzburg: Müller, 1981.

———. "'Ethik und Äesthetik sind Eins': Wittgenstein and Trakl." *Modern Austrian Literature* 23, no. 2 (1990): 55–70.

———. "Wittgenstein: Ein österreichisches Rätsel." *Das Fenster* 38 (Autumn 1985): 3714–3719.

Janik, Allan, and Stephen Toulmin. *Wittgenstein's Vienna*. Chicago: Dee, 1996.

Jaspers, Karl. "Wahrheit und Unheil der Bultmannschen Entmythologisierung." *Merkur* 7, no. 11 (69) (1953): 1001–1022 and 7, no. 12 (70) (1953): 1108–1126.

Jünger, Ernst. *Der Arbeiter* (1932). In *Sämtliche Werke*, Vol. 10: *Essays II*, 9–317. Stuttgart: Klett-Cotta, 2015.

———. *Blätter und Steine*. Hamburg: Hanseatische Verlagsanstalt, 1934.

———. "Über die Linie." In *Anteile: Martin Heidegger zum 60. Geburtstag*, 245–284. Frankfurt: Klostermann, 1950.

Jünger, Friedrich Georg. "Trakls Gedichte." *Text + Kritik* 4/4a, 3rd ed. (January 1973): 2–15. First published in 1964.

Kaiser, Gerhard. "Brot und Wein: Epiphanie statt Kommunion." In *Gedichte von Georg Trakl*, edited by Hans-Georg Kemper, 142–153. Stuttgart: Reclam, 1999.

Kamuf, Peggy. *Book of Addresses*. Stanford, CA: Stanford University Press, 2005.

Keiling, Tobias. "Dwelling after 1945: Heidegger among the Architects." In *Heidegger and the Human*, edited by Jeff Malpas and Ingo Farin. Albany, NY: SUNY Press, 2022.

Kemper, Hans-Georg, ed. *Interpretationen: Gedichte von Georg Trakl*. Stuttgart: Reclam, 1999.

Killy, Walther. "Gedichte im Gedicht. Beschäftigung mit Trakl-Handschriften." *Merkur* 12, no. 12 (130) (December 1958): 1108–1121.

———. *Wandlungen des lyrischen Bildes*. 5th ed. Göttingen: Vandenhoeck & Ruprecht, 1967.

Kierkegaard, Søren. *Der Pfahl im Fleisch*. Translated by Theodor Haecker. Innsbruck: Brenner, 1914. First published in *Der Brenner* 4, no. 16 (May 15, 1914): 691–712, and no. 17 (July 1, 1914): 797–814.

———. *Eighteen Upbuilding Discourses*. Edited and translated by Howard V. Hong and Edna H. Hong. Princeton, NJ: Princeton University Press, 1992.

Kießig, Martin. "Kristallene Tränen, geweint um die bittere Welt: Georg Trakl zum Gedächtnis." *Bücherwurm* 25, nos. 4–5 (1939): 70–73.

Kiessling, Friedrich. "Fruchtbare Zerrissenheit: Der *Merkur* in der frühen Bundesrepublik." *Zeitschrift für Ideengeschichte* 8, no. 1 (Spring 2014): 87–100.

Kisiel, Theodore. "Notes for a Work on the 'Phenomenology of Religious Life' (1916–19)." In *A Companion to Heidegger's Phenomenology of Religious Life*, edited by S. J. McGrath and Andrzej Wierciński, 309–328. Amsterdam: Rodolpi, 2010.

———. "The Siting of Hölderlin's 'Geheimes Deutschland' in Heidegger's Poetizing of the Political." In *Heidegger und der Nationalsozialismus II: Interpretationen*, edited by Alfred Denker and Holger Zaborowski, 145–154. Freiburg: Alber, 2009.

Kisiel, Theodore, and Thomas Sheehan, eds., *Becoming Heidegger: On the Trail of his Early Occasional Writings, 1910–1927*. 2nd ed. London: Routledge, 2009.

Klessinger, Hanna. "Schuld und Erlösung: Zur Dostojewskij-Rezeption in Georg Trakls Lyrik." *Jahrbuch der Deutschen Dostojewskij-Gesellschaft* 20 (2013): 32–50.

Klettenhammer, Sieglinde. "Hans Limbach als Schriftsteller und 'Brenner'-Leser." *Mitteilungen aus dem Brenner-Archiv* 5 (1986): 38–49.

Kluge, Friedrich. *Etymologisches Wörterbuch der deutschen Sprache*. 4th ed. Straßburg: Trübner, 1889. Translated into English by John Francis Davis. London: Bell & Sons, 1891. 25th ed., edited by Elmar Seebold. Berlin: De Gruyter, 2011.

Kommerell, Max. *Briefe und Aufzeichnungen 1919–1944*. Edited by Inge Jens. Olten: Walter, 1967.

———. "Die Sprache und das Unaussprechliche: Eine Betrachtung über Heinrich von Kleist." In *Geist und Buchstabe der Dichtung*, 243–317. Frankfurt: Klostermann, 2009.

———. "Hölderlin's Empedocles Poems." Translated by Christopher D. Merwin and Margot Wielgus. In *Philosophers and Their Poets: Reflections on the Poetic Turn in Philosophy since Kant*, edited by Charles Bambach and Theodore George. Albany, NY: SUNY Press, 2019.

———. "Immermann und das neunzehnte Jahrhundert." In *Essays, Notizen, poetische Fragmente*. Edited by Inge Jens, 187–222. Olten: Walter, 1969.

———. *Jean Paul*. 5th ed. Frankfurt: Klostermann, 1977.

———. "Vom Wesen des lyrischen Gedichts." In *Gedanken über Gedichte*, 4th ed., 9–56. Frankfurt: Klostermann, 1985.

Kudszus, W. G. *Poetic Process*. Lincoln: University of Nebraska Press, 1995.

Kunisch, Hans-Peter. *Todtnauberg: Die Geschichte von Paul Celan, Martin Heidegger und ihrer unmöglichen Begegnung*. Munich: dtv, 2020.

Kurrik, Maire Jaanus. *Georg Trakl*. New York: Columbia University Press, 1974.

Krell, David Farrell. "Derrida, Heidegger, and the Magnetism of the Trakl House." *Philosophy Today* 64, no. 2 (Spring 2020): 281–304.

———. *Lunar Voices: Of Tragedy, Poetry, Fiction, and Thought*. Chicago: University of Chicago Press, 1995.

———. *Phantoms of the Other: Four Generations of Derrida's Geschlecht*. New York: State University of New York Press, 2015.

———. "Schlag der Liebe, Schlag des Todes: On a Theme in Heidegger and Trakl." *Research in Phenomenology* 7 (1977): 238–258.

———. "We, the Unborn: On Derrida's *Geschlecht III*." *Research in Phenomenology* 51, no. 1 (2021): 1–19.

Lachmann, Eduard. "Ende des Brenner." *Merkur* 8, no. 10 (80) (October 1954): 993–995.

———. "Hölderlin und das Christliche." *Der Brenner* 17 (1948): 171–189.

———. *Kreuz und Abend: Eine Interpretation der Dichtungen Georg Trakls*. Salzburg: Müller, 1954.

———. "Trakl und Hölderlin: Eine Deutung." In Georg Trakl, *Nachlass und Biographie: Gedichte, Briefe, Bilder, Essays*, 161–212. Salzburg: Müller, 1949.

Lacoue-Labarthe, "Présentation," in Martin Heidegger, *La pauvreté (die Armut)*, 7–52. Strasbourg: Presses universitaires de Strasbourg, 2004.

Land, Nick. "Narcissism and Dispersion in Heidegger's 1953 Trakl Interpretation." In *Fanged Noumena: Collected Writings 1987–2007*, edited by Robin Mackay and Ray Brassier, 81–122. New York: Sequence, 2019.

Lasker-Schüler, Else. *Die gesammelten Gedichte*. Leipzig: Weiße Bücher, 1917.

Leitgeb, Josef. "Die Trakl-Welt: Zum Sprachbestand der Dichtungen Georg Trakls." *Wort im Gebirge* 3 (1951): 7–39.

Laitinen, Kauko. "A War-time Guest Lecturer in Helsinki—in Memory of Professor Tsutomu Kuwaki (1913–2000)." In *Yoki hito wo shinobu. Ko Kuwaki Tsutomu shi tsuitou bunshu* (Tokyo: Hokuou Bunka Kyoukai, 2002), 62–63.

Levinas, Emmanuel. *Humanism of the Other*. Translated by Nidra Poller. Urbana: University of Illinois Press, 2006.

———. *Otherwise Than Being: Or Beyond Essence*. Translated by Alphonso Lingis. Pittsburgh: Duquesne University Press, 1998.

Lindenberger, Herbert. "Georg Trakl and Rimbaud: A Study in Influence and Development." *Comparative Literature* 10 (1958): 21–35.

Lyon, James K. "Altered States of Consciousness: Trakl and the Mystical Experience." In *Internationales Georg Trakl Symposium*, edited by Joseph Strelka, 78–93. Frankfurt: Lang, 1984.

———. "Georg Trakl's Poetry of Silence." *Monatshefte* 62, no. 4 (Winter 1970): 340–356.

Malabou, Catherine. "Négativité dialectique et douleur transcendantale: La lecture heideggerienne de Hegel dans le tome 68 de la Gesamtausgabe." *Archives de philosophie* 66, no. 2 (Spring 2003): 265–278.

Mann, Klaus. *Der Wendepunkt: Ein Lebensbericht*. Frankfurt: Fischer, 1963.

Marder, Elissa. "Still (Un)Born: Derrida, Heidegger, Trakl." *Philosophy Today* 64, no. 2 (Spring 2020): 343–360.

McLary, Laura A. "The Incestuous Sister or the Trouble with Grete." *Modern Austrian Literature* 33, no. 1 (2000): 29–65.

McNeill, William. "Heidegger's Hölderlin Lectures." In *The Bloomsbury Companion to Heidegger*, edited by François Raffoul and Eric S. Nelson, 233–235. New York: Bloomsbury, 2013.

———. "Life Beyond the Organism: Animal Being in Heidegger's Freiburg Lectures, 1929–30." In *Animal Others*, edited by H. Peter Steeves, 197–248. Albany, NY: SUNY Press, 1999.

———. "Remains: Heidegger and Hölderlin amid the Ruins of Time." In *Philosophers and Their Poets: Reflections on the Poetic Turn in Philosophy since Kant*, edited by Charles Bambach and Theodore George. Albany, NY: SUNY Press, 2019.

———. *The Fate of Phenomenology: Heidegger's Legacy*. Lanham, MD. Rowman & Littlefield, 2020.

McNulty, Jamie. "Heidegger and the Poets: We Need to Talk about Trakl." *Existential Analysis* 31, no. 1 (2020): 82–96.

Mendes-Flohr, Paul. "Martin Buber and Martin Heidegger in Dialogue." *The Journal of Religion* 94, no. 1 (January 2014): 2–25.

Mengaldo, Elisabetta. "Tönend von Wohllaut und weichem Wahnsinn': Religiöse Motive und elegische Dichtung bei Georg Trakl." In *Ästhetik, Religion und Säkularisierung*, Vol. 2: *Die klassische Moderne*, edited by Silvio Vietta and Stephan Porombka, 73–87. Munich: Fink, 2009.

Methlagl, Walter. *Brenner-Gespräche: Aufgezeichnet in den Jahren von 1961 bis 1967*. Edited by Christine Riccabona, Ursula A. Schneider, und Erika Wimmer. Forschungsinstitut Brenner-Archiv, Universität Innsbruck, June 2014. www.uibk.ac.at/brenner-archiv/publikationen/links/brenner_gespraeche.pdf

———. "'Der Brenner': Weltanschauliche Wandlungen vor dem ersten Weltkrieg." PhD Dissertation, Leopold-Franzens-Universität Innsbruck, 1966.

———. "Hans Limbach: 'Begegnung mit Georg Trakl.' Zur Quellenkritik," *Mitteilungen aus dem Brenner-Archiv* 4 (1985): 3–46.

———. "Nietzsche und Trakl." In *Frühling der Seele: Pariser Trakl-Symposion*, edited by Rémy Colombat and Gerald Stieg, 81–118. Innsbruck: Haymon, 1995.

———. "Theodor Haecker und 'Der Brenner.'" *Literaturwissenschaftliches Jahrbuch* 19 (1978): 199–216.

———. "'Versunken in das sanfte Saitenspiel seines Wahnsinns . . .': Zur Rezeption Hölderlins im 'Brenner' bis 1915." In *Untersuchungen zum "Brenner,"* edited by Walter Methlagl, Eberhard Sauermann, and Sigurd Paul Scheichl, 35–69. Salzburg: Müller, 1981.

Methlagl, Walter, Eberhard Sauermann, and Sigurd Paul Scheichl, eds. *Untersuchungen zum "Brenner."* Salzburg: Müller, 1981.

Meyer-Kalkus, Reinhart. "Zerwürfnis mit Nachspiel: Erinnerungen an Ingrid Strohschneider-Kohrs." In *In memoriam Ingrid Strohschneider-Kohrs*, edited by Helmut Berthold and Jürgen Stenzel, 39–50. Wolfenbüttel: Lessing-Akademie, 2016.

Meyknecht, Werner. "Das Bild des Menschen bei Georg Trakl." *Der Brenner* 15 (1934): 48–85.

———. *Das Bild des Menschen bei Georg Trakl*. Quakenbrück: Kleinert, 1935.

Michel, Robert. "Vom Podvelež." In *Die Verhüllte*, 108–135. Berlin: Fischer, 1907.

Michel, Wilhelm. *Das Leben Friedrich Hölderlins*. Frankfurt: Insel, 1967.

Mieszkowski, Jan. "The Next Word (or something like it)." *MLN* 129 (2014): 606–620.

Millington, Richard H. *Snow from Broken Eyes: Cocaine in the Lives and Works of Three Expressionist Poets*. Bern: Lang, 2012.

Milton, John. *Paradise Lost*. Edited by Scott Elledge. 2nd ed. New York: Norton, 1993.

Mitchell, Andrew J. "Contamination, Essence, and Decomposition: Heidegger and Derrida." In *French Interpretations of Heidegger: An Exceptional Reception*, edited by David Pettigrew and François Raffoul, 131–50. Albany, NY: SUNY Press, 2008.

———. "Die Politik des geheimen Deutschland: Martin Heidegger und der George-Kreis." *Existentia* 23, nos. 1–2 (2013): 41–64.

———. "Entering the World of Pain: Heidegger." *Telos: A Quarterly Journal of Critical Thought* 150 (2010): 83–96.

———. "Heidegger's Breakdown: Health and Healing Under the Care of Dr. V. E. von Gebsattel." *Research in Phenomenology* 46 (2016): 70–97.

———. "Heidegger's Later Thinking of Animality: The End of World Poverty." *Gatherings* 1 (2011): 74–85.

———. "Heidegger's Poetics of Relationality." In *Interpreting Heidegger: Critical Essays*, edited by Daniel O. Dahlstrom, 217–231. Cambridge: Cambridge University Press, 2011.

———. *The Fourfold: Reading the Late Heidegger*. Evanston, IL: Northwestern University Press, 2015.

Moore, Ian Alexander. *Eckhart, Heidegger, and the Imperative of Releasement*. Albany, NY: SUNY Press, 2019.

———. "Homesickness, Interdisciplinarity, and the Absolute: Heidegger's Relation to Schlegel and Novalis." In *Brill's Companion to German Romantic Philosophy*, edited by Elizabeth Millán and Judith Norman, 280–310. Leiden: Brill, 2019.

———. "Memory and Mystical Detachment in Paul Celan's Eckhart-Poems," *Essays in Medieval Studies* 36 (forthcoming 2022).

———. "On the History and Future of Heidegger's Literary Estate, with Newly Published Passages on Nazism and Judaism: A Review of Klaus Held's *Marbach-Bericht*." *Gatherings: The Heidegger Circle Annual* 10 (2020): 222–238.

———. "Science, Thinking, and the Nothing as Such: On the Newly Discovered Original Version of Heidegger's 'What Is Metaphysics?'" *Review of Metaphysics* 72 (March 2019): 529–562.

———. "'statt aller / Ruhe': Divine Dispossession in Celan's Critique of Eckhart," *International Yearbook for Hermeneutics* 20 (2021): 306–330.
Morat, Daniel. *Von der Tat zur Gelassenheit: Konservatives Denken bei Martin Heidegger, Ernst Jünger und Friedrich Georg Jünger, 1920–1960.* Göttingen: Wallstein, 2008.
Moreiras, Alberto. "'Another Topology for New Tasks' (Derrida, *Of Spirit* 132–33): Derrida on Heidegger on Trakl. Zusage." *Política común* 14 (2020). https://quod.lib.umich.edu/p/pc/12322227.0014.005?view=text;rgn=main
Morgan, Ben. "Georg Trakl (1887–1914) in Context: Poetry and Experience in the Cultural Debates of the Brenner Circle." *Oxford German Studies* 41, no. 3 (December 2012): 327–347.
Most, Glenn W. "Heidegger's Greeks." *Arion: A Journal of Humanities and the Classics* 10, no. 1 (Spring–Summer 2002): 83–98.
Mullins, David Michael. "Count Heidegger." *Política común* 14 (2020). https://quod.lib.umich.edu/p/pc/12322227.0014.003/--count-heidegger?rgn=main;view=fulltext
Murdoch, Brian. *The Apocryphal Adam and Eve in Medieval Europe: Vernacular Translations and Adaptions of the* Vita Adae et Evae. Oxford: Oxford University Press, 2009.
Muschg, Walter. *Die Zerstörung der deutschen Literatur.* Bern: Francke, 1956.
———. *Von Trakl bis Brecht: Dichter des Expressionismus.* Munich: Piper, 1961.
———. *Pamphlet und Bekenntnis: Aufsätze und Reden.* Edited by Peter André Bloch in collaboration with Elli Muschg-Zollikofer. Olten: Walter, 1968.
Neske, Günther. "Nachwort des Herausgebers." In *Erinnerung an Martin Heidgger*, edited by Günther Neske, 293–302. Pfullingen: Neske, 1977.
Neri, Matteo. *Das abendländische Lied: Georg Trakl.* Würzburg: Königshausen & Neumann, 1996.
Nielsen, Cathrin. "Der Schmerz: Zu Heideggers Trakl-Deutung." In *Das Spätwerk Heideggers: Ereignis–Sage–Geviert*, edited by Damir Barbarić, 143–62. Würzburg: Königshausen und Neumann, 2007.
Nietzsche, Friedrich. *Kritische Studienausgabe.* Edited by Giorgio Colli and Mazzino Montinari. 15 vols. Munich: Deutscher Taschenbuch, 1999.
Noack, Hermann. "Gespräch mit Martin Heidegger." *Anstöße: Berichte aus der Arbeit der Evangelischen Akademie Hofgeismar* 1, no. 2 (1954): 30–37.
Novák, Aleš. *Heideggers Bestimmung des Bösen.* Nordhausen: Bautz, 2011.
Novalis. *Gedichte, Die Lehrlinge zu Sais.* Edited by Johannes Mahr. Stuttgart: Reclam, 1984.
———. *Heinrich von Ofterdingen.* In *Schriften*, edited by Ludwig Tieck and Fr. Schlegel. 5th ed. Part One. Berlin: Reimer, 1837.
Ortega y Gasset, José. "Anejo: En torno al 'Coloquio de Darmstadt, 1951.'" In *Obras completas*, Vol. 9, 2nd ed., 625–644. Madrid: Revista de Occidente, 1965.

Otto, Rudolf. *Das Heilige: Über das Irrationale in der Idee des Göttlichen und sein Verhältnis zum Rationalen*. Breslau: Trewendt und Granier, 1917.

Palmier, Jean-Michel. "*Entretien avec Jean-Michel Palmier*, réalisé par Peter Živadinović (en 1980)." In *Jean-Michel Palmier: Arts et société*, edited by Dominique Berthet and Jean-Marc Lachaud, 77–118. Paris: L'Harmattan, 2012.

———. "Préface à la nouvelle édition (1987)." In *Situation de Georg Trakl*, 17–23. Paris: Belfond, 1987.

———. *Situation de Georg Trakl*. Paris: Pierre Belfond, 1972.

———. "Situation de Georg Trakl." PhD Dissertation, Université Paris-Nanterre, 1970.

Panzig, Erik A. "*gelâzenheit* und *abegescheidenheit*—zur Verwurzelung beider Theoreme im theologischen Denken Meister Eckharts." In Andreas Speer and Lydia Wegener, eds., *Meister Eckhart in Erfurt*, 334–356. Berlin: De Gruyter, 2005.

Paul, Hermann. *Deutsches Wörterbuch*. Halle: Niemeyer, 1897.

Pestalozzi, Karl. "Einzelinterpretation und literaturwissenschaftliche Synthese bei Emil Staiger." In *1955–2005: Emil Staiger und* Die Kunst der Interpretation *heute*, edited by Joachim Rickes, Volker Ladenthin, and Michael Baum, 13–30. Bern: Lang, 2007.

Peters, Wolfgang A. "Durch Sprechen zur Sprache." *Die Zeit* (26 October 1950). www.zeit.de/1950/43/durch-sprechen-zur-sprache?utm_referrer=https%3A%2F%2Fwww.google.com%2F

Petzet, Heinrich Wiegand. *Auf einen Stern zugehen: Begegnungen und Gespräche mit Martin Heidegger 1929–1976*. Frankfurt: Societäts-Verlag, 1983.

———. "'. . . Reif ist die Traube / Und festlich die Luft . . .': Zu einem Bilde von Juan Gris." In *Martin Heidegger zum siebzigsten Geburtstag: Festschrift*, edited by Günther Neske, 239–248. Pfullingen: Neske, 1959.

Phillips, James. *Heidegger's Volk: Between National Socialism and Poetry*. Stanford, CA: Stanford University Press, 2005.

Pimentel, Dror. *Heidegger with Derrida: Being Written*. Translated by Nessa Olshansky-Ashtar. Cham: Palgrave Macmillan, 2019.

Pindar. *Die Dichtungen und Fragmente*. Translated by Ludwig Wolde. Leipzig: Dieterich, 1942.

———. *Pindar*. Translated by Franz Dornseiff. Leipzig: Insel, 1921.

———. *Pindari carmina cum fragmentis*. Edited by Hervicus Maehler. 2 vols. Leipzig: Teubner, 1971.

Pinthus, Kurt, ed. *Menschheitsdämmerung: Ein Dokument des Expressionismus*. Hamburg: Rowohlt, 1959. First published in 1920 with the subtitle *Symphonie jüngster Dichtung*.

Plath, Sylvia. *Collected Poems*. Edited by Ted Hughes. New York: Harper & Row, 1981.

Plato. *Plato's Republic: The Greek Text*. Vol. 1. Edited by B. Jowett and Lewis Campbell. Oxford: Clarendon, 1894.

Podewils, Clemens: "Erörterung eines Trakl-Gedichts." *Die Neue Zeitung* (October 11–12, 1952).

Pöggeler, Otto. "Neue Wege mit Heidegger?" *Philosophische Rundschau* 29, nos. 1–2 (1982): 39–71.

Polt, Richard. *Time and Trauma: Thinking through Heidegger in the Thirties*. London: Roman & Littlefield, 2019.

Pound, Ezra. *ABC of Reading*. London: Faber and Faber, 1961.

Powell, Jeffrey. "The Way to Heidegger's 'Way to Language.'" In *Heidegger and Language*, edited by Jeffrey Powell, 180–200. Bloomington: Indiana University Press, 2013.

Powell, Jeffrey, ed. *Heidegger and Language*. Bloomington: Indiana University Press, 2013.

Rainer, Ulrike. "Georg Trakls 'Elis'-Gedichte: Das Problem der dichterischen Existenz." *Monatshefte* 72, no. 4 (Winter 1980): 401–415.

Raja, Srinivasa N., et al. "The Revised International Association for the Study of Pain Definition of Pain: Concepts, Challenges, and Compromises." *PAIN* 161, no. 9 (September 2020): 1976–1982.

Raffoul, François. "Sexual Difference and Gathering in *Geschlecht III*." *Philosophy Today* 64, no. 2 (Spring 2020): 325–341.

Rapaport, Herman. *Derrida on Exile and the Nation: Reading Fantom of the Other*. London: Bloomsbury, 2021.

Rey, W. H. "Heidegger–Trakl: Einstimmiges Zwiegespräch." *Deutsche Vierteljahrsschrift für Literaturwissenschaft und Geistesgeschichte* 30, no. 1 (1956): 89–136.

Rickes, Joachim, Volker Ladenthin, and Michael Baum, eds. *1955–2005: Emil Staiger und Die Kunst der Interpretation heute*. Bern: Lang, 2007.

Riese, Walther. *Das Sinnesleben eines Dichters: Georg Trakl*. Stuttgart: Pürttmann, 1928.

Rilke, Rainer Maria. *Briefe*. 2 vols. Edited by Karl Altheim. Wiesbaden: Insel, 1950.

Röck, Karl. *Tagebuch 1891–1946*. 3 vols. Edited by Christine Kofler. PhD Dissertation, Leopold Franzens Universität Innsbruck, 1975.

Roesner, Martina. "De la tautologie: Heidegger et la question de l'esprit." *Les Études philosophiques* 1 (January: 2006): 63–88.

Roi, Jim. "Open letter to David Krell." www.academia.edu/33147012/Open_Letter_to_David_Farrell_Krell-06-12-16-Final.pdf

Rosenthal, Adam D., and Rodrigo Therezo, eds. "*Geschlecht III* and the Problem of 'National Humanism.'" Special issue of *Política común* 14 (2020).

Rovini, Robert. *La fonction poétique de l'image dans l'œuvre de Georg Trakl*. Paris: Belles Lettres, 1971.

Rusch, Gebhard, and Siegfried J. Schmidt. *Das Voraussetzungssystem Georg Trakls*. Wiesbaden: Springer Fachmedien, 1983.

Safranski, Rüdiger. *Ein Meister aus Deutschland: Heidegger und seine Zeit*. Munich: Hanser, 1994.

Sappho. *If Not, Winter: Fragments of Sappho*. Translated by Anne Carson. New York: Vintage, 2002.
Sauerbruch, Ferdinand, and Hans Wenke, *Wesen und Bedeutung des Schmerzes*. 2nd ed. Frankfurt: Athanäum, 1961. First published in 1936.
Sauermann, Eberhard. *Die Rezeption Georg Trakls in Zeiten der Diktatur: Stigmatisierung, Instrumentalisierung und Anerkennung in NS-Zeit und DDR*. Innsbruck: StudienVerlag, 2016.
———. "Trakl-Lektüre aufgefunden." *Mitteilungen aus dem Brenner-Archiv* 7 (1988): 58–59.
———. "Zu Valenzverstößen in poetischer Sprache: Befremdende Transitivierungen bei Georg Trakl." In *Studien zur deutschen Grammatik*, edited by Erwin Koller and Hans Moser, 335–356. Innsbruck: Inst. für Germanistik, 1985.
———. "Zur Authentizität in der Trakl-Rezeption: Zugleich eine Antwort auf Methlagls Untersuchung des Limbach-Gesprächs in 'Erinnerung an Georg Trakl.'" *Mitteilungen aus dem Brenner-Archiv* 5 (1986): 3–37.
Savage, Robert. *Hölderlin after the Catastrophe: Heidegger–Adorno–Brecht*. Rochester, NY: Camden, 2008.
Schaber, Johannes. "Der Theologiestudent Martin Heidegger und sein Dogmatikprofessor Carl Braig." *Freiburger Diözesanarchiv* 125 (2005): 332–347.
Schade, Oscar. *Altdeutsches Wörterbuch*. Halle: Waisenhaus, 1866.
Schelling, Friedrich Wilhelm Joseph. *Philosophische Untersuchungen über das Wesen der menschlichen Freiheit und die damit zusammenhängenden Gegenstände*. Edited by Thomas Buchheim. 2nd ed. Hamburg: Meiner, 2011. Translated by Jeff Love and Johannes Schmidt as *Philosophical Investigations into the Essence of Human Freedom*. Albany, NY: SUNY Press, 2006.
Schildt, Axel. *Medien-Intellektuelle in der Bundesrepublik*. Edited by Gabriele Kandzora and Detlef Siegfried. Göttingen: Wallstein, 2020.
Schlier, Paula. "Geburt der Dichtung." *Der Brenner* 17 (1948): 9–16.
Schlosshotel Bühlerhöhe, ed. *Die Geschichte der Bühlerhöhe: 1913–1993*. Bühl: Schlosshotel Bühlerhöhe, n.d.
Schmidt, Dennis J. *Between Word and Image: Heidegger, Klee, and Gadamer on Gesture and Genesis*. Bloomington: Indiana University Press, 2013.
———. "Black Milk and Blue: Celan and Heidegger on Pain and Language." In *Wordtraces: Readings of Paul Celan*, edited by Aris Fioretos, 110–129. Baltimore: Johns Hopkins University Press, 1994.
Schmitt, Hans-Jürgen, ed. *Die Expressionismusdebatte: Materialien zu einer marxistischen Realismuskonzeption*. Frankfurt: Suhrkamp, 1987.
Schopenhauer, Arthur. *Die Welt als Wille und Vorstellung*. 4 vols. Zurich: Diogenes, 2017.
Schürmann, Reiner. *Des hégémonies brisées*. 2nd ed. Zurich: Diaphanes, 2017. *Broken Hegemonies*. Translated by Reginald Lilly. Bloomington: Indiana University Press, 2003.

———. "'Only Proteus Can Save Us Now': On Anarchy and Broken Hegemonies." Edited by Francesco Guercio and Ian Alexander Moore. *Graduate Faculty Philosophy Journal* 42, no. 1 (2021): 53–90.
Seebold, Elmar. *Chronologisches Wörterbuch des deutschen Wortschatzes*, Vol. 2: *Der Wortschatz des 9. Jahrhunderts*. Berlin: De Gruyter, 2008.
Sembera, Richard. "Unterwegs zum Abend-Lande: Heideggers Sprachweg zu Georg Trakl." PhD Dissertation, Albert-Ludwigs-Universität zu Freiburg i. Br., 2002.
Sharp, Francis Michael. "On Reading Trakl." In *Internationales Georg Trakl-Symposium*, edited by Joseph Strelka, 154–161. Bern: Lang, 1984.
Silesius, Angelus. *Cherubinischer Wandersmann*. Edited by Louise Gnädinger. Stuttgart: Reclam, 1984.
Smith, David Nowell. *Sounding/Silence: Martin Heidegger at the Limits of Poetics*. New York: Fordham University Press, 2013.
Sokel, Walter H. *The Writer in Extremis: Expressionism in Twentieth-Century German Literature*. Stanford, CA: Stanford University Press, 1959.
Sommer, Christian. "*Das harte Geschlecht*: Derrida Reading Heidegger in *Geschlecht III*." Translated by Katie Chenoweth. *Philosophy Today* 64, no. 2 (Spring 2020): 441–449.
Speidel, Hans. *Aus unserer Zeit: Erinnerungen*. Frankfurt: Propyläen, 1977.
Staiger, Emil. *Die Kunst der Interpretation: Studien zur deutschen Literaturgeschichte*. Zurich: Atlantis, 1955.
———. "Zu einem Gedicht Georg Trakls." *Euphorion* 55 (1961): 279–296.
Steiner, George. *Martin Heidegger*. Chicago: University of Chicago Press, 1989.
Stieg, Gerald. *Der Brenner und die Fackel: Ein Beitrag zur Wirkungsgeschichte von Karl Kraus*. Salzburg: Müller, 1976.
———. "'Frühling der Seele.'" In *Frühling der Seele: Pariser Trakl-Symposion*, edited by Rémy Colombat and Gerald Stieg, 163–168. Innsbruck: Haymon, 1995.
———. "Une lettre de Heidegger à Jean-Michel Palmier (de 1972) justifie-t-elle la nouvelle édition de 'Situation de Georg Trakl' (en 1987)?" *Austriaca* 13, no. 25 (1987): 175–177.
Storck, Joachim W. "Hermeneutischer Disput: Max Kommerells Auseinandersetzung mit Martin Heideggers Hölderlin-Interpretation." In *Literaturgeschichte als Profession*, edited by Hartmut Laufhütte, 319–343. Tübingen: Narr, 1993.
———. "'Zwiesprache von Dichten und Denken'—Hölderlin bei Martin Heidegger und Max Kommerell." In *Klassiker in finsteren Zeiten—1933–1945*, Vol. 1, 345–364. Marbach: Deutsche Schillergesellschaft, 1983.
Strohschneider-Kohrs, Ingrid. "Die Entwicklung der lyrischen Sprache in der Dichtung Georg Trakls." *Literaturwissenschaftliches Jahrbuch der Görresgesellschaft* 1 (1960): 211–226.
———. "Ein Gedicht Georg Trakls." *Studium Generale* 5, no. 2 (1952): 69–74.

———. *Fast schon jenseits der Welt: Georg Trakls Gedicht "Klage."* Warmbronn: Keicher, 2010.

Stroomann, Gerhard. *Aus meinem roten Notizbuch: Ein Leben als Arzt auf der Bühlerhöhe.* Edited by Heinrich W. Petzet. Frankfurt: Societäts-Verlag, 1960.

———. "Der ärztliche Rat." *Merkur* 9, no. 5 (87) (May 1955): 451–57.

———. "Karl Geiler †." *Merkur* 7, no. 10 (October 1953): 977–78.

———. "Mittwoch-Abende auf Bühlerhöhe." *Das literarische Deutschland*, 20 March 1951.

Taylor, Charles. "Heidegger on Language." In *A Companion to Heidegger*, edited by Hubert L. Dreyfus and Mark Wrathall, 433–455. Malden, MA: Blackwell, 2005.

Therezo, Rodrigo. "From Neutral Dasein to a Gentle Twofold: Sexual Difference in Heidegger and Derrida." *Philosophy Today* 63, no. 2 (Spring 2019): 491–511.

———. "Heidegger's National-Humanism: Reading Derrida's *Geschlecht* III." *Research in Phenomenology* 48 (2018): 1–28.

———. "When Silence Strikes: Derrida, Heidegger, Mallarmé." *The Oxford Literary Review* 40, no. 2 (2018): 238–262.

Theunissen, Michael. *Pindar: Menschenlos und Wende der Zeit.* Munich: Beck, 2000.

Thomä, Dieter. *Die Zeit des Selbst und die Zeit danach: Zur Kritik der Textgeschichte Martin Heideggers 1910–1976.* Frankfurt: Suhrkamp, 1990.

———. "Sprache: Von der 'Bewandtnisganzheit' zum 'Haus des Seins.'" In *Heidegger Handbuch: Leben–Werk–Wirkung*, 2nd ed., edited by Dieter Thomä, 295–304. Stuttgart: Metzler, 2013.

Thomas Aquinas. *Opera omnia S. Thomae.* www.corpusthomisticum.org

Thonhauser, Gerhard. *Ein rätselhaftes Zeichen: Zum Verhältnis von Martin Heidegger und Søren Kierkegaard.* Berlin: De Gruyter, 2016.

Tezuka, Tomio. "An Hour with Heidegger." In Reinhard May, *Heidegger's Hidden Sources: East Asian Influences on His Work*, translated by Graham Parkes, 59–64. London: Routledge, 1996.

Trakl, Georg. *Aus goldenem Kelch: Die Jugenddichtungen.* 2nd ed. Salzburg: Müller, 1939.

———. *Die Dichtungen.* 6th ed. [Edited by Wolfgang Schneditz.] Salzburg: Müller, 1938.

———. *Die Dichtungen: Erste Gesamtausgabe.* Edited by Karl Röck. Leipzig: Wolff, 1917.

———. *Gedichte.* Leipzig: Wolff, 1913.

———. "Gedichte." *Merkur* 4, no. 7 (29) (July 1950): 760–765.

———. "Gedichte zur Erinnerung: Abendländisches Lied, Frühling der Seele, Gesang des Abgeschiedenen." *Der Brenner* 16 (1946): 11–13.

———. "Gesang des Abgeschiedenen." *Der Brenner* 4, no. 13 (April 1, 1914): 578–79.

———. "Nachgelassene Gedichte." *Merkur* 12, no. 12 (130) (December 1958): 1101–1108.

———. *Nachlass und Biographie: Gedichte, Briefe, Bilder, Essays*. Edited by Wolfgang Schneditz. Salzburg: Müller, 1949.

———. "Passion." *Der Brenner* 4, no. 10 (February 15, 1914): 431–433.

———. *Poesías*. Translated by Wolfgang von Harder, Narciso Pousa, and J. Rémy. With a study by Martin Heidegger, translated by Hernán Zucchi. Buenos Aires: Cármina, 1956.

———. *Sämtliche Werke und Briefwechsel*. Innsbrucker Ausgabe. Edited by Eberhard Sauermann und Hermann Zwerschina. 6 vols. Frankfurt/Basel: Stroemfeld/ Roter Stern, 1995–2014.

———. "Untergang." *Der Brenner* 3, no. 11 (March 1, 1913): 475.

———. "Zwei Gedichte." *Der Brenner* 3, no. 10 (February 15, 1913): 425.

Trakl, Georg, and Martin Heidegger. *Il canto dell'esule / La parola nella poesia*. Edited by Gino Zaccaria with Ivo De Gennaro. Milan: Marinotti, 2003.

Travers, Martin. "'Die Blume des Mundes': The Poetry of Martin Heidegger." *Oxford German Studies* 41, no. 1 (2012): 82–102.

Trawny, Peter. "Politik und Dichtung bei Heidegger: Stefan George und 'das geheime Deutschland.'" *Existentia* 16, nos. 1–2 (2006): 11–22.

Troeltsch, Ernst. "Zur Religionsphilosophie: Aus Anlaß des Buches von Rudolf Otto über 'Das Heilige' (Breslau 1917)." *Kant-Studien* 23 (1919): 65–76.

Uhsadel, Walter. "[Review of] Heidegger, Martin: Unterwegs zur Sprache." *Theologische Literaturzeitung* 86 (1961): 217–221.

Vallega-Neu, Daniela. *Heidegger's Poietic Writings: From* Contributions to Philosophy *to* The Event. Bloomington: Indiana University Press, 2018.

Vesper, Will. *Das harte Geschlecht*. Hamburg: Deutsche Hausbücherei, 1931.

Vezin, François. "Trakl au pays de Rimbaud." *Heidegger Studies* 1 (1985): 129–135.

Vietta, Egon. *Die Seinsfrage bei Martin Heidegger*. Stuttgart: Schwab, 1950.

———. "Die Vorträge Martin Heideggers 1949–1951." *Universitas* 6 (1951): 1359–1361.

———. *Georg Trakl: Eine Interpretation seines Werkes*. Hamburg: Ellemann, 1947.

———. "Georg Trakl in Heideggers Sicht." *Die Pforte* 5 (1953): 351–355.

———. "Martin Heidegger über Georg Trakl." *Frankfurter Allgemeine Zeitung*, October 9, 1952.

Vietta, Silvio. "Briefwechsel mit Egon Vietta." In *Benn-Handbuch: Leben–Werk–Wirkung*, edited by Christian M. Hanna and Friederike Reents, 274–275. Stuttgart: Metzler, 2016.

———. "Dialog mit den Dingen." In *Erinnerung an Martin Heidegger*, edited by Günther Neske, 233–237. Pfullingen: Neske, 1977.

———. "Egon Vietta und Gottfried Benn—Kritischer Dialog in schwierigen Zeiten." In *Gottfried Benn—Wechselspiele zwischen Biographie und Werk*, edited by Matías Martínez, 273–294. Göttingen: Wallstein, 2007.

Vietta, Silvio, ed. *Lyrik des Expressionismus*. Tübingen: Niemeyer, 1976.
Vietta, Silvio, and Hans-Georg Kemper. *Expressionismus*. Munich: Fink, 1975.
Von Herrmann, Friedrich-Wilhelm. *Wege ins Ereignis: Zu Heideggers "Beiträgen zur Philosophie."* Frankfurt: Klostermann, 1994.
Wagner, Richard. *Tristan und Isolde: Complete Orchestral Score*. New York: Dover, 1973.
Wasmuth, Helge. *Kindertageseinrichtungen als Bildungseinrichtungen: Zur Bedeutung von Bildung und Erziehung in der Geschichte der öffentlichen Kleinkinderziehung in Deutschland bis 1945*. Bad Heilbrunn: Kinkhardt, 2011.
Weininger, Otto. *Geschlecht und Charakter: Eine prinzipielle Untersuchung*. 10th ed. Vienna: Wilhelm Braumüller, 1908.
Welte, Bernhard. "Erinnerung an ein spätes Gespräch." In *Martin Heidegger/Bernhard Welte: Briefe und Begegnungen*, edited by Alfred Denker and Holger Zaborowski, 147–150. Stuttgart: Klett-Cotta, 2003.
Weichselbaum, Hans. "Ein überraschender Fund: Georg Trakls Gedicht *Hölderlin*," *Mitteilungen aus dem Brenner-Archiv* 35 (2016): 169–172.
———. " 'Eine bleiche Maske mit drei Löchern': Zu Georg Trakls Selbstporträt." *Mitteilungen aus dem Brenner-Archiv* 31 (2012): 37–43.
———. *Georg Trakl: Eine Biographie*. Salzburg: Müller, 2014.
———. "Unbekannte Gedichte und Prosa Georg Trakls entdeckt." In *Autorschaft und Poetik in Texten und Kontexten Georg Trakls*, edited by Uta Degner, Hans Weichselbaum, and Norbert Christian Wolf, 405–423. Salzburg: Müller, 2016.
Wild, Heinrich, ed. "Der Brenner-Verlag: Eine Gesamtbibliographie. 1910–1954." In *Nachrichten aus dem Kösel-Verlag: "Der Brenner": Leben und Fortleben einer Zeitschrift*, 30–44. Munich: Kösel, n.d.
Wild, Markus. "Heidegger and Trakl: Language Speaks in the Poet's Poem." In *Paths in Heidegger's Later Thought*, edited by Günter Figal et al., 45–63. Bloomington: Indiana University Press, 2020.
———. "Heidegger, Staiger, Muschg: Warum lesen wir?" In *Heidegger und die Literatur*, edited by Günter Figal, 107–130. Frankfurt: Klostermann, 2012.
Wills, David. "Which Way Back (way back)?" *Philosophy Today* 64, no. 2 (Spring 2020): 451–465.
Windelband, Wilhelm. *Präludien: Aufsätze und Reden zur Philosophie und ihrer Geschichte*. 2 vols. 6th ed. Tübingen: Mohr, 1919.
Wittgenstein, Ludwig. *Geheime Tagebücher 1914–1916*. Edited by Wilhelm Baum. Vienna: Turia & Kant, 1991.
Wolfson, Elliot R. *Heidegger and Kabbalah: Hidden Gnosis and the Path of Poiēsis*. Bloomington: Indiana University Press, 2019.
Xolocotzi, Ángel. *Facetas Heideggerianas*. Mexico: Los libros de Homero, 2009.
Yu, Pauline. "The Poetics of Discontinuity: East-West Correspondences in Lyric Poetry." *PMLA* 94, no. 2 (March 1979): 261–274.

Ziarek, Krzysztof. *Language after Heidegger*. Bloomington: Indiana University Press, 2013.
Zhuangzi. *The Complete Works of Zhuangzi*. Translated by Burton Watson. New York: Columbia University Press, 2013.
Zweig, Stefan. *Die Welt von Gestern: Erinnerungen eines Europäers*. Frankfurt: Fischer e-books.
Zwerschina, Hermann. "'Erinnerungen' an Georg Trakl und 'Erinnerungslücken': Probleme ihrer Edition." In *Edition von autobiographischen Schriften und Zeugnissen zur Biographie*, edited by Jochen Golz, 264–76. Tübingen: Niemeyer, 2012.

Index

Abendland (German noun), 2, 4, 9–10, 30, 62–63, 99–101, 107, 185, 195, 199, 213, 327n18, 329n24; as distinct from the temporally more primordial notion of *Abend-Land*, 202; as more primordial notion than those of West or Occident, 39
Abraham, 86–87
absence, 55, 65, 74, 158
Achilles, 148
Adenauer, Konrad, 13, 202
Adorno, Theodor, 15, 213, 323n52
Aeschylus: his *Agamemnon*, 334n17
aesthetic: beauty, 55; escapism, 71; satisfaction, 70; status of colors, 163
Allemann, Beda, 18, 258, 308n31, 317n11
Agamben, Giorgio, 47, 175
alētheia/a-lētheia (Greek noun), 55, 111, 128, 131, 155–156, 162, 336n37
algontology, 130, 134
algos (Greek noun), 111, 119, 130–133
alienation, 86, 117, 122, 128, 134, 212, 325n9, 326n13
anarchy, 4, 106, 131, 213
Anaximander, 146
androgyny, 175, 187, 347–348n25

animal(s), 2, 5, 37, 48, 89–90, 151, 157, 174–175, 185, 188–189, 193–200, 206, 213, 344n2, 344n5, 345n9, 348–349n35
animal rationale (Latin phrase), 114, 122
animality, 82, 175, 195–200, 348n34; humanimality, 199–200
anthropology, 32, 205, 269
anxiety, 117, 178
appropriative event (*Ereignis*), 111, 118, 127, 134, 156, 162, 209, 339n13
Aquinas. See Thomas Aquinas, Saint
Arendt, Hannah, 8–9, 245, 262–263, 346n19
Aristophanes, 112
Aristotle, 320n21, 335n37; Plato and, 334n18; Thomas Aquinas and, 113, 122;
—works: *De anima*, 104; *Metaphysics*, 334n20
Aristotelianism, 173, 334n18
Athena (Greek goddess), 149, 339n14
atonement (*Sühne*), 5, 15, 70, 78, 95, 321–322n45; *See also* expiation
attunement, 155
Augustine, Saint, 55, 108;
—works: *De civitate dei*, 332n48

Austria(n), xiv, 1, 2, 4, 11, 18, 21, 31, 48, 72, 85, 102, 144, 154, 175, 212–213, 266, 333n10
autobiography, 3, 35, 39

Baader, Franz Xaver von, 204, 206, 351n8
Bach, Johann Sebastian, 75;
—works: *Matthäus-Passion*, 190
Bacon, Francis, 121
Badiou, Alain, 8
Bambach, Charles, 303n4, 351n2, 351n3
Baptism, 204, 349n3
Barth, Emil, 21, 34, 309n39, 310n42
Basil, Otto, 32, 333n10
Bauch, Kurt, 17, 244, 333n11
Baumann, Gerhart, 261–262
Bayerische Akademie der Schönen Künste, 12
Beauvoir, Simone de, 182;
—works: *Das andere Geschlecht*, 182
beget (English verb), 137, and *Geschlecht*, 174–175; and *austragen*, 56, 58, 186; *See also* birth, unborn
being (*Sein*): and/as pain, 4, 59, 111–112, 116–119, 121–127, 129–135, 137, 201–202, 205, 207, 333n4, 336n37
beings (*Seiendes*): in their difference from being, 59, 117, 124, 127, 143, 200; as a whole, 121, 149
Benjamin, Walter, 47, 81, 316n5
Benn, Gottfried, 15, 17, 62, 212, 250–251, 253, 308n32, 310n44, 311–312n46, 319–320n21, 352n6
Bense, Max, 15, 308n31
Benz, Richard, 14
Bergson, Henri, 248
Bernard, Claude, 121
Bernasconi, Robert, 112

beyng (*Seyn*): as distinct from being (*Sein*), 111, 117, 125
Bible, the, 56, 63, 71, 79, 205, 320n30, 326n10, 349n3, 350n6;
—Genesis: 1:2, 105; 2:24, 41–42; 32:24, 77;
—Exodus: 19:5, 339n13;
—Leviticus: 25:13, 326n10;
—Deuteronomy: 4:24, 349n3;
—Psalms: 37:5, 79; 119, 85–86, 326n10; 129/130, 325n9;
—Ecclesiastes: 4:12, 91;
—Isaiah: 38:1, 75; 55:12–13, 90;
—Matthew: 3:11, 349n3; 4:3, 167; 5:3, 70, 90, 205; 11:15, 39; 18:3, 105; 19:4–6, 41; 22:42, 35, 232; 27:46, 190; 28:19–20, 136;
—Mark: 10:5–9, 41; 15:34, 190;
—Luke: 3:16, 349n3; 4:3, 167; 12:37 and 13:29, 75; 14:26, 94;
—John: 1:1, 324n63, 340n21; 3:8, 201; 10:9, 76; 14:2, 75;
—Acts: 2:3–4, 349n3;
—Romans: 5:3, 121; 6:11, 96; 6:23, 90;
—1 Corinthians: 7:9, 334n17; 15:26–28, 206; 15:28, 92; 15:55, 90; 15:55–57, 192;
—2 Corinthians: 12:7, 320n31;
—1 Thessalonians: 2:2, 135;
—Titus: 2:14, 339n13;
—Hebrews: 11:13–16, 86; 12:29, 349n3;
—1 Peter: 2:4–6, 136;
—Revelation: 2:1 and 21:21 and 22:2–3, 77; 14:3, 87
biography, 3, 12, 22, 27, 30, 32, 35, 37, 39, 69, 71, 93, 135, 164, 215, 329n25
biology, 121, 166, 174, 185, 344n5
birth, 125, 319n20, 339n14; *See also* beget, unborn

Blanchet, Vincent, 155–156, 338n7
Bloom, Harold, 306n18
blue (color), 4, 28, 68, 73, 88–90, 94, 99–100, 140, 143–144, 151, 155–163, 168, 176–177, 180, 185, 187, 189–191, 193–200, 213; See also chrusology, gold
body: and soul, 36, 43, 48, 63, 85–86, 119–121, 128, 326n10, 344n3; and blood, 47, 59, 72, 77, 213; and pain, 116, 131, 133–134, 140, 224; as a translation of Geschlecht, 92
Boehme, Jakob, 157, 171, 204, 206, 340n22, 350n8
Böhm, Wilhelm, 163, 165, 341n33
Bonaventure, Saint, 143
Boss, Medard, 17, 216, 309n37, 317n11
Braig, Carl, 248, 337n2;
—works: *On Being: An Outline of Ontology*, 143
bread: and wine, 3, 28–29, 35, 45–47, 54–55, 59, 77–78, 95, 100, 161–162, 213, 323n53, 350n6; See also Eucharist
Brenner Circle, 3, 23, 33, 35, 39, 91, 314n60
Der Brenner, 3, 9–10, 15, 23, 26, 32, 34, 40, 70–72, 108, 118, 139, 215, 243, 245, 248, 269, 305n13, 310n42, 311n45, 313n52, 315n72, 322n46, 322n49, 322n50, 329n25, 348n29
Brentano, Franz: his book *On the Manifold Meaning of Being in Aristotle*, 248
bridal. *See* marriage
Britting, Georg, 12, 22–23
brother: as figure in Trakl's poetry, 46, 66, 89–90, 92, 100, 157, 162, 165, 167, 178–179, 181, 183, 188, 212, 235, 327n18, 342n40, 345n18, 346n18
Buber, Martin, 15
Buddha, 41, 229
Bühlerhöhe (spa resort and sanatarium), 3, 12–14, 17–20, 22, 24, 26–27, 30–31, 40, 47, 50, 56, 60, 134–135, 138, 239, 241, 244–245, 251, 258, 261–262, 305n13, 306n22, 307n28, 308n32, 311n46, 317n12, 319n19, 325n5
Bultmann, Rudolf, 308n31
Buttlar, Herbert von, 20, 309n35, 317n12
Büttner, Herman, 178

Caputo, John, 332n4
causality, 61, 150, 320n28, 351n8
Celan, Paul, 4–5, 8, 15, 163, 168–169, 258, 261, 303n4, 320n23, 331n42, 333n4, 343n43, 343n46; his suicide, 168;
childhood, 89, 178, 182–183, 192
Christ (Jesus), 26, 39–41, 46–47, 56–57, 59, 65–66, 70, 75–77, 87, 91, 94, 96, 136, 188, 190, 192, 206, 209, 212, 229–231, 314n64, 321n32, 321n34, 322n46, 328n18, 339n13, 343n1; his body and blood, 47, 59, 77
Christianity, 2–3, 22, 26, 29, 35–37, 39–42, 55, 63–67, 69–71, 76, 87, 91, 95, 98, 103, 121, 136–137, 145, 153, 157, 175, 201, 204, 209, 213, 310n41, 311n46, 313n52, 316n2, 322n46, 327n18, 330n27, 334n18, 349n3; as distinct from Christendom, 35, 39, 64, 66
chrusology, 146, 152; *See also* blue, gold

Cicero, 127
Circle of Friends of European Thinking, 14
circularity, hermeneutic, 84, 117
clearing (*Lichtung*), 31, 88–89, 111, 124, 127, 139, 134, 151–152, 162, 264, 286–287
cleave (*reißen*), 59, 124–125, 129, 334n24; *See also* rift
Club zu Bremen, 12
cocaine, 1, 140, 265; *See also* drugs, narcotics
color, 63, 90, 148, 154, 157–160, 165, 175, 302n6, 340n23, 344n2; of being, 156; Celan's view of Trakl's use of, 168, 343n43; Heidegger's theory of, 144, 163; the holy and, 145, 153; light and, 143–144; poetic, 4, 213
Communion, Holy. *See* Eucharist
compassion, 37–38, 140, 208, 226, 312n46; *See also* sympathy
concealment (*lēthe*), 4, 55–56, 128, 131, 151–154, 156, 160, 187, 248, 336n37
condensation (*ge-dichten*), 28, 83–84, 324n4; *See also Gedicht*
corruption. *See* decay
cross (Christian), 56–57, 65, 71, 76, 94, 123, 136, 187, 190, 192–193, 220
crucifix. *See* cross (Christian)
countenance, 38, 91, 160, 167, 182, 184, 196, 198, 226, 231, 247

Däubler, Theodor, 23
Dallago, Carl, 40–41, 69, 91, 226–231, 315n69, 322n46, 350n6
Dante: his *Paradiso*, 202
Dasein (German noun), 118, 336n37; non-gendered status of, 340n16
de Man, Paul, 351n3

death, 37, 87, 89–90, 92, 96, 137, 140, 157–158, 169, 175, 177, 187, 193, 195, 199, 206, 212, 217, 303n1, 331n41, 342n40, 343n1, 347n25; and being, 70; as concealment, 56, 153; and/as depature, 28, 95, 98; Heidegger's, 106; and love, 2; and pain, 77–78, 114; Trakl's, 18, 30, 72, 101, 225, 345n17
decay, 1–2, 5, 23, 36–37, 43, 85, 90, 93, 96, 103, 109, 137, 141, 157–158, 167, 173, 177, 189, 197–198, 207, 212, 222, 234, 310n41, 322n46, 333n10
deconstruction, 82, 106, 117, 119, 204, 325n6, 343n41
Democratis, 334n17
Departure (*Abschied*), 4, 27, 29, 37, 95, 98, 125, 129; *See also* detachment
Derrida, Jacques, 1, 4, 7, 39, 45, 65–67, 82–83, 85, 95, 99, 101–103, 106–107, 109, 167, 174–175, 184, 188, 200–201, 203–207, 302n6, 304n5, 324n3, 327n18, 331n40, 343n41, 344n6, 345n14, 350n8;
 —works: *L'animal que donc je suis*, 200; *De l'esprit*, 201, 321n33, 350n8; *Geschlecht III*, 1, 65, 107, 201, 203, 301n1; *The Phantom of the Other*, 82
despair (*Verzweiflung*), 35, 37, 55, 63, 65, 69, 90–91, 117, 122, 232, 252, 321n32, 327n18, 336n40
destiny, 66, 107; of the West, 12, 265; of thinking and poeticizing, 47, 102
detachment (*abegescheidenheit, Abgeschiedenheit*), xiii, 4, 28, 37, 58, 81–83, 95, 98–100, 102–103,

105–109, 132, 177, 185, 208, 213, 302n6, 324n3, 331n41
Detsch, Richard, 65
Deutsches Literaturarchiv Marbach, xiv, 114, 245, 341n37
dialogue (*Gespräch*): of Heidegger with Kommerell, 47; of Heidegger with Trakl, 2, 63, 67, 101, 135, 250; of poetry with thought, 27, 102; of Trakl with Pindar, 4, 144
Dickinson, Emily, 111, 163
difference, 3, 5, 20, 42, 58, 61–62, 79, 92, 96, 112, 124–126, 143, 156–157, 167, 183–184, 186, 195–196, 198, 319n21, 326n10, 351n10; ontological, 5, 129; racial, 5, 157; sexual, 2–3, 5, 42, 66, 82, 91–92, 96, 157, 173, 175–176, 183–186, 188, 200, 213, 315n69, 327n18
Dilthey, Wilhelm, 254
Dionysius Thrax, 100, 330n26
discord (*Zwietracht*): and animality, 193, 196; of difference, 96; of *Geist*, 204; as inevitable, 201; polemical, 156; between the sexes, 42, 179, 182, 185, 197, 203
dissension, 5, 96, 98, 173, 178, 205, 214; *See also* discord
dissemination, 81, 83, 106–107, 132, 134, 167, 174, 201
divinities. *See* fourfold, god(s), godhead
Dostoevsky, Fyodor, 42, 71, 78, 254, 315n71, 322n46
—works: *The Bothers Karamazov*, 231, 321n44; *Crime and Punishment*, 42, 71, 231
downfall (*untergehen, Untergang*), 37, 91, 96, 100, 174, 184, 333n10

downgoing, 157, 181
drugs, 11, 154, 266; *See also* cocaine, narcotics
dwell (English verb), 4, 11, 13, 17, 20, 43, 46, 56, 62, 73, 85, 99, 100, 129, 130, 141, 154, 159, 162, 222, 252, 264, 327n18

earth, 4, 29, 36–37, 54, 59, 63, 76, 85–87, 89–90, 95–96, 100, 109, 154, 159, 177, 187, 194, 210, 221, 226, 234, 270–271, 325n9, 326n10, 326n13, 350n6; and sky, 20, 47, 50, 56, 77, 153, 213
East: and West, 14, 254, 309n37
Eden (Garden of), 90
Eliot, T. S., 14
Elis Fröbom (character in E. T. A. Hoffmann's "The Mines of Falun"), 190
Elisha, 190
Emerson, Ralph Waldo, 49
Endymion (in Greek mythology), 190
Es ist (phrase in Trakl's poetry), 12, 36, 85, 88, 93, 194, 241–242, 271; and *Es gibt/Il y a*, 31, 259–260
Esterle, Max von, 164
Etymologicum Magnum, 130
etymology, 1, 4, 29, 51, 82, 93, 95–96, 99–100, 112, 123–124, 126, 131–132, 134, 153, 166, 174, 178, 189, 319n16, 320n28, 330n26, 332n4, 335n32, 342n39
Eve, 46, 77, 324n57
evil, 43, 117, 167, 179, 181, 328n21, 350n6, 349n3; and innocence, 32, 90, 182, 309–310n41; and good, 36, 207, 310n41; Heidegger's analysis of, 5, 112, 204–205, 350n5; Schelling's analysis of, 206–207

Eucharist, 45, 59, 78
Europe, 14–15, 101–102, 127, 131, 329n22
experience: lived (*Erleben*), 121, 133; as German *Erfahrung*, 122
expiation, 3, 70, 328n18; *See also* atonement
expressionism, 1, 4, 8, 11, 14, 18, 144, 173, 212–213, 250, 320n21, 345n17, 352n6; understood as precursor to facism, 26, 311n45

faith, 59, 66, 86, 145, 175; and the thinking of being, 67, 69; as one of two thorns in Heidegger's side, 63; of Trakl, 40, 79, 91, 136
Fall, the, 76–77, 86, 90
Fichte, Johann Gottlieb, 39
Ficker, Ludwig von, 5, 7–9, 14, 21–23, 26–27, 30, 33–34, 40, 43, 50, 70, 79, 85, 95, 108–109, 134–135, 138–140, 164, 226, 239–240, 242, 245, 249, 255–256, 258, 261, 303n2, 304n6, 305n11, 305n13, 306n24, 310n44, 311n46, 312n47, 312n48, 313n52, 313n53, 314n64, 320n21, 321n45, 322n46, 329n25, 336n40, 336n41, 337n43, 341n33, 345n17
fire, 13, 83, 90, 204, 208, 210–211, 221, 349n3, 350n4; *See also* flame
flame, xiii, 13, 89, 129, 132, 136–137, 142, 203–204, 208–209, 213, 223, 255, 327n18
flesh (*Fleisch*), 63, 92, 158, 332n4, 350n6; One, 41–42, 91, 231
Flickenschildt, Elisabeth, 18
Focke, Alfred, 26, 135, 243, 309n41, 310n44, 311n46, 312n50, 322n46, 345n11

foreigner. *See* stranger
fourfold, the (earth, sky, divinities, mortals), 20, 47, 56–57, 59, 153–154
fremd (German adjective): as Old High German *fram* ("on the way"), 1, 29, 36, 82, 85, 93, 96, 107, 177, 194, 262
freedom: of being, 209; of the human being, 206; of the individual against all collective slogans, 14; in Schelling, 207
Friedrich, Hugo, 15, 304n6
friend: as figure in Trakl's poetry, 179, 349n35
Fühmann, Franz, 71, 111, 304n6

Gadamer, Hans-Georg, 20, 50, 309n35, 317n12
gather (verb). *See* gathering
gathering (*Versammlung*, *rassemblement*), 55–56, 83, 132, 141, 204–205, 209, 222, 240, 324n3, 339n15; of color, 158, 160, 185; and detachment, 81–84, 99, 104, 106–107; and dispersion, 3; as the *Ge-* of *Gedicht/Gewalt/Gebirge*, 52, 150, 187; gentle/peaceful, 4, 29, 96, 100, 129, 135, 150, 196, 208; gigantomachia between Derrida and Heidegger over, 167; of/and pain, 111–112, 123, 125, 130, 132–135, 201, 207–208, 349n35; and sheltering, 51; and Theia, 152
Gebsattel, V. E. von, 306n21
Gedicht (German noun), 28, 50, 52–54, 83–84, 95, 98–99, 102, 109, 178, 184, 304n6, 314n56, 318n13, 321n45, 329n25; *See also* condensation
Geiler, Karl, 14, 307n24

George, Stefan, 10, 20, 22, 35, 62, 211, 268, 301n2, 306n18, 316n5, 317n12
generation: as translation of *Geschlecht*, 5, 96, 157, 173, 184, 344n5; as translation of *Generation* as distinct from *Geschlecht*, 137, 249
gentle (*sanft*), 4, 42, 46, 54, 75–76, 87, 89, 92, 112, 123, 130, 134–135, 137, 156–159, 162–163, 165–166, 173, 179, 182, 184–185, 190, 195, 204–205, 210, 235, 249, 327n18, 339n15, 342n38; See also gentleness
gentleness (*Sanfte*), 29, 96, 129, 172, 193, 196, 198, 203, 208, 223, 232, 349n35; See also gentle
Gerhardt, Paul, 325n9
German (language): archaic, 29, 85, 93, 224; Gothic, 224; Old High, 1, 28, 83, 85, 93, 129, 166, 342n39; Middle High, 103–104, 109; modern, 102–103, 178
Germany, xiv, 8, 13, 38, 100, 102, 202, 212, 214, 225, 232, 258, 351n1; See also Secret Germany
Geschlecht, 5, 29, 32, 35–37, 42, 64, 82, 87, 91–93, 95–96, 98, 109, 115, 137, 161, 166–167, 171, 173–177, 182, 187–188, 191–192, 196–200, 207, 209, 233, 328n18, 329n23, 336n39, 343n1, 348n29, 349n4; One, 41, 91, 101, 104, 157, 167, 184–185, 187, 199, 202, 344n2
gesture, 47, 56, 316n6, 319n20; Kommerell's theory of, 48–49
Ginsberg, Ernst, 310n44
Gnosticism, 206
god(s), 26, 28–29, 36, 40–41, 43, 45, 49, 55, 64, 66–69, 71, 73, 75–77, 86, 90–92, 95, 100, 104–106, 109, 122, 129, 139, 141, 144–145, 147, 150–152, 157, 162, 165, 173, 186, 190, 206–207, 212–213, 218, 221–222, 226, 229, 235, 243–244, 247, 257, 303n2, 321n32, 322n46, 325n9, 329n25, 334n18, 338n11, 339n13, 343n1, 344n5, 349n3
godhead, 145, 147, 151–152, 160, 338n11, 340n16
Goethe, Johann Wolfgang von, 70, 123, 144, 163
gold (color), 4, 36–37, 53–54, 56–57, 59–60, 63, 66, 73, 76, 78, 109, 140–141, 144–156, 158–160, 163, 165, 168, 172, 181–183, 187, 192, 337n5, 339n11; See also blue, chrusology
grace, 75, 78, 130, 134, 182; and faith, 66; tree of (figure), 54, 56, 76–77, 153, 318n14
Greece, Ancient, 57, 121, 160, 212, 325n5
Greeks: their age understood as pinnacle of human achievement, 41, 230; their experience of being, 146, 149, 155–156, 160, 195, 270; their conception of *hubris*, 102; their poets and authors, 4, 108, 144, 150, 154, 180, 314n63, 338n7; their sailors/soldiers, 148
Gründgens, Gustaf, 18
guilt (*Schuld*), 28, 70–71, 95, 179–180, 243, 310n41, 321n44, 322n45
Günther, Johann Christian, 139

Habermas, Jürgen, 15
Haecker, Theodor, 23
hagiography, 3, 33, 35
Hamacher, Werner, 111, 207

Hamann, Johann Georg, 319n21
Hamburger, Michael, 341n36
happiness, 38–39, 121, 225, 264, 340n15; *See also* joy
Hardenberg, Karl von, 87
Hartung, Hans, 310n44
Hattingberg, Immo von, 17, 306n22
Hauser, Kaspar, 347n24
Hebbel, Christian Friedrich, 263
Hebel, Johann Peter, 10, 263, 305n14, 344n5
Hegel, Georg Wilhelm Friedrich, 21, 87, 117, 122–124, 132, 134, 207, 248, 254, 309n38, 325n10, 335n34;
—works: *The Science of Logic*, 132
Heidegger, Elfride, 258
Heidegger, Fritz, 216–217
Heidegger, Heinrich, 216, 309n37
Heidegger, Martin: color theory of, 144, 154, 163, 213; eschatology of, 207; hermeneutics of, 8, 36, 63, 66; history of being of, 201, 205, 268; marginalia of, 2–3, 5, 9, 32–33, 35, 40, 69, 97, 103, 115, 165, 171, 176, 208–209, 215–237, 319n21, 330n32, 333n10, 342n38, 345n10, 346n22; theory of difference of, 3, 58; use of etymology of, 1, 4, 29, 51, 82, 93, 95–96, 99–100, 123–124, 126, 131–132, 153, 166, 174, 319n16, 320n28, 335n32, 342n39;
—works: *Anaximander's Verdict*, 144, 146; *The Appropriative Event*, 115, 129; *Being and Time*, 32, 52, 71, 126–127, 145, 252, 264, 269, 325n6; *Beiträge*, 1, 156, 213–214, 352n9; "Bremen Lectures," 13, 17, 319n19; *Country Path Conversations*, 150; "Evening Stroll on Reichenau Island," 10–11; *Logging Paths*, 146; *Introduction to Metaphysics*, 150; "Language," 3, 7–8, 17–18, 20–21, 27, 29, 46–47, 49–51, 54, 58, 60–62, 69, 74, 79, 108, 125, 127, 144, 153–154, 239–240, 256, 303n5, 309n36, 317n11, 318n13, 318n15, 319n18, 319n19; "Language in the Poem," 1, 3–5, 7–8, 15–17, 21, 23, 27–28, 33, 42, 50–51, 62, 64, 66, 74, 82, 95, 108, 135, 138, 144, 156–157, 166, 173, 177–179, 181–182, 188, 192, 194, 196, 198–200, 203, 208, 239, 242, 245, 251, 265, 301n2, 304n5, 305n13, 312n49, 318n13, 319n18, 320n21, 327n18, 345n17, 346n22, 348n29, 348n35, 351n8; "Legacy of the Being-Question," 156; "Letter on 'Humanism,'" 15, 112, 145, 151; *Nachlass*, 9; *On Pain*, 4, 111–115, 117–118, 120, 122–126, 128–129, 133–134, 332n4, 334n18; *On the Way to Language*, 8, 47, 303n4, 309n37, 316n11, 319n18, 328n22, 336n40, 343n41; "Time and Being," 1; *What is Called Thinking?*, 15; "Wherefore Poets?," 23
Heidegger, Thomas, 216–217
Heinrich, Karl Borromäus, 34, 38, 71, 98, 178, 226, 331n41
Helios (Greek god), 147, 150–151, 339n14
Hell, 5, 40, 70, 79, 229
Hellingrath, Norbert von, 11, 211, 314n62, 337–338n5, 341n36
Heraclitus, 124, 146, 317n11, 320n24

Herder, Johann Gottfried, 319n21, 333n4; theory of language of, 20, 318n16
Hertz, Peter D., 303–304n5
Hesiod, 150;
—works: *Theogony*, 150–151
Heyer, Gustav Richard, 17
Hilpert, Heinz, 19
Hinze, Diana Orendi, 313n53
historiography, 32, 135
history, 4, 14, 32, 81, 132, 136, 198, 201, 205, 212, 215–216, 268, 344n5
Hofmannsthal, Hugo von, 21–22, 35, 62, 309n38
Hölderlin, Friedrich, 2, 8, 11, 13, 22, 39, 47, 57, 59, 67, 87, 92, 109, 112, 144, 155–156, 161, 163–164, 170, 181–182, 202, 211–213, 248, 251, 253, 263, 268, 303n3, 306n16, 306n17, 310n42, 314n62, 316n4, 320n23, 326n10, 331n43, 337n5, 341n35, 341n36, 343n40, 344n5, 346n18, 348n26, 351n2, 351–352n3, 352n5; madness of, 4, 145, 164–169, 343n46; as paragon poet, 10, 69; self-marginalia of, 33;
—works: "Der Archipelagus," 334n24; "Autumn," 337n5; "Bread and Wine," 165; "Half of Life," 306n16; "Der Ister," 128; "Mnemosyne," 128; "Patmos," 212; "Remembrance," 33, 337n5
holy, the, 4, 13, 55, 68, 77, 144–145, 148, 150–161, 163, 165, 168, 177, 196–198, 337–338n5, 346n18, 349n35
home, 23, 40, 56, 61, 72, 75, 78, 83, 85–86, 90, 96, 101, 200, 203, 213, 216–217, 226, 254, 258, 325n9, 326n10; *See also* homecoming, homeland, promised land
homecoming, 202, 236; *See also* home, homeland, promised land
homeland (*Heimat*), 2, 37, 69, 93, 96, 100, 102, 159, 197, 202, 209, 305n14, 330n34; *See also* home, homecoming, promised land
homosexuality, 66, 185, 188
Horwitz, Kurt, 21–22, 26, 34–35, 63–65, 215, 232, 310n44, 312n50, 314n64, 321n41
Horwitz, Ruth, 26, 29, 244, 310n44
humanimality, 199–200
humanism, 122; of the face, 196; national, xiv
Humboldt, Wilhelm von, 319n21
Husserl, Edmund, 117, 119, 145, 252;
—works: *Logical Investigations*, 248

idiom, 31, 51, 82, 101–102
Immermann, Karl, 20, 309n35
incest, 1, 179–180, 191–192; and Christ's crucifixion, 192; as synecdoche for sin, 191; between Trakl and his sister, 70–71; in Trakl's work, 2, 4, 65, 87, 90, 167, 179–180, 327–328n18
individuation, 178, 197–198
ineffable, the (*Unsägliche*), 49, 61; *See also* unsayable
iniquity. *See* sin
insurgency. *See* insurrection
insurrection (*Aufruhr*), xiii, 29, 96, 129, 179, 197–198, 204–209, 223
intimacy, 20, 33, 58, 62, 112, 132
Ireland, Julia, 305n14

Jaspers, Karl: critique of Rudolf Bultmann of, 308n31

Jerusalem, New, 56, 76
joy, 40, 43, 89–90, 106, 109, 137, 228, 347n25; See also happiness
Jünger, Ernst, 15, 22, 33, 112, 114–116, 118, 130–131, 311n44, 333n10, 333n12;
—works: *Leaves and Stones*, 115, 333n10; "On Pain," 116, 333n11, 334n20; "Total Mobilization," 115; *The Worker*, 113–116
Jünger, Friedrich Georg, 22–23, 258, 308n32
justice (*Gerechtigkeit*), 30, 42–43, 43, 63, 149, 231

Kafka, Franz, 212, 252
Kaspar Hauser, 347n24
Käster, Erhart, 251, 323n52
Kierkegaard, Søren, 65, 71, 118, 248
Killy, Walther, 168, 209, 218, 255–256, 314n56, 331n46, 343n43
Kleist, Heinrich von, 20, 48, 61, 317n12, 318n13
Klostermann, Vittorio, 310n44
Kluge, Friedrich, 93, 174–175, 189, 349n4
Klunker, Wilhelm, 310n44
knowing, absolute, 117, 122–123, 207
Koch, Dietmar, 113
Kokoschka, Oskar, 72, 157, 212
Kommerell, Max, 17–20, 45, 47, 50, 56, 61, 309n35, 309n36, 316n3, 316n4, 316n5, 319n21; his theory of gesture, 48–49, 316n6;
—works: "Language and the Inexpressible," 20, 48, 50, 317n12, 318n13
Krane, Wilhelm von, 310n44
Kraus, Karl, 23, 34, 54, 72–74, 79, 319n21, 322n49, 322n50, 323n52, 329n25

Krell, David, 1, 137, 179, 302n6, 327n18, 332n4, 336n39, 345n10
Kubin, Alfred, 333n10
Kunisch, Hans-Peter, 261
Kütemeyer, Wilhelm, 310n44
Kuwaki Tsutomu, 20, 309n37

Lachmann, Eduard, 21–23, 244, 310n42;
—works: *Cross and Evening*, 22, 309n41; "Trakl und Hölderlin," 320–321n32
Lacoue-Labarthe, Philippe, 211
Langen, Grete, (née Trakl), 30, 109, 140, 180, 322n46, 348n25;
—works: "Helian's Song of Fate," 347–348n25
language: as expression, 55, 153, 318–319n16, 320n21; self-speaking of, 3, 8, 53, 62, 83, 303n4, 318n16
Latin(ate), 58, 98–99, 103–104, 109, 130, 133, 137, 189, 202, 241, 268, 319n20, 329n23, 329n24, 330n34, 349n3
Lasker-Schüler, Else, 67, 345n17
Laslowski, Ernst, 242
legein (Greek verb), 111, 132–133, 242, 339n15
Leibniz, Gottfried Wilhelm, 175
Leitgeb, Josef, 23, 34, 313n52
letting-be (*Seinlassen*), xiii, 108–109, 130, 156, 158, 209, 214
Levinas, Emmanuel, 196, 313n55, 321n44, 326n10, 348n30
Liliencron, Detlev von, 70
Limbach, Hans, 34, 38, 40–42, 226, 315n69, 315n70, 346n22
Lissner, Erich, 310n44
Li-Tai-Pe, 7, 303n1
logos (Greek noun), 111, 152, 167, 317n11

Loos, Adolf, 72
love, 11, 38, 43, 54, 70, 75–76, 95, 137, 191, 196, 202, 226, 234, 315n1, 351n10; anarchic, 4; between brother and sister, 71, 266; and death, 2; of deconstruction, 82; of dissemination, 107; as letting-be, 108–109
Lukács, György, 26
lunar, 141, 160, 162, 177, 178–181, 185, 219, 222, 234–235, 324n5, 345n15; See also moon, mooness, Selene, selenic
lupē (Greek noun), 133, 335n37
Luther, Martin, 67–68, 79, 85, 90
Lutherbibel, 190
Lyon, James, 309n41

madness, 2, 37–38, 46, 138, 144, 157, 162–167, 169, 172, 176–177, 193, 213, 302n6, 311n46, 342n38; of Hölderlin, 4, 145, 164–169, 343n46; of Nietzsche, 41
Maeter, Ragnvi, 258
Mahrholdt, Erwin, 34–38, 98, 109, 224, 315n66, 341n25
Mallarmé, Stéphane, 263, 319n21, 343n41
Manggold, Walter, 310n44
Mann, Thomas, 72
marriage, 91, 271, 327n16, 328n18, 347n25
Martin-Heidegger-Archiv, 97, 217, 305n11
Martin-Heidegger-Gesellschaft, 112
Marxism, 26, 311n45
Mary (mother of Christ), 65, 321n35
maternity, 56, 151, 175, 186, 213, 340n16
Meister Eckhart, xiii, 11, 28, 31, 86, 103–106, 109, 118, 178, 201, 208, 241, 325n10, 326n11, 330n32, 331n41, 331n42
melancholy, 10, 23, 35, 43, 63, 72, 85, 172, 224, 232, 234, 264
Mercury: German Journal for European Thinking, 3, 14–15, 21, 23, 26, 135, 209, 253, 308n31, 310n42, 328n18, 343n41
Meßkirch, 97, 200, 216–217
Meßkirch Castle, 215
metaphysics, 79, 95, 107, 116, 120, 124, 150, 195; culmination of, 135; as domain of beings, 117; dualistic, 36, 206; end of, 214; inauguration in Ancient Greece of, 121; of language, 318n12; Occidental, 30, 126; of pain, 113; of Platonism and Christianity, 209; substance, 149, 207, 339n13; and the will, 334n18
meter, 77–78, 324n59
Methlagl, Walter, 305n13, 315n69
Michel, Robert, 72
Michel, Wilhelm, 168
middle voice, 150, 320n28
Milton, John, 68;
—works: *Paradise Lost*, 69, 112
Mitchell, Andrew, 175, 199
monism, 98, 206
monk(ess): as figure in Trakl's poetry, 1, 183, 186–187, 263–264
moon, 11, 57, 180–181, 183, 187, 221, 323n51, 324n5; See also lunar, mooness, Selene, selenic
mooness, 180–181, 324n5; See also lunar, moon, Selene, selenic
Moras, Joachim, 26
Mörike, Eduard, 10, 59–60, 70, 155, 241, 263, 308n31, 320n26, 339n14;
—works: "On a Lamp," 59–60, 155; "September Morning," 155

mortal(s), 20, 47, 52, 56, 59, 93, 108, 153, 160, 172, 175, 181, 195, 198–199, 233, 235, 321n32, 332n4; See also fourfold
mourning, 137, 155
Munch, Edvard, 347n24
Muschg, Walter, 8, 307n31; critique of Heidegger of, 303n3, 308n31, 333n4
music, 51, 71, 82–83, 163, 165, 173, 190, 193, 213, 301n2, 325n9, 342n38

narcotics, 111; See also cocaine, drugs
nationalism, 100–101, 103, 212, 329n22, 330n29
National Socialism, 26, 63, 306n18, 328n20, 344n5
Neoplatonism, 204
Neugebauer, Klaus, 113
Neumann, Gerhard, 261
Newton, Isaac, 163
Nicholas of Cusa, 105–106
Nietzsche, Friedrich, 15, 21, 63, 116, 230, 251, 309n38, 315n69, 320n21, 344; doctrine of eternal return of, 135, 172; idea of active nihilism of, 135; idea of the Dionysian of, 31, 135, 250; madness of, 41, 231;
—works: *Thus Spoke Zarathustra*, 63, 135, 250, 265; *Will to Power*, 248, 254
night, 11, 23, 56, 87–89, 99–100, 123, 140–141, 151, 155, 157, 159–162, 166, 172, 177, 179–181, 185–187, 189–190, 194–196, 198, 247, 323n51, 328n18, 342n40, 349n35; See also nocturnal
nihilism: active, 135; of body and soul, 128; modern, 351n3

nocturnal, 46, 151, 167, 180–183, 193, 199, 235, 342n38; See also night
Novalis, 10–11, 87, 92, 157, 160, 171, 190, 199, 321n35, 326n10, 340n22, 348n35

Odysseus, 101
Oedipus, 39, 168
ontology, 146; as algology, 112; and evil, 207; as gathering of being, 132; phenomenological, 145; the poetry of Pindar as, 152; regional, 175
Orpheus, 71
Ortega y Gasset, José, 14, 17
Oschwald, Maria, 217
other, the: and love, 109; and the same, 3; relation to as double homosexuality, 66; sex (book by Beauvoir), 182
Otto, Rudolf, 145, 150, 337n3;
—works: *The Holy*, 145
Otto, Walter Friedrich, 18

Paeschke, Hans, 23, 253
pain, 2, 54–55, 58, 77–78, 113–122, 124, 127, 131, 136, 140, 142, 172, 175, 197, 201–202, 205, 207, 209, 213–214, 236, 246, 250, 324n59, 332n4, 333n7, 335n25, 335n30, 335n34, 335–336n37, 344n5, 349n35; as or in relation to being itself, 111–112, 123, 126, 130, 132, 333n4; Heidegger's genealogy of, 133; as inter-section of thing and world, 59, 125; incest and, 4; ontic, 134–135; of Trakl, 137–138, 157, 208; as truth, 128–129
Palmier, Jean-Michel, 32, 263, 266, 304n11, 314n56, 314n57;

—works: *Situation de Georg Trakl*, 32, 265, 314n59
Parmenides, 146
parting. *See* departure
Paul, Jean, 48–49, 257
Paul, Saint, 67, 204
Pentecost, 204, 349n3
Petzet, Heinrich Wiegand, 26, 250, 310n44, 312n48, 331n46
phenomenology, 117–119, 126, 145, 252, 340n21
Picard, Max, 310n44
Picasso, Pablo, 8, 17
pilgrimage, 20, 53, 75, 86, 187, 210, 221, 325n9; *See also* wandering
Pindar, 4, 57, 60, 62, 78, 143–156, 158, 160, 163, 325n5, 337–338n5, 338n7, 338n11, 339n13, 339n14, 339n15, 340n16, 343n46;
—works: 5th Isthmian, 57, 60, 144, 146, 148, 152–154; 7th Olympian, 339n14; 10th Olympian, 325n5; 8th Pythian, 155, 337n5
Pinthus, Kurt, 172–173, 344n4
place (*Ort*), 4, 28, 30, 35, 51, 64, 75, 81, 83–85, 98–100, 102, 106, 163, 202, 301n2, 318n15, 329n25
placement/emplacement (*Erörterung*), 27, 39, 62, 64, 67, 83, 107, 109, 180, 186, 253, 309n37, 318n15
Plath, Sylvia, 143
Plato, 29, 85, 107, 204, 320n21, 326n10, 334n18
Platonism, 35–36, 63, 86, 95, 155, 198, 204, 209, 326n10
Plotinus, 204
Podewils, Clemens von, 17–18, 22–23, 249, 252–253, 258, 310n44, 313n52

Podewils, Sophie Dorothee von, 249, 252, 310n44
Pöggeler, Otto, 8
polysemy, 5, 81–82, 106, 157, 173
positive sciences, 175
Pound, Ezra, 324n4
Preetorius, Emil, 17–18, 253
prelapsarian state. *See* Fall
presence, 4, 50, 55, 60, 71, 260; metaphysics of, 107
promise, 86, 91, 153, 173, 183, 190, 193, 202–204, 209, 212, 240, 327–328n18; *See also* promised land
promised land, 4, 29, 62, 202, 213; *See also* home, homecoming, homeland, promise
Phidias, 149
Phylakidas of Aegina, 148
psychoanalysis, 27
physics, 114, 117, 181
psychology, 111, 117, 119–121, 129, 131, 166, 207
putrefaction. *See* decay

Rahner, Karl, 331n46
reconciliation, 123, 134, 177, 327–328n18
redeem (English verb), 43, 92, 109, 129, 167, 318n12, 339n13; *See also* redemption, salvation
redemption: Christian, 3, 64, 76–77, 87; eschatological, 91; and penitence, 193; religious, 56, 70, 72, 310n41; and ruin, 167; spiritual, 5, 92; for the West, 157; *See also* redeem, salvation
Reifenberg, Benno, 310n44
releasement (*Gelassenheit*), xiii, 96, 103, 107, 109, 129–130, 150, 208–210, 214, 223, 305n14; *See also* detachment
religion, 26, 40, 67–68, 74, 315n69

reticence, Trakl's. *See* Trakl
Rey, W. H., 258
rhyme, 55, 69, 78, 348n28
Ricœur, Paul, 266, 313n55
rift (*Riß*), 49, 59, 124–125, 127
righteousness. *See* justice
Rilke, Rainer Maria, 7, 10, 22, 34–35, 62, 248, 252, 254, 263, 268, 306n18, 315n70
Rimbaud, Arthur, 31, 109, 157, 260, 270, 332n49
Röck, Karl, 269, 321n40
rot. *See* decay
Roth, Matthias, 27, 34
Russia, 42, 70, 231; as Trakl's dreamland, 212

Saint-Exupéry, Antoine de, 108, 332n47
save (English verb). *See* salvation
salvation (*Heil*), 5, 13, 20, 29, 41, 43, 56, 62, 76, 78, 87, 91, 93, 107, 130, 134, 153, 161, 195, 202–203, 207, 229, 253
salvific. *See* salvation
Sappho, 84, 163, 180–181, 320n21, 324–325n5
Satan, 202
scattering. *See* dissemination
Schelling, Friedrich Wilhelm, 5, 186, 202, 204, 206–207, 254, 350n8, 351n10;
—works: *Freiheitsschrift*, 206
science, 95, 175, 335n37; Hegelian, 123; *See also* scientific worldview
scientific worldview, 29, 108; *See also* science
Schifferli, Peter, 310n44
Schlier, Paula, 23, 305n13, 310n44
Schmerz (German noun), 53–54, 58, 77–78, 111–114, 118–119, 128, 130, 132–136, 139, 172

Schmidthüs, Karlheinz, 310n44
Schmitt, Carl, 15
Schoenberg, Arnold, 72
Scholl, Arnold, 310n44
Schopenhauer, Arthur, 70, 113, 122, 334n20
Schowingen-Ficker, Birgit, 261, 310n44
Schürmann, Reiner, 213–214, 331n41, 352n9;
—works: *Broken Hegemonies*, 213
schweigen (German verb): used transitively, 31, 263
Secret Germany, 2, 30, 102, 211, 213, 351n2
secularization, 13, 29, 57, 79
Selene (Greek goddess), 150; *See also* lunar, moon, mooness, selenic
selenic, 186; *See also* lunar, moon, mooness, Selene
sensation: and gold (color), 148–149; and feeling, 119, 133; and sense-making, 124
sheltering, 4, 51, 128–129, 134, 151–152, 156, 158–161; *See also* gathering, truth
Shoah, 13, 163
show (*zeigen*), 128, 257; and sign (*Zeichen*), 124, 126–128
show oneself (*sich zeigen*). *See* show
Silesius, Angelus, 104–105, 109, 150, 339n14
sin (*Sünde*), 59, 70–71, 79, 90, 92, 96, 191, 205, 310n41, 321n45
singular(ity), 54, 56, 84, 99, 132, 178–179, 187, 220, 304n6, 331n42
sister, as figure in Trakl's poetry, 46, 64–66, 71, 89–90, 92, 142, 167, 178–183, 186, 188, 190–191, 200, 213, 222, 234–236, 321n34, 324n5, 328n18; *See also* Langen

sociology, 27
Socrates, 150, 326n10
Sonnemann, Ulrich, 323n52
Sophocles: his *Antigone*, 146, 163
soul (*Seele*), 4, 23, 28, 31–32, 43, 49, 68, 87, 94–95, 98–100, 104, 106–107, 111, 123, 129, 153, 172, 214, 224, 232, 235–236, 241, 247, 263, 328n18, 331n40, 349n35, 351n8; and body, 36, 43, 48, 63, 85–86, 119–121, 128, 326n10, 344n3; as "something foreign or strange on earth" (*ein Fremdes auf Erden*), 29, 36, 85, 89–90, 93, 96, 109, 194, 216, 271
space: and *Abend-land*, 202; as figure in Trakl's poetry, 187, 210, 221; and time, 14, 27–30, 55, 81, 99–100, 103–104; of the unsayable, 8; and/between words, 49, 184, 208, 223, 236, 343n41, 346n22
Spengler, Oswald, 116
spirit (*gheis, Geist*), xiii, 14, 31, 38, 41, 49, 65, 69–70, 79, 82, 86–87, 92, 95, 105, 129, 132, 136–137, 139–140, 142, 157, 160, 166–167, 178–179, 182, 198, 201, 203, 205–207, 209–210, 213, 223–225, 241, 247, 276, 306n23, 327n18, 331n40, 342n40, 349n3, 351n8, 351n10; understood as Indo-Germanic *gheis* rather than Greek *pneuma* or Latin *spiritus*, 1, 5, 29, 96, 129, 133, 202, 204, 208, 224, 349n4; as Hebrew *ruah/ruach*, 106, 202, 331n40, 349n3; of Trakl's poetry, 4, 63, 215, 339n15
Stadler, Ernst, 18, 306n24
Stalder, Willy, 310n44
Staiger, Emil, 60, 155, 308n31, 311n46, 320n26
Stieg, Gerald, 327n15
Stifter, Adalbert, 163
still (English verb, *stillen*): as both to pacify and to breastfeed or suckle, 61, 186
still(ness) (*Stille*), 15, 36, 38, 49, 61, 88–89, 92, 100, 109, 139, 157, 159, 161–162, 166, 176, 178, 182–183, 185–186, 219, 226, 264, 328n18, 342n39; peal of (*Geläut der Stille*), 50, 62, 108, 318n14, 320n28
Stramm, August, 212
stranger (*Fremder, Fremdling*): as figure in Trakl's poetry, 3, 32, 39, 84, 86–87, 95–96, 98, 100, 157–160, 178–182, 194–195, 198, 200, 213, 224–235, 247, 265, 269, 325n9, 326n10, 327n14, 342n40, 345n18, 350n6
strangeress (*Fremdlingin*): as figure in Trakl's poetry, 181–183, 346n19
Strohschneider-Kohrs, Ingrid, 165, 167, 255–256, 313n52, 314n56, 341n37
Stroomann, Gerhard, 3, 12–14, 17–18, 21–22, 240, 242, 245, 307n24, 310n42, 311n46, 312n47, 313n52
sublation (*Aufhebung*), 123–124, 134
suffering (*Leid*), 36, 38, 41, 46, 76, 69, 92, 112, 118, 123, 131, 133–138, 167, 172, 190, 207, 224, 226, 233, 236, 252, 255, 310n41, 320n30, 334n17
Swabia, 101, 164, 202
sympathy, 27, 95, 139–140, 172–173, 226, 231, 233, 236, 304n6; *See also* compassion

Szklenar, Hans, 314n56

Tannert, Hannes, 20
Tabu: Es ist die Sele ein Fremdes auf Erden (biopic), 12
tautology, 51, 61, 205; as more than redundancy, 319n17
teleology, 61, 103, 106, 150
temporality, ecstatic, 55, 334n24
Tezuko Tomio, 254
Theia (Greek goddess), 57, 147–148, 150–152, 160, 186, 338–339n11, 340n16
theologian(s)/theological. *See* theology
theology, 39, 41, 64, 66, 86, 103, 143, 145, 152, 205, 248, 252, 321n34, 331n46
theosophy, 150, 204, 206, 350–351n8
Third Reich, 11, 13, 306n17
Therezo, Rodrigo, 343n41
Thomas Aquinas, Saint, 65, 103, 113, 122, 206;
—works: *Quaestiones disputatae de veritate*, 334n20; *Summa theologiae*, 334n20
threshold (*Schwelle*), 3, 54, 58–59, 78, 138, 162, 176–177, 199, 219–220
Thun, Roderick von, 310n44
Toshio Hosokawa, 342n37
Towarnicki, Frédéric de, 263
Trakl, Georg: his death, 18, 101, 140, 208, 265; as Christian poet, 2–3, 35, 40–41, 63–67, 70–71, 87, 98, 103, 188, 213, 228–229, 232, 243, 312n46, 314n64, 315n71, 321n32, 322n46, 330n27, 332n4; his figure of Elis, 32, 90, 182, 190, 200, 327n14, 346n18; his gravesite, 30, 134; his pessimism, 40; his reticence, 38–41, 139, 227, 315n70;

—works: "Abendland," 345n17; "Afra," 22, 30, 212, 305n11, 312n47; "Autumn Soul," 26, 28, 32, 93–96, 98–100, 102, 243, 347n24; "To the Boy Elis," 182, 195, 345n18; "Bright Spring," 135–136; *Die Dichtungen*, 9, 21, 32–34, 63, 97, 165, 171, 178, 181, 186, 208, 215–216, 218, 232–233, 269, 310n42, 310n44, 312n49, 312n49, 336n40, 341n25, 342n38, 346n22, 352n4; "Downfall," 38, 329n25; "Elis," 22, 190, 329n25; "Evening Song," 31, 263, 269, 329n25; *From a Golden Chalice: Poems of His Youth*, 135; "Gródek," xiii, 4, 27, 32, 37, 64, 97, 101, 134, 136, 138–141, 176, 188, 204, 208–209, 222, 309n39, 336n39, 345n15; "The Heart," 183; "Helian," 22, 165–166, 342n38, 343n43, 345n18, 352n5; "Hölderlin," 4, 164, 167–168; "In the Dark," 31, 262–263, 269; "Into an Old Family Album," 171, 173, 215, 232–233, 342n38; "Lamentation," 37, 64–65, 139, 188, 321n32, 342n37; "Nightsong," 195–196; "Nook in the Forest," 165; "To Novalis," 87; "Out of the Depths," 31, 258, 260, 325n9; "Passion," 65, 188, 191, 193, 200, 234–235, 342n38, 348n29; "Psalm," 31, 34, 73–74, 76, 181, 241, 258, 260, 323n51, 325n9; "Revelation and Downfall," 182, 267–268, 329n25; *Sebastian in Dream*, 22, 72–73, 200, 234; "Song of the Departed One," 38, 92, 99–100, 161, 176, 178–179,

185, 218–219, 223, 305n13, 329n25, 345n10; "Song of the Occident," 41, 91–92, 101, 144, 157, 159, 184, 249, 305n13, 349n35; "Sonja," 22, 42, 231; "Spiritual Twilight," 179–180, 198–199, 208, 234–235, 324n5, 343n40; "Springtime of the Soul," 4, 29, 85, 87, 92–93, 191, 194–195, 234, 305n13, 325n9, 327–328n18; "Summer's Decline," 144, 158, 194–195, 236; "Surrender to the Night," 186, 209–210, 218, 220–221; "The Thunderstorm," 31, 241; "Whispered in the Afternoon," 165, 232–233; "In Winter (A Winter Evening)," 3, 20, 47, 53, 55–57, 61, 63, 69, 71–72, 74–75, 77–79, 90, 125, 144, 153–154, 177, 210, 240, 304n6, 319n18
transcendence, 29, 39, 41, 95, 140, 243–244, 327n18
transcendental signified, 107
Troeltsch, Ernst, 145
Trinity, 104
truth, 27, 73, 124, 130, 168, 196, 199, 231, 263, 315n1, 327n18, 333n17, 336n37; and appearance, 63; of/and being/beyng, 118, 121–122, 126–127; in Germanic sense of sheltering, 128–129, 134, 163; and the human being, 117; and language, 47; as un-concealment, 131, 134, 151
twilight (*Dämmerung*), 144, 157, 172–173, 180, 193–195, 235, 247, 249

unborn: as figure in Trakl's poetry, 32, 37, 64, 137, 139, 142, 208, 223, 227, 237, 247, 315n70, 345n15; *See also* beget, birth
unholy, the, 43, 85, 163, 167
univocity, 45, 95, 102, 157, 316n2
unsaid, the. *See* unsayable
unsayable, the (*Unsagbare*), 8, 48–49, 105, 131, 240, 314n56; *See also* ineffable
unspoken, the, 39, 84, 152, 318n13, 342n37; language as the speaking of, 20, 47, 49–50, 61, 153
uselessness: as what is most necessary, 83, 118, 130

Van Gogh, Vincent, 159
Vietta, Egon, 310n44, 311–312n46, 318n13, 320n30
Vietta, Silvio, 312n46
violence, 8, 26, 29, 67, 89, 150, 213, 287, 327n18
Virgil, 91
Vita Adami et Evae, 77

Wagner, Richard, 328n20;
—works: *Die Walküre*, 191; *Götterdämmerung*, 172; *Tristan und Isolde*, 328n20
wandering, 84, 93, 98, 100, 106, 129, 162; *See also* pilgrimage
war, 66, 70, 95–96, 136–138; holy, 68; WWI, 1, 22, 37, 42, 106, 139, 212, 253, 266, 336n39; WWII, 11, 13, 216, 258, 304n6, 305n13, 314n64, 336n39
wed(ding). *See* marriage
Weichselbaum, Hans, 165
Weininger, Otto, 37, 224–225;
—works: *Sex and Character*, 42
Weisgerber, Antje, 18
Whitman, Walt, 315n69; Trakl's opinion of, 40, 228

wild blue game (*ein blaues Wild*): as figure in Trakl's poetry, 158–160, 189–191, 193–200, 213, 349n35
will (English noun), 116, 121, 135, 207, 334n18
Windelband, Wilhelm, 145
without why (*ohn warumb*), 93, 104–106, 109, 150, 205
Witt, Franz, 310n44

Wittgenstein, Ludwig, 7, 72, 322n49
Wolff, Kurt, 23, 212, 352n6

Yeats, William Butler: his poem "The Second Coming," 106
youth(ess): as figure in Trakl's poetry, 182–183

Zeus (Greek god), 149, 339n11
Zhuangzi, The, 118

www.ingramcontent.com/pod-product-compliance
Ingram Content Group UK Ltd.
Pitfield, Milton Keynes, MK11 3LW, UK
UKHW041915140426
5217IPUK00013B/160